# WOMAN IN THE MISTS

'Farley Mowat's book ought to be force-fed to everyone engaged in conservation' *Daily Mail*

'I was simply not able to put the book down' Barbara Amiel, *The Times*

'A rare and gripping look at the tragically mingled destinies of a heroically flawed woman and her beloved mountain gorillas amid the high mists of the Parc des Volcans' *New York Times Book Review*

'An intriguing biography . . . an engaging, fluidly written and judicious study of a remarkable woman' *Kirkus*

Farley Mowat, author of such bestselling works as *A Whale for the Killing*, *Never Cry Wolf*, *People of the Deer*, *And No Birds Sang* and *Seas of Slaughter*, has long spoken out against man's destruction of the earth and its creatures. A recipient of Canada's highest literary honour Farley Mowat ranks as one of our most distinguished storytellers and naturalists. He is an author uniquely able to portray the courageous life of Dian Fossey.

# WOMAN IN THE MISTS

## THE STORY OF DIAN FOSSEY
### AND THE MOUNTAIN GORILLAS OF AFRICA

## FARLEY MOWAT

Futura

A Futura Book

Copyright © 1987 by Farley Mowat Ltd.

First published in the United States of America in 1987 by
Warner Books, Inc., 666 Fifth Avenue, New York, NY 10103.
Published in Canada under the title *Virunga, The Passion of Dian Fossey*.

First published in Great Britain in 1988 by
Macdonald & Co (Publishers) Ltd
London & Sydney
This Futura edition published in 1989

ISBN 0 7088 4251 8

Printed and bound in Great Britain by
Hazell Watson & Viney Limited
Member of BPCC plc
Aylesbury, Bucks, England

Futura Publications
A Division of
Macdonald & Co (Publishers) Ltd
66–73 Shoe Lane
London EC4P 4AB
A member of Maxwell Pergamon Publishing Corporation plc

FOR NYIRAMACHABELLI
and for those she loved

# ACKNOWLEDGMENTS AND CREDITS

As will be seen, a great many people have contributed to this book in one way or another. I am grateful to them all, but the following deserve my special thanks.

Wade Rowland, my associate in this project, who scoured three continents in pursuit of interviews and who was responsible for locating and gaining access to Dian Fossey's personal archives. His contributions have been invaluable.

Mary Elliott, my secretarial assistant, who deciphered Dian's sometimes nearly illegible notes and journals and who typed the several versions of the manuscript with magical speed and precision.

Lily Poritz Miller, my editor, who rescued the book, and me, after I became so embroiled in Dian's life that I thought myself lost forever.

Rosamond Carr, Dian's closest friend in Rwanda.

Stacey Coil and Ian Redmond of the Digit Fund, who staunchly continue to serve the cause of the mountain gorillas.

Contributions to the Digit Fund will be gratefully accepted if sent to:
The Digit Fund
P.O. Box 4557
Triphammer Mall
Ithaca, NY 14852

Grateful acknowledgment is given to the following for their kind permission to use material:

Kelly Stewart, Ph.D., for the poem on pages 109–110.

*The New York Times* for portions of articles which appear on pages 269–270 and on page 275. Copyright © 1981–1982 by *The New York Times,* reprinted by permission.

The Associated Press for portions of an article which appears on page 336, reprinted by permission.

Houghton Mifflin Company and Hodder & Stoughton, Ltd. for excerpts from *Gorillas in the Mist* by Dian Fossey, which appear on pages 30, 101, 102, 115, 185–186, 189, and 198. Copyright © 1983, reprinted by permission.

Ian Redmond for the original sketches for the endpapers and frontispiece.

Richard and Kitty Price for access to the letters and papers of Dian Fossey.

# AUTHOR'S NOTE

Dian Fossey never spoke about writing her autobiography, but that she someday hoped to do so is evident from notations in her journals and from the fact that she went to great pains to amass and preserve an extraordinarily complete personal archive.

This massive collection included the correspondence received by her since the days of her youth together with copies of most of her own letters. In addition, she preserved her own writings and musings, both published and unpublished; a comprehensive file of what was written about her; a set of daily journals; an enormous mass of observations of both animals and people, together with a miscellaneous collection of documents covering every aspect of her years in Africa.

When my associate in this project, Wade Rowland, uncovered Dian's archives, I was jubilant. It appeared to be the sort of treasure trove every biographer dreams of acquiring. However, as I immersed myself in this detailed record of a human life and began to listen to Dian's own voice telling her own story, I felt much less comfortable with my role as her biographer. In truth, I began to feel like an intruder. Consequently, I made the decision to abandon the usual biographer's role as recorder and commentator and to settle for something in the nature of an editorial collaborator.

Insofar as I have been able to make it so, what follows is Dian Fossey's own account of her life. Her voice is paramount throughout, and I have muted mine—a claim which may inspire some initial incredulity in those who know me.

To make this work, I have arranged that Dian's own words be set in a distinct typeface. I have occasionally reshaped awkwardly phrased source material into descriptive scenes and dialogue. But in all such cases, the reworked version remains faithful to the record.

I never met Dian Fossey in the flesh, but I have lived with her on terms of intense intimacy for more than a year. Having read thousands of her letters, her diaries and journals, her printed words, and having listened to scores of people who knew her in life, she has become as achingly familiar to me as if we were of one blood.

I would be happy if we were.

*Port Hope, Ontario*
*Canada*
*June 1st, 1987.*

# WOMAN IN THE MISTS

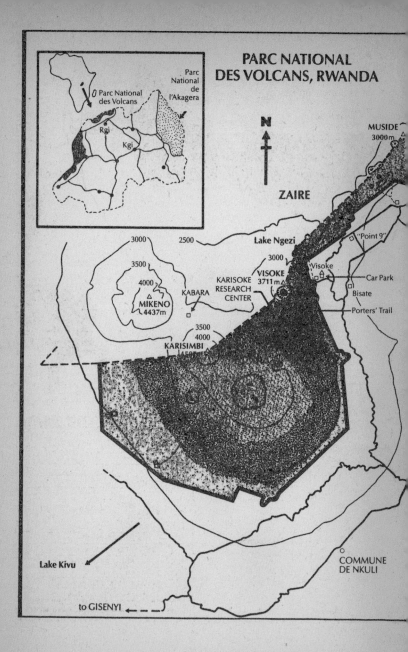

# PARC NATIONAL DES VOLCANS, RWANDA

Parc National de l'Akagera

Parc National des Volcans

Rgi

Kgi

**N**

MUSIDE
3000 m

**ZAIRE**

3000    2500    **Lake Ngezi**

3500         3000

4000        **VISOKE**
              3711 m △

**MIKENO**
4437m

KABARA

KARISOKE
RESEARCH
CENTER

"Point 9"

Visoke

Car Park

Bisate

Porters' Trail

3500
4000
**KARISIMBI**

**Lake Kivu**

**COMMUNE
DE NKULI**

to GISENYI

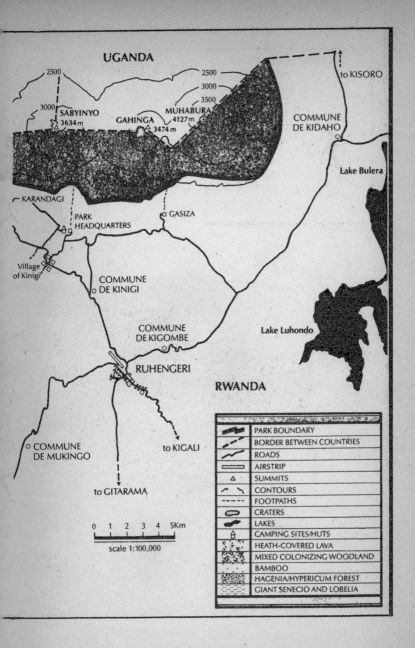

UGANDA

2500                    2500
                        3000
                        3500

3000  SABYINYO        MUHABURA           COMMUNE
      3634 m   GAHINGA  4127 m           DE KIDAHO
               △ 3474 m

                                                    Lake Bulera

KARANDAGI

        PARK          GASIZA
        HEADQUARTERS

Village
of Kinigi

        COMMUNE
        DE KINIGI

                                        Lake Luhondo

        COMMUNE
        DE KIGOMBE

               RUHENGERI

                            RWANDA

COMMUNE
DE MUKINGO        to KIGALI

        to GITARAMA

0   1   2   3   4   5Km

scale 1:100,000

to KISORO

| | |
|---|---|
| | PARK BOUNDARY |
| | BORDER BETWEEN COUNTRIES |
| | ROADS |
| | AIRSTRIP |
| △ | SUMMITS |
| | CONTOURS |
| - - - | FOOTPATHS |
| | CRATERS |
| | LAKES |
| | CAMPING SITES/HUTS |
| | HEATH-COVERED LAVA |
| | MIXED COLONIZING WOODLAND |
| | BAMBOO |
| | HAGENIA/HYPERICUM FOREST |
| | GIANT SENECIO AND LOBELIA |

KARISOKE RESEARCH CENTER

(Based on sketches drawn from memory by Ian Redmond, April 25, 1987)

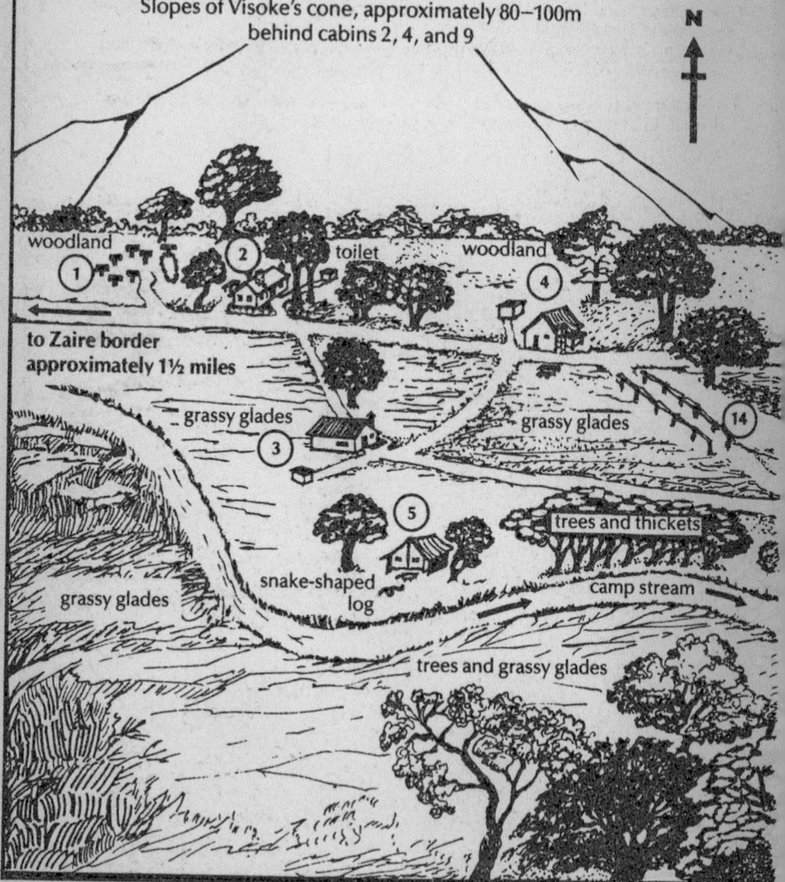

Slopes of Visoke's cone, approximately 80–100m behind cabins 2, 4, and 9

N

woodland

① ② toilet woodland ④

to Zaire border approximately 1½ miles

grassy glades ③ grassy glades ⑭

⑤ trees and thickets

snake-shaped log camp stream

grassy glades

trees and grassy glades

1. Gorilla graveyard, Dian's grave on right (east) of other graves.
2. Dian's cabin (known as "The Mausoleum" by Dian)—internal brick chimney
3. Guest cabin
4. Middle cabin
5. Tent cabin—safari tent with corrugated roof—my favorite.
6. First cabin—the one in early N.G. photographs, mine for 1976–1978
7. Kitchen/laundry shed
8. Hen house—also used more recently for path guards to sleep in on patrols!
9. Workers' house "The Men's House"—small windows and 1 big bed—their choice!
10. Men's fire pit for cooking beans and potatoes and sitting around.
11. Meteorological center—installed a few months before Dian died.
12. Used to be called "Kelly's Cabin" or Bottom Cabin
13. Fire pit and wood chopping area and outdoor table and bench. Site of old flagpole (Rwandan + N.G. flags)
14. Most paths have gravel from stream (gray lava pebbles and boulders) where mud and fences of long thin hyperlcum saplings along 18" high uprights thus:

All cabins have "long drop" toilets nearby—deep hole with box with hole in top over it and simple roof with matting around for walls.

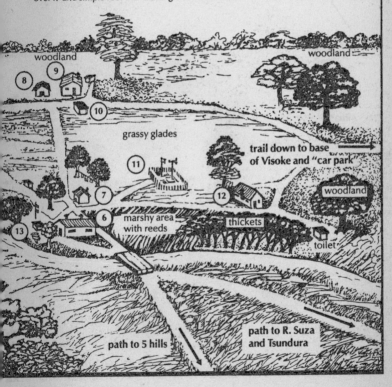

woodland

woodland

8

9

10

grassy glades

trail down to base of Visoke and "car park"

11

woodland

7

12

6

marshy area with reeds

thickets

13

toilet

path to 5 hills

path to R. Suza and Tsundura

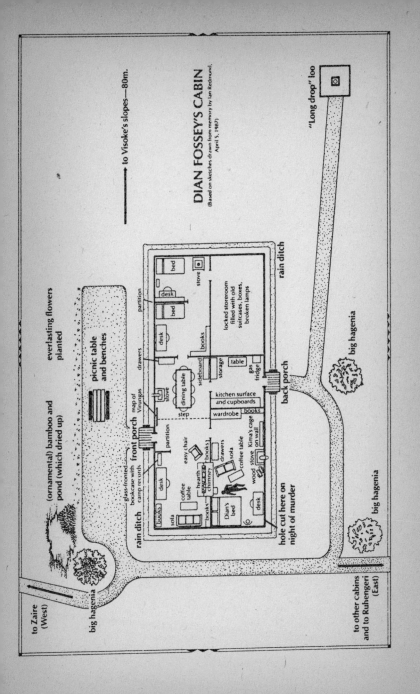

**DIAN FOSSEY'S CABIN**
(Based on sketches drawn from memory by Ian Redmond,
April 5, 1987)

→ to Visoke's slopes—80m.

to Zaire (West)

big hagenia

(ornamental) bamboo and pond (which dried up)

everlasting flowers planted

picnic table and benches

rain ditch

rain ditch

front porch

glass-fronted bookcase with camp records

desk

sofa

books

coffee table

books

hearth chimney

easy chair

partition

map of Virungas

drawers

stove

dining table

sideboard

desk

books

partition

desk

bed

desk

bed

stove

storage

table

gas fridge

locked storeroom filled with old suitcases, boxes, broken lamps

step

wardrobe

books

kitchen surface and cupboards

back porch

rain ditch

Dian's bed

books

drawers

sofa

coffee table

wood stove

Kima's cage on wall

desk

hole cut here on night of murder

big hagenia

big hagenia

"Long drop" loo

to other cabins and to Ruhengeri (East)

# 1

**N**either destiny nor fate took me to Africa. Nor was it romance. I had a deep wish to see and live with wild animals in a world that hadn't yet been completely changed by humans. I guess I really wanted to go backward in time. From my childhood I believed that was what going to Africa would be, but by 1963, when I was first able to make a trip there, it was not that way anymore. There were only a few places other than the deserts and the swamps that hadn't been overrun by people. Almost at the end of my trip I found the place I had been looking for.

Right in the heart of central Africa, so high up that you shiver more than you sweat, are great, old volcanoes towering up almost fifteen thousand feet, and nearly covered with rich, green rain forest—the Virungas.

Going to Africa was one of many dreams that filled Dian Fossey's lonely childhood. Her father, George Fossey, son of an English immigrant, was a big, affable, outdoorsy type who loved his little daughter but hated his impoverished life as an insurance agent in San Francisco. In consequence he drank too much, which got him into trouble with the law and finally brought on a divorce that took him out of Dian's life in 1938 when she was six. A year later her mother, Kitty, married Richard Price, an ambitious, hard-driving building contractor. In the beginning, George Fossey tried to keep in touch with Dian, sending her pictures of himself in his navy uniform during the war; but even his name was taboo in the Price household and eventually he drifted out of sight.

Although she dutifully called him Daddy, Dian's stepfather

never adopted her. Richard Price was a stern traditionalist who believed that children should be properly disciplined. Until she was ten, Dian was not even permitted to take her evening meal with Richard and Kitty, but ate in the kitchen with the housekeeper. "I had always been brought up to think that children dined with adults when they were becoming adults," Price offered in justification.

Like many lonely children Dian loved animals and took comfort from their undemanding acceptance of her; yet she was not permitted any pets of her own except for a goldfish, upon which she lavished the affection that had few other outlets. The death of the fish left her desolate.

**I cried for a week when I found him floating belly up in the bowl in my room. My parents thought it was good riddance, so I never got another. A friend at school offered me a hamster, but they considered it dirty, so that was out.**

Although the Prices seemed wealthy, Dian did not receive much financial assistance from them when she entered the adult world. In the main, she supported herself after she completed high school. In 1949, while at Marin Junior College taking a business course, which she despised, she worked as a clerk at the White House Department Store. As a university undergraduate she spent holidays and weekends doing clerical and laboratory jobs, and she once had a job as a machine operator in a factory.

One of the few bright episodes in her early life was learning to ride. The rapport she had with horses won her a place at a dude ranch in Montana during the summer of her twenty-first year; but she lost this—"the best job I'd ever had"—when she contracted chicken pox. A young man who knew her at the ranch remembered her as being "completely wrapped up in animals—the horses, dogs, a pet coyote, anything that walked or flew. She liked people well enough, but didn't seem to rely on them as much as the rest of us do."

Rejecting Richard Price's decision that she seek a career in business, Dian began setting her own course and in 1950 enrolled as a preveterinary medical student at the University of California campus in Davis. She was determined to share her life with animals; but although she did extremely well in such studies as writing and art, botany and zoology, she had no affinity for the "hard" sciences. To her enormous disappointment she failed her second year, brought down by chemistry and physics, which she simply could not master.

Undaunted, she decided to work with damaged children. She transferred to San Jose State College, graduating in 1954 with a degree in occupational therapy. During the succeeding nine months she interned in several hospitals. She dealt with tuberculosis patients in one of these, an experience that left an indelible impression on her.

The job she chose after graduation was about as far removed from California as she could get and still remain in the United States. Except for brief, ritual visits with the Prices, she never returned to the scene of her birth and early years.

The new focus of her life, Korsair Children's Hospital in Louisville, Kentucky, was a rambling half-timbered old building, exactly to her liking.

It's a Shriners' hospital and I'm surprised they hired me without Shriner pull. I'm to be the director of the occupational therapy department, which makes me feel quite inadequate. My assistant is a fifty-year-old woman, and that makes me feel a little like a louse, but everyone is relaxed and friendly. The children come direct from the backwoods. They are brought out of the hills by truck, jeep, even on horseback. I'm excited because within the next month I am going in with the doctors on one of their "collecting" trips. We may even go to the area where four sheriffs have been shot in the last three years. These children have a variety of physical and emotional disabilities and are lost in this world of ours. All are much younger than their years and are like wild animals penned up with no hope of escape. They need a tremendous amount of care and kindness to make them feel life is worth living.

Although she had lived in a big city most of her life, Dian hated urban constraint, so her first concern after settling in at Korsair was to find a place to live, well beyond Louisville's city limits. Eventually she rented a dilapidated cottage on a sprawling, century-old farm called Glenmary.

The owners encouraged her to pitch in with the seasonal farm chores, and she was able to put her knowledge of veterinary medicine to constructive use. She was in her element.

Never have I seen any place as beautiful as this is now in autumn. At Glenmary the creeks are full of the golden, red, green, and brown leaves from the forests. The pastures are still vivid green and are framed by trees that you would swear were on fire. When I wake up in the morning, I just run to the windows all over the house and am blinded by the beauty. Quite often I'll see a raccoon or possum scurrying by, or else the ninety head of Angus cattle will be taking their morning meal off my backyard. When I come home from work, I have to take about twenty minutes to feed the multitude of barn cats and the big white shepherd dog

3

from over the hill who stops by for a handout, along with our own farm dogs, Mitzi, Shep, and Brownie, who have adopted me as one of their own.

A warm friendship developed between Dian and Mary White Henry, secretary to the chief administrator at the Korsair Children's Hospital. Mary White was the daughter of a well-known Louisville heart specialist and she introduced Dian to Louisville society.

Now in her twenties, she was not conventionally beautiful, but a number of the men she met found her attractive. She was exceptionally tall and slender with gleaming dark hair, intense and searching eyes, strong features, and a coltish grace. Some of the city's most prominent men courted her, yet none of them appealed to her. More to her liking was Franz Forrester, a shock-headed young Rhodesian whom she also met through her friendship with the Henry family.

Franz was the youngest son in a displaced Austrian family who owned extensive agricultural and business interests in Africa. Called Pookie by his intimates, he came as close to evoking a serious response from Dian as any man she had so far met—though that was not very close.

**He's from Southern Rhodesia and he's a dream, but younger than I am, the son of an Austrian count claiming imperial blood. He has all these great plans for us, but I really don't think I can afford the time.**

Dian might have slipped away from Franz Forrester as she had done from previous admirers, but he was persistent beyond all others.

**Letters, letters, letters from New York, London, Ireland, Paris, Rome, and South Africa. The ladies in the local post office are beside themselves. Now Pookie is back in town from New York and sets the sky as the limit for fun and frolic in Louisville. Not long ago he sent me a "pouf"—phew! It's a footstool, I guess. The top is certainly right off a zebra's back. It's not bad except that it looks like a tumor rising out of my vicuña floor rug. The dogs attacked it on sight, but now the smell has so permeated the house, I guess they think it belongs.**

Dian met an even more impressive man through Mary White. As a favor to Mary, one day she drove to a monastery called Gethsemane, two hours from Louisville, to pick up a writer who had been on retreat. While there, Dian encountered a vibrant Irish priest with sparkling blue eyes, contagious enthusiasm, and a considerable interest in the mundane.

**I can't believe it. This Trappist monk, Father Raymond, who**

4

wrote the best-selling book *The Man Who Got Even with God,*
obviously has a liking for me. Last Sunday Mary White called to
say he was coming to Louisville and wanted to see me. Well, that
was about the most rewarding experience in my life. Talking to
him is like sitting on top of a live volcano. You're constantly
exploding one idea on top of another. You leave his presence, and
thoughts, like lava, continue pouring over you for days. I'm not
going holy holy, but this was an experience of a lifetime. He is
quite a man!

He must have been. Less than a month later, in a letter to her
mother, Dian noted as a casual aside that she had converted to Catholicism. Although it proved to be a transient conversion, it horrified the family.

Kitty Price was inconsolable. "I can't stop crying long enough to
reason it out," she sobbed into the telephone the night she heard the
awful news. "I can't believe you would take such a serious step without considering us."

Kitty and Richard Price had not even begun to suspect what
Dian was capable of doing with her own life.

While Dian developed an intimate relationship with Father
Raymond, Franz Forrester remained in hot pursuit and even offered
to pay her way to Africa, on a one-way trip.

Dian was already intrigued by Africa. In 1957 she had met a
traveler just back from that far country, a dashing reporter on the
Louisville *Courier Journal,* whose excitement about his trip had been
contagious. She was in love with the world he described and perhaps
a little in love with him.

**The thought of being where the animals haven't all been
driven into little corners attracts me so much. If he goes back to
Africa, as he hopes, I'll be right behind him!**

Then the journalist moved to Florida and dropped out of Dian's
life. But the dream of Africa remained.

In 1960 Mary White made an African safari, and Dian's dormant
desire was rekindled. In one of the most painful decisions of her life
she turned down Mary's invitation to go along. The truth was she
could not pay her way. However, she made up her mind she would
find the funds to make a safari on her own in the not-too-distant future. "I am saving every penny for Africa," she wrote her mother
soon after Mary's departure, perhaps in the faint hope that the Prices
would offer some assistance.

Despite its attraction, she would not accept Franz Forrester's offer. Marriage to him as the price of getting to Africa was not accept- .

able. She would go under her own steam or not at all. She began accumulating literature on safaris, but was appalled by the costs. Still, she was determined to reach Africa before 1963 ended.

By June of that year she had made tentative arrangements to hire the services of a Nairobi safari guide and was desperately trying to raise the requisite five thousand dollars. She pleaded with the Prices to back a bank loan; and although they initially agreed, they withdrew the offer on the grounds that the venture was both rash and dangerous. Eventually she mortgaged her income from the hospital for the next three years to a loan company at the usurious interest rate of twenty-four percent.

Her family was outraged by the size and nature of the debt she had incurred. Even her maternal aunt and uncle, Flossie and Bert Chapin, who had sometimes helped her financially during her university days, were scandalized. "It's madness," they told her. "If you had any sense, you'd call the whole thing off!"

Dian held adamantly to her course but tried to soothe her relatives by assuring them she would recoup the money by writing about her experiences and selling photographs and even motion pictures.

She read everything about Africa she could find. She was particularly impressed by American zoologist George Schaller's book, *The Year of the Gorilla,* in which he described his pioneering study of the rare mountain gorillas in the Belgian Congo. The subject offered such exciting journalistic possibilities that Dian decided to extend her safari from four to six weeks in order to visit the Virunga volcanoes in central Africa, the home of the mountain gorilla.

During the preparations for her journey she had continued her correspondence with Franz Forrester and had agreed to visit his family estate. "I have my riding attire all cleaned and ready, for riding is a big thing at Pookie's home," she told her mother. She also packed hiking boots and an army surplus poncho, together with a box of purloined Howard Johnson sugar cubes and American Airlines soap bars to hand out to the natives.

Dian had suffered from allergies all her life and was worried about how much they might trouble her in Africa. "About three Saturdays ago I ate a tiny, insignificant plum," she wrote home, "just to test if my allergies were under control. Well, within an hour my eyes swelled shut, I had a temperature of 102°, I threw up, and my throat swelled shut. I was really frightened." She was also subject to debilitating asthma attacks and was a frequent victim of pneumonia. Just after graduation from college she saw an X ray of her lungs, which were so scarred that she described the photos as looking like a street map of Los Angeles superimposed on a street map of New York. An essential part of Dian's safari luggage consisted of a medicine chest weighing forty-four pounds.

She had her immunization shots.

**I have been on the Camille list again due to all the inoculations. They seem to be giving me the diseases instead of preventing them. I feel like a character out of an Ernest Hemingway novel, what with the fever-delirium-chills-recovery sequence.**

A month before her scheduled departure for Africa she contracted pneumonia again. She made the best of it. "Except for the expense," she told her mother, "this is the best going-away present, since now I can have a week off from work just to rest!"

Her itinerary included Kenya, Tanganyika, Uganda, the Belgian Congo, and Southern Rhodesia. She departed September 26, 1963, with high expectations—and sixty pounds of excess luggage. During the descent into Cairo, where her plane would refuel for the long leap south to Nairobi, she became feverish and nauseated. The next thirty-six hours were a blur: crowds and noise, hot-water bottles, and half-digested meals in seedy hotels. But the symptoms vanished as mysteriously as they had occurred, and three days later she was traveling on a bus from Nairobi to Treetops, the elite up-country lodge of the Mount Kenya Safari Club, where she was to meet her white hunter guide. Pending his arrival, there were other fascinating Africans to meet.

**Bristly warthogs and baboons everywhere. Buffalo, then rhino, but too dark to photograph. Sykes monkey, Colobus monkey, crested cranes . . .**

Exhaustion felled her the day after her arrival at the luxurious lodge, and she slept until seven in the evening. Then she freshened up, dressed, and put her long black hair up in a French roll. Striving to appear sophisticated, she added earrings and a flashy ring her mother had given her.

With the hope that she looked glamorous enough for the posh surroundings, she swept out onto the patio where she was met by actor William Holden, owner of Treetops. He invited her to his table for dinner, together with a Texas oil tycoon, a millionaire big game hunter from Scotland, and two white hunters. Her eyes grew luminous with excitement as she listened to these "old hands" talk, but she herself said little. "These people really know the Africa I've so far only dreamed about."

Two nights later John Alexander, her own mail-order white hunter, arrived at Treetops with two other clients in tow. He was so

7

preoccupied with them that he hardly gave Dian a second glance. She had imagined a close association with an epic African hero—and her Great White, as she came to call him, was too busy to talk to her until the next day. She went to bed sick with dysentery and disappointment, but woke early in the morning and got gamely into her safari clothes, ready to go when her guide arrived. As the hours passed and he did not appear, she was virtually in tears—of rage.

**I'm disgusted with him! Ten-thirty already! I wish to hell he'd get here.**

John Alexander eventually picked her up in his Land Rover and they drove into Nairobi, then continued south to the northern rim of Tanzania's Serengeti Plain.

Once they were on the move, Dian relaxed a little and wondered whether her first assessment of her companion had been too harsh. Certainly he knew the animals she so much wanted to see and where to find them. As the days wore on, she worked her cameras mercilessly, begrudging every wasted opportunity to see and photograph more creatures.

"Shall we stop for a rest and lunch?" John Alexander asked wearily one day at noon.

"No! I'm just getting started, so let's not dawdle."

By October 3 they had reached Tsavo in the southeast corner of Kenya, where Dian spent the morning photographing elephant, baby rhino, and buffalo. That night she again suffered from dysentery and vomiting and awoke absolutely drained. Nevertheless, she insisted they move on at dawn and had to curb her temper as she waited for her increasingly lethargic guide.

**Alexander cranky, but who cares! Up at 6:30 and out. Buffalo pictures mainly. No lion. Breakfast watching baboons, and he eats like one!**

A few days later they drove into the Ngorongoro Crater, a famous landmark in Masai country in northern Tanzania. Since childhood Dian had suffered from a paralyzing fear of heights, and as the road into the crater dropped precipitously, she cowered on the floor of the Land Rover with her head covered, emerging only when they reached level ground.

**The floor of the crater is a vast plain with some swamp area and a small lake. The Masai graze their cattle there and the warriors still kill lion in spite of the government's efforts. The flies literally obscure the babies' faces. The moment we stepped out of the truck, the flies and people descended on us—but spray took care of the flies and shillings took care of the people. No picture can**

be taken for less than a shilling. I also have a huge bag of beads—really beautiful, gaudy things. Their eyes would light up, they would whistle, ooh and aah and grab, but I still couldn't save a shilling.

If the Masai were something of a disappointment, so was her guide.

Saw five male lion, herds of wildebeest, zebra, impala . . . Charged by one rhino, but Alexander wouldn't hold the car still long enough for a decent cine of the charge, so most of that twenty feet of film will be a series of bumps and sky. I'm not pleased with him, but I guess I should be grateful that he's not a drinker, which makes him a rarity in these parts. He's reliable as far as driving, finding game, etc., and he won't risk any dangers. But God, he is a bore and I feel as though a huge tsetse fly were hovering over my head all the time I'm with him. He's very, very, very, very British, and I have a new term for them now—White Masai: arrogant, proud, and completely lacking in substance. A native only has to sneeze in front of them and they are off on a rampage of muttering, vengefulness, and oaths.

Oh, but I really find this Alexander hateful. Yesterday I was tempted to abandon him and his Land Rover when he claimed some African had given him a bit of lip. It spoiled a whole afternoon of game-viewing for me. But on the other hand, when this jerk wants something, he's as obsequious as a lamb. He may be tall and handsome, but to me he's ugly.

After a week on the road Dian put her camera gear in top order and made herself as presentable as possible for a visit to Olduvai Gorge on the southern border of Serengeti National Park. She was hoping to meet Dr. Louis Leakey, the celebrated paleoanthropologist.

Leakey had been uncovering hominid fossils in Olduvai Gorge since the early 1930s. His discoveries had clearly established that man had been around far longer than anyone had suspected, and that his roots were in East Africa, not Asia, as had previously been believed. His interpretation of the place these fossils held in man's family tree had made Leakey a figure of enormous controversy among his scientific brethren; but the public loved him for his ability to make an obscure branch of knowledge exciting and accessible. By the 1960s he had reached such a pinnacle of fame that it was a major triumph for any journalist to obtain an interview with him.

Dian had decided to take a chance on finding Leakey at his camp, although the likelihood that he would be there was remote. He was sixty years old now and preferred to be in Nairobi, far from the heat and harshness of the gorge.

Seen through a curtain of shimmering heat, the Olduvai field camp looked deserted and unimpressive—a few drab tin huts and some dusty Land Rovers and small trucks. However, as Dian and Alexander bounced into the parking area trailing a thick cloud of red dust, several natives and a noisy pair of dalmatians appeared out of nowhere; and when a wildebeest with a Sykes monkey riding on its back trotted by, Dian recognized them as some of Leakey's famous pets.

Then, with delight, she spotted Leakey himself striding toward her, white hair blowing in the wind, patches on the knees of his khaki boiler suit, two days' growth of salt-and-pepper stubble on his chin.

Always one to rise to the occasion when a good-looking woman was at its center, Leakey grasped Dian's hand in both of his, and she responded with such warm and prolonged pressure, and such a look of frank admiration, that he became as affable with this intruder as if she had been a welcome and invited guest.

He questioned her about where she had been; then about what she still wished to see and do. "I particularly want to go to the Virunga volcano country to meet the mountain gorillas," she told him.

Leakey eyed his dusty, gangly, yet attractive visitor speculatively. "Are you merely interested in gorillas as a spectator or as a journalist?"

"Much more than that, Dr. Leakey," she responded earnestly. "Someday I plan to come here to live and work."

"Indeed. Well, the study of the great apes is a neglected and tremendously significant field, you know. It could shed a great deal of light on the evolution and behavior of our own early, apelike ancestors. . . . But now you're here. Would you like to tour the dig? Can't go myself, but one of the men will take you around."

"That would be wonderful, but could I possibly take your photo first? You know, the best thing about coming on this safari is my good fortune in meeting you." Dian gave Leakey the smile of a woman who knows she is being admired.

Accompanied by a sullen Alexander, who had been totally ignored during this interchange, Dian followed the guide to view and photograph the age-old burials. Then they moved on to a current dig where workers were carefully uncovering the fossilized skull of a giant giraffe. While maneuvering to get a picture, Dian slipped and wrenched her ankle. Grimacing with pain, she muttered to Alexander, who was close behind, "Oh, shit! I think I'm going to vomit!"

He gave her a look of distaste, taking due note of her return to the irritable Dian Fossey he had come to know so well, now that she was out of Leakey's presence.

"Well, how about carrying me back?" she demanded. "I can't get up that hill on only one foot!"

When they returned to the camp compound, Leakey showed great solicitude, insisting on personally examining and bandaging Dian's ankle, while his wife, Mary, fetched her a cold and soothing drink. As they parted, Leakey put his hand lightly on Dian's shoulder—a somewhat awkward gesture since he had to reach up to her.

"Go and see your gorillas if you can manage that ankle. I think you will. You strike me as that sort of person. And keep in touch."

Uncertain whether he meant this last remark or was simply being polite, Dian was nevertheless in psychic ecstasy—if in considerable physical pain—as Alexander gunned the Land Rover back up the dusty road.

Through the next four days Dian and John Alexander worked their way northward, skirting Lake Victoria, then on through lush jungle toward Kampala in Uganda. Continual disagreements between them sometimes left Dian shaking with fury. They argued about everything, but mostly about the progress of the safari and whether Alexander was earning his daily fee. He was extremely reluctant to take her into the Congo to see the gorillas.

"You really try to get away with murder," she told him angrily. "I'm here to see as much as I can, and I'm not leaving until I see the Virunga gorillas."

"It's not that easy," he argued stubbornly. "There are political problems in the Congo, and my Land Rover and equipment have to have extra insurance. Are you prepared to pay for that?"

"I *told* you I've run out of money," she retorted furiously.

Alexander grunted and speeded up the truck.

**This blasted white hunter has not even made arrangements to get a visa for the Congo, and he keeps coming up with all kinds of new expenditures—the cost of his visa, repair on the Land Rover, gifts for mountain guides, and now extra insurance! He's going to get a blank check—which is all I have left!**

Her ankle was slowly improving but she still couldn't get a boot on that foot, so she lived in her shoes.

11

I'm grateful to have left Kenya and Tanganyika behind because that also means the end of the British for a while. There are few Europeans in Uganda, and the Congo has only French and Belgians, far more broad-minded than the English. There are so many native tribes around Lake Victoria that it's impossible to distinguish one from the others. Indians are thrown in to boot, and hundreds of different types of half-breeds. The costumes are as mixed up as the skin colors—and they are all staring at me! I found two little Masai boys on the plains who were all dyed with red ocher. They were wonderful—as shy as the animals of being photographed, but I snapped away.

On the morning of October 15 the pair arrived at the village of Kisoro and its Traveler's Rest hotel, near the Uganda-Congo-Rwanda border. By now they were hardly exchanging a word, but Dian was glad of the silence for it enabled her to absorb the African scene without distraction.

The Traveler's Rest sits within hiking distance of mountain gorilla country on the western slopes of the Virunga volcano chain, and during the eight years Walter Baumgartel had been the hotel's proprietor, he had become something of an expert on these elusive animals. A stop at the Traveler's Rest was almost mandatory for anyone wanting news of the gorillas. On this occasion Baumgartel informed Dian and Alexander that the world-renowned wildlife photographers Joan and Alan Root were currently on Mt. Mikeno, in the Congo section of the Virungas, where they had been filming gorillas for some weeks. Reluctantly the white hunter agreed to try and reach them.

They crossed into the Congo and a day later reached the jumping-off point for the climb to Mt. Mikeno. By late that evening they had completed the ascent.

We are now at a base camp high up on the Virungas. The Great White and I climbed Mt. Mikeno from a small village of thatched huts and hundreds of blacks at the base of the mountain. After hours of haggling over loads and money, we hired eleven porters and two guides. The altitude here is 11,400 feet, so you can imagine what happened to my lungs on the way up. It took six and a half hours to get to this camp and I thought I would die. My rib cage was bursting, my legs were creaking and in agony, and my ankle felt as though a crocodile had his jaws around it. How those porters do it, each carrying around thirty pounds on his head, I'll never know.

Halfway up, the leading guide was charged by a gorilla! All I could hear were the screams of the animal, and by the time we got to the spot, the gorilla was probably a mile away. I was extremely disappointed not to see him, and even more so when they all described the incident in such fast Swahili I couldn't understand a word. Of course, the Great White is reluctant to translate!

Yesterday we started out early to track the family of gorillas we had heard on the way up. We found fresh tracks—much bigger than my foot. And fresh nests and wild celery croppings. But after six hours of hacking our way through dense jungle, I had to give up. There's little water available in volcanic mountains, and my tongue was literally stuck to the roof of my mouth and my lips were sealed together from thirst. My right ankle was all but useless, and my whole body was one big sheet of pain.

When I reached camp, our cookboy, Manual, came running, looked at me, and started screaming for help. I didn't realize what I must have looked like—swollen lips, bloodshot eyes, phlegm running from my mouth. He brought me water, made tea, and took off my shoes. I collapsed.

A few days later Alan Root and his wife, Joan, who were living in a rickety cabin nearby and resented our invasion, took pity on me and asked if I wanted to go out with them. He seems like a gentle, soft-spoken person, but I feel a little uncomfortable with him. He looks sort of studious in his gray, plastic-rimmed glasses, and he's probably stooped from bending over to get just the right shot. It's obvious he's confident in his photography and knows he's one of the best in the world. And his wife, Joan, seems made in his image. They handled the terrain like pros, while I panted along behind.

The terrain was unbelievable, almost straight up, and we had to hang on to vines to get along or go on hands and knees. For a long time we found no sign of gorillas, but then we came upon a bedding place where thirteen of them had slept the night before.

There followed the experience that would determine the future course of Dian's life.

Sound preceded sight, and odor preceded both in the form of an overwhelming, musky, barnyard yet humanlike stench. Then the thin mountain air was shattered like window glass by a high-pitched series of deafening screams. Nothing can possibly prepare one for such a terrifying avalanche of sound. The only thing that prevented me from fleeing down the misted slopes of the volcano was the presence of Manual behind me and the Congolese tracker, Sanweke, guiding Alan Root ten yards ahead.

We all froze where we stood hip deep in a soaking-wet bed

13

of stinging nettles surrounded by a seemingly impenetrable wall of foliage. For a minute the chill, fog-dripping forest was unbelievably silent, then it was rent by even more ferocious screams punctuated by thunderous, drumlike tattoos. Once more we froze until the forest was hushed.

We could see only a few feet into the lush, green mass, but Sanweke now very carefully and almost silently began cutting a window through it with his *panga* bush knife. Alan motioned me forward and I crept to his side, both of us stooping low. He pointed, and I peered through the opening. There they were: the devilmen of native stories; the basis of the King Kong myth; the last of the Mountain Kings of Africa.

A group of about six adult gorillas stared apprehensively back at us through the opening in the wall of vegetation. A phalanx of enormous, half-seen, looming black bodies surmounted by shiny black patent-leather faces with deep-set warm brown eyes. They were big and imposing, but not monstrous at all. Somehow they looked more like members of a picnic party surprised by interlopers. Their bright gazes darted nervously from under their heavy brows as they tried to determine if we were dangerous. They were evidently wondering if it was safe to stay or if they had better run for it.

"*Kweli nudugu yanga!*" These words in Swahili, whispered by the awestruck Manual, who was also seeing his first gorilla, summed up exactly what I was feeling.

"Surely, God, these are my kin."

I left Mt. Mikeno next day, never doubting that somehow I would return to learn more about the Virunga gorillas.

After three and a half hours spent struggling down the mountain through thunder, lightning, and mud, Dian reached the Traveler's Rest, freezing and covered in muck from head to foot.

Walter Baumgartel greeted her warmly, and after a good night's sleep Dian awoke to the sounds of chickens clucking and Baumgartel's Siamese cat lapping fresh cream from a bowl on the terrace. When she looked out the open window, she saw Baumgartel striding across the tidy courtyard in his pyjamas, bringing a pail of hot water for her bath. In the background the blue-green Virungas seemed to dissolve in the pale morning mist. She watched them slowly retreating into their own mystery.

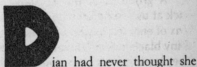ian had never thought she would be as pleased to see Franz Forrester as she was in the moment when she stepped off the plane in Salisbury and searched the crowd in the arrivals area for a friendly face. There was the doggedly devoted Pookie, accompanied by his smiling, handsome mother. They took her off to the elaborate family town house where Dian unburdened herself of the troubles she had endured with her white hunter.

"Don't let it spoil your trip, my dear," Mrs. Forrester consoled her. "Just put him out of your mind."

Next day Dian and Franz drove two hundred miles south to the wide sweep of the home farm—a tobacco plantation near Victoria. Here she met Franz's elder brother, Alexie. Shirtless, dark-haired, tall and brawny, he was riding a tractor in a tobacco field when she first saw him. She was impressed.

**The Forresters' farm is truly lovely—horses, gardens, tennis, a big, gracious house that fits the count's background, and lots of black servants. I like them all, but Alexie is quite remarkable. I think he is inclined to be arrogant, but there's something powerful about him I never felt with Pookie. He's thirty-one, single, and just about the best-looking man I've ever laid eyes on. Pookie sulked last night as Alexie and I really hit it off and kind of ignored him all day.**

**Pookie wants me to go off on a tour and see Victoria Falls, but if I go I won't see Alexie again. And so-o-o-o . . .**

Politeness overcame passion and she took the tour. But it was not the last she was to see of Alexie.

She heard from him soon after she'd returned to work at the Korsair Children's Hospital.

**Alexie! Oooh what a letter! He has been traveling in Mozambique to survey tobacco plantations and opportunities, but says there's not much security there for whites. *It is not the place to get married in and raise a family and work for a future*, he says. He seems terribly eager for my advice and thinks he'd like to come over here and go to Notre Dame University for a while, if I approve!**

Dian approved, though cautiously. "I believe you would like this country but doubt you would care to live here. I'd be happy to show you 'my' farm and introduce you to the Angus family—all ninety of them."

The following autumn Alexie flew to New York, then on to Notre Dame to register. Dian had anticipated an early reunion with him, but as she soon discovered, it was first things first with Alexie. Although he phoned her frequently, he did not come to Louisville. "It's three hundred miles from South Bend," he told her, "and I don't have the time to spare just yet."

It was not until Thanksgiving that he found the time.

**Alexie has just left after his week here. . . . I really need all of *this* week to recover; tornadoes and hurricanes have a lot to learn from him! It seems he has taken a part-time job that occupies his weekends, thus he hasn't been able to make it down here and was too embarrassed to go into details before.**

At first he seemed stiff and distant in his city clothes, but when he shed them for farm attire to help with the chores at Glenmary, he exuded the same appeal she had felt when she met him on a tractor at his family's estate. They became lovers. But when he returned to Notre Dame, he left behind him a confused and resentful woman.

**I cannot as yet express what I feel or don't feel about him. I can say this, though—I will have nothing to do with him seriously until he is through taking his bows. I would say he is suffering from a rather enlarged cranium, and rightly so, because everybody in his university, business, and social world is apparently approaching him on bended knee just to share the aura of his personality and brilliant magnetism.**

The brief relationship between them already seemed to be waning. Dian immersed herself into her several projects. In addition to her regular job at the hospital, she gave slide shows to local service clubs for a small fee; she was trying to sell her 16mm safari film to a television program, *Bold Journey*; she was attempting to interest the *National Geographic* in her still pictures of the Karamojong tribe; and she was working on several magazine articles.

Dian spent at least three hours each night writing—usually scratching out half of what she had written the night before. One piece, entitled "I Photographed the Mountain Gorilla," ended:

**It was with no small degree of reluctance that I departed from the Virungas, the Roots, Sanweke, and the gorilla families I had come to know and respect for their individuality, their independence, and their majesty.**

**I am deeply concerned over their future. How much longer will they continue to thrive, in view of the many opposing interests threatening their habitat—poachers, agriculturalists, and pastoralists? Will an uneasily settled, newly independent Congo cease to care about the anthropoid treasures it harbors? Will the gorilla, like so many other wild animals, merely become the hapless victim of our times, whose future bends to the will of frenzied human aggrandizements?**

This article produced only rejection slips from *Saturday Evening Post, Life,* and *Reader's Digest.* Long discouraging months were to pass before any of the African material found a publisher. Eventually, the Louisville *Courier Journal*'s weekend color supplement printed stories and photos by Dian on the gorillas; on her meeting with the celebrated paleoanthropologist, Louis Leakey, at Olduvai; and on other aspects of the safari. When she received her first check, for one hundred dollars, she was so proud that she photographed herself holding it and sent the picture to her mother in California.

With the publication of the safari articles, Dian became a minor celebrity in Louisville.

**Next Saturday night I have to go to Jim and Ann Pope's house for dinner with my safari movies to show the mayor, the Louisville zoo director, and others. I'm a bit nervous that the zoo director will detect my ignorance. At any rate, I have my new suit and pearls, so at least I'll look all right if I call a kongoni a hartebeest.**

Dian's rejections by national publications made her realize that her writing was not up to professional standards, so she enrolled in the Famous Writer's School, a correspondence course fronted by well-known American authors.

Applying her lessons diligently, she began a novel for young people, set in Africa.

When her friend Mary White asked how it was going, Dian

replied glumly, "The keys are sticking from my sweat dripping on them, and I'm trying desperately to finish the stupid thing before it finishes me!"

She eventually sent the manuscript to the Doubleday publishing company and with a delirious sense of freedom went back to helping on the farm in her spare time and running through the fields playing with the dogs.

At Christmas, Alexie turned down Dian's invitation to return to Louisville. She was furious and spent the holidays with her parents in California, doing a slow burn. On her return:

**I collected the mail, which included two pious "forgive me"-type letters from Alexie. Then a phone call, and another lo-o-ong letter. He is coming, finally, on the twenty-eighth for four days. Just between us, I shall be very happy to see him, but I hope I don't show it!**

And after the visit:

**Yes, Alexie now says he wants to marry me. I am adamant, though, about waiting until my African safari debt is paid off, and that is another seventeen months and fifteen days away. A lot can happen in that time, but it is a chance we both have to take.**

Doubleday's response to her manuscript arrived. The editors felt her book should be directed to the adult market so she could take fuller advantage of the wealth of material.

"With due respect to their opinions," she told a friend, "I can't see why the book can't sell to both the juvenile and adult markets. I refuse to drop my characters—they're a product of my Smith Corona womb and just can't be aborted now."

Doubleday advised they were returning the manuscript with a draft of suggested revisions. However, the changes asked for were so extensive that she lost hope and abandoned the book.

Dian had almost given up again on Alexie Forrester when he wrote to say that his mother was coming to the United States and was eager to meet her parents.

This announcement came on such short notice that by the time Dian could call and warn her mother, the Countess Forrester had already arrived in San Francisco—with Alexie in tow. Mrs. Price was in a frenzy.

"I would have liked to entertain them properly," she wailed, "but how can I with so little time?"

"You don't have to do anything special," Dian told her.

"I presume since they're coming here your friend must have serious intentions?"

"That's difficult to know."

"Then what is this all about?"

"Don't take it so seriously, Mother. Mrs. Forrester has a sister in San Francisco, a Roman Catholic nun, and she's probably going mainly to see her."

Alexie and his mother arrived at the Prices' home for dinner, accompanied by Sister Maura, a senior administrator in the California Catholic school system. Kitty and Richard gave the visitors a cordial reception, though Kitty was so nervous she was shaking. She felt that her daughter's entire future lay in her hands. And marriage into such a distinguished family was more than she could have dreamed of for her only child.

As Dian may have anticipated, the Forresters were not impressed by the Prices. Though Alexie and his mother did their best to conceal this fact, Sister Maura was openly hostile. From her rigidly Catholic point of view, the Prices were living in sin since Kitty had been divorced. Dian's already shaky relationship with Alexie was further jarred by this unpleasant complication.

Dian again immersed herself in her own work, still trying to rid herself of the safari debt. She was living so close to the bone that she was occasionally negligent about her rent, and at one point the power company cut off her electricity.

This period of drab endeavor was relieved by the attentions of a handful of well-to-do Louisville admirers. Although Dian found these men and their lives superficial in the extreme, she was not above using her experiences with them to impress her society-conscious mother, and perhaps to excuse her failure to ensnare the illustrious Alexie.

"My social life is a whirl. Cream of Louisville society. Mostly I've been seeing this teddy-bear type who maintains a job at the university here but really doesn't have to work. Very leisurely. We went to his sister's house for an afternoon of riding—very plush, with a stable full of show horses and jumpers and a groom for each horse. During cocktail hour I showed the African movies. Then he dragged me to some in-laws for the most ostentatious birthday party, which took place in a house that must have been spread over at least an acre— Olympic-sized swimming pool, tennis courts, formal gardens, and a go-go girl rented for the evening, plus a combo. So, you see, I don't have much time to brood about Alexie, though he still calls all the time."

In his abrupt and unpredictable way, Alexie suddenly appeared in Louisville, playing the ardent suitor. He demanded, rather than proposed, marriage and insisted on setting a date for the following August. Dian allowed herself to be swept along but not overwhelmed by him.

**He has promised me an engagement ring made from a family heirloom belonging to the Austrian royals, but what he gave me was a silk negligee covered with lace—breathtaking but somewhat impractical.**

**Anyway, the weekend was a dream. One of the happiest I've ever had. We spent the day at Glenmary just talking about our love and at night went to Mrs. Henry's—Mary White's mother— and I got all dressed up in borrowed plumes. We went to the Old House for chateaubriand and wine, then on the town and danced to dawn.**

When Alexie returned to Notre Dame, Dian's skepticism about a future with him had been somewhat dispelled. But not for long. Within a month he had changed his plans.

"He now wants to postpone the wedding for two years!" she wrote to the Prices. "He says, being a student, he feels he's not ready financially to take on a wife! Of course, I would intend to work, but that doesn't seem to be his style. He feels some horrible stigma attaches to the working wife. That aunt of his, the nun, influenced him greatly. I know she didn't like me—or you, I might add. You know, being divorced and so on. Anyway, please don't be heartbroken because I'm not. I've made it clear I don't intend to wait around for another two years if he can't make up his mind."

A few weeks later, in March 1966, Dr. Louis Leakey, whom she had not seen or heard from since her visit to Olduvai Gorge three years earlier, arrived in Louisville on a lecture tour—and the course of Dian's life was irrevocably changed.

**3**

The auditorium was filled almost an hour before the lecture began, and I had to sit nearly at the back. I had brought along the three articles I'd written for the Louisville *Courier Journal* about my African safari. After Dr. Leakey had given his talk, which enthralled the audience, I nervously joined the line of people eager to speak with him. When my turn came, he gave a crinkly smile of recognition and gave my hand a good long squeeze. I was so surprised he knew me that I just pushed my damp and wrinkled articles into his hand with the rushed explanation that he might be interested in reading the article on Olduvai.

His eyes narrowed into the perceptive squints that I was later to know as his "keen" look. "Miss Fossey, isn't it? Please wait until I've finished with all these people." Not knowing what to expect, I waited at the back of the stage until finally he came over and started throwing a barrage of questions at me. Had I gone to Kabara? With whom did I go? Why did I go there? How often had I been able to see the gorillas? What was my current profession, and what were my plans for the future?

I told him that all I really wanted was to spend my life working with animals—that had always been my dream, and I was especially interested in the gorillas on the Virunga mountains.

Leakey was again struck by the intensity of this tall, handsome woman who had lingered in his memory long after their first meeting.

"And how is your ankle? Did it heal properly?"

She looked at him, astonished that he recalled the incident, then laughed. "Yes, you bandaged it beautifully. Not a bone out of place."

"Come to my hotel tomorrow morning at eight. You might be just the person I have in mind to start a long-term study of gorillas."

During that night half my mind was already planning resolutely for the dozens of things that would need to be done before leaving for the Virungas, while the other half kept admonishing, "It's not possible. Things just don't happen like this!" In the morning I rushed off to the hotel on my way to work, wearing my weary white hospital garb, though I'd been sorely tempted to don my treasured safari clothes.

Our interview lasted about an hour. Dr. Leakey did most of the talking. He praised Jane Goodall, then in her sixth year studying chimpanzees. Using her as his prime example, he told me of his conviction that women made far better field students of animals than men because of their patience and capacity to give more fully of themselves.

He said he had "already tested" twenty-two applicants for the gorilla field work and had not been satisfied with any of them. I found myself wondering why I, just an occupational therapist, should be considered above others much better qualified. Though I had an absolute conviction that I could succeed, I nonetheless found myself giving Dr. Leakey reasons why I should not be selected:

Number one, I had no means of funding myself. He waved this off as a minor problem, totally confident that it was one he was especially capable of handling. I told him that although I'd had two years of preveterinary medicine before switching to occupational therapy, I had no training in anthropology, ethology, biology, zoology, or any of the other "ologies." Leakey scoffed, "I have no use for overtrained people. I prefer those who are not specifically educated for this field since they go into the work with open minds and without prejudice and preconceptions." Then I brought up my age—thirty-four. "But this is the perfect age to begin such work," Leakey said. "You have attained maturity and won't be apt to take rash actions."

We then discussed George Schaller's work, and just as I felt the meeting was drawing to a close, he suddenly asked, "Have you had your appendix out?" When I answered no, he launched into some hair-raising stories of people who had been struck down by appendicitis in remote regions and suffered lingering deaths. He concluded, "So you will have to have your appendix removed."

For the next few weeks I carried on my duties with the crippled children whom I dearly loved, giving no indication of the excitement bubbling inside me. Of course, the first priority was to get rid of the appendix, which seemed a small sacrifice for such an opportunity.

Paying the full cost of the operation was impossible on my loan-repayment budget, so I had to let a doctor friend in on my secret. I asked if he knew a surgeon who would attend to it as though it were a necessary appendectomy. The surgeon was found, the date was set, and it was only left up to me to convincingly feign appendicitis. Two days of pitiful moans and side-clutching (sometimes the wrong side) was persuasive enough.

The operation was routine, except for my waking up in the recovery room and yelling, "Are the gorillas really worth this?"

When I arrived home from the hospital, there was a letter from Dr. Leakey. "Actually, there isn't any dire need for you to have your appendix removed," it began. I nearly burst my stitches in indignation.

But my exasperation turned to joy when I read on to discover he was formally offering me the job, if I still wanted it, and if he could corral a suitable grant.

The letter read like a gilt-edged invitation to heaven. Dr. Leakey told her that he would try to arrange for all her travel expenses and the money needed to set up a camp and pay for one or more African helpers, her food, and photographic supplies. He would try to raise enough to pay her a small salary, as he had done for Jane Goodall, with the expectation that she could earn additional funds by writing articles about her research.

He cited the National Geographic Society as likely to act as her sponsor if she agreed to give them first refusal on photographs and articles. After she had established a rapport with the gorillas, Dian might need the services of a film cameraman, who could be attached to the camp, to produce a television movie from which she should receive a substantial amount, Leakey surmised. And, he concluded, National Geographic might want a popular book from her in addition to the scientific one she, of course, would write.

He wanted her out in the field "as soon as possible" but still had no word on permission for her to go to Kabara and was intending to visit the ambassador for the Congo Republic, in Nairobi, to tend to the matter.

Two days after receiving Leakey's offer, Dian submitted her resignation to Korsair Children's Hospital. Her plan was to drive her ancient Saab to the Prices' home in California, where she would await word from Leakey on grants and travel permits.

When she told Alexie of her decision, he was incredulous, then furious.

"You must be out of your mind! A white woman alone in that part of Africa? Are you trying to commit suicide?"

The Prices were even more shaken than when Dian had announced she had converted to Catholicism.

"What's come over you?" Kitty cried. "Why are you doing this to us?"

"Mother," Dian pleaded, "it's an incredible offer. I'll never have such an opportunity again in my life. I just won't turn it down."

"Opportunity? To live with wild gorillas and wild natives?"

"You don't understand, Mother. I'll be doing utterly fascinating research, the first of its kind."

"Why can't you be like other girls?" her mother moaned. "Look at Mary White, how happy she is. What have *you* done with your *real* opportunities?"

"I'm different from Mary. I want different things."

When Dian shared her plans with Father Raymond, the Trappist monk who had introduced to her Catholicism, he seemed relieved that she was steering away from Alexie Forrester, of whom he may have been a little jealous.

"This African research project is a gift from God," he wrote the Prices. "She will never be satisfied with the common, ordinary things most girls of her day are satisfied with. She requires some truly stupendous accomplishment before she will be at ease on earth. She will never be perfectly satisfied until she is the saint she longs to be. . . ."

Resolutely Dian clung to her decision.

**Now it was time to take the next step toward Kabara, which meant severing the deep attachments of many years in Louisville. Leaving the place I'd grown to love—the children, my home, the farm dogs, and my friends—was one of the most difficult things I've ever had to do.**

She drove to California but found that staying with the Prices was particularly uncomfortable after several years spent on her own.

As the months dragged by with no further instructions from Dr. Leakey she slipped into a depression. Though she studied Swahili and audited a class in primatology at Stanford University, she began to think she had lost the gorilla project as well as everything else. In desperation she wrote to Leakey:

"On August 1, I left everything I owned and loved in Kentucky

24

to come to California. I did this on the basis of your correspondence, which made a departure date seem imminent. I realize that unforeseen hindrances have arisen that you are certainly not accountable for, but I cannot endure another three months of nonproductivity. It is for this reason that I must ask you for a definitive date of departure. . . .

"If you think that more than a month will elapse before you can send for me, then I most definitely shall have to set about finding another occupational therapy job somewhere in the States. . . . This is certainly not the way I'd hoped things would turn out, but I'm neither financially nor constitutionally able to endure another month of idleness."

Shortly thereafter, Leakey cabled that the Wilkie Foundation, which for years had supported Jane Goodall, had agreed to provide a grant to establish the gorilla project. Although it would be another few weeks before National Geographic funding fell into place, the Wilkie money was enough to get things moving.

Dian's luggage included an Olivetti typewriter and four cameras together with tripod, lenses, and countless rolls of film. She boxed enough paper, notebooks, envelopes, carbon paper, pens, and typewriter ribbons to equip a moderate-sized office. She also purchased at least a three-year supply of heavy-duty clothing, including jeans, parkas, and army surplus ponchos.

Finally, on December 15, 1966, Dian Fossey departed for Africa.

Her mother was almost too upset to bid her farewell, but Richard Price spoke on her behalf. "I need not tell you that your mother is heartbroken," he said sternly. "I can only hope you will learn something sensible from this experience, though I'm not sure what."

Dian journeyed by way of Louisville, where she again said good-bye to Mary White, to Mary's ailing mother, Mrs. Henry, to Father Raymond, and to her associates and the children at the Korsair hospital. She also phoned Alexie, who was still angry. "If that's your calling, I can't stop you, but I think you'll wish you'd decided differently," he told her.

"I'm not forgetting you, Alexie, and I am not saying good-bye."

In Washington, D.C., she visited her National Geographic sponsors.

**Unfortunately, as I was preparing to leave California, I had come down once again with pneumonia, and it goes without saying that I presented a sorry specimen of an "intrepid gorilla girl" to my sponsors and everyone else I met. I was to learn later that**

25

the National Geographic Society's vice-president for research wrote to Dr. Leakey expressing his serious misgivings about my ability to do the job.

In London she spent two days with Jane Goodall's mother and sister. While waiting for the night flight to Nairobi, heavily dosed with antibiotics, coughing and shaking with fever, her attention was caught by an announcement on the public address system.

"Paging Mrs. Root. Will Mrs. Root please come to the BOAC information desk for a telephone call." The name didn't register until I chanced to look up and see Joan rushing over to the nearest courtesy phone, where a call from Alan was awaiting her. I flew across the lobby, trailing wads of Kleenex, and arrived at her side to hear her say: "Alan, guess who's here? It's Dian from Kabara." A murmuring followed on the line. "What are you doing here?" she asked. "I'm going to study the Virunga gorillas at Kabara." I could hear Alan's squawks of incredulity.

Our flight was called, and as we waited to board I explained briefly how it had all come about. I could sense that Joan, too, thought the whole scheme was preposterous. We switched to the topic of their latest filming project in the Galápagos. It was only later that I was to realize how very fortunate this unexpected meeting was for me.

I was met in Nairobi on the morning of December 22 by Dr. Leakey's secretary, Mrs. Crisp, and within minutes we were speeding away from the airport to a small hotel near the Coryndon Museum where he had his offices. Stepping from the car onto the slick stone patio of the hotel, I felt both feet slide out from under me and made as graceful a landing as possible on both knees. As I sat back and watched the blood gush, Mrs. Crisp said, as only a British woman could: "Oh, what a pity, you've laddered your stockings!" I burst into hysterical laughter, which no doubt gave Mrs. Crisp pause to reflect on the recruiting abilities of her employer.

First day back in Africa or not, I pleaded the need for sleep. Later in the afternoon I was awakened by a phone call from Dr. Leakey, asking me to meet him at the museum the next morning. He seemed very fit, far more so than when I'd last seen him in Louisville, and his enthusiasm for seeing another of his projects launched matched my own. He introduced me to his staff, then we hastily drew up a list of essential materials I'd need to collect before leaving for Kabara. Though the Congo was in political tur-moil, and I still had not received official government permission

26

to work in the Parc des Virungas, neither of us gave a thought to making a reconnaissance trip. Many people thought this was a foolhardy way to begin a long-term research project, but we were both far too anxious to get started.

As it was, I had to endure the delay imposed by the Christmas holiday. Dr. Leakey wanted me to share Christmas with Jane Goodall and her husband, Hugo van Lawick, who were going to be camping at Lake Beringo for a few days. I felt more than a little uncomfortable, but Dr. Leakey had made up his mind and there was no changing it.

Jane and Hugo welcomed me graciously into their midst. Their combi van held a little artificial Christmas tree and was festooned with balloons. The presence of a rapidly decaying ostrich egg in the combi added a nontraditional scent to the occasion.

A disastrous polio epidemic had recently struck down many of the chimps at Jane's Gombe research station. A precious shipment of polio vaccine had arrived, and she and Hugo were anxious to return to begin distributing it in doctored bananas. Dr. Leakey thought it advisable for me to go to Gombe with them to see how their camp was run.

I traveled to Gombe with an imitation-leopard-skin carryall bag my parents had given me years earlier. Because of its striking realism, I asked Jane if it shouldn't be hidden somewhere in the cabin lest it frighten the chimps when they arrived for their bananas. Jane assured me that the animals wouldn't pay any attention to it, but I tucked it far back in a corner of the main room. The first couple of chimps to arrive caused no problems, simply grabbing their bananas and leaving. Then a sharp-eyed female spotted the bag. She let out a piercing scream and fled, followed by several others who had not even had an opportunity to see the bag. I quickly hid it in an adjoining room, but it was several hours before the chimps returned to the door.

On my return to Nairobi the Kabara preparations began in earnest. Joan Root provided invaluable advice and assistance in shopping for food and other camp needs. Finally, only the choice of a vehicle remained, and Dr. Leakey would entrust this to no one but himself. We went to a garage in Nairobi where he almost immediately picked out a secondhand Land Rover. It had a canvas roof, couldn't be locked properly, and suffered from mysterious internal ailments. Dr. Leakey took it on the test run of its life through the streets of residential Nairobi. Pedestrians and law-abiding vehicles scattered as the Land Rover's brakes, gears, and engine were put through their paces. When it finally wheezed back to the garage, it had won Dr. Leakey's approval.

That afternoon I found myself, accompanied by one of Dr. Leakey's African workers, frightening the stripes off zebras and stampeding other forms of wildlife in the game park where I'd gone for instructions in the fine art of driving a Land Rover. The fact that the African spoke no English and I spoke very little Swahili didn't much hinder communication between us—his facial expressions and gestures clearly conveyed his emotions, ranging from mild apprehension to sheer horror at the way I handled the car while simultaneously trying to view the game and look up words in my English/Swahili dictionary. When he left me after our "lesson," I'm sure he was convinced I wasn't going to make it safely out of Nairobi, much less all the way to the Congo.

He wasn't the only one in Nairobi harboring reservations about my chances for success. Alan Root considered the proposed venture sheer madness. He let Dr. Leakey know, in no uncertain terms, what he thought about sending a totally inexperienced girl some seven hundred miles across Africa to the Congo without even the documents required for her to begin her research.

Blissfully unaware of their confrontation, I was busily involved in the near-impossible chore of squeezing all my gear into the Land Rover, which I'd named Lily. Then, two days before my scheduled departure, Alan told me he intended to accompany me in his own Land Rover to make sure I at least reached the right country, and to assist me with the formalities of gaining permission to set up a research camp. I knew this meant a great sacrifice of time for him, but it's difficult to see how I could have begun the project at that time without his assistance.

I met Mary Leakey shortly before I left Nairobi; this was our first meeting since 1963. Her greeting was one I've never forgotten:

"So you're the girl who's going to out-Schaller Schaller, are you?"

It was an intimidating thought to carry with me.

**4**

The heavily laden, two-car convoy bearing Dian Fossey to the Virungas bounced along the dusty roads across the savannas and through the jungles of Kenya and Uganda.

Four days out of Nairobi, Alan Root and Dian reached the Traveler's Rest hotel in Kisoro, Uganda, just five miles from the Congolese frontier.

Walter Baumgartel welcomed Dian back. When he heard that she was undertaking a serious study of the mountain gorillas, he was both delighted and aghast.

"For years I've been trying to get something like this started, but I dread the thought of your going into the Virungas alone right now."

He warned Dian that Kivu province was in a state of incipient revolt against the central Congolese government and that the military, which was undisciplined at the best of times, had grown dangerously unpredictable in its treatment of foreigners.

Taking Alan Root aside, Baumgartel warned him too.

"You know how rough things can get. Use your influence. Perhaps we can persuade her to stay here and work with the gorillas on Mt. Muhabura, at least until the Congo quiets down."

Root grinned and shrugged. "You don't know this one, Walter. She'll go to Kabara come hell or high water. But we'll see. Maybe the border will be closed."

The border was open, and although there were some difficulties with her documents, Root's composure and assurance got them into the Congo. Next day they arrived at the Parc des Virungas headquarters in Rumangabo, where they hired two reliable camp workers and picked up a pair of armed park guards who were to accompany them to the campsite. They left their vehicles in the tiny village of Kibumba at the base of Mt. Mikeno; and just as Dian had done three years earlier, they hired a score of local men to carry her equipment and supplies four thousand feet up the mountain to the Kabara meadow, where Dian intended to spend the next two years.

**This return climb was really poignant. There were vistas along the trail that left me speechless with their majesty. The far sweep of the volcanoes seemed never to end. There were some wondrous, sprawling hagenia trees lining the trail that seemed so familiar I wanted to rush up to them to shake branches. The heaviness of limb and shortness of breath that come with the attitude were also vividly familiar.**

**Under Alan's supervision, the porters climbed quietly, but we saw no trace of gorillas. We did see plenty of buffalo and elephant spoor, and that was an encouraging sign. Most encouraging of all, when we reached the Kabara meadow, we saw that it had remained unspoiled; in fact, it seemed scarcely to have changed at all in the three years since I'd last been there.**

Root could stay for only two days so the two of them worked around the clock, dividing their energies between the tedious but necessary chores involved in setting up camp and reconnoitering for gorillas. Alan gave Dian a crash course in tracking.

**We found fresh tracks of a gorilla group in the relatively flat saddle area adjacent to the mountain. In my excitement I promptly took off on the trail swath left by the gorillas through dense foliage in the certainty that I would encounter the group at any moment. Some five minutes of "tracking" passed before I was aware that Alan was not behind me. Perplexed, I retraced my steps and found him patiently sitting at the very point where we had first encountered the trail.**

**With the utmost British tolerance and politeness, Alan said, "Dian, if you are ever going to contact gorillas, you must follow their tracks to where they are going rather than backtrack trails to where they've been." That was my first lesson in tracking, and one that I've never forgotten.***

On the eve of Alan's departure, Dian was thrilled to hear gorillas hooting and beating their chests in the forest no more than half a mile

*From *Gorillas in the Mist* by Dian Fossey.

away from camp. Early the next morning, January 15, 1967, the day before Dian's thirty-fifth birthday, Alan made a last check of the camp—the patched-up cabin where the African workers would stay; Dian's tent with its freshly dug rain gutters; the latrine pit and its burlap modesty screens; and the rain barrels in which drinking water would collect. Satisfied, he wished her luck and headed back down the mountain.

I'll never forget the feeling of sheer panic that I felt watching him depart. He was my last contact with civilization as I had known it. I found myself clinging to the tent pole simply to avoid running after him.

The strangeness of the near-total isolation stayed with me for several weeks. I could not listen to the shortwave radio Dr. Leakey had kindly insisted I take along because, if anything, it increased my sense of desolation. I couldn't read any of the popular or scientific books I'd brought, or even use my typewriter. All of these connections with the outside world simply made me feel lonelier than ever.

Four days after Alan Root's departure, the Congolese tracker, Sanweke, arrived at camp. As a youth he had tracked gorillas for Carl Akeley, and later he had done the same for George Schaller. He had also guided Joan and Alan Root. Dian had met him during her 1963 visit to Kabara, when she had learned to appreciate his remarkable abilities. His was a familiar face, and with his arrival her initial overwhelming sense of aloneness subsided somewhat.

January 19: Left camp at 8:30 with Sanweke, along Bitshitsi trail. About half an hour out we found a single, fresh gorilla foraging trail to the right. We followed it through high nettles and saw that it joined up with four other trails. We heard a shrill bark, went in that direction across the main path and crossed on a log over a ravine, then up the hill along many feeding trails, down an extremely steep ravine and straight up the slopes of Mikeno, where we found the group's night nests. Solid dung in each and all along the trail. We returned toward Bitshitsi and in about ten minutes saw an adult gorilla sunning to our left. It barked shrilly upon seeing us and disappeared. We went further down the trail and turned and crossed the ravine again. At that point the entire slope was in the open sun and here we encountered an adult male—a blackback—approximately eight to nine years old, who sat watching us, but displaying no fear. Time was 11:10. He gave small hoots, more like burps, before his chest beats (each five to eight thumps) and ended two of his chest beats with branch grabbing. Between three and five minutes elapsed between chest beatings, during which time two older females appeared. . . . Then the silverback boss of the family appeared from behind the young male after screaming *wraaagh* several times.

This first real contact, lasting more than three hours, involved a family of nine gorillas that Dian named Group 1. It was the beginning of a series of contacts that continued until the rains set in and the gorillas moved far down the slopes below the camp where fog, mud, and torrential runoff made tracking them extremely difficult. By the end of January, Dian had racked up more than twenty-four hours of observations, which she carefully detailed each evening in her typewritten notes.

In these early days her approaches to the animals were often clumsy. She was too persistent in pursuit, which disturbed and provoked them.

January 26: I left camp alone at 9:00 as Sanweke had malaria. At 9:20 I heard a bark to the right, not far from the Bitshitsi trail. . . . It was Group 1. . . . I take another few steps so as to be in the clearing when the animals see me, and I almost bump into the blackback male. I measure later; we were six feet apart. He stands up, blinks his eyes, opens his mouth, screams, and runs about fifty feet through the brush behind him, screaming and tearing at the undergrowth. There's quite a bit of screaming now from all sides, and a mother with infant, a juvenile, and an old female take to a tree. Old female and juvenile beat trees and chests and then juvenile runs to old female. Mother sits there holding branch with right arm and infant in left arm. She lets go of the branch and beats her chest, hitting the infant in the process. She stands up on the limb, wants to get down, but keeps looking at me hesitantly. Then in a split second she shoves the infant onto her back and leaps a good eight feet from the higher branch to a lower one covered with moss. She clings there for just a second with all four extremities and then leaps ten feet to the ground. As she lands, she gives a piercing scream and the infant lets out a long, high-pitched cry. I'm really worried about both of them, for it's not my intention to cause them harm. Just then the old female does the same thing, only when she reaches the lower branch she rolls off it and must have hit the ground on her back. She lets out a terrible scream and about four others in the bush join in.

Dian had learned from Schaller's books that it was best to remain visible to the animals at all times, but not to frighten them with a sudden appearance. She soon found that this approach had the added advantage of capitalizing on the gorillas' highly developed curiosity, attracting them to her. She tried to further arouse their curiosity by softly talking to them, but that frightened the animals away. She switched to imitating the gorillas' own vocalizations, particularly the deep, rumbling *naooooom* that sounded a little like purring, and which she would describe as a "contentment vocalization." She also mimicked mannerisms such as self-grooming and nibbling on wild celery stalks, and maintained a submissive crouch in the animals' presence.

There were inevitable setbacks.

**Today Sanweke and I were charged by two gorillas and it wasn't a bluff charge—they really meant it. We were about one hundred and fifty feet directly downhill from a group when a silverback and a female decided to eradicate us. They gave us a split second of warning with screams and roars that seemed to come from every direction at once before they descended in a gallop that shook the ground. I was determined to stand fast, but when they broke through the foliage at a dead run directly above me, I felt my legs retreating in spite of what I've read about gorillas not charging fully. I paused long enough to try to dissuade them with my voice, which only seemed to aggravate them more, if possible; and when their long, yellow canines and wild eyes were no less than two feet away, I took a very ungainly nosedive into the thick foliage alongside the trail. They whizzed on by, caught up in their own momentum. It's a good thing they didn't come back to attack, for I was certainly in no position to defend myself. It may have taken only a split second to dive into that foliage, but it took about fifteen minutes to extract myself—what a tangle!**

As the gorillas began to reveal their individual personalities, Dian gave them names. First, No-nose: **I think she is an old female, and she is the only one I've dared to name, but this is the only way I can think of her—she looks as if she has no nose.** Then came Ferdinand, her name for a big blackback, followed by a whole rush of christenings: Pucker, Mzee, Solomon, Dora, Hugger, Scapegoat, Popcorn, Tagalong, Mrs. Moses, Cassius, Monarch . . . even an adolescent male named Alexie.

Before long Dian developed an acuity for spotting trail signs that was matched by only the best African trackers. She learned that branches bent by passing animals point in the direction of travel. Gorilla knuckle prints show clearly in damp earth, and chains of dung deposits are laid neatly along a travel trail when a group is moving normally. Culs-de-sac created by individual animals that wander off the main trail to feed can be identified by taking the time to see whether there is a top layer of foliage bent back toward the main path along which the animals have been traveling. She learned to look far ahead along the line of travel to see if vine growth on trees had been disturbed or if bark had been damaged.

Dian also discovered that the gorillas' distinctive barnyard odor clung to the foliage, so the animals could sometimes be tracked by their scent, if one was willing to do it on hands and knees. Their dung, too, provided invaluable clues to a group's proximity, size, and composition, and even its collective state of mind. The freshness of a dung deposit could be tested by its relative warmth and by the number of flies and/or eggs or maggots on it. Different-sized gorillas left different-sized dung deposits, so a careful examination revealed much about the number and ages of the animals in a given group. As for the group's state of mind—dung from undisturbed gorillas had the same general smell and consistency as horse manure, but gorillas in flight or frenzy became diarrheic.

Two months after arriving in Kabara, Dian received a long letter from the associate editor of *National Geographic* magazine, setting out the Society's expectations.

**They want to do the entire works, just as was done with Jane Goodall: television special and magazine series and a popular book. They want me to start planning the first article now. I would get two thousand dollars for the article and any pictures of mine would bring fifty to two hundred dollars depending on page size.**

The opportunity to be published in *National Geographic* had appealed to Dian from the beginning, and she commenced work on an article almost immediately.

It was at this time that she began having problems with poachers.

Virunga poachers came mainly from among the pygmy Batwa people (often abbreviated to Twa), who hunted forest antelope (duikers, bushbuck, and bongo) and other game using snares, spears, and bows and arrows. Their skill at tracking and trapping was legendary. In earlier times these people had wandered freely in the forests, leaving farming to the more numerous Hutu tribesmen—people of Bantu stock. Although hunting in the park was forbidden, that was where the antelope lived, so the Batwa accepted the small risk of getting caught.

**Now in the March rainy season most of the elephant and buf-**

falo and some gorilla have gone down the mountain to lower altitudes. In an attempt to locate gorilla, Sanweke and I descended the eastern side of the volcano in an area that turned into rain forest and was filled with Twa hunters. We met four of them in the deepest, darkest park of the forest, and while Sanweke held his gun on them, I took their spears and pangas. Sanweke intended to march them out of the forest to the nearest village, but one by one they slipped away from him because I couldn't keep up and he had to keep his eye on me. That was easily the most horrible day of my life. We walked thirty-seven miles in all, through forest, mountains, and villages, before reaching the park headquarters because we couldn't return the way we descended due to the presence of the Batwa. Six hours of this walk was in the dark and about twelve hours in the pouring rain.

Finding enough nourishing food was another problem for Dian. She was not very good at adapting her cooking and eating habits to locally available products. She had a hen she called Lucy, and later acquired a cock, Dezi. She also tried to grow a vegetable garden. The hen provided her with an occasional egg, but the garden was trampled so often by night-wandering elephants and other wildlife that she finally abandoned it.

On my monthly shopping trip I buy potatoes, carrots, artichokes, lettuce, and whatever else looks appealing at the village of Kibumba at the base of the mountain. Then I drive to the small town of Goma to visit English-speaking friends and buy canned goods, and then go to Kisoro, two hours away from the base of the mountain, to pick up my mail at the Traveler's Rest and have a good meal.

Much to my sorrow, the variety of canned goods is truly poor. The meat in particular. I can only get canned frankfurters, corned beef, and several varieties of "luncheon meat," all of which are horrible. So I substitute tuna and cheese, and as fast as my poor hen can lay an egg, I claim it. She's doing very well now, for I cook her a bowl of porridge each morning (with raisins in it, of course), and as soon as she is finished she lays a Grade A, superlarge. But no porridge, no egg. I also give her a slice of butter and cheese each evening.

Food would frequently spoil or she would find that she had not bought enough, then Dian would be reduced to living on potatoes. This was not quite so unendurable as running out of cigarettes, something she also managed to do regularly.

Still, none of this was enough to dampen her enthusiasm. In her letters home she described the joy of life on the meadow and among the gorillas:

"I'm all curled up on my cot with the interior of my tent looking like a Salvation Army fire sale—wet, muddy clothes hanging everywhere around the pressure lamp in the vain hope that they will dry. Everything I own is wet.

"The nights have truly been spectacular though, for there is a full moon and for some reason the sky clears in the evening. The volcano Karisimbi looms up fifteen thousand feet or so to the left of my tent, and its snow-peaked cone seems to pierce the heavens, with all the stars—looking like small, twinkling moons at this altitude—paying homage to it. When the moon is full, there is an uncanny, silvery glow over the meadow, the hills around it, and the mountain, and I can see all sizes and shapes of eyes reflecting its light along the fringes of the meadow. Last night a large herd of buffalo fed about fifty yards from my tent without seeing me sitting on my 'front porch' in the shadows.

"The night really comes alive with sounds never heard in the day. There is the trumpeting of elephants ringing up the gorge between the mountains, the snorting of the buffalo, the chest beating and hooting of lone gorillas, the barks of the duiker, the soft, mounting cry of the tree hyrax—a rabbity little animal unlike any other creature on earth—that ends up with an abrupt sound like someone with a bad cold blowing his nose, and lastly the weird cries, hoots, shrieks, and laments of the nocturnal birds."

Dian was now feeling much less of a transient at Kabara; and in her hunger for a sense of permanence, as well as her need for a little more comfort, she took over one of the two rooms in the men's cabin.

I've just about finished fixing up a room in the hut, and it looks great. The ugly wooden walls are matted with two-tone grass mats the natives made for me, and the wooden supports are hidden by bamboo that was cut down the mountain a way and is a beautiful shade of moss green now. I have pictures, skins, tusks, and horns hanging here and there, and I've made curtains out of some African printed material. A fireplace will be built next week.

Work is going well, for I've been following one gorilla group around all month, and now I'm able to get within thirty to sixty feet of them and they are not afraid of me. To be perfectly frank, I think they are quite confused as to my species! I've gotten them accustomed to me by aping them, and they are fascinated by my facial grimaces and other actions that I wouldn't be caught dead doing in front of anyone. I feel like a complete fool, but this technique seems to be working, and because of the increased proximity I've been able to observe a lot never recorded before.

Last week two of them approached me to within twenty feet, and the rest of the group remained at thirty-five to sixty feet for over an hour! There aren't words to describe what a thrill that was, and as long as I live I'll never forget it. At the same time I was slightly apprehensive because I was directly downhill from them and without a tree to climb or hide behind should anything have happened. I had to use my "threat face" once—don't laugh, it's quite effective—when one of the silverbacks began to get carried away with his bluffing tactics of running, chest beating, and breaking down trees. Needless to say, I was dutifully impressed with his prowess, but decided our proximity was being strained, so turned a horrible grimace on him, which had the effect of a flower on Ferdinand: immediately he sat down and began to eat, nervously and with one eye on me, but at least his hands were harmlessly occupied, and finally he just stood up and walked away.

It was really an hour that made everything else worthwhile, and my only regret is that no one was there either to witness or photograph it.

My field notes, of course, are just about ready to squeeze me out of the tent as they are quite voluminous after almost six months. This month I've been doing a great deal of work on what might optimistically be called thesis preparation—analyzing, classifying, charting and graphing, etc.—and now something complete and compact is growing out of all those pages and pages, and I'm rather proud of what's being created.

Now in June the rainy season has subsided to a great extent, and many elephant and buffalo are in the area because the local pond is the only source of water for some miles around. I feel as though I'm walking through the Denver stockyards, with animals behind every tree. I don't mind the elephant so much because there's no danger of stumbling across one of them. But the buffalo are often hidden by the foliage, and it's hard to tell who's more shocked when we "bump" into one another. The other day I was crawling under a long log, following a typical gorilla trail, when I noticed that the slender tree trunk I was about to grasp seemed to be moving. I pushed aside a few vines and found myself a foot away from a buffalo's leg! The silly thing wasn't aware of my presence, so I crept back farther beneath the log and let loose with some hog-calling yells that sent the entire herd into a frenzy. I'll bet they're still running.

There are two Egyptian geese on the pond, which though lovely to look at, are not musically inclined. I've named one Olivetti and the other Corona Smith. They've taken to briefly visiting the meadow to exchange threats with my rooster, Dezi, who considers himself king of the mountain. Dezi has already succeeded in cowing two white-necked ravens, who now have to come to the tent instead of the hut (the tent is outside of Dezi's domestic range) for the food I give them. It's quite impossible to sleep there in the morning, what with the cock crowing, the ravens cawing, and the geese clicking.

One issue that threatened to wreck Dian's mountain paradise was her relations with her camp workers. Her problems with the camp cook were the first to cause her serious concern.

My cookboy, Phocas, came back after a nine-day absence, and although I was all set to fire him, I couldn't find a decent substitute. He does his work perfectly, but he's so rude and insolent I hate having him here. At any rate, I told him he was on trial this month and I've tripled his workload and treat him like dirt. This is what I should have been doing all along, for he's finally toeing the mark and actually seems to respect me for the first time. The same holds true with the park guards. You can't be nice to them. If you give them a cigarette one day, they want the pack the next. So I go around giving orders and grumbling, but it makes me lonely—I've no one to talk to now that I've just about mastered Swahili.

Ultimately things got so bad that she felt compelled to appeal to Leakey for help:

"Dr. Leakey, I don't like writing the following any more than you're going to enjoy reading it, but the fact remains that I must have some 'help' up here as soon as possible, if only for a few weeks.

"Now that the novelty of my being here has worn off, the guards have become increasingly insubordinate, and the growing problems with discipline have me defeated. The lying, stealing, complaining, and begging, manifest all along, are just one part of it and don't really affect my work. However, shooting at animals grazing on the meadow or disobeying my orders when in contact with a group of gorillas has definitely had an effect on my observations this month, and I don't wish it repeated. . . .

"Please know I dislike asking for help but, under the present circumstances, consider it mandatory."

In a letter to the Prices, she spoke more bluntly:

"My current mood is somewhat black, and I've no business writing in this frame of mind. These Africans may yet be my undoing. Much as I dislike having to do it, I've written Dr. Leakey for help in the form of a cussing, wog-whacking 'mzunga'—a white person—to enforce some discipline. Since I've been here alone for so long, they are beginning to bully me because, to their way of thinking, I'm a lone entity. . . . Sanweke has been horrible this month, threatening to shoot at game and not obeying my orders while we are in contact with the gorillas. On the 15th I had to release my stored-up wrath and sent him packing down the mountain. On the next night I awoke to the sound of gunfire because the cookboy, who is terrified of being up here alone, was shooting at a herd of elephants who'd come onto the meadow to graze. I was furious, and naturally I didn't see a sign of gorilla for days after. Sanweke has since returned with another guard and all are as obedient and docile as the first week I was here, but I've told them their individual actions have been reported to the big chiefs of the study and of the park, and that they are in for it. Leakey had better not let me down or I stand to lose a lot of face."

Dian corresponded as much for personal release as to share her experiences with the people she had left behind. When she went on her monthly shopping trips and collected her mail at the Traveler's Rest, there was usually a letter from the Prices or Mary White or occasionally from Alexie. These always had a depressing effect on her, with their not-so-veiled suggestions that perhaps she was learning a hard lesson and would soon return to civilization somewhat wiser.

There were times of loneliness and stress when she herself was tormented by doubts and fear, isolated as she was in this remote corner of the central African highlands. Her problems with insubordination and bullying were not imaginary. Such difficulties had also been experienced by Joan and Alan Root, Walter Baumgartel, and others who had predicted failure for Dian Fossey's gorilla study.

n July 9, 1967, Dian returned from her day in the forest with the gorillas to meet, with shock, a new and larger problem. Lounging about the camp was a ragtag group of soldiers and porters. They were under orders from the Parc des Virungas' director, Anicet Mburanumwe, to escort her off the mountain.

Rumangabo, the 7 July 1967

Dear Miss Dian Fossey,

According to the bad situation of our Congo which started the other day before.

Yesterday I would like to advise you to get out of the bush as soon as possible, you may come and stay here or at Goma for the time being up to new order, other wise we don't like you to ruin your life when you are meet at our Parcks.

I hope that you will understand my advise friendly.

Yours affectionately.
MBURANUMWE, Anicet

The letter had been written just two days after European mercenaries serving the rebel leader Moise Tshombe took Kisangani and Bukavu and thus put the entire eastern region of the Congo under a state of siege. Antiwhite sentiment amongst government troops and the populace in general was rampant. The frontier between the

Congo and Uganda had been sealed off. Commercial air traffic was suspended, as were mail and telephone services. Atrocities were being committed by soldiers on both sides. Considering these circumstances, director Mburanumwe's advice was reasonable, but Dian saw it as an outrageous infringement on her personal freedom.

Since her work kept her isolated, she knew little about the upheavals in the region. Beyond the desire for stability she had no interest in central African politics and so did not comprehend how serious the Congolese crisis had become by the summer of 1967. Still, the director's "advice" was backed by force, and she had no choice in the matter but to descend from her aerie.

On July 12 she wrote the Prices:

"Three days ago I became a very ungrateful and unhappy refugee. I have yet to thank the park officials for snatching me from the certain jaws of rape, malice, and murder—that's what they keep telling me they snatched me from—and I can't get used to the idea that I must stay in the Congo and am not allowed to leave until the borders are opened. I don't understand what the heck is going on. I can figure out that it is *matata mkubwa*—big trouble—because of Tshombe and the mercenaries, but why it means I must leave the work, peace, and joy of my mountain meadow, I've yet to figure out."

Packing up her research station on such short notice was no easy matter.

I have to admit I spent a great deal of time in tears, especially when the mats were stripped from the walls of the hut, my tent was taken down, and all the work I'd done for the past six months was undone. I never fully realized what that place meant to me until I had to give it up, not knowing if I would be able to return or not.

By the time I reached the village below I thought I was steeled against further emotional outbreaks, but many of the women and children had gathered to say *kwa heri*—good-bye—and I started crying all over again, causing great wailing and mourning. I'm sure all this sounds like something out of a Grade C movie—I know I felt kind of hammy walking stalwartly in front of my line of sweating porters through the village huts with the mountain rising majestically behind me, and the tears brimming in my eyes while I said to those who had gathered to pay their respects, "I shall return." Come to think of it, I don't even think a Grade C movie would accept that line!

The forty-five-minute drive from the village to the park headquarters was really a nightmare, with troops everywhere and roadblocks and barricades at every turn. At each place some ass in a military uniform, full of beer and carrying a machine gun, would interrogate the driver and really glare at me. It was all so stupid and unnecessary.

I'm now penned up in the huge castle built by the Belgian colonial administrators at park headquarters and am receiving visiting "dignitaries." I think everyone in the area has been here at least twice, dragging all their relatives and children behind. I made a mistake by inviting the first batch into the two-acre living room and serving tea. They stayed four hours, during which not more than two intelligible sentences were exchanged! I also made a mistake by playing football with the children—they were using the inflated bladder of a sacrificial cow—and now they are here constantly.

I chose a small room in the front of the castle that commands a wonderfully spectacular view of the Virungas. However, it puts me on permanent exhibition, and the porch is usually lined with spectators! I can also see one of the military roadblocks down in the valley from my window, and the day it is gone is the day I'm going to get to the Traveler's Rest to find out what's going on and to post and pick up mail.

In her book, *Gorillas in the Mist*, Dian tells that she spent an extremely unpleasant two weeks at park headquarters in Rumangabo and for the first week was unable to discover why she was being forbidden to leave for Kisoro in Uganda. From bits and pieces of conversation I learned that the park headquarters was being secured for the visit of a general who would soon be arriving at Rumangabo from the besieged town of Bukavu. It was only after a "visit" to the army camp that I realized, on reading a military cable, that I was earmarked for the general. With chances for my release lessening each hour I remained in captivity, I decided to escape.

Dian's version of the adventure she was living through was colored by the writer in her. When she was taken to military headquarters in Goma, it was at her own request because she wanted to resolve a bureaucratic muddle that had arisen over the registration for Lily, her Land Rover. Her contact with the dreaded military consisted of an afternoon spent filling out motor vehicle registration forms. As for "the general"—it seems probable that his ominous and lecherous shadow was created to add zest to the story.

What actually happened is detailed in two sworn affidavits written by Dian soon after the events described had taken place. One was prepared for the American embassy in Rwanda, the other for Louis

Leakey. They are somewhat less thrilling than her published version, though harrowing enough in their own right.

The tale begins on June 1. While on one of her regular shopping trips to Kisoro, Congolese customs officials at the frontier noted that Dian's permit to keep Lily in the Congo was due to expire in a week. They reminded her that if she neglected to renew it, she would forfeit a three-hundred-dollar bond she had posted on first taking the Land Rover into the country. Dian argued that there had been an error in filling out the form and that she actually had another month to go.

The customs men obligingly agreed to take her word for it on the understanding that she would return in a month to pay the fee and complete the necessary forms. She did return on July 1, but by then the understanding had apparently been forgotten, and she found herself sinking into a kind of bureaucratic quicksand that seemed likely to swallow, if not Lily, then several hundreds of dollars in fines and forfeits. She protested long and loud and, when that failed, recruited the assistance of park director Anicet Mburanumwe and drove with him to the main customs office at Goma to complain to higher-ups. She was advised to discuss the matter with the chief customs officer at the frontier, who had been away but would be back on July 10.

So she returned to her Kabara camp, where larger events intervened, and on July 9 she was escorted down to park headquarters.

On July 10, Dian sought permission from the park authorities to visit the frontier and straighten out the vehicle problem once and for all; but it was not until a week had passed that the military situation was sufficiently stabilized for her to go anywhere. On that day she left for the frontier with a park guard as driver and accompanied by the bilingual secretary to the park director, who had been instructed to assist her in sorting out her difficulties.

At the border they found the chief Congolese customs officer drunk, disheveled, and in an ugly mood. He waved her papers aside and ordered some soldiers to seize Lily and impound it as an unregistered vehicle.

Dian was livid, and her reaction, as recorded in the affidavit she prepared for Leakey, was completely in character.

**I immediately jumped back into the car, grabbed the key, put it in my pocket, and settled myself behind the steering wheel. The secretary tried to make himself invisible, and the driver tried to take a stand to protect me but was pushed aside by the military men who came trotting up, also full of native gin.**

**Now, let me make myself quite clear: no one threatened me**

with a gun nor was I touched by any of these soldiers after the initial attempt by one to jerk me from the car. I have a beautiful command of international cuss words that they seemed to understand. However, the hour and a half that followed is kind of like a bad dream. Each soldier was ordering me out, screaming, yelling, threatening, and the big man was outscreaming them all. Since I wouldn't leave, he then started with the "prison" routine and ordered the man nearest me to take me to prison along with the driver and the secretary. By now the secretary was whiter than I and said it would be a good idea for me to leave the car. But the driver was still ready to pounce if anyone touched me, so I continued to cuss and threaten anyone of the military who got too close to me.

The standoff ended when the head customs man produced a document from the capital, Kinshasa, ordering the military to seize all improperly registered vehicles. In the face of this indisputable authority, Dian had to back down. Through her driver she asked the customs officer if he would accept a three-hundred-dollar cash payment in lieu of impounding the car.

This immediately pacified him until he realized I would have to go across the border to Kisoro to get the money. Then he flew into another screaming, mouth-drooling rage that even frightened the military. Finally he consented, but only under the conditions that he retain my passport and that I be accompanied by a Congolese guard. I wasn't too happy about letting my passport go but felt it was cheaper than losing the car. Nor was I happy about the drunken Congolese military who crawled into the front seat and ordered me to sit on his lap. The driver told him to leave me alone, I told him to leave me alone, and on we went to Kisoro, where I spilled my troubles to Mr. Baumgartel.

Baumgartel was appalled. He fully understood the risks involved in confronting the Congolese military under conditions of martial law. His hotel was already crowded with frightened European guests who had taken refuge from the chaos in the Congo and were full of stories of atrocities. He urged Dian to remain with him in Kisoro, at least until stability had returned to Kivu province, but Dian was no more inclined to take his advice this time than she had been when she first entered the Congo with Alan Root. She had no intention of letting anything so trivial as an armed insurrection interfere with her work. She cabled Leakey that she was safe in Kisoro and needed three hundred dollars.

Meanwhile, Baumgartel had enlisted the aid of a captain in the

Uganda Rifles, who sent Dian's Congolese guard packing in the direction of the border. Realizing he could not sway Dian, but always the friend in need, Baumgartel arranged for her to borrow the money she required.

The following morning Dian, her driver, and the very unhappy bilingual secretary returned to the frontier escorted by the Ugandan captain. The customs chief contentedly accepted the money, returned her passport, and put her papers in order. Once this transaction was concluded, she thanked the Ugandan officer and drove off—not back to the security of Kisoro—but on to park headquarters at Rumangabo.

In her absence, Baumgartel and his refugee guests had been astonished to see a light aircraft risk being shot down by trigger-happy soldiers on both sides of the border as it circled the village and landed at a disused airstrip near the hotel. On receiving Dian's cable, a distraught Leakey had chartered the plane to fly her back to Nairobi.

Far from intending to flee the Congo, Dian was determined to return to Kabara. She pointed out to the park director that there had never been an official order from the military forbidding her to stay up there. She had assessed the risks, she said, and was willing to take her chances. Perhaps intimidated by her vehemence, or simply sick of her intransigence, the director acquiesced.

Next day she drove on to Kibumba, the village at the foot of the mountain, where she unloaded her equipment and arranged for porters. She then returned to park headquarters for a second load and to pick up two park guards. While there she dashed off a note to Leakey:

"I got the same guards who helped me take the tent down, for I haven't the slightest idea how to get the damn thing up again. Then, when I was on my way out the door, Anicet's secretary came in with a telegram from the military camp saying on no condition should I be allowed to go back up the mountain.

"Dr. Leakey, this hit me even worse than the first letter from Anicet on the 9th! I don't think you can realize what this delay is costing me at this crucial time of habituating my gorillas. I *know* these park people don't know beans about what I'm trying to accomplish. Two weeks lost *now,* just when I was on the verge of complete habituation, is the exact equivalent of two *months* lost, and for no reason at all."

The following day, again accompanied by a park official, Dian drove to military headquarters at Goma to appeal the decision. She was told politely enough that it would be at least two and perhaps four months before she could be allowed to climb to Kabara again.

Returning angrily to her palatial quarters, she brooded over the view of Karisimbi. The "castle" now felt like a prison to her. Lawlessness in the surrounding region was increasing day by day, as were the numbers of soldiers and the flow of banana beer. She began to be awakened by unseen visitors pounding on her bolted door. She asked for and received an armed sentry.

It was finally clear to her that nothing was to be gained by her remaining. On July 26 she once again stowed her field notes, one of her chickens, and most of her equipment in Lily and drove back to the frontier.

**Upon reaching Bunagana I was told the border was closed and the keys were gone. I waited there five hours until a priest from the Congo came and gained admission to Uganda as he had a sick person with him who required hospitalization there. Once it was apparent that the men at the post had the keys, I was able to bribe them to open the gate for me.**

It was not quite that easy. Dian had no remaining cash, so she had to persuade the guards to let her drive on to Kisoro where she could get more. History repeated itself. It was agreed, on condition that one of the guards go too.

When Dian's Land Rover once again rattled up the dusty driveway of the Traveler's Rest and skidded to a halt at the front door, Walter Baumgartel was there to see her stumble out of the driver's seat drenched in sweat and close to collapse. She ran past him into the hotel, where she was solaced by half a dozen other refugees. Meantime, Baumgartel confronted an unhappy Congolese soldier who insisted he had orders to bring Dian back to the border post as soon as she raised the money she had promised. In his memoirs, *Up Among the Mountain Gorillas,* Baumgartel recalled the scene:

" 'Miss Fossey is not your prisoner,' I said. 'She is going to stay here. If she wants to return, I shall tie her to that tree out there!'

" 'But I have guaranteed to bring her back,' her guard protested. 'They will shoot me if I don't.'

" 'Better to shoot you than her,' I said. Eventually he left."

The following day the American ambassador to nearby Rwanda arrived at the Traveler's Rest to take Dian to his embassy in the Rwandan capital of Kigali, preparatory to sending her on to Nairobi where Leakey anxiously awaited her. She was gently interrogated by embassy staff, then asked to prepare an affidavit testifying to her treatment at the hands of the Congolese.

"Did you suffer any material losses?" she was asked.

"Some of my camp gear—a tent and things like that and, oh, yes, one of my pet chickens was kidnapped."

"Miss Fossey, were you ill-treated or physically abused in any way?"

"Well, I was cussed out in French and Congolese. And a soldier tried to pull me out of my car but didn't make it. No, I was not abused."

A widely circulated story maintains that Dian was raped by Congolese soldiers—gang-raped in some versions. However, the record that she herself wrote only a few days after her escape makes no reference to rape, attempted rape, or indeed to assault of any kind. Nor is there even a suggestion of rape in her other accounts of what took place. Finally, Dian herself consistently and vehemently denied the story.

Myths—especially racist and salacious ones—die hard.

**6**

The unsung little country of
Rwanda in which Dian now found herself was one of the smallest,
most densely populated, and poorest in Africa. Its nearly five million
people lived in an area not quite as large as the state of Maryland.
Perched high on the continent's central plateau only a few miles
south of the equator, Rwanda had once been heavily and lushly forested. Now, with about four hundred persons living off the produce
of each square mile, the land had been almost totally given over to the
farmer and the charcoal-maker. The only remaining forests, and the
only survivors of the once-abundant wildlife, existed somewhat pre-
cariously in two national parks—A'kagera in the northeast, and the
Parc des Volcans in the higher reaches of the Virunga mountains to
the northwest.

Although overfarmed and overcrowded, Rwanda was and is dra-
matically beautiful. Its rugged, closely terraced hills resemble a terres-
trial version of the huge and chaotic swells of the Atlantic Ocean,
with the cluster of old volcanoes looming to the north like magical
snow-capped islands against a vibrant tropic sky.

Dian had neither the time nor the inclination to admire the scenery during her first few days in the country. "She was completely
preoccupied—obsessed, really," according to Rosamond Carr, one of
the first white people Dian met in Rwanda.

Rosamond Carr was a petite fifty-three-year-old American expa-
triate who had been living in the shadow of the Virungas for thirty
years. She made her living growing flowers on her small plantation
and selling them to hotels and resorts around nearby Lake Kivu and
in the capital, Kigali. One day near the end of July 1967, Mrs. Carr

was invited to lunch at the home of the American military attaché in Kigali.

"I dropped in on the ambassador's wife on my way, and she said to me, 'Rosamond, you are going to meet a really very strange girl at lunch today. She is Dian Fossey, who has been studying gorillas in the Congo and has only just escaped from there. She's looking for a place to camp, but be careful. She is really *very* odd.'

"Odd? Well, I suppose she had a reason to be so considering the absolutely desperate experience she'd just been through. Anyway, I went on to lunch at the Frayzes', and that first meeting with her was something I could never forget. She was so attractive—so *vital*. I mean, she was absolutely stunning with her hair in this long black braid flung carelessly over one shoulder and a glowing look in her face. She had on the most beautiful dress you could imagine. A pale lilac color—I mean, absolutely from a tip-top shop. And then, the poor little thing—the poor *tall* thing—she had very large feet and the only shoes she'd managed to keep were tennis shoes that were filthy and *enormous*. And so here she was with this beautiful dress, her lovely hair, and those awful shoes!

"I immediately saw what the ambassador's wife had meant, because she had this absolutely wild look in her eye.

"We went in to a beautiful lunch with crystal and silver. We all sat down and Dian immediately pulled out a notebook—the cheap kind you can pick up for ten francs here. She just ignored her hosts, the Frayzes, stared straight at me, and demanded, 'Mrs. Carr, I have some questions for you.' The questions were numbered, one to about twenty. She'd ask one, check it off, and move right on to the next. The first was, 'May I use your plantation as a base camp to start my studies of gorillas again?'

" 'Well,' I said, 'you can, but you won't find gorillas on the Rwandan side of Mt. Karisimbi.' She said, 'Oh, no, you're absolutely wrong about that. The gorillas are there.' And I replied rather definitely, 'I'm sorry, they're *not* on this side of Karisimbi.'

"She'd never been on this side of Karisimbi, but she was so certain she was right, and she just went on firing these questions at me. The poor Frayzes—their luncheon was anything but a social occasion, I'm afraid."

During those first few days in Kigali, Dian had no more time to waste on social amenities than on the scenery. Apprehensive as to how Leakey would react to her "failure" in the Congo, she was determined to establish a foothold for a research station on the Rwandan side of the Virunga chain before having to face him in Nairobi. She had already sought permission from the Rwandan authorities to set up camp in the Parc des Volcans, adjacent to the Congolese Parc des Virungas and Kabara. Unfortunately, she had not been able to find anybody who knew where the gorillas were. Because Rosamond Carr lived close to the forested lower slopes of the volcanoes, she had hoped for help from her. Mrs. Carr did not disappoint her.

"The one person who has the answers you need," she told Dian after the lunch was over, "will soon be flying into Nairobi from Paris. You'll be in Nairobi and can see her there. Her name is Alyette de Munck, an utterly charming Belgian lady who has lived in Africa the best part of her life, mostly near the volcanoes that she knows like the palm of her hand because she loves them dearly and has climbed all over them."

Mrs. Carr went on to explain that Alyette de Munck and her husband, Adrian, had raised one son of their own, together with the three children of Alyette's sister, on a plantation in the Congolese province of Kivu. As the troubles in the Congo had begun to grow serious, the young people had been sent off to finish their schooling in Belgium. When Kivu sank deeper into lawlessness, the de Muncks sold their Congo farm and bought another in nearby Rwanda, just a mile or two down the trail from Rosamond Carr's cottage.

"Unhappily," Mrs. Carr continued, "Adrian died suddenly in Paris only a week ago. Alyette will be desolate. It will do her good to have a new involvement, and you and your gorillas might be just the thing."

August 12, 1967, found Dian pacing the dusty, fly-infested lounge of the Nairobi airport, impatiently awaiting an incoming Air France flight from Paris. When the plane finally arrived and its passengers disembarked, she anxiously scanned the crowd. Finally she spotted a slight and pretty woman about ten years her senior who was being greeted by three very young men. Dian held back for a few moments, not wanting to intrude upon what was clearly an intensely emotional reunion.

She herself had reached Nairobi a week earlier, nervous and worried. As if having to abandon the gorilla study in the Congo and her harrowing experiences thereafter had not been enough, she was unemployed and virtually penniless. Nor was she confident of the reception she could expect from Dr. Leakey, who prided himself on always having been able to carry on his scientific work in Africa and the Middle East under the most trying political conditions. Would he think she had exaggerated the danger that had forced her to abandon the Kabara camp? Even if he did understand the difficulties, would funds be available to establish a new camp elsewhere?

Her fears had evaporated when she was greeted on arrival at the airport by a beaming and affectionate Leakey, who gave her a bear hug and was effusive in his praise of her courage and ingenuity in escaping from the Congo. He took her to a hotel then out for an intimate dinner, after which they discussed the options open to her. Leakey spoke enthusiastically of the need for someone to start a long-term study of orangutans in Borneo or of lowland gorillas in West Africa.

Dian was not enthused. She was resolutely committed to the mountain gorilla, and she told him so.

"I'm going to stay with them, Dr. Leakey. Nothing will stop me from doing that. They interest me more than anything on earth! Will you help me get started in Rwanda?"

Leakey was charmed by her spirit and determination.

"I wouldn't dare stand in your way," he told her, laughing. "Just promise me you'll stay away from the Congolese border. And that you'll come back to Nairobi at once if you ever again find yourself threatened by the military."

A week later he called her to his office in the museum to give her the splendid news that the Wilkie Foundation had agreed by cable to provide the funds for her to begin again in Rwanda. Soon thereafter, the National Geographic Society also agreed to the enforced change of venue for the gorilla study.

The three young men who had been awaiting Alyette de Munck at Nairobi airport were her son, her nephew, and a close friend of theirs. All three had recently graduated from Louvain University, for which achievement they were being given a six-week safari in East Africa by Alyette and her husband. They had been on passage from Belgium when they heard of Adrian de Munck's death and had only just reached Nairobi themselves. Now they were prepared to abandon their great adventure, but Alyette would not hear of it.

"Nonsense!" she told them firmly. "Adrian would not wish it! You must carry on!"

Invited to dine at their hotel that evening, Dian had at first tried not to intrude herself and her difficulties into this sad reunion. But her companions were fascinated by her gorilla stories and showered her with questions. The three young men were particularly admiring, and she responded with vivacity and warmth. Her presence lifted the pall from the little party, and Alyette was grateful. Before the evening was out, Dian had been invited to use the de Munck plantation as her base camp while she explored the Rwandan side of the Virungas. Alyette volunteered to lend a hand establishing a new research camp as soon as a suitable location could be found. They all arranged to meet at the de Munck plantation a week hence.

A few days later Dian flew happily back to Kigali, resurrected the battered Lily, loaded her with supplies, and set off toward the Virungas along the only paved road in Rwanda. She drove for several hours through densely populated mountain foothills to a side road just west of the provincial capital of Ruhengeri—itself a nondescript collection of low, cement block and mud-brick buildings.

The side road started out well enough, a sandy set of ruts skirting a steep valley carpeted with the tiny two-acre plots of Rwandan farmers and dotted with grass-roofed, wattle and straw rondel houses and granaries. As Dian looked out over the valley through the blue haze of smoke from charcoal cooking fires, the scene seemed oddly desolate. There were no power or telephone lines, no mechanical or electrical noises, no busy cars or trucks or tractors. But gradually she began to discern movement and when she stopped from time to time, became aware of the susurrus of thousands of human voices. The valley was unobtrusively alive with people going about their daily chores, tending the tiny plots of rich, red volcanic soil that provided their sustenance.

Descending into the valley, the road quickly deteriorated into a boulder-strewn track traversing rough lava flows, a trail that might have been designed as a torture test for truck tires. Now the farmers' huts were only a few yards away on either side, and a steady stream of barefooted people moved in both directions along the track, many of them balancing plastic water jugs, gourds of *pombe,* or woven potato baskets on their heads. Most of the women had children strapped to their backs. They all seemed remarkably fit and contented, though Dian knew that many were or would be victims of yellow fever, cholera, malaria, typhoid, and a host of other virulent diseases.

Dian eventually reached the de Munck farm, only to find that the mistress was absent. All she could learn from the household staff was that something bad had happened to the boys, and Mrs. de Munck had gone to see about it.

With a chill presentiment in her heart, Dian bounced on up the lava trail toward Rosamond Carr's cottage.

Just when it appeared that Dian's dust-encrusted vehicle would not tolerate another moment of this punishment, a high evergreen hedge guarding a crushed-stone driveway appeared. Turning in, she had the sensation of having fallen through a hole in time to emerge, blinking, in a kind of nursery-book paradise.

Ahead was a low, vine-covered cottage, surrounded by acres of beautifully cultivated flowers and shrubs of every description. After long hours of driving through the parched, khaki countryside, the bright colors were as refreshing as a splash of cold water. Jersey cows were grazing toward a line of ancient pines. To the left of the house was a broad sweep of carefully manicured lawn, and beyond that rose the immense, brooding shape of Mt. Karisimbi. Still farther off was the smaller, more regular profile of Mt. Visoke, another of the eight volcanoes—two of them still active—that make up the Virungas.

As Lily ground to a stop, Rosamond appeared at the door as impeccably groomed as if she had just stepped from the pages of *Country Life*. Her face, however, was darkly shadowed. Dian followed her into a chinz-bedecked living room. "Where is Mrs. de Munck?" she asked anxiously. "I stopped at her place and the servants wouldn't tell me anything. What's wrong?"

"Something dreadful has happened, dear," Mrs. Carr replied distractedly. "As you know, the plan was for Yves, Philippe, and Xavier to drive across Kenya to Kisoro, spend a night at Walter Baumgartel's place, then come on to the plantation here next day. But, Dian, they never arrived! After three days, Alyette drove across the Uganda border to the Traveler's Rest."

Walter Baumgartel met Mrs. de Munck at the hotel door. An indescribable foreboding of disaster seized him, and he could hardly get out the words, "What brings you here, madame?"

"I am looking for my boys. They should have arrived days ago. Maybe they have had some trouble with their Land Rover and I can help them."

In what Baumgartel called "one of the most awful moments of my life," he had to tell her that the boys had arrived at his inn three nights earlier—and had left the following morning. "She and I both knew they could not have reached Rwanda," he remembered. "One would have heard of anything that happened to a white person there. They must have taken the wrong road and driven into the Congo where all hell was breaking loose by then."

Mrs. de Munck made frantic inquiries through her many contacts in Uganda and the Congo. She learned that the three young men had indeed taken a wrong turn on leaving the Traveler's Rest and had arrived at the Congolese frontier at Bunagana. There they had been arrested as spies and mercenaries. Then, in a grotesque misunderstanding, a well-meaning Congolese army officer at Goma told her by telephone, "You'll have to be very brave, madame—the boys are not transportable." From this she concluded they had been wounded—and set about trying to hire an ambulance. Before she could find one, she learned from officials at the Belgian embassy in Kigali that the three young men had been killed by the Congolese military.

"When I told Dian what I knew about it," Mrs. Carr recalls, "she nearly went berserk. I think all the emotions she had bottled up during her own experience in the Congo just broke through. I finally calmed her down, and then she said, 'Well, I will spend the night here with you, then I must go to her.' In the morning we went together to Ruhengeri where Alyette was staying, and Alyette embraced Dian and they cried and Alyette said how much she wanted—*needed*—more than ever to help Dian."

During the bleak days that followed, Dian did what she could to comfort Alyette, though she herself was on the brink of a nervous collapse.

She wrote to the Prices: "There is nothing I can tell you now that would make sense—too much has happened. You can't know the horror and grief of this country. Each letter I finish sounds like a newspaper release. It is remote; it just doesn't sound believable, thus I've given up.

"I only write to say I'm well and being taken care of physically. But mentally I don't know if I'm strong enough to take much more.

"At Rumangabo, the place I escaped from, my three new friends—Yves, Philippe and Xavier—were killed by the Congolese. We have all agreed that the mother of one of the boys, Madame de Munck, must never be told the truth, but they were reportedly tortured for eighteen hours—castrated, ears cut off, eyes gouged out, burned, hung on racks, finally eaten. The Congo can't be covered by the press, like Vietnam, thus no one knows what really happens. But what goes on there makes the rest of the world seem like a playground.

"Have been staying with Madame de Munck and the grief that tears me apart for her is almost impossible to bear. Worse yet is the frustration that comes from my own ineptitude at dealing with this situation. No one in the States would or could believe it."

The letter, scribbled on aerogram paper in a moment of black depression, was to have a galvanizing effect on the Prices.

Gradually the traumatic effects of this dire tragedy subsided, and by September Dian was installed in "the upper house" on the de Munck plantation, at the foot of Karisimbi. From there she began probing the forests for traces of gorilla habitation. She planned to begin her survey as close as possible to the gorilla ranges with which she had been familiar in the Congo and then work her way eastward, deep into the rain forests on the Rwandan side of the border. On her first day out she climbed with her porters and a park guide to alpine meadows at twelve thousand feet where she camped within shouting distance of the Congolese border. It had been a depressing trek—the slopes were infested with lyre-horned cattle ranging through the hagenia forest zone where gorillas might otherwise have been expected.

The following morning produced a more optimistic result.

**We were only about half an hour from the border, and I couldn't resist the impulse to check a portion of the Mikeno-facing slopes of Karisimbi inside the Congo where my old Group 2 gorillas often ranged. Luck seldom plays a part in this type of work, but on that day it certainly did. I literally bumped right into Group 2 without even having to track. It had been nineteen weeks since I'd last seen them, but they definitely recognized me and held their ground at fifty feet after some initial alarm cries and chest beating. I was thrilled to note that one of the females had given birth during my absence, and all the animals seemed in good health. As happy as the contact made me, it also reinforced my desolation at having lost these animals permanently.**

Turning her back upon the Congo, Dian then struck out to the east, into the unfamiliar forests of the Rwandan slopes of Mt. Karisimbi. For ten days she explored and each day became increasingly alarmed and incensed at the vast number of cattle roaming illegally in the national park with their Tutsi herders. Worse, she was constantly finding and destroying poachers' traps. Worse still, she was forced to watch in helpless anger while her park "guide" accepted duiker meat and bribe money from the numerous poachers they encountered. It seemed to her that this part of the park, at least, was beyond redemption, and for the first time she began to wonder whether Rosamond Carr had been correct in thinking there were no gorillas left in Rwanda.

On the tenth day of her search Dian traversed the barren upper alpine reaches of Karisimbi's northern summit to see what the other side of the mountain might have to offer. From her thirteen-thousand-foot lookout she could see arrayed before her, curving in a gentle arc into the eastern haze, the entire range of the Virungas. With mounting excitement she swept her binoculars over the rolling saddle terrain between Karisimbi and Mt. Visoke to the north. To her delight, the habitat appeared to be exactly right for gorillas. This, she felt immediately, was where she should set up her camp.

Early in the morning of September 24, 1967, Dian and Alyette de Munck made a last check of the contents of their heavily laden vehicles and set out down the volcanic track toward the highway. Dian's vintage Land Rover blazed a trail through pelting rain and deepening mud for Alyette's Volkswagen "combi" van. Their destination was the plantation of a Dutch foreign-aid worker who lived conveniently close to Mt. Visoke. As overseer of a Common Market scheme to introduce the pyrethrum plant as a cash crop in Rwanda, he knew the mountain region and its people well and had agreed to help get Dian's equipment up the mountain.

Dian had only recently learned of the pyrethrum project and was appalled at its effect on the Parc des Volcans. Under this ambitious foreign-aid project, ten thousand hectares—more than a third of the land previously enclosed within the park boundaries—was being cleared of bamboo and hagenia forest and turned over to farmers. These smallholders received their tiny plots free, on the condition they devote half the land to the cultivation of pyrethrum, the daisy-like flowers of which were dried and shipped to Europe to be used in the manufacture of an organic pesticide. The Rwandan government and the aid workers saw the project as a way of easing, in some small measure, the pressure of Rwanda's exploding population. But for Dian the scheme was an abomination that would shrink the already inadequate remnant of forest range suitable for gorillas past the danger point for their survival. In the coming months she would mount an angry—and unsuccessful—campaign against the pyrethrum project.

The Dutchman had agreed to arrange porters for the climb up Visoke, and the two women found forty shivering men awaiting orders in a tin-roofed pyrethrum-drying shed at the foot of the mountain. The rain was now alternating with hail that beat down on the tin roof with a thunderous din, and the porters were noisily demanding either a delayed departure or higher wages for venturing out in such weather. In the minds of these two determined women there could be no question of delay, so while Mrs. de Munck negotiated payment, Dian set about assigning loads. Soon the men were strung out, barefoot, in single file along the muddy path leading to the foot of Visoke's steep slopes, their burdens balanced atop their heads as they slogged through the glutinous mud. The two women fell in at the rear of the line.

They marched for four kilometers through the ravaged and still-smoldering remains of virgin forest before reaching the new park boundary, 8,600 feet up on Visoke's mist-veiled slopes. Dian was astonished afresh at the mass of people they encountered along the way. The curious stares of innumerable men, women, and children followed every step of the journey.

The Parc des Volcans began where the clearing and cultivation ceased. One moment the party was in recently cleared, already densely populated farmland, the next they were in the looming silence of the dripping, moss-shrouded forest. They climbed for three hours, following a steep and muddy trough made by herds of elephant and buffalo. Twice Dian ordered a halt and prepared to pitch her tents in what seemed to her a suitable campsite; but each time the chief porter and guide objected, assuring her there was a better spot farther on. At 4:40 in the afternoon, with sunlight finally gleaming through the canopy of foliage, they found themselves emerging into a long, narrow meadow on a 10,000-foot-high plateau where the saddle joining mounts Visoke, Karisimbi, and Mikeno reaches its highest point. The clearing was richly carpeted with grass, surrounded by heavy forest, and dotted with ancient, moss-draped hagenia trees. A swift-flowing stream tumbled through the meadow. It was, as the porters had promised, an ideal campsite. It was also the most beautiful place Dian had ever seen.

The porters set about erecting the tents, one for Dian and, at the other end of the clearing, one for the camp workers she would recruit that evening from among the porters. They had been at work only a few minutes when the unmistakable *pok-pok-pok* of gorilla chest beating reverberated through the gathering darkness on the steep slopes behind the camp.

Lying exhausted in her cot that night, Dian savored the moment.

**H**er acute sense of destiny moved Dian to record the precise time of the founding of the research camp she would name Karisoke—from mounts Karisimbi and Visoke. It was 4:30 P.M., September 24, 1967.

Had she fully divined the nature of that destiny, she might also have noted the time that evening of the appearance of a hundred-odd head of cattle and two Watusi herders who slowly drove their animals through the meadow across the creek from her tents. Or she might have noted the arrival time of two Batwa poachers who strolled nonchalantly through the clearing carrying bows, arrows, and spears, and who volunteered to show Dian the location of a gorilla family they had encountered only forty-five minutes from the camp.

Dian chose to ignore the herders for the moment, but was hard-pressed to decide whether to run the poachers out of camp or accept their offer. In the end she followed them to the gorillas, but issued a stern warning that from this day forward neither cattle herding nor poaching would be tolerated in her part of the park.

This news must have been greeted with incredulity by the Tutsi and Batwa alike. Both peoples had ranged the Virunga slopes since time immemorial—the Tutsi using the meadows and open woods for grazing, and the Batwa hunting everywhere for meat and hides, both for their own use and to sell to the Hutu farmers down below. Although the park had been legally off limits to hunters and herders since its establishment by the Belgians several decades earlier, the mountain people had long since worked out a comfortable arrangement whereby they supplied the poorly paid park guards with meat and milk, and sometimes cash, in exchange for immunity. Although this arrangement was so well established as to be virtually sacrosanct,

Dian decided that the park rules had to be enforced. She was so adamant about this that she was soon at loggerheads with Alyette de Munck and Rosamond Carr.

"You really must consider the traditions of the local people," Alyette advised. "They depend, you know, on what they can get from the land. You must be fair to them."

Dian was unmoved.

"The Batwa are poachers pure and simple," she insisted. "They set their snares everywhere for the antelope and hyrax, and that's bad enough, God knows, but they often end up catching gorillas too. I know, I know, the adults can break free, but they can be maimed for life by the wire nooses. And we both know some poachers deliberately kill gorillas and make souvenir ashtrays out of their dried hands to sell to the horrid tourist trade, and sell skulls and heads to the so-called sportsmen who want African trophies for their rec rooms. Poachers catch baby gorillas for sale to zoos, too. There *has* to be strict enforcement of the park laws or there won't be any gorillas left, and very little else either."

Nor did Rosamond Carr's protests on behalf of the Tutsi cattle herders make much impression on Dian's resolve.

"The herders ruin the habitat, Rosamond, because they have far too many cattle. They keep ten times what they need, just for prestige. There are so many up here now—they churn the ground until it looks as if it were plowed. They crush the plants the gorillas eat, shut them out of the best feeding areas, and force them higher and higher up the slopes into the cold and wet until they get pneumonia. Those high altitudes are deadly for them. Let the Tutsi cut down their herds to only what they need and graze them outside the park."

Her disagreements with Alyette and Rosamond forced Dian to realize that very few people placed the same paramount priority on the survival of the gorillas that she did. But she remained inflexible.

I came onto an empty poacher's camp today. There was one flea-bitten, rack-ribbed dog guarding a lean-to fitted into a huge hagenia tree. The only other signs of life were fresh footprints that led up and down the trail. A newly killed duiker was lying on top of the roof of the lean-to. I offered the duiker to the tracker as bait to help me destroy the sixty bamboo sticks that the poachers had just brought up from below to use for setting snares. He went about the task willingly, helping me to break the heavier pieces. Once we had broken all the potential traps, I turned my attention to the inside of the lean-to and found a big bag of millet, which I threw to the four winds, a couple of hundred yards of rope especially woven for snare traps, and several *chungas* or big iron pots for cooking. Although I am not a thief at heart, I do believe in making things difficult for poachers, so I tied the *chungas* onto my African along with the snare rope and the duiker, and we left the camp apparently undetected except for the dog, who'd been regarding our doings with a malevolent eye from the nearby foliage. For all I know, the poachers were lined up beside him, glaring, but that doesn't matter. At least I left the tattered red rags that one of them had left out to dry in the late afternoon sun— I've not been reduced to stealing a man's clothing!

The point of this story comes from the fact that I was accompanied by my friend Alyette de Munck, who has known Africa since birth. Because of this continent she has lost her son and nephew, and yet nothing can discourage her love of the land—and love is a trite word to describe such an affinity. So because of this poacher's camp, a harmless afternoon's stroll, which had previously been filled with the beauty of an isolated river flowing deep within the jungle fastness of wild orchids and liana and senna, turned into a heated argument between the two of us.

As I stood there breaking bamboo snares one by one, she stood apart and in a very firm way asked what right I had, an American here in Africa for only a few months, to invade the rights of the Africans whose country this was. I kept on breaking traps, though I couldn't help but agree with her—Africa belongs to Africans.

My friend continued to plead her case.

"These men have a right to hunt. It's their country! You have no right to destroy their efforts."

Maybe she is right, for the country African living on the fringes of a park area has little alternative but to turn to poaching for his livelihood. But at the same time, why should one condone a man if he openly breaks the law—why shouldn't you take whatever action you can against him. The man who kills the animals today is the man who kills the people who get in his way tomorrow. He recognizes the fact that there is a law saying he mustn't do this or that, but without the enforcement of this law he is free to do as he chooses. If I can enforce the written rules of a supposedly protected park against the slaughter of animals, then I must do it. And so I continued to break bamboo, the reliable and flexible trap of the last game in Africa.

In a manner as unpredictable as their relationship had always been, Dian and Alexie maintained contact by mail—she in desultory fashion, while he wrote increasingly often and with supreme confidence that she would follow where he chose to lead.

**Alexie's recent letters are mainly about leaving Notre Dame and transferring to the Chicago School of Divinity to major in comparative religion for his Ph.D. I am now expected to hurry back to the States and live with him in Chicago in a blissfully married state until he gets his degree, then his field work will take us to South America or northern Africa, where we will be happy ever after. Unfortunately I can't seem to find my rose-colored glasses anymore, though he still seems to have his.**

Seeking allies, Alexie kept in touch with the Prices, and the news of Dian's and the de Muncks' chilling experiences in the Congo spurred the three of them into action.

In the last days of September Alexie met the Prices in New York. An engagement ring was purchased, a flight booked, and Alexie dispatched on a rescue mission to bring Dian back to civilization. He boarded his plane confident that when offered the take-it-or-leave-it choice between marriage and continuing her studies, she would choose marriage.

When he came face to face with her in her mountain camp, he was horrified. Dressed in torn jeans and faded windbreaker, her long hair matted with the rain, her eyes bemused, she seemed like some barbaric creature of the jungle.

Alexie delivered his ultimatum—me or the gorillas—and was stunned when Dian turned him down. He persisted.

"Marry me," he pleaded, "and I'll give up university. We'll go to Rhodesia and take up farming. I don't want us ever to be separated again."

Dian would not be moved. "Not possible, darling. You'd be giving up too much. We've both got a lot of things to do."

"Then we can do them together. If you *must* stay here, how would it be if I stayed on too . . . *for a year* . . . on condition that you'd leave this place then?"

"Alexie, it wouldn't work. Go back and get your Ph.D. Do what you have to do and I'll do what I have to do. Perhaps in two years' time, well, we'll see how things look then."

He left the camp heartbroken—and humiliated. At Kisoro he

wrote a farewell letter to Dian and left it in the care of Walter Baumgartel. He wrote, telling Dian to keep the ring or throw it into the stream near camp if she chose. His last words to her were, "You saw me cry, and that, my dear, was the last tear I will ever shed for you."

Although relieved that the affair was at an end, Dian was defensive too.

**He came up here like Sir Galahad, but who asked him to rescue me? He criticized everything here; said that the Rwandans hated me, that they called me a wild woman and wanted me out. Said I was making life impossible for my mother. He as good as forced me to throw him out.**

She told Leakey something of what had happened, and he replied, "I am delighted at the news that you have found a good place on Karisimbi, with plenty of gorillas, and I do hope that now things will become reasonable once more. In particular I hope that the young man who you say that you are having to be rude to realized that you don't want him in your life. You've got such important things to do."

During the succeeding weeks, Dian found two more gorilla families, which meant that she was virtually assured of being able to locate at least one group to observe on any given day. Her total hours of gorilla observations were mounting swiftly.

Other aspects of her life were also going well.

She was making headway on an article for *National Geographic*. Three publishers had written to her expressing interest in a book to be based on her experiences with the gorillas. She heard from Cambridge University in England that she had been accepted for Ph.D. studies on the basis of her preliminary field notes, and she began preparing to attend her first semester there in the autumn of 1968. Meanwhile, she was reveling in the Virungas.

**I've been doing a great deal of survey work in the areas around the volcanoes. Because of this I've seen the most fantastically gorgeous country I never dreamed existed. Yesterday I found a river that tumbles down from Mt. Karisimbi to the Congo by a series of spectacular waterfalls. . . . I really felt as though I was the first white person ever to see it and gave up all thoughts of looking for gorilla for that day.**

Despite the physical hardships and the loneliness, Dian was now finding her solitary life a deeply satisfying experience. She observed herself in a series of highly evocative, somewhat transcendental musings.

I must say, despite the leaks, my canvas tent is a happy roof. It beams with the morning sunshine when the day is bright, and it frowns a little darker whenever I open my eyes to the prospect of a drippy dawn. I'm lucky in having a tea-boy who, no matter how much I cuss him out for bringing tea at six, brings tea at six. He pecks once at the tent pole with the teapot lid and then runs like hell. Six o'clock is not such an unholy hour, in fact it is the normal hour of awakening in most countries, but I guess I'm getting to be an old lady—six seems very early to me.

When the moon is full here it seems a sacrilege to be inside one's tent, for outside are screaming the violet, iridescent demands of snow-peaked volcanoes and etchings of lacy mosses and leaves against the silver-blue sky. Each tree assumes its own character when silhouetted against the moonlit sky—some are sinister, some are comical, but none is just a plain tree and none belongs to the daylight world. Walt Disney would be pleased to know Mr. Pluto—a gangly hypericum tree whose moss-tipped limbs exactly resemble Pluto, even to the whiskers. But even Mr. Pluto is just another tree in the daylight world.

To leave the kerosene lamps of the tent and to go outside on such a night is to be automatically captured in spite of one's best intentions. Inevitably the nipple of Karisimbi is shining with snow, and the sparkle of that triangle can only be matched by the tusks of The Loner elephant wading through the creek just outside the tent. When I go out on such a night, he raises his tusks and trumpets as if to say the night belongs to him and I am the intruder. When this happens I relinquish the silhouettes of the trees, the silver phosphorescence of Karisimbi and the golden glow of my campfire, for it is true, the night belongs to the animals and I am an intruder. At the same time, I wonder why it is that the elephant and buffalo will crowd around the area of my camp on such a night. Is it because they feel safer, or does the spectacle of the moon here make them as oblivious to any potential dangers as it does me?

On such nights I feel that it is mandatory to track The Loner as he scratches himself and feeds his way along the meadow. My voice seems to fall on his ears like so much empty air, and he pays no attention to me or my shadow in spite of the fact that I'm near enough to reach out and touch him. The buffalo, however, are not quite as moon-touched: your presence is signaled by snorts and bellows before you pick up their elongated yellow eyes around the edges of the meadow.

And why is it on such nights that Visoke always chooses to hide her mediocre appearance in veils of cloud while Karisimbi and Mikeno trumpet the moon and insist upon showing off their splendid peaks to full advantage under the silver reflection of the full moon? Also, why is it that the owls and hyrax refuse to add to the litany of the night when the air is silver and bright? They refrain on these magical nights, thus giving sound only to the tumble of the creek, the snorts of the buffalo, and the trumpet of the elephant. They save their presence for the dark nights, as if they know they would only be superfluous on the nights of the full moon.

There is an opening in the trees of my meadow that lets me see the heavy, ordinary rain clouds blanketing the lowlands on my magical moonlit nights up here. I'm sorry for those below me who cannot feel the moon the way it shines up here, even though they know the daily sun as I can never know it.

Why should most African novels begin with, "It was a hot night, there was a full moon, the hyena was calling, the mosquitoes were swarming," etc.? Why should I apologize for saying it's always cold here. Actually I'm lucky ever to see the moon, and as for a bug—bless his soul, he's a brave one, he is, if he comes up to Karisoke. Wouldn't it introduce it better if I say I'm a noncommercial nobody—I have a clean tent and take a hot bath each night, but I'm not on a Kenyan safari; I see more really infested sores and goddamned chronic cases of leprosy than Schweitzer, but I'm certainly no missionary. . . .

Yesterday I spent the usual day—six hours of climbing in and out of ravines on seventy percent slopes, and I screamed like a baptized baby over the worst of them for I know one fear, and that is acrophobia. Maybe I'm in the wrong line of work. I'm beginning to think so just because of my inability to control this particular line of thinking—fear of heights.

People have many fears, some deserved, some pretense, some either heard or read about, and some that seem to need cherishing because they elicit sympathy and thus bring attention. I can't recall that my acrophobia can be attributed to any of these

64

**attention-getting aims, but it is real nonetheless. It is the only thing I feel brave about in spite of all the accolades for working in the Congo or here with the gorillas. The only peril I really face in this work is sliding across a moss-slippery rock face of seventy percent of slope, something a two-year-old could jump across, but which still reduces me to shivering weakness.**

In her isolation, Dian thought more often of her father, George Fossey. Though her parents had divorced when she was six and her mother married Richard Price a year later, she had a soft spot in her heart for her real father. She still kept with her a picture of him in navy uniform taken during the war. As Dian grew older, she had sometimes yearned to see him. Finally, in 1959, a letter from her father reached her in Louisville, and she began a sporadic correspondence with him.

She sometimes wrote from Karisoke, pouring her heart out, as if to a stranger for whom she had an instinctive liking. He was very proud when a newspaper in San Rafael, California, carried a story about Dian and her African adventures, identifying her as the daughter of George and Kathryn Fossey of Fairfax, California.

**I had another letter from Daddy. He has not been well, but his wife seems to be taking care of him. I wonder what he would think of the Virungas? He always did love the wilderness, but never had a chance to enjoy it very much. Perhaps I'm here because of that. . . .**

As 1967 ended and the new year began, Dian wrote to Leakey: "It seems impossible that a year has gone by since beginning the study in the Congo, for I haven't accomplished half of what I intended during that time. I have chalked up 485 hours of observation, and although this puts me ahead of Schaller, it's less than what I'd hoped for. Now, of course, I'm anxious to know what the next 485 hours of observation will bring and hope that I will know twice as much as I do now.

"Had several good contacts with Group 8 two weeks ago— unfortunately deep into the Congo and six hours from camp, so I couldn't follow them further. The young adult, Peanuts, and the blackback, Samson, approached me to twelve feet; and as has been the case from our first contact, this small group of six members was receptive and calm, and their response behavior was at a minimum. Also was able to follow a badly wounded silverback—the third dominant in Group 4—for two days before losing the trail. However, from trail signs today it appears that he is now recovered enough to follow his group, although still at a day's distance. Have also recorded some excellent play sequences in this group that involve the dominant silverback, Uncle Bert, with younger members."

The observation of play was of particular importance. Dian was beginning to suspect that play was an aspect of gorilla behavior generally concealed from human observers, and for that reason had in the past been accorded far too little importance in studies of the apes' daily lives. That the gorillas were allowing Dian to observe their play showed how well she was being accepted.

The one constant thorn in her side was the presence of human intruders, and she told Leakey, "I will be going to Kigali January 23 for a visa extension and renewed permission to work in the park. At that time I intend to make an urgent request to the ministry to do something about the cattle and the poachers as the situation is past the point of tolerance. Now that the rainy season is over, there has been a tremendous influx of cattle and men, and the constant bawling of the cattle and yelling of the men has driven the gorilla out of the area, with the exception of one group that now clings to the summit of Visoke. It is a deplorable situation."

The result of her complaints was a commitment by L'Office Rwandais du Tourisme et des Parcs Nationaux (ORTPN) to increase patrols by armed park guards and an understanding whereby Dian would be able to call on the guards for assistance to help drive herders and their cattle out of the park. She began employing their services almost immediately, organizing cattle drives down Visoke's slopes. However, as she explained to Leakey, "The park guards do not stay in the park, and they only come up here once a month or when I send for them. Unfortunately, last week when the conservateur, who is the top park official, and a guard climbed, they were attacked by herdsmen whom they met on the lower trail, so their enthusiasm for trying to patrol this area is somewhat diminished as the guard's head was really mashed a bit."

She had some problems with her own African camp workers but was now better able to handle them.

**One of my two trackers increased his use of hashish and really made life miserable for me during the month of November**

and most of December. I hated to let him go because he was a good tracker, but had to do so when he became violent. He returned last week and I had to shoot over his head to get rid of him—he left immediately. I then reported the use of my pistol to Mr. Descamps, a Belgian adviser to the park authorities, as I want it on the record, and he in turn drew up a convocation, or warrant, for this man's arrest should he return.

Two other problems plagued Dian—her ailments and her growing notoriety.

In April 1968 she was eagerly awaiting Leakey's decision whether she could attend a primate symposium scheduled for June in the United States.

"A lesser reason for wanting to go to America is the fact that my teeth are beginning to rot and chip out in spite of the fact that I spent most of my savings before coming here to have them 'fixed up' just to prevent such a thing from happening. A friend of mine in America would be able to repair them much cheaper and faster than could be done in Africa, but again, this is not justification for making the trip, it is only an added incentive. Meanwhile, I'm saving all the chips and packing my gums with stuff that my tent boy brings up from his village every week—it helps to relieve the pain even though it looks like a combination of *merde* and vacuum-cleaner sweepings."

In the same letter she noted: "Some screwy British female psychiatrist has been trying to get up here—Descamps stopped her, and apparently she finally returned to Kigali spreading stories about my being charged and embraced by male gorillas, and now the American ambassador thinks I'm due for hospitalization any day. . . . Descamps told me of fourteen other people he's turned away, mainly just curiosity-seekers and missionary types from Rwanda, and this makes me mad for I don't feel that Descamps should have to worry about protecting me from 'the public.' "

Dian received word from Leakey the following month that grant money had been found to send her to the States for the primate symposium. For two days she was walking on air, her mind a world away from the forests of central Africa, as she silently rehearsed the stories she would soon be relating to friends in Louisville—between visits to her dentist.

Then a telegram arrived from Alan Root to tell her he had been hired to visit Karisoke in June to begin documenting her work on film for a *National Geographic* article.

The necessity to forgo the conference and remain at Karisoke for a few more months was made less painful when Leakey agreed to send her back to the States in October as a consolation.

By the time Alan arrived, Dian's venerable canvas tent had been replaced by a two-room cabin about twelve by twenty feet, crudely constructed of timber posts and sheathed in corrugated metal—a project initiated, financed, and supervised by Alyette de Munck. Dian painted the exterior of the cabin green so that it would blend into the background and decorated the interior with rush mats, skins, masks, and other local artifacts. She hung curtains made of bright yellow African printed cotton in the big front window. When she was finished, her cabin and its surroundings had an air of permanence. Karisoke was no longer just a name—it was a place in being.

fter spending so much time alone, Dian felt she was getting a little "bushy." So she welcomed Alan Root's company during the summer of 1968. It was a productive time for both. While Alan shot hundreds of feet of cine film of the gorillas and took scores of still photographs, Dian and her Rwandan trackers ranged far and wide on the steep slopes of Visoke and Karisimbi, exploring her little empire and getting to know its natural inhabitants. By summer's end she had located nine gorilla groups, or families, and had named and could identify by name each of nearly eighty individuals.

Alan Root had to leave at the end of August, but the National Geographic Society arranged for Robert Campbell, another Nairobi-based wildlife photographer, to carry on filming and to maintain the camp at Karisoke while Dian was away on her autumn trip to the United States.

Dian showed the quiet young Scotsman the ropes and introduced him to the camp staff and the gorillas. It was at this juncture that she learned in a telegram from her stepmother, Kathryn, that George Fossey had committed suicide.

In death, George became more real to Dian than he had perhaps ever been, and she grieved for him. It was a grief that needed sharing, but there was no one at camp to share it with except the newly arrived Bob Campbell. He turned out to be a sympathetic listener—so much so that Dian was moved to show him the first, anguished letter she had ever received from her dead father.

April 15, 1959

My Dearest Dian,

    I imagine you will be surprised to hear from me, but I just received your address from R. S. in Carte Madera. He got it from some girl in Larkspur who went to school with you. About a year and a half ago I wrote to Hazel asking for your address but never had an answer from her.

    I am married again, my baby, to a very wonderful person and we are very happy. It happened two years ago. At present we are living in Inverness on Tomales Bay. It is very beautiful up here. Deer in the place plus raccoons and quail. I have been so anxious, my darling, to write to you and to know how you are and what you are doing. I understand that you gave up the idea of veterinary and agricultural work and decided on occupational therapy.

    PLEASE write to your daddy and tell him all about it. Also if you have a picture of yourself PLEASE send it to me. Kathryn is very anxious to see and meet my beautiful daughter and suggested that maybe we might take a trip to see you if you would like us to. Do you come out to the coast at all? . . .

    PLEASE, my baby, write to me and tell me all about yourself. I have been so anxious to know about you, what you are doing, etc. . . . PLEASE, my baby, please write.

> All my love
> Your Dad
> George Fossey

Dian seldom made a show of her deepest emotions and for a time regretted having exposed her sorrow—which was as much for her own lost childhood as for her lost father. However, Bob Campbell's quiet but compassionate response reassured her.

**Bob is so kind. He listens but doesn't speak about such things in an embarrassing way. We get on well together and I really hope he will be able to stay on after I return.**

On September 24, 1968, Dian departed from the tiny airport in Gisenyi for Kigali, there to catch a connecting flight to Nairobi. She was on her way home to the United States for the first time in nearly two years. But those two years had forged a different woman with a new life, and there was now some doubt as to where "home" really was.

70

She spent three days in Nairobi, consulting with Dr. Leakey and looking after outstanding Karisoke business. Then it was on to Cambridge, England, to meet Prof. Robert Hinde, who had been Jane Goodall's Ph.D. thesis adviser and would be hers; after that to Washington, D.C., for discussions with the National Geographic Society's Research Committee about future funding of Karisoke and to screen the film taken by Alan Root. Only when her business was completed was there time to savor the old life that now seemed to lie so far behind her.

From Washington, Dian traveled to Louisville. She visited the farm cottage, now occupied by a couple whom she did not know. She spent most of her time at the home of Mary White's mother, Mrs. Henry, where she found some small measure of remembered pleasure. But for the most part Louisville was a disappointment. She was impatient with the uninformed and sometimes patronizing reactions to her tales of Africa and found Louisville life much less engaging than she had remembered it.

On first arriving in the United States, Dian had dutifully placed a call to Kitty Price. "Do you think you'll have time to see your mother?" Kitty had asked plaintively.

"Of course. As soon as I'm finished with my work and get my teeth fixed."

But Dian was in no hurry. She spent several days sorting and cataloging the hundreds of slides she had taken at Kabara and Karisoke and had forwarded to Mrs. Henry for safekeeping. She spent a day in the hospital undergoing minor surgery to remove a growth on the cornea of her right eye; and many hours in her dentist's chair.

Finally the time came to seek the warmth of California sunshine and endure a cool reunion with the Prices.

"The life you lead," Kitty cried reproachfully, "it's tearing us apart. Why are you punishing us like this?"

"It's my career, Mother. It's my life's work."

"Your life's work!" Kitty looked to her husband for support.

"Those gruesome letters you write. They have a terrible effect on your mother. Do you have to put her through all that?"

"I'm just writing the truth . . . sharing what I do with you. And it's what I *want* to do. You have to understand that. I'm thirty-six years old, and it's my life."

During the rest of her stay an uneasy armistice prevailed between Dian and the Prices. Her treatment of Alexie Forrester especially rankled them, but this was a subject she would not discuss.

**Lots of yak yak about Alexie. What a chance I'd lost! Mother really cried about that and she said I was a fool. Too bad *they* couldn't marry him!**

Despite everything, the Prices could not suppress a certain pride in Dian's burgeoning fame. When she left for the long trip back to Africa, they gave her a battery-powered cassette player, for which she chose some favorite tapes—classical piano, the Beatles, Frank Sinatra, Edith Piaf, some jazz, and the sound track from the movie *Dr. Zhivago*.

Flying first to London, Dian checked into a hotel and slept off her jet lag before joining Robert Hinde and Louis Leakey for dinner, which Louis cooked at the home of Jane Goodall's mother, an old and very dear friend of his. Dian was unimpressed by his culinary efforts.

**Leakey had slaved over two roasted ducks with African-style dressing and other exotic dishes he makes up as he goes along. He loves to cook and Mrs. Goodall lets him, but it takes some tolerance to clean up the kitchen after he is finished with it!**

Three days later she was back in central Africa, to be greeted at the little Gisenyi airport by the loyal Rosamond Carr, who had guessed she would be returning that day and had arranged to have Dian's Land Rover waiting for her.

**I set off the next day, Sunday, to let the porter wogs in the village at the base of the mountain know I had returned. . . . They were waiting also, just on a hunch, and shed real tears when they saw that I was back—I really can't get over this. After leaving them some messages to take up to Robert Campbell on the mountain, I drove on to Kisoro, spent the night at Traveler's Rest, did food shopping early on Monday morning, and then returned and climbed up to camp. I found everything running smoothly, although my wogs were a little drippy to see me and carried on like crazy—simply can't understand why they like me, as all I do is cuss them out from morning to dusk.**

**Bob Campbell was willing to spend another night and catch me up on all that had happened since I'd left, which was really nice of him since I was already so far behind schedule. He left on Tuesday morning. Since then I've wasted six days trying to find the gorilla groups, which has been very frustrating to me.**

It was some weeks before she was able to locate them all. Her study area seemed to be ever-expanding, and she reluctantly concluded that she would need help if she was to continue to keep track of all nine groups, let alone survey the remainder of the Virungas to discover how many gorillas still existed in the region.

Her feelings about sharing Karisoke with other whites were ambivalent. Although she looked forward to the occasional visits of close friends like Rosamond Carr, Alyette de Munck, and Alan Root, she had come to love and value her solitude and the feeling of being in charge of human activity in camp and in the surrounding forests and meadows. Nevertheless, she now urged Leakey to find a photographer willing to spend a prolonged period at Karisoke to document the gorillas' lives in still and motion pictures; and she also asked for a student or two to work on a census of the gorilla population:

"Robert Campbell would do well, but if not available I would ask that whomever you choose be self-reliant and willing to set up his own camp some ten minutes or so away from this one, which I hope you don't consider an eccentric request. I have found that too much time is lost from field notes and related work when I have to cook for people or sit around in the evenings talking. If you think he would be happy under these circumstances and isn't an overly gregarious sort, then I should certainly get on with him."

Dian had great difficulty locating Group 5, and when she eventually found the gorillas ranging in the saddle between Visoke and Karisimbi, several miles from camp, she had a terrifying encounter.

**The infants and juveniles approached ahead of the silverbacks, and the latter, imagining the youngsters to be in danger, became very threatening. Then one of the "show-off" juveniles fell out of its tree almost onto my lap, which prompted a series of charges from both silverbacks wanting to "protect" their young.**

**The aggressive behavior when the very young approached me without the "sanction" of the silverbacks makes me wonder if I'm ever going to be able to literally mix with the groups.**

She need not have worried. A month later she cabled Leakey:

ALL 6 MEMBERS OF GROUP 8 APPROACHING ME FROM 5 TO 10 FEET. EXPECT PHYSICAL CONTACT WITHIN A WEEK. JUST HAD TO SHARE MY EXCITEMENT WITH YOU—DIAN.

However, the physical contact that would signal the ultimate triumph for her unorthodox habituation techniques and be her reward for months of patient observation was delayed while she suffered a wrenching, two-month interruption in her field work.

On February 24, 1969, Dian returned to camp with her tracker to find an urgent message waiting from a doctor friend in Ruhengeri. A young gorilla had been captured by poachers and was now in the hands of the park conservateur, who was keeping it in a tiny cage near his office.

Dian trekked down the mountain next morning and drove to Ruhengeri. Her objective was a dilapidated army barracks currently being used to house the park administration. As she drove into the dusty parade square, her attention was caught by a mob of chattering, laughing children crowding into the doorway of a lean-to garage. Pushing her way past a brand-new Land Rover, Dian discovered that the object of attention was á young gorilla crouched in a tiny, almost totally enclosed cage. The animal—a three-year-old male—feebly bared his teeth at her as she shooed the children away and opened its cage door to get a closer look. The poor creature appeared to be mortally sick and its stench was overpowering.

Outraged, Dian stormed into the conservateur's office.

"Where did this baby come from," she demanded, "and what are you doing with it?"

Although somewhat cowed by her fury, the conservateur managed a brave front. He explained that he had hired a notorious poacher named Munyarukiko to capture an infant gorilla.

"Why?" raged Dian.

"Some nice German visitors, they want a mountain gorilla, better two, for show at the Cologne Zoo."

It appeared that the Germans had agreed to give the conservateur a Land Rover as payment in advance, to be followed by a large sum of money for "conservation work" in the park. Furthermore, the conservateur was to get a free air trip accompanying the merchandise to Cologne.

"Unfortunately, as Mademoiselle can see for herself, the young gorilla, he is not fit to go."

Dian later discovered that the order from the Cologne Zoo had been filled at the cost of slaughtering all ten adults of a gorilla group as they tried to protect their young on the south slopes of Mt. Karisimbi. The poachers had wired the little captive hand and foot to bamboo poles and kept it that way for three or four days. Later it was placed in a cage that afforded it neither room to stand up or turn around. Eventually it was brought to Ruhengeri with its limbs still bound. When Dian found it, it had been in the conservateur's possession for two or three weeks. The wounds from the wire bindings at its wrists and ankles had become badly infected; it was seriously malnourished, dehydrated, and having difficulty breathing.

Convinced that the infant could survive no more than a day or two longer in Ruhengeri, Dian was ready to make any sort of bargain with the conservateur so long as she would be allowed to take the animal back to Karisoke where she could care for it. She hurriedly struck a deal whereby she would attempt to nurse the infant back to health, at which time it could be shipped off to Cologne.

While her staff converted the storeroom of her cabin into a gorilla nursery supplied with plenty of foliage for nesting and eating, Dian made a breakneck trip to Kisoro to purchase antibiotics, salves, glucose, vitamins, canned milk, and other supplies. Then her porters carried the infant, whom she named Coco, up to Karisoke in a borrowed child's playpen with boards fastened across the top.

Field studies were forgotten as she nursed the young gorilla day and night, coaxing it to drink medicine-laced milk, even sleeping with it in her own bed during one period of crisis. Each day the nursery room was stripped, disinfected, and restocked with fresh grass and branches. By the fifth day Coco had begun to show some slight signs of improvement.

Then, on March 4, came another shock. Hearing voices, Dian went to her cabin door and saw a group of porters approaching, carrying a wooden barrel suspended between two bamboo poles. She guessed immediately what it contained.

One of the porters handed her a note from her friend in Ruhengeri. "They've got another one for the Cologne Zoo, and the conservateur wants you to look after it. I think he was afraid to write to you himself, but here it is."

That evening she dashed off a letter to Leakey's secretary:

"I'm going round the bend. They've captured a second baby, a female approximately three years of age, but it's in much better shape than the first one, which I'm afraid is going to die.

"I put them together in the nursery this morning with no trouble at all, but there now lies the problem of the second one's becoming infected by the first, and I'm unsure whether to start it out on antibiotics before it needs it."

She described the regime of feeding and medication she had been following for Coco, continuing, "This is all I know how to do—maybe it's all wrong, but by the time you get the letter, it will be too late to change. Anything you can suggest I would greatly appreciate. . . .

"One very interesting fact is that the new baby also has webbed toes on its right foot, as does the first. I had thought they might be from the same family due to their reactions to each other, and this webbed toe trait seems to indicate it's true. . . . Needless to say, it is impossible for me to continue with my field work right now. Am taking notes around the clock on the babies, but haven't yet begun to type them up."

Three weeks later both infants were doing well, and she again wrote Leakey's secretary.

"For approximately three hours each day I play mother gorilla and go out and search for the best the forest has to offer in the way of vegetation delicacies, including ripe blackberries, and if you ask me, they never had it so good!

Their dung is now perfect, if you can describe dung that way. My only concerns are the horrid facial sores on the female, whom I've named Pucker, which are spreading and far from healthy looking. I have the perfect medicine for these, but it sets back our rapport considerably whenever I try to apply it, and then it takes several days for her to trust me again . . . and now Coco has started one on his face.

"I am also taking Coco out into the forest and turning him loose, when he will let go of me, that is, but he is very timid outside. I feel almost certain that Pucker would follow us, but I would prefer to have someone around before I try letting her out too—she is the most obstinate, bullheaded animal I've every met, and it would be just like her to climb to the top of a seventy-foot hagenia and not come down. . . .

"I still am unable to go out for observations on the groups, but I'm filling up notebooks on the behavior of these two monsters, which of course is almost identical to that of wild infants and fascinating to observe at such close quarters! Because of the addition of the second one, at least I can dispense with TLC (tender loving care) during the night hours, but they do consume most of the day. And now they are having to learn the meaning of 'no,' which is rather comical as they are so obstinate. I've ceased to begrudge the loss of days in the field, for the time being at least, as what I can record now is a valuable addition to the study."

In her few free moments Dian pounded furiously at her battered Olivetti, firing off angry letters to the mayor of Cologne, the head of the Cologne Zoo, the Fauna Preservation Society in England, and anyone else she could think of who might help prevent the exporting of the young animals.

But all to no avail.

The "conservateur" is absolutely impervious. He climbed to camp yesterday to insist that the gorillas be in Kigali on April 4 in order to depart for Germany on the 5th, yet he hadn't a clue as to how to go about it and asked me to handle everything for him. He was extremely nervous, and from the few facts I could obtain from him, this definitely seems to be a private matter between ORTPN—the Tourism and National Parks Department—and the Cologne Zoo. I would guess they've felt some pressure from previous letters I've written to conservation authorities, thus the speedup in departure time, some three weeks ahead of schedule. Obviously I can't keep the animals forever, nor would I want to as it is a bit much, but I am seeking a deal at least to let Bob Campbell get here for pictures of them. Dr. Leakey has arranged for Bob to come back for a six-month stay. With his support maybe I can still get the Rwandan authorities to consider an alternative for the babies—I'm sure a return to the wild would still be feasible.

A delay was to be the best she could arrange, however, and Campbell arrived just in time to help build the gorillas' shipping crates. Four days before the deadline for their departure, Dian made one final, futile attempt to save them.

Saturday I received a very strong cable opposing their export from the Fauna Preservation Society, which I'd hoped would give me one last chance to return them to the wild. Armed with this cable, Polaroid pictures of cage, babies, etc. and Alyette de Munck as interpreter, I set off for Kigali last Tuesday morning. The trip was a failure with regard to returning the babies to the wild. The director of Tourism and National Parks Service would not hear of it and was very snotty about the delay. However, the two days weren't entirely wasted. I had the chance to tell my story to some other government officials, and they were appalled, or so they said, by what ORTPN had done. I gave them some Polaroids taken by Campbell of the babies, which pleased them immensely.

The ORTPN director offered to have the conservateur capture two more gorillas for me! These people have no sense of guilt whatsoever. I must now compile another report based on what I learned in Kigali—it was the initial fault of the Cologne Zoo in seeking these two gorillas. I had a good session with a member of the German embassy in hopes of thwarting further captures for that particular country. I've received a rumor that two more zoos in Germany are seeking gorillas, but I can hardly put that in the report since it is rumor only.

The "babies" left for Cologne by jetliner on May 3 and, thanks to Dian's meticulous travel preparations, arrived in good condition.

They died in their cage at the zoo within a month of each other, in 1978, after nine years of time-serving for the entertainment of that most superior primate—Homo sapiens.

Dian's life did not quiet down with the departure of Coco and Pucker.

On May 10 about 1:30 in the morning I awoke to find the opposite wall and ceiling above the fireplace a solid sheet of flames! With great calm and presence of mind I ran screaming and yelling out of the house, fell over the first fenced path I encountered, managed to return with two containers of water from the kitchen, and was throwing these on the walls when my men came running with more water—oh, what a mess, but we did get it out.

Then the next day my beloved chickens began to die—all had names and were pets of several years—from a disease brought up from the village by chicken bought for eating. I can't kill mine. I immediately put them in individual boxes that lined the cabin, for segregation, medicine, and warmth, but out of nineteen, only two are still alive and I think one is on its way tonight.

Repairing her charred cabin gave Dian an excuse for a general improvement of the campsite. Alyette de Munck volunteered her contracting skills and in four days had supervised the erection of a new, corrugated-iron kitchen and food storage building. This permitted the dismantling of the old kitchen, which had been slapped together out of tin sheets and canvas, and the striking of the original food storage tent, which was suffering from terminal jungle rot. The camp now consisted of two permanent metal-sheathed shacks and two tents: one for the camp workers and one for Bob Campbell, both situated some distance down the meadow from Dian's cabin.

It was not until nearly two months after the departure of Coco and Pucker that field work settled back into its "normal" routine. Bob Campbell had to be trained in gorilla tracking and contact etiquette, a chore Dian enjoyed since her liking for the quiet, sensitive Scot was growing day by day. The real difficulty hinged on the fact that a prolonged drought had driven the gorillas to seek new feeding grounds beyond their normal ranges, and it required several weeks to locate them all again.

By early July Dian was picking up on her observations where she had left off in May.

**Yesterday and today afforded two wonderful contacts with Group 8, mainly Peanuts, who is curious and playful enough to seek proximity. He showed reasoning ability yesterday when he sought to obtain a candy bar I had laid down by my side.**

**I'd made a big thing of this candy bar, imitating the vocalizations of Coco and Pucker whenever they were eating favorite foods while I unwrapped it and nibbled on the end. Peanuts was in a real frenzy by the time I laid it down and turned partially away, yet instead of just reaching out for it, which he could easily have done, he tried to slowly pull the foliage stalks upon which it was lying toward him. He almost had it when suddenly it slipped through the matted vegetation and onto the dirt below and out of sight. Was he mad!**

The problem of finding a student for the gorilla census work seemed to have been solved with the enlistment of a young Englishman Leakey had met in Nairobi. However, as Dian was to discover over and over, people working with gorillas in the isolation of the Virungas required physical and mental abilities that most either did not possess or, lacking her own dedication to the animals, did not care to exercise.

The student was given a crash course in gorillas and before long found himself encamped with a native tracker on a mountain some miles from Karisoke. His field notes, brought to Dian by runner, quickly became so bizarre that Dian grew concerned about his mental stability. Then she learned from her staff that he had become a heavy user of hashish. By mid-September Dian was asking Leakey's permission to fire B——.

B—— was forthwith given his walking papers, but the traumas of the past months had taken their toll on Dian, and this latest setback with the census that was so important to her research was the last straw. Her health had also taken a sudden and disturbing turn for the worse. Severe chest pains led her to fear she had contracted tuberculosis. The threat of this dire disease had haunted her childhood and her dread of it had been intensified by her experiences with it when she had worked for a brief time with tuberculosis patients at the City of Hope Hospital in Duarte, California. When a doctor at a Seventh-Day Adventist school near Rosamond Carr's plantation tentatively confirmed her suspicion, she became so alarmed that she wrote to Leakey telling him she had to see him in Nairobi.

As always, Leakey was frantically busy—dashing down to Olduvai, flying off to raise money and receive awards in England, Europe, and the United States, but he had a clear week starting October 8 and he asked Dian to come to Nairobi then.

Leakey made no attempt to hide his pleasure when he met her at the airport. Tall and straight, comfortable in jeans and workshirt with her long, thick hair close-braided, she was one of the most striking women he had ever seen.

"I don't like doing this," she told him in explanation of her visit, "but I'm nearly at my wits' end. Everything's ganged up on me. I miss Coco and Pucker more than words can say, and I hate to think what will happen to my babies in Cologne. I'm desperate to continue with the census work, but it's impossible without decent help. The poachers and herders are driving me crazy. And to top it off, I'm afraid I've got tuberculosis."

"Ah, my dear," Leakey said cheerfully, "what you need is a proper little holiday. Need one myself, come to think of it. You leave it to me and I'll get something going. Meantime, I shall take you to the best doctor in Kenya and arrange to have him check your lungs."

Dian underwent a series of tests and was given some drugs for the treatment of her symptoms, but a diagnosis could not be completed for several days. Undeterred, Leakey pushed ahead with his plans, and one bright morning he and Dian left Nairobi for a safari through the grassy plains of south-central Kenya. In the company of this enthusiastic and much admired—if somewhat elderly—companion, Dian put her worries behind her.

The guided Kenyan safari organized by Leakey was a far cry from the exhausting journey Dian had made with John Alexander, her "Great White" hunter, six years earlier. The vehicles were well-sprung and air-conditioned. Camp facilities were elaborate, including sleeping tents with attached shower stalls and big, cozy beds. Superb food was accompanied by vintage wines. Under such sybaritic conditions, Dian succumbed to the romance of star-filled nights on the sweet-smelling savanna. Leakey did more than succumb—he fell deeply, wildly in love.

After a week they returned to Nairobi just in time for Leakey to fly off to London. On the day of his departure he wrote Dian *three* letters which were as ardent as those of any heavily smitten teenager. He was distraught that they were to be separated by so much space and time but solaced himself with memories of the "heavenly week we had" and with the conviction that they now belonged to each other.

**I**n letter after letter over the next few weeks Leakey continued to pour out his passion for Dian; but it was a one-way flow, and his pleas for a response from her became ever more plaintive. Back in Nairobi in mid-November, he was becoming desperate to see her or at least to hear from her. He proposed that they make another safari together, and when this elicited no response, he wrote to tell her that he was giving her a ruby but needed to discuss the setting and ring size with her. "I want you to have it soon as a deep token of my caring. . . ."

Leakey's letters had an inhibiting effect upon Dian. As she tried to think of how best to answer one of his outpourings, another would descend upon her. She was embarrassed that the great Louis Leakey, that paragon of strength and purpose, should have become so besotted. She may also have been feeling guilty, since she was becoming ever more interested in Robert Campbell.

Eventually she wrote Leakey a short and rather formal note to accompany a report on a visit she had recently made to Kabara. Perhaps she hoped his ardor would be diminished by it and that their old relationship could be restored, but this was not to be.

Leakey's reply exuded enormous happiness and relief at having heard from her, and he was authentically pleased to be the bearer of good news from the doctor who had tested her for tuberculosis and who was now convinced she was free of the disease.

Moved by gratitude and perhaps pity for this sixty-seven-year-old lover, Dian responded with a warm and cheerful letter full of news about the gorillas, although sparing about her own feelings. In her journal she wrote distractedly: **Don't know what to do about L. God—what a mess.**

His reply, which seemed to arrive by the next post, was ecstatic. It included plans to meet her in Cambridge—a prospect that did not delight her, for she had hoped her long absence in England would cool his passion.

From the hour of her return to Karisoke, Dian had been buried under a mountain of field notes that had to be worked into shape in preparation for her first semester at Cambridge.

She was also extremely busy in the field. Early in November she chanced a journey across the mountains to Kabara in the Congo, although she was fully aware that she might be imprisoned should she be caught by park guards or the military. However, she badly wanted to know what had become of her Kabara gorilla groups.

Although the distance as the crow flies was little more than five miles, it took Dian and two trackers five hours of slogging through a steady downpour to reach that familiar meadow. Once there, she managed to contact only one of her former study groups, which she found sadly depleted. She encountered no soldiers or park guards, but discovered a great deal of evidence of poaching, and the whole region was overrun with cattle. She and her two men took the considerable risk of destroying more than sixty poacher's snares and demolished several shelters erected by Congolese cattle herders, but this was hardly more than a gesture. Sadly, she estimated that fewer than half the gorillas she had known at Kabara in 1967 still survived.

Not long after her return from this adventure she found herself at even greater hazard.

**On November 17 I was just barely nipped by a sickly poacher's dog on the lower leg, and since it amounted to nothing, I joked about it. But much to my embarrassment, everyone became most upset due to the fact that the incidence of rabies among wild dogs in Rwanda is sixty percent, and of course rabies is one hundred percent fatal without the series of injections.**

**Everyone pleaded with me to get the injections, but I refused as I just didn't have the time—Leakey heard about it and even went out to the airport in Nairobi and had needles, serum, etc., sent to me, but I didn't use them. By my next trip off the mountain, in December, I'd forgotten all about it. I went down to post my mail, shop, and send Bob Campbell off on his way to Nairobi to spend Christmas with his wife. I returned to the mountain, looking forward to the next few weeks alone so as to get all in readiness for going to England. But soon I began to ache all over,**

became almost too weak to stand, alternately sweating and chilled, was dizzy with buzzing ears, and my temperature was a neat 105°F!

No joking now. I thought I did have rabies—my one medical book on the mountain gave these as initial symptoms—so I knew I was going to die and was really quite provoked as I wasn't ready yet. Late that evening I crawled to the front door, shot my pistol off to bring the wogs running, and ordered two of them to run directly down to the home of the nearest European, at park head-quarters, to ask for medicine as I was very sick. I was proud of these chaps for taking off in the middle of the night with only a flashlight for protection, because the area is thick at night with buffalo, which are the one thing the Africans fear.

I then spent the night just trying to stay awake by dividing my delirium time with reading a pocket book, for I didn't dare to sleep. By 5:30 the next morning the mattress was soaked with perspiration, yet I was freezing.

Then M. Descamps knocked on the door, and that silly little Belgian looked like a guardian angel. His first words were *"Mon Dieu!"* as I seem to have been a wee bit blue by then. He ordered the boy to bring a freezing tub of water, hauled me out of bed, and wrapped me in dripping wet, cold towels, which can only be described as pure agony! After some ten or twenty minutes of this fever-reduction therapy I was ordered to change clothes, then *"allez!"* out the door to a waiting teepoy—an elongated basket affair with stout rims and handles manned by six Africans. I was trussed up into the basket along with piles of blankets, and before I could say *kwa heri,* the men began carting me off in such a silent and gentle way that I really had no sensation of movement be-yond the passage of tree boughs over my head. It was a rather strange experience. I didn't really possess all of my faculties, and yet I was so aware of the silence of the porters and the sparkling, crisp beauty of the morning.

When we finally reached the Land Rover, I was becoming more aware of my surroundings. I was taken to the nearest hospi-tal and checked in as a rabies patient by all the French-speaking doctors and nurses in Ruhengeri. No one spoke English and I guess I learned more French during the next three days than I'd learned during the past three years.

That day seemed to be a succession of one painful needle af-ter the next, all accompanied by torrents of French. This is a French-run hospital for wogs, so in between the constant comings and goings of the European staff, there was the wailing of sick babies, the buzz of flies, and the smells of their cooking seemed to permeate my room. To be sure, there were comic highlights—like the French nurse who seemed to eat garlic with every meal and would come into my room to inquire, *"Comment ça va?"* exuding odors that would cause me to head for the nearest basin.

After three days and nights of this, I figured that my mind was going to crack before my body, so I packed up my knapsack and readied myself to face the doctor to tell him I was leaving. Among my complaints was the fact that there was no drinking water available except what the nurses would bring me from their homes, and the food came from a horrible hotel in Ruhengeri, delivered by the proprietor, who breathed fumes of whiskey and who had to have fixed the toast and tea for the next morning the night before as he never woke up before noon.

Just as I was ready to leave, Mrs. Carr drove up. She had heard that I was in trouble and just dropped everything to come to my rescue—I don't know when I've been so happy to see anybody in my life. Within an hour I was released and on my way to her plantation, where I had to continue the rabies injections for another eleven days. Once there, I was given a lovely bedroom overlooking acres of beautiful garden and was really waited on hand and foot by her staff, all of whom are spoiled rotten, until the rabies series was terminated.

On December 30 I left for camp, and happily this was the same day that Bob Campbell returned to Ruhengeri, so we climbed back up the mountain together, taking a very long time to do so.

As 1970 began, the perennial rain and mist vanished and the forest again glowed with sunshine, tempting Dian out of the cabin in search of the gorillas even before she had recovered her strength. Accompanied by Bob Campbell, she experienced ten near-perfect days that came to a deeply symbolic climax when Peanuts, the young blackback of Group 8, reached out in what was the first friendly physical contact ever recorded between a wild mountain gorilla and a human being.

Peanuts left his tree for a bit of strutting before he began his approach in my direction. He is a showman. He beat his chest, he threw leaves in the air, he swaggered and slapped the foliage around him, and then suddenly he was at my side. His expression indicated that he had entertained me—now it was my turn. He sat down to watch me "feeding," but didn't seem particularly impressed, so I changed activities; I scratched my scalp noisily to make a sound familiar to gorillas, who do a great deal of scratching.

Almost immediately Peanuts began to scratch. It was not clear who was aping whom. Then I lay back in the foliage to appear as harmless as possible and slowly extended my hand. I held it palm up at first, as the palms of an ape and a human hand are more similar than the backs of the hand. When I felt he recognized this "object," I slowly turned my hand over and let it rest on the foliage.

Peanuts seemed to ponder accepting my hand, a familiar yet strange object extended to him. Finally he came a step closer and, extending his own hand, gently touched his fingers to mine. To the best of my knowledge this is the first time a wild gorilla has ever come so close to "holding hands" with a human being.

Peanuts sat down and looked at my hand for a moment longer. He stood and gave vent to his excitement by a whirling chest beat, then went off to rejoin his group, nonchalantly feeding some eighty feet uphill. I expressed my own happy excitement by crying. This was the most wonderful going-away present I could have had.

The icing on the cake was that Bob Campbell recorded the event on film in a sequence that *National Geographic* splashed over a two-page spread. The expression on Dian's face is one of pure ecstasy.

A week later, on January 11, 1970, Dian was wandering the narrow and venerable streets of Cambridge, trying to find her way to Darwin College, where she was to begin her first three-month term as a doctoral student in one of the world's most ancient and prestigious centers for the study of natural science.

At first she was charmed by her surroundings and stimulated by the company of her fellow Ph.D. students, but she soon began to have second thoughts.

During the winter in this part of England it is dark until about 9:00 or 9:15 in the morning, then there are a few periods of gray that last until about 4:30 to 5:00 P.M., at which time it becomes dark again. I feel like a mole. Robert Hinde, my doctoral adviser, picks me up about 8:30 for the drive to the Maddingley lab where I spend the days working on my field notes and using computers and sonographic equipment to work up the data.

I'm not particularly happy here as there are so many thousands of rules to follow, the town is so crowded and rushed, the people so terribly self-important, the air so heavy, gray, and smoggy all of the day, and there is no privacy whatsoever. I guess it will all just take getting accustomed to—never had this problem of adjustment in Africa, but now it seems as though I must rely on others for everything, a situation I detest.

Leakey, out of touch and frustrated in Nairobi, continued to plead for news—and for some recognition of his love, but with no success.

Dian wrote briefly that she felt confined and alienated in Cambridge and did not care for all the formalities and protocol. "I don't feel at ease with the people, and the whole thing doesn't seem worth it."

Leakey responded with some news to lift her spirits. He was attempting to persuade Robert Hinde to try and get the time she must spend in England reduced and even suggested that she might forget about earning her Ph.D. He just wanted her to be able to present her data "in the best possible way to the scientific world." He planned to be in London by February 5 or 6, he told her, and would meet with her then.

Since Leakey's travel depended on grants from various foundations, he had to hew to a strict itinerary, but when he boarded the BOAC jet for London at Nairobi airport early in February 1970, he was eagerly looking forward to the dinner and "quiet talk" with Dian he had managed to wedge into his schedule.

It was not to be. Leakey was felled by a heart attack shortly after arriving in London and was rushed to a hospital.

Dian wrote to him immediately, but it was nearly a month before she took the ninety-minute train ride into London to visit him in his convalescence. There is no record of what took place between them, but at least there was no rupture in their relationship.

Leakey made a good recovery and, against the advice of friends and medical advisers, continued to work and to travel incessantly. He saw Dian only on a few occasions when their paths crossed in their travels, and she was always careful to limit their encounters to settings where decorum would be preserved.

Nevertheless, Leakey continued to pour out his unrequited love in letter after letter, scratched out in his nearly illegible scrawl, and in notes furtively scribbled at the bottom of their "official" correspondence, which he'd dictated to a secretary. For a time he encouraged Dian to write to him at his personal postal box in Nairobi, assuring her that only he would see the letters.

He pressed her endlessly to accept the ruby which had now been set in a ring. Although she eventually did so only with reluctance, it became one of her most precious possessions.

The last letter from him surviving in her files was written early in January 1972 when she was again at Cambridge.

He was despondent; everything seemed to be going wrong for him in his fund-raising efforts. The people who promised to support Birute Galdikas's study of orangutans had reneged. He was having trouble getting money for his own research and for a research station at Tigone. He closed with the wish that she could be "near him to calm the awful uncertainty and give him peace." Perhaps he knew his time was running out. Later that year a second heart attack would put an end to Louis Leakey's life and loves.

# 10

Dian never really enjoyed Cambridge, but by the time she was preparing to leave the university in March 1970 at the end of her first three-month semester, she had reluctantly come to accept the necessity of going there.

**You have to obtain a union card in the scientific field. Without a Ph.D. at the least, it is very hard to get adequate grant support or to get really good students to come and work on your project. Without that Big Degree, you don't cut much ice no matter how good you are.**

She planned to return to Cambridge in October for a six-month stay, but was faced with the problem of finding someone capable of caring for the camp and the gorillas during her absence.

This time there was no shortage of candidates. The publication of a cover story by and about her and the gorillas in the January 1970 edition of *National Geographic* magazine had made her moderately famous, and her mail was filled with requests from all sorts of people wanting to come to Karisoke. However, she had little use for most of these volunteers.

**It may sound terribly conceited, but I don't want my camp overrun with hippies, freeloaders, or other similar unqualified, adventure-seeking people who will "work for nothing." This kind can always spend their time protesting in America—I don't want them here.**

At last she found a candidate who seemed ideal. He was a one-time schoolteacher who had returned to Liverpool University to gain a bachelor's degree in zoology, following which he had studied captive orangutans. He had written Dr. Hinde in Cambridge looking for doctorate-level research work, and Hinde had passed his letter on to Dian.

"I've finally found the right man for the job," she wrote Leakey. "His name is Alan Goodall—no relation to Jane! I know that you would like him, Louis, for he's honest, forthright, intelligent, completely dedicated, has a good sense of humor, common sense, humility, and, above all, maturity. This young man is definitely the one to replace me when I'm away from camp, or for that matter to help me out in pursuit of special study topics when I'm there, for it has gotten to be too much to cover for one person."

Alan Goodall was married, and when Dian interviewed him at Cambridge, he and his wife were expecting their first child. After her disastrous experience with the dope-smoking census taker, Goodall seemed to represent the kind of stability and maturity for which Dian was looking.

Since he was a family man with responsibilities, Dian agreed that he should be paid a small salary (fifty pounds a month) and provided with transportation to Rwanda for his wife and child.

Leakey objected. "Don't you think you're being overly generous? After all, I'm the one who has to raise the money."

"Generous!" Dian flared back. "Not everyone can work for nothing! If I can't get some decent help, I may be forced to abandon the whole project!"

Leakey capitulated. It was agreed that Goodall would take charge of Karisoke while Dian returned to Cambridge for her next two semesters.

Back in the Virungas for the summer, Dian spent every possible hour with her gorillas. She was often accompanied by Bob Campbell, who was shooting still pictures to illustrate a second *National Geographic* article scheduled for October 1971, as well as cine footage for the planned television special. Close contact with the gorillas was now routine, and though working under extremely difficult conditions, Campbell was able to record some remarkable moments of communion between the two species.

Dian took considerable pleasure in his presence. Ever since sharing her grief with him over her father's death, she had felt an affinity with this unassuming man who worked so unremittingly and uncomplainingly. She sometimes wondered what his life was like in Nairobi, but although she knew that he had a wife, she never probed into his personal affairs.

During the progress of his assignment, the relationship between them was gradually transformed from that of two professionals to an intensely personal rapport. For his sake, Dian began dyeing her hair to hide the gray that, at thirty-eight, had begun to salt it. Campbell brought out the domestic impulse in her. She delighted in cooking for him and on his birthday and other festive occasions would prepare elaborate meals. For his part, Bob Campbell had a calming influence on her mercurial personality.

From time to time he returned to his home in Nairobi, and Dian dreaded these departures. She missed him deeply and sometimes turned to drinking at night to dull the loneliness. During his absence, she would spend hours sewing curtains or making other wifely improvements to his quarters in preparation for his return.

Her private life did not, however, interfere with her gorilla studies—or with her war against poachers and herders. She was indefatigable and implacable at breaking snares, destroying shelters, and chasing cattle to the park boundaries. A ghastly incident occurred in May, to which she reacted with such ferocity that she horrified herself.

A poor buffalo had gotten wedged into a tree fork, and some Tutsi herders had come along and found it that way. They cut the meat off its hind legs and left it alive and horribly tortured when my men found it some time later. I loaded my little pistol and went to find the poor animal, which was still full of courageous bluff—snorting with every inch of life left within it and trying so hard to defend what remained of its life. I detested killing such a display of courage, and of course I was crying my eyes out when I pumped the bullets into its skull. I don't think I will ever forget those eyes.

Killing that poor animal has done something to me that I didn't think possible, for now I am finding myself out to avenge the cruelty of the Tutsi by crippling their cattle with bullets. I used to shoot above or below or near the cattle of the Tutsi, but now I shoot them in their hind legs and have crippled several since the buffalo was found.

Obviously this makes me no better than the Tutsi who hacked off the hind legs of the buffalo, but suddenly the entire area is devoid of cattle and once again the buffalo, elephant, and gorilla are able to return to their ranges.

By September Dian had settled Alan Goodall at Karisoke and was off for Los Angeles en route to Cambridge again. Los Angeles was to be the scene of an event that more than any other marked her emergence as a naturalist of world stature. Once again she owed the opportunity to Louis Leakey, who had arranged for her to be the featured speaker at a thousand-dollar-a-plate fund-raising dinner for the Leakey Foundation. Dian was somewhat intimidated at the prospect of keeping an audience of such wealth and breadth of knowledge entertained for an hour; but from the moment she walked, stunningly dressed, to the podium in the darkened ballroom and, in the soft Southern inflections she had acquired in Louisville, introduced the first of her remarkable gorilla slides, her audience was enthralled.

The thunderous applause at the end of her talk was a moment of pure triumph that, ironically, marked the decline of her dependence on Leakey. Soon she would have the academic credentials to run Karisoke on her own; and she was now confident she had the personal influence to sustain it financially. When she walked into the conference room at National Geographic headquarters in Washington a week later to argue for a renewal and enlargement of her research grant, she succeeded without any support from Leakey.

Under Dian's tutelage, Alan Goodall had learned the routine of life at Karisoke, observing the gorillas and engaging in antipoaching and antiherding activities. But he found it difficult to adjust to the isolation of the camp and to the physical hardships involved in tracking gorillas through dense forest and across rugged terrain at high altitude and in weather that was all too often abysmally bad.

After being bluff-charged once or twice by silverbacks reacting to his unaccustomed presence, he began to wonder whether he had the stamina to live with much more of that. In fact, on the very day of Dian's departure for Los Angeles, he had tried to resign. While busily completing her packing, Dian talked him out of it. In his own book, *The Wandering Gorillas,* Goodall recalled the moment:

"She listened sympathetically to my tale of woe before telling me that she, too, had been very depressed when she first started her study three years earlier. She recalled that when her friend Alyette de Munck left her alone on the mountain for the first time, she had run and locked herself in her cabin when one of the African staff came to speak to her. Later, upon translating his words with the aid of her *Upcountry Swahili* book, she had discovered that he had merely asked her if she required hot water! Such is the fear of the unknown."

Although by Dian's rigorous standards Goodall's research observations left something to be desired, there was no denying that he was a determined and energetic conservationist.

On one occasion he actually shot a fleeing poacher with the .32-caliber pistol Dian had left with him. Exactly where he hit the man is unclear—Goodall admits to hitting him in the leg, but Dian believed he was wounded in the back. The poacher turned up at Ruhengeri hospital for treatment and was placed in a bed next to one being occupied by Alyette de Munck's gardener. When Mrs. de Munck learned of the shooting from her gardener, she stormed up the mountain to Karisoke where she confronted Goodall. He tearfully confessed, and she read him the riot act. Fortunately for him, the Rwandan authorities chose to turn a blind eye to the incident.

Early in November Alan heard a rumor that villagers at the foot of Mt. Karisimbi had killed several gorillas. He spent half a day getting to the scene, accompanied by his wife and Guamhogazi, one of the camp workers. They found five mutilated bodies—two silverbacks, one blackback male, and two mature females. The animals, which happily did not belong to any of the study groups, had been killed just outside the existing park boundary. They were, however, inside the *earlier* boundary that was still visible in the form of a thin line of stumps. The bodies had been too badly mutilated by dogs, hyenas, and other scavengers for the cause of death to be properly determined, but Goodall deduced from the many small stones lying near the corpses that they had been stoned to death by frightened villagers. The fact that only the bodies of adult gorillas had been found led him to believe that an infant had been captured during the massacre.

Dian was desolated by Alan's hastily written report of the macabre incident, when it reached her at Cambridge. She discarded the hypothesis that the animals had been stoned to death, although she knew how frightening gorillas could be when threatened and how terrified most farmers were of them. Noting that the gorillas had been killed in the same general area in which Coco and Pucker had been captured, she concluded that they had been slaughtered by poachers during the capture of one or more infants destined for the zoo trade.

Furious, she pounded out a letter to the park conservateur accusing him of being behind the killings and threatening him with the wrath of international public opinion. She wrote equally angrily to his boss, the director of Tourism and National Parks. And she wrote to a friend employed by Sabena Airlines in Kigali, asking him to watch cargo manifests for the shipment of a baby gorilla. She also wrote to every conservation organization she could think of to alert them to the slaughter. She asked Alyette de Munck to use her African staff to ferret out information on the slaughter from local villagers. When despite all of this she was unable to get to the bottom of the killings, she vowed never again to be at such a loss for information. Thereafter she developed a network of informants in Ruhengeri and Kigali to keep her abreast of the activities of any person engaging in the illegal traffic in endangered animals.

Dian returned to Karisoke on March 12, 1971, and more than ever it felt like coming home. But on the very first evening she had a run-in with Alan Goodall, who had been somewhat cavalier in his treatment of her cabin.

"My God," she scolded, "look at the mess. What do you think this is—some transient shelter?"

"Now wait a bit, Dian! I've tried to keep the place as neat as possible."

"Neat? Hell, this is my home! It looks like a pigsty. You don't realize what this place means to me. You come in here, use my stuff, don't even bother to put it back. This isn't a commune!"

After Dian's return—and Goodall's departure—a new cabin was built to replace the tent in which Bob Campbell had spent the better part of the previous year. Soon thereafter, a fourth cabin was constructed to house a succession of students engaged for the long-delayed census of the park's gorilla population.

The first census students had already begun work by the time Dian returned to Karisoke. They were two American girls, Jacqueline Raine and Marshall Smith. Cambridge student Nick Humphrey would arrive soon after, to be followed by Sandy Harcourt, Graeme Groom, and many others. Initially the students were based in bush camps in remote areas of the park where the gorilla populations had not yet been surveyed. Later, as the census work was completed and the emphasis switched to research into gorilla behavior, students who were gathering material for their own doctoral theses lived at and worked from Karisoke proper.

Well before her second departure for Cambridge there had been talk between Dian and Bob Campbell of his ending his ten-year marriage. However, when he and Dian were reunited at Karisoke in March of 1971, he confessed that he had not told his wife of what was happening, much less broached the subject of divorce.

Although Dian was deeply distressed by what she viewed as

cowardice on his part, she nevertheless forgave him and the affair continued.

Dian was convinced that for the first time in her life she was genuinely in love. Although her experience with her own family had made her leery of permanent arrangements between man and woman, Bob inspired a great desire within her for a traditional and enduring relationship. Each time he went off to his home in Nairobi, she hoped and willed that he would cut the knot; but always he returned to Karisoke to admit that nothing had been done.

So the summer passed with no resolution of their relationship. Then, in late November, Dian discovered she was pregnant.

It was not easy for a white woman to procure an abortion in Catholic Rwanda. The abortion was eventually done by a Belgian woman doctor working across the border in the Congo, who agreed to drive to Gisenyi to perform the operation.

December 1: **Appointment at 11:00. I've never been through anything like it and seem to have forgotten a great deal since then. I swallowed my tongue during surgery and was turning purple before it came up. Drove to Rosamond's in back of Bob's car. Mt. Nyiragongo erupting all night—had injection to make me sleep.**

After spending four days recuperating at Rosamond Carr's home near Gisenyi, Dian insisted on going back to camp. Despite Rosamond's protestations, she drove herself to the foot of the mountain and then made the climb. That afternoon she began hemorrhaging.

**Was terrified so plopped straight into bed and was there when Bob came in from the gorillas and found me. Did not tell him what was wrong and don't think he guessed how bad it was.**

Although she succeeded in concealing the scale of the bleeding from Bob, he stayed close to camp for the next three days. On the third day Dian sent a note down to the Ruhengeri hospital asking for medication. The porter returned with pills and a message from the disapproving Dr. Weiss ordering her to come to the hospital at once for proper treatment. Dian ignored this message and stilled Bob's apprehensions by assuring him that the medicines she had received would stop the hemorrhaging.

She was wrong. On the fourth day she was too weak to get out of bed. Bob had arranged to fly to Nairobi that day to visit his wife, and he left camp at about ten in the morning. However, in Ruhengeri he paused to question Dr. Weiss about Dian's condition. He was so disturbed by what he heard that instead of continuing on to the airport in Kigali, he hastily hired ten porters and a native litter and by 2:30 that afternoon was back at Dian's bedside.

"You *must* come down to the Ruhengeri hospital," he insisted. "You simply can't stay here alone. You might well die!"

Too weak to resist any longer, Dian was carried down the mountain. After Campbell delivered her to the hospital, he extracted from her the promise that she would not leave until the problem was cleared up. Content with that, he continued on his way to Nairobi.

Two days later Dian was still bleeding so profusely that, to save her life, Dr. Weiss performed an emergency operation.

**They give me a shot that nearly puts me out as I am very weak now. Heard myself yelling after surgery was over—was embarrassed. They gave me plasma. . . . Feel rather sluggish when I wake up. Try to talk with Dr. Weiss but don't get message across. Stay on cigarette diet until 5:00 P.M. Work on National Geographic manuscript most of the day and night. Dr. Weiss told me something had been left in, and that caused the trouble. Now, no more bleeding.**

Just two days after the second operation she insisted on returning to camp despite the angry remonstrances of Dr. Weiss.

"You are being foolish, mademoiselle. There may be more complications. If you do not stay here I take no responsibilities. It is stupid what you have done, and stupider still to leave here now."

**He was not very nice to me, but I respect him for his integrity, although I don't know if he has told the truth. One of the nurses came in all dripping with false sympathy because, she said, I couldn't have a baby now. Dr. Weiss says nonsense, but I can't stand the way they all look at me, as if I were a criminal. I have to get out of here.**

Although she was in a black mood for the next two weeks—or perhaps *because* of her dark depression—Dian worked herself to the limit of her endurance. Both Rosamond and Alyette had invited her to spend Christmas down below, but for Dian there could be no question of leaving Karisoke at this season of the year, which was the time when poaching became most intense, and there was no one but her at Karisoke to protect the gorillas.

On Christmas Eve she distributed the many gifts she had bought for the camp staff during her last trip to the United States and England and shared a few bottles of beer with her men. Back at her own cabin she continued to drink in solitude until she fell asleep.

She observed Christmas Day by staying in her cabin writing letters and working on the monthly research report for the National Geographic Society. Bob Campbell would be away for some time, and in his absence she made plans to build him a new privy, food storage box, and cold box for his cabin. But her mood was, to put it mildly, rather grim.

**Went out this morning and furious to see cows all over camp. Got pistol and killed one poor old cow with a single shot in the spine at the neck. It fell to its knees, dropped its head, and was immediately dead. Two Tutsi herders were hanging around. They were afraid but I screamed at them to come and get their cow. Some fourteen men came to cow's body next morning to move it across the meadow and cut it up. They were afraid I'd shoot them too —all very obsequious.**

On January 5, 1972, after hearing the barking of Twa hunting dogs for several days, she went on a single-handed antipoaching patrol.

**D day. I go to Group 5. They awake slowly and feed off into Camp Gully and beyond, and then I go to the poacher trail and, finding no footprints, track down to the lower meadow, where, lo and behold, after half an hour's wait, two of them appear. I let them get closer before firing three shots at intervals. Talk about run! I waited a bit but they didn't return so I came back to camp. My men were very impressed.**

Two days later a group of armed park guards arrived at Karisoke with eight captured Tutsi herders in tow. As it was then late in the afternoon, the guards received permission to stay at Karisoke overnight with their prisoners.

**I scold them all. Take amulet band of monkey fur away from one. Next day put on a black magic show for the prisoners, and conservateur climbs up to take part. We put on masks, use kerosene in fire—very effective. All of them terrified.**

Dian had at least some sympathy for the cattle herders, even though she was unforgiving of their trespass in the park. She was much harsher with captured poachers. The application of "black magic" to both groups of offenders was a carefully contrived tactic that she had devised during the winter of 1970–71. It involved the use of a variety of magic tricks of the kind that can be purchased in novelty stores, together with ferocious Halloween masks and other intimidating disguises. The idea was to terrorize the herders and poachers into mending their ways. It was from such comparatively innocent actions that Dian later gained a reputation for "dabbling in witchcraft."

She knew about sorcery as it was practiced locally and respected its power over the native people. Walter Baumgartel had regaled her with many a story about the sometimes-fatal effects of curses and other forms of black magic, as had Rosamond Carr and Alyette de Munck. Dian had already fired one camp worker for stealing a lock of her hair, which, she noted contemptuously, "the silly fool intended to use on me as a love potion." She was not at all worried, but could not tolerate the lack of respect the act implied.

On another occasion she was asked for a loan by one of her camp staff so that he could pay a sorcerer to lift an evil spell cast on him by an irate poacher. She at first refused, but acquiesced when she noted an alarming deterioration in the man's health. She was not sure, she told a friend, but she thought she might have saved his life.

On January 20, 1972, Bob Campbell returned to Karisoke after an absence of forty-two days, carefully counted by Dian and during which she had made many improvements to his cabin.

**Bob comes back at last about 5:30—he is very happy to see me and shows it more than ever. We unpack in his cabin and he tells me about that woman J——. I'm really defeated by this. It is as though half of me has died. He comes over for dinner. Afterward very clamorous.**

They took up their romance, but Dian no longer believed that Bob was being straight with her. Her fears seemed to be confirmed when she opened a letter at the Ruhengeri post office one afternoon while the two of them were in town for supplies. It was from a mutual friend who knew nothing of the personal relationship between them. The gist of it was that Campbell had let it be known that he would soon be leaving Karisoke. When Dian taxed him with this, he did not deny it.

Dian was silent during the six-hour trip back to Karisoke, but felt she was very near a nervous breakdown. **Never have I known such sorrow,** she noted in her journal.

That night they sat silently in her cabin in the soft light of the kerosene lamp until Bob could stand no more. "Well," he said, "I guess I might as well pack and get out. Is that what you want me to do?"

Dian met his glance but was too miserable to risk an answer.

"I suppose I had it all coming," he continued bleakly. "I deserve to have everything catch up with me. I told you you'd hate me some-day."

However, the prospect of parting with Bob Campbell was too

painful for Dian to bear, and so as they had always done in the past, they avoided the problem by making love.

It was a transient solution. Night after night through the next two months they would return from tiring days spent tracking, observing, and photographing the gorillas, to engage in interminable, soul-searching talks that ended either in fierce arguments, lovemaking, or both. And nothing was resolved.

In late March, when Bob left Karisoke for another two-week break in Nairobi, Dian told him tenderly how much she loved him. "Then trust me a little more," he begged, and his eyes filled with tears.

As she watched him descend the mountain behind his porters, her heart was filled with hurt and anger. The evening was so long and lonely that she escaped with a sleeping pill.

When Bob was three days overdue returning, panic welled up in her. She stood outside her cabin for hours, looking down the porters' trail for any sign of his return. She watched and listened and grew even more alarmed.

Two days later he walked into the meadow and she was ecstatic. But the seeds of mistrust had taken root and Dian no longer believed that he would leave his wife for her. Although they remained together physically, it was a time of mounting sadness and distress for both.

Eventually it became unendurable. On May 29, 1972, Bob Campbell left Karisoke for the last time. It was a harrowing departure.

**"I love you, Dian—I just don't know how to say it." Bob told me this today while he was crying, crying, crying. I told him I wanted him to be happy and he hid his head and cried and cried.**

Two days later:

**I began drinking early and thus by afternoon was finished. Gave poor little Nemeye undeserved hell about some tents. Fell into bed at last after writing some terrible letters and cables to him, but they won't be sent. God, I hope someone comes up here soon.**

No one came, and rather than seek solace with friends down the mountain, she stubbornly remained at camp. For the next two months she was overwhelmed by despair, often drinking her days away. She left much of the monitoring of the gorilla groups to her chief trackers, Nemeye and Rwelekana. The only real work she accomplished was to strip and redecorate Bob Campbell's cabin. It was not until mid-July, when she had completed this task, that her mood began to improve and she once again immersed herself in her work.

As in the past, contact with the gorillas proved to be the best of all therapies.

July 12: I go out in A.M. to find Group 4 in Amok's area, but Uncle Bert seems upset and, although not seeing us, gives loud warning. Anyway, I left Nemeye behind and joined the group for a while before they took off into a ravine and up a steep slope I couldn't climb. Watched them feed, then let them go. Returned to camp briefly, then on to Group 5, which Nemeye had found on second hill in saddle. Had very nice short but close contact with them. Home tired. A bongo, a rare antelope, at night near my window gave two barks. Heard Uncle Bert chest beat around 10:30—sounded high up the mountain. Will visit him again tomorrow.

July 13: Saw a hyrax briefly at 8:40 A.M. Had a fabulous contact with Group 4. I tried an experiment—showing the animals a mirror—and it really succeeded, with Simba and others ever so curious. I was thrilled beyond words by the way they gathered and stared into it as ladies will. Uncle Bert and the young blackback, Digit, watched, then walked away as if such foolishness bored them.

Have been teaching Kanyaragana how to cook American, and tonight he did a grilled cheese sandwich covered with jello! Where have I gone wrong?

# 11

**D**ian was emerging from the depths of her despair into one of the sunniest, most productive periods of her life. With her academic credentials well on the way to being secured, and with regular help provided by some of the students from Cambridge and elsewhere who were eager to work at Karisoke, Dian was able to devote much more of her time to doing what she loved best—being with her gorillas.

In 1972 there were ninety-six gorillas in or on the fringes of the study area, living in eight family groups. While students and the staff of trackers kept tabs on the others, Dian spent much of her time with Group 4, which had accepted her presence so completely that she had virtually become an adopted member of the family.

This was the group to which the poachers had led her on her first day at Karisoke. At that time it consisted of fourteen members led by an aged silverback whom she named Whinny because of his strange, horselike cries. When Whinny died in 1968, Dian and a group of porters tied his body to bamboo poles and transported it to the hospital in Ruhengeri, where an autopsy was performed. The patriarch, whom she estimated to have been about thirty years of age, had been suffering from at least three potentially fatal ailments: peritonitis; an infection of the skull lining that may have been meningitis; and advanced deterioration of the lungs, which had accounted for his distinctive "whinny."

There were two younger silverbacks in the group, Uncle Bert and Amok, but it was to Uncle Bert that the mantle of leadership fell. His half brother, Amok, seemed to Dian to be suffering from some sort of chronic ailment, which caused him to behave unpredictably.

He became a lonely outcast on the fringe of the group, until one day he disappeared.

Uncle Bert, affectionately so called for the well-to-do uncle who had sometimes come to Dian's financial rescue during her younger days, did in fact have a distinctly avuncular nature and was often to be found frolicking with the group's youngsters. Dian named the eldest blackback, or nonmature male, Digit, because he had a twisted, broken finger. She estimated his age at five when she first encountered him in 1967. In 1972 he was still young enough to join in the acrobatic play of the youngsters but was beginning to accept some responsibility for protecting the family.

Of the group's two senior females, the cantankerous Old Goat seemed the natural matriarch. Mrs. X, another older female, was in less robust physical health and grew progressively weaker after Whinny's death, until she too vanished.

In this, the fifth year of her study, Dian watched the group change and evolve through three deaths, three births, and the emigration of three young females. In the detailed recording and interpretation of such inter- and intra-group changes over long periods lay the unique value of Dian's study. But, as she was well aware, it would not be possible to claim that the social relationships of the mountain gorillas were really understood until the animals had been observed through several generations.

Dian was often mobbed by the youngsters of Group 4, who treated her almost as one of themselves. Digit in particular seemed to welcome her presence. On such occasions note-taking would be forgotten and Dian would revel in the pure joy of being accepted. She groomed her friends and allowed them to groom her. She dozed with them in the sun. She tickled the infants and exchanged commiserative belches with the older females. These intimate contacts she described as "just too thrilling for words," and she was often moved to tears by them.

I received the impression that Digit really looked forward to the daily contacts with Karisoke's observers as a source of entertainment. . . . He seemed pleased whenever I brought strangers along and would completely ignore me to investigate any newcomers by smelling or lightly touching their clothing and hair. If I was alone, he often invited play by flopping over onto his back, waving stumpy legs in the air, and looking at me smilingly as if to say, "How can you resist me?" At such times, I fear, my scientific detachment dissolved.*

*From *Gorillas in the Mist.*

As Digit matured and grew more serious, the bond between them remained.

Contacting Group 4 one cold, rainy day, Dian resisted the urge to join Digit, who was huddled against the downpour about thirty feet away from the other animals. She did not want to intrude upon his growing independence, so leaving him to his solitude, she settled herself several yards from the main cluster of humped forms that were scarcely visible in the heavy mist. After a few minutes she felt an arm around her shoulders and looked up into Digit's warm, gentle brown eyes. He stood pensively gazing down at her before patting her head then settling down by her side.

I laid my head on Digit's lap, a position that provided welcome warmth as well as an ideal vantage point from which to observe his neck injury. The wound was no longer draining but had left a deep scar surrounded by numerous seams spidering out in all directions along his neck.

Slowly I took out my camera to take a picture of the scar. It was too close to focus on. About half an hour later the drizzle let up, and without warning Digit stretched back his head and yawned widely. Quickly I snapped the shutter. The resultant photograph shows my gentle Digit as a King Kong monster because his wide-mouthed yawn displayed his massive canines in a most impressive manner.

Digit's neck wound had been sustained during a violent encounter between Group 4 and Group 8. Digit, now acting as his group's self-appointed peripheral sentry, was the first to face the intruders and fought to hold them off. The wound he received as a result became deeply infected, and as his health deteriorated, he became more and more withdrawn until Dian feared he might be going the way of Amok. Happily, he proved her wrong.

The depth of Dian's affinity for the gorillas was largely incomprehensible to others, nor could she easily articulate it. Sometimes she came close.

I heard a noise in the foliage by my side and looked directly into the beautifully trusting face of Macho, who stood gazing up at me. She had left her group to come to me. On perceiving the softness, tranquillity, and trust conveyed by Macho's eyes, I was overwhelmed by the extraordinary depth of our rapport. The poignancy of her gift will never diminish.*

No one who has spent time in the company of wild mountain gorillas can escape the recognition of kinship, but Dian took that for

*From *Gorillas in the Mist*.

102

granted. The essential words in this revealing passage are *softness,* *tranquillity,* and *trust,* three elements so painfully lacking in many of her relationships with her own species.

Gorillas were far from being her only animal friends. Her pet rooster, Dezi, enjoyed the company of an ever-growing harem of hens protected from the stewing pot by Dian's tender sensibilities. And she fretted endlessly if either Charles or Yvonne—two ravens whom she fed on food scraps—failed to appear at mealtime. She even watched affectionately as mice scurried across her cabin floor during the quiet evenings. **Mice mating tonight—two up and boxing in middle of floor—really comical.** She lavished affection on her dog, Cindy, and her monkey, Kima. In 1969, while stopping for gas at a village filling station, she had been approached by a "shifty-eyed" man who offered to sell her the mysterious contents of a straw basket for the equivalent of about thirty dollars. Dian seized the basket, removed the lid, and found the disheveled little monkey Kima huddled at the bottom. Placing the basket firmly on the seat beside her, she started her Land Rover and drove off—after intimidating the unhappy salesman with a ferocious diatribe on the illegality and immorality of catching monkeys.

Against the advice of friends, including Louis Leakey and Rosamond Carr, both of whom had owned monkeys and knew what a handful they could be, she decided to adopt the two-year-old female. She curbed Kima's destructive tendencies to some extent by providing her with stuffed toys that she first made out of socks and later purchased ready-made in the United States. Nevertheless, Kima periodically wrought havoc in the camp. Although amply provided with bamboo shoots, fruits, and vegetables, the monkey developed a passion for human food, including beer, and after that no one's dinner or pombe was ever safe.

Kima was allowed to roam the camp during the day, terrifying visitors—particularly African ones—whom she would attack, screaming and biting. She frequently bit Dian's hands when being brought unwillingly indoors for the night. Occasionally the bites were serious—one of them severed a muscle at the base of Dian's index finger. That particular wound remained painful for weeks, but Dian never held it against Kima. At night or in bad weather, the monkey had the run of the cabin and frequently slept with her mistress. Dian tolerated her destructive binges, apparently feeling they were a penalty to be paid for having domesticated the animal in the first place.

Cindy had come to Dian as a pup in the summer of 1968, a gift from European friends "down below"—as she referred to the world beyond the volcanoes. This was the dog Dian had yearned for and been denied all through her childhood. Of all her animal friends, the big brown boxer became the most beloved.

When Cindy was about nine months old, she ambled down the porters' trail one day while Dian was off somewhere with the gorillas, and disappeared. When Dian returned to camp, wet and weary, to be told by her staff that Cindy was missing and had probably been stolen, she was transformed into an avenging fury. Whipped by Dian's tongue, the trackers traced the dog along the trail until its pawprints merged with and disappeared amongst the bare footprints of a group of men. She had evidently been seized and carried off by cattle herders or by poachers. Dian thereupon devised a desperate stratagem to recover her. Together with her men, Dian rounded up several dozen Tutsi cattle and corralled them near her cabin. She then instructed her trackers to shout the message through the forest that she would shoot a cow for every day that Cindy remained missing.

Near morning the unfortunate Tutsi herder whose cattle Dian was holding hostage timidly ventured to the edge of the camp clearing to report that the dog had been located in the *ikibooga,* or hunting camp, of a group of poachers led by a Twa named Munyarukiko. This was the same man who had captured Coco and Pucker after slaughtering most of the gorillas in their group.

The *ikibooga* was too far away from Karisoke for Dian to reach quickly, considering the state of her lungs, so she armed her camp staff with Halloween masks and firecrackers and sent them off. Hours later they returned with the dog. They laughed uproariously as they told a vastly relieved Dian of the poachers' terror-stricken flight in the face of their masked and explosive attack. The cattle were returned to their owners; the camp staff was rewarded; and life at Karisoke settled down.

A year later Cindy was again stolen by the incorrigible Munyarukiko and his band. This time she was rescued by the father of the same Tutsi herder who had located her after the first dognapping. In returning her, this tall, dignified old man earned a healthy cash reward and Dian's undying gratitude, which would one day be translated into a job for his son at Karisoke.

Dian had to wait until February 1972 to even the score with Munyarukiko, but when the opportunity came, she savored it to the full.

**Come home from Group 5 and find park guards here with Munyarukiko. Really pleased! It took four of them to catch him. Even then he escaped while the guards were talking to me and made a run for it, but they caught him again and brought him**

back. I spit on him and hit him, and then we went through the magic routine, this time with tear gas added. Then we tied him up with chains in the men's cabin.

In the morning Dian accompanied Munyarukiko's armed escort down the mountain to the office of the prefect of police in Ruhengeri, where he was locked up. A few days later he was sentenced to two years in prison for poaching. Dian gave each of the four park guards twenty-five dollars, a small fortune for them and no trivial amount for her either, but she looked upon it as an investment in improved park patrols.

Dian had no tolerance for those who abused animals.

When I was working on the ranch in Montana, there was a real jerk hunter type who delighted in snaring ground squirrels alive. He would then hang them kicking and wiggling from a fence and practice shooting them with his big game rifle. When I told him to stop, he simply laughed and told me where to go. He was practicing for the hunting season when he would go after deer and anything else that moved. Well, somebody must have poured some mud in his rifle because one day, *blooey*, it blew up in his hands and the shock broke his nose. Couldn't have happened to a nicer guy!

On a visit to Ruhengeri, Dian and a student were driving along the crowded, dusty main street when they saw a man beating a sick and half-starved Alsatian. Almost before the combi could be stopped, Dian shot out the door and across the road to the rescue. The dog's tormentor fled, but Dian learned from bystanders that the dog belonged to an American woman married to an African. She lifted the animal into the back of her combi and drove to the woman's house, there to inform her through clenched teeth that, like it or not, the dog was going to Karisoke to be looked after until it regained its health. The owner, who was considerably shorter than Dian, wordlessly acquiesced, although she later gathered enough courage to telephone Dian's hotel to accuse her of stealing the animal.

At Karisoke a grumbling student was assigned to construct a chicken wire dog-run and, under Dian's supervision, nursed the animal back to health. It was eventually returned to its owner with stern instructions for its future care and a warning that it would be removed for good if it was again mistreated.

Dian continued to view most of the students coming to work at

Karisoke with a jaundiced eye. She especially disliked their book-bound softness and their youthful preoccupation with self, which she called "me-itis." She may also have envied them their youth and lack of responsibilities.

**I've just returned from a visit to Kabara. I had to set up six nasty little census workers there some four days ago, so I didn't get to really enjoy, remember, and breathe the spot with all of its beauty until today, when I came back through the saddle with just one porter. . . . Changing nappies for six kids at Kabara took most of the joy out of the four days.**

Of a dozen or more students from universities in Britain and the United States who worked at Karisoke between 1970 and 1974, no more than four met with her approval. These were the ones who, in Dian's view, placed the interests of the gorillas above their own. They showed their worth by adopting Dian's own Spartan attitude toward the discomforts of their surroundings: by being willing to risk life and limb in the continuing battle against poachers and herders, by unflagging devotion to the task of locating and observing the animals no matter what the weather, and, most of all, by treating the gorillas with respect, recognizing that these superb creatures were according them a great privilege by tolerating the human presence.

One student stood out among that small handful of worthies: a Cambridge undergraduate named Sandy Harcourt. He had first approached Dian after an informal slide show she had given at Cambridge, asking if there was any chance to work for her at Karisoke. His academic credentials were impressive and she liked his lean, hawkish good looks. She agreed to hire him for three months in the summer of 1971 to help with the census. With her encouragement he returned the following year to begin a behavioral study of gorillas for his Ph.D.

Dian saw little of Sandy Harcourt during his three-month census stint since he spent most of that time in remote bush camps. However, when he returned to begin work on his Ph.D. study in June of 1972, just days after Dian's final break with Bob Campbell, she put him in the cabin the photographer had vacated and which she was painstakingly redecorating.

Short, wiry, and given to rolling his sleeves up above his elbows to display his sinewy arms, Harcourt possessed classic, angular Anglo-Saxon features. Dark-haired and dark-eyed, he had the intensity of a young Battle of Britain pilot. He was twenty years Dian's junior, and she found him endearing. Before many months had passed, he was signing his notes to her "All my love, Sandy," and her replies began, "My dearest Sandy."

Dian's journal reveals the tenderness she felt for him.

We went down the mountain to Ruhengeri for some shopping errands and on the way back ran into some Tutsi herders and their cattle. Sandy took out after them like a tiger, and a Tutsi youngster got so scared he ran to me for shelter. When Sandy got back to camp he was crying and yelling with anger and frustration at finding cows on the trail where Group 6 was this morning. I gave him a strong gin and tonic and he apologized for losing control. Poor boy, I feel so sorry for him, but he must learn to live with it. A week ago we were out to Group 5 and I was so tired by the time we found them. Had a horrid coughing fit, but Sandy was so sweet and gentle with me. He is a joy to have at camp.

In November, Dian left Karisoke in the care of Sandy Harcourt and another highly regarded Cambridge student, Ric Elliott, while she flew to the United Stated to assist in editing the National Geographic film shot by Bob Campbell and Alan Root. From Washington she would fly on to Cambridge for another three-month stint at university.

Parting from Sandy was not easy.

I had cooked a farewell breakfast, which turned out all burnt and horrid. He sat there without eating, very quiet, then just broke up. He said he didn't know how he was going to stay on without me and grabbed me so hard he left a huge bruise on one arm. We were both in tears when I went down the mountain.

Harcourt was determined to earn Dian's admiration, and to this end he devoted himself almost fanatically to fighting poaching and to driving the Tutsi cattle off the mountain.

Harcourt had been looking for Group 5, which had taken to ambling about in the farmers' fields near the foot of the mountain. Harcourt was uneasy that they came "so close to the wogs." Believing that the massacre of the gorilla group during Goodall's time at Karisoke had been intended as retaliation for Goodall's antipoaching activities, Harcourt feared similar vengeance might be visited on Group 5 because he had now shot several poachers' dogs and a cow. He told Dian that he regretted the shootings but that he'd become so angry at the poachers that "all I remember not to do is actually shoot a person."

When he told her of having beaten a Tutsi, she was very concerned; however, he justified his actions because the man had tried to "brain" him. If the police investigated him, he would be able to plead self-defense.

On her return to Karisoke, Dian and the students continued the campaign of harassment against the herders. Early in July 1973, she and Sandy and Ric Elliott went on a cattle raid. Much of the day was spent rounding up cows scattered over the rugged, heavily forested terrain. Finally, the herd was driven down the trail to the shambas below, where it stampeded through fields of potatoes and peas. The Hutu farmers were justifiably incensed and swarmed angrily around the exhausted trio of whites. A shoving match developed between Sandy and some of the men; then one of the farmers grabbed Ric Elliott and tried to tie him up. With the situation threatening to get completely out of hand, Dian pulled her gun and covered their retreat up the mountain.

She seemed to be winning the battle against the herders, but the severe measures she sometimes felt compelled to take sickened and depressed her.

Near the end of August the study area was inundated with cattle in what seems to have been a final concerted effort by the Tutsi to reassert their ancestral claims to the region. Dian and her students reacted with a ferocity that won the war—but the resultant shooting spree left a score of cattle dead and dying and Dian in the depths of self-disgust.

I hate myself for doing this. The poor cows just won't die, won't die. I can't stand seeing this. I climbed to Thermos Ridge to get away. The fog swirled in and then rain, rain, and more rain. I lay on the grassy ridge in a break in the fog and looked down on camp and wondered why I bothered. In another couple of years or so I'll be dead, and the cabins will probably end up rusty skeletons when the wogs get through with them. One Ph.D. and a lot of rot will come out of the study—that's about it!

The whole problem of cattle in the park came to a head late in 1973 when Dian was summoned to the Ruhengeri office of a new prefect of police, appointed after a coup d'état had turned Rwanda into a military dictatorship.

I was scared shitless, as it was about the cows and I was determined to go to jail first before paying for killing them. As it turned out, the new prefect was wonderful, spoke perfect English (he's ex-ambassador to America, Kenya, Paris, and Belgium), and shrugged the whole thing off. I used my chief porter, Gwehanda-goza, as a witness, so he in turn has told all of the people that the prefect is on our side. On only two occasions since then have stray cattle shown up, but we don't think it wise to kill them anymore. I've had enough.

**12**

**A**nother of the handful of students destined to leave a lasting imprint arrived at Karisoke in the summer of 1973. She was Kelly Stewart, daughter of actor James Stewart. Although raised in Hollywood, she was the antithesis of the bubble-headed "valley girl." With her wire-rimmed glasses and schoolmarmish hairstyles, the young Stanford student was Central Casting's stereotype of what a bookish female zoologist ought to be like. But her mordant wit and sparkling intelligence were atypical. These qualities, together with the fact that she soon proved her mettle in the daily routine of collecting gorilla data while coping with foul weather, spider bites, nettle rashes, and dysentery, endeared her to Dian.

This was the first time another woman had been in camp on a more-or-less permanent basis; and despite the twenty-year difference in their ages, she and Dian quickly became close, sharing confidences and sometimes getting together in the evenings for a drink.

Kelly wrote amusing doggerel about her encounters with the study groups. Asked by Dian for a report on the sexual behavior of the gorillas she was observing, Kelly submitted one in verse form:

Introduction      As regards gorillas in the wild
There's little known, in fact,
About behavior relating to
And surrounding the sexual act.
Data gathered in the field
Are presented in this text
To clarify some aspects of

|                | Wild gorilla sex. |
| Periodicity    | Though swollen labia in chimps |
|                | Are rather hard to miss, |
|                | The vulvas of gorillas show |
|                | More subtlety than this. |
|                | We measured cycles from the times |
|                | We saw our subjects mate. |
|                | Oestrus was about two days, |
|                | And cycles, twenty-eight. |
| Copulation     | Initiators of the cops |
|                | Were usually quite plain. |
|                | The females start the engines of |
|                | The copulation train. . . . |

"Wow, she is so clever!" Dian commented admiringly after reading the report. She was so delighted that she rewarded Kelly with a Raggedy Ann gorilla doll.

By autumn Dian's admiration had begun to cool somewhat, even as Sandy Harcourt's mounted. For a time Kelly tried to maintain a balanced relationship between the three of them, but without much success.

**Kelly up to my cabin at 8:30 to "return" Cindy—her kindness is killing. The fact is, she is just plain nosy about where I am and what I'm doing. Sandy's cabin lights went off early, and hers much earlier, but then come on again, and her curtains firmly drawn. Whom do they think they're kidding?**

As the months slipped by, Dian tended to be more and more irritated, not to say jealous, as Kelly and Sandy became increasingly enamored of each other. It was not that Dian had any passionate feelings for Harcourt, but she did have a proprietary interest in him and resented having to compete with a "fat, pimply young girl who ought to stick to the job she came up here to do."

Doubtless it was fortunate for all concerned that Dian had to leave Karisoke in late October to undertake a lecture tour that would take her and the newly completed National Geographic film about the gorillas right across the United States. Following that, she would spend a further, and final, four months at Cambridge.

This time there was no tender parting between her and Sandy. "No tears, no kiss, he was just plain sulky." Part of his disaffection may have been due to the fact that he was temporarily losing both women in his life, since Kelly would also be departing for Cambridge to begin her own doctoral program under Robert Hinde.

During the California part of her speaking tour, Dian met Kelly's parents and some of her famous friends, including Alfred Hitchcock.

**Wow, what a house the Stewarts have. Quite a jump for Kelly from this to Karisoke. Her parents couldn't do enough for me and I really liked them both. Told them, without a lie, that Kelly was one of the best students I've ever had. Hitchcock wanted to know how scary gorillas are. I think he wants to make a chiller/thriller about them. I told him they were about as dangerous as pet lambs, and he simply grunted and went off to talk to someone else.**

The Stewarts' warm welcome helped ease the antipathy Dian had been feeling toward their daughter. By the time Kelly reached England, Dian was happy to see Kelly again and to hear the latest news from Karisoke. Although the friendship had lost some of its intimacy, the two women enjoyed one another's company, often dining or going to the cinema together. Occasionally they rubbed each other the wrong way.

"I'm sorry my relationship with Sandy seems to stand between us," Kelly ventured one evening as they were leaving a movie house in Cambridge.

Dian was glad of the darkness. "How does it stand between us? I don't follow you."

"Well, I know you're annoyed at us—but I really like the guy."

"My only concern is that the work gets done properly," Dian cut her off.

"You don't care for him, do you?" Kelly persisted.

"Why don't you drop the subject. Sandy is young enough to be my son."

Despite such moments of irascibility, Dian did everything she could to help Kelly get financial backing so that she could return to Karisoke.


It was early May of 1974 before Dian flew back to Africa. Although she was essentially finished with Cambridge, she felt no great sense of relief, nor was she full of anticipation at the prospect of going home. As she stared out the aircraft window at the blank face of the clouds below, she felt apprehensive. During the long stay in England her health—especially that of her lungs—had deteriorated. She had always been careless of her body and unwilling to accept its limitations—or the limitations of increasing age. Now she was entertaining doubts about her physical ability to continue on her chosen path.

There was also Sandy Harcourt to be considered. From the tone of the letters he had written to her during her six-month absence, it was apparent that he had begun to see himself as cock of the walk at Karisoke—and to regard Kelly Stewart as the lady who ought to share it with him. Dian foresaw—and dreaded—an exhausting conflict.

She postponed the inevitable by staying in Nairobi for a week. But this time the city was no great source of solace. Shopping and some socializing at the American embassy could not obliterate the memory of Louis Leakey, who had died from a second heart attack late in 1972. She vividly remembered the intensity of his love for her and the comfort and compassion he had offered. Perhaps she wished she had accepted all of that, as she had accepted the ruby ring that had been his last gift to her.

The day came when she could postpone her return to camp no longer.

I flew into Kigali Saturday, and on Sunday, May 5, hired a car to take me to Ruhengeri, where I checked into the hotel. Very frightened about climbing the mountain so decided not to go today. I drank a little, wrote a little about the Harcourt problem to Joan and Alan Root, then went for a walk and saw some Africans I knew, who stopped to gossip. That felt better, so went back to the hotel and had a sleep.

When I came down for dinner, there was Kelly waiting. She'd come down the mountain to have a "chat" before I climbed. Kind of pouring oil on sort of thing. "Are you still my friend?" she asked me after dinner. I said I'd have to wait and see. "I've never felt so tender toward a boy as I do toward Sandy," she told me. "Well, then have fun," I said, "but I guess you're doing that." "Oh, no," she denied. "If you think we've gone to bed together, you're wrong. He's afraid to."

That did it. The oil she was pouring caught on fire, and I was out of there and upstairs to my room before she could get her mouth shut.

I climbed next day with Gwehandagoza and a crowd of porters to carry all the stuff I'd brought back, mostly for the men, from England and the States. Took me nearly three hours and I was beat. Cindy and Kima were very happy to see me and so were the men, but no sign of Sandy. He'd been living in my house and it was a bloody mess. Couch was filthy, everything was filthy. Old shoes, sweaty clothes. Furniture missing. I was furious.

Later he came back from the gorillas *and walked right by my house*. Two hours later he came up. "Thanks so much for taking care of my things," I told him. "Well," he said, "you haven't been very nice to me." And then had the nerve to say I could come down to "their" cabin for dinner. It took all my courage to go down. I told them, "I'm about as welcome here now as the plague." Kelly's face simply turned white and I had to leave. Kima bit me when I tried to get her in the house.

There was no communication between the warring camps through the next week, then Sandy—probably at Kelly's insistence—sent Dian an olive branch.

He acknowledged that the previous year, there had been an "unnecessary misunderstanding" about his relations with a female census worker, but he insisted that if Dian thought something similar was happening between him and Kelly Stewart, she was wrong. He apologized for any "misunderstanding" and signed the note, "Love, Me."

Dian dismissed this overture as a "silly note" that did not deserve a reply, but she too realized that the impasse could not continue and on May 15 went down to Harcourt's cabin to try and restore some degree of amicability. Sandy was not cooperative.

He got mad, clenched his fists, gritted his jaws over very small things. I came back to my cabin MAD and remain MAD. My lungs are hurting like hell.

Kelly, who had been trying desperately to restore peace, now began to break down. She sent a note to Dian "full of bloody fucking mad, etc." A day later she followed it with an abject apology. This did the trick. Dian was glad of the chance to end hostilities and that night visited Kelly and Sandy, each in their separate cabins, then had them up to hers for a nightcap.

A period of uneasy truce followed at Karisoke with each of the warring parties hunkered down in defensive positions, holding on to ground gained, firing no shots. Having reestablished working relationships, Dian began working flat out on her thesis.

Harcourt seemed content for the moment to revert to a subordinate role, although he had piled up such an impressive number of hours in the field that he was fast becoming the world's second authority on mountain gorillas.

At the end of May Dian began feeling very ill and was convinced pneumonia was about to strike again. The prospect worried her as it never had before. **For the first time ever I don't think I have enough resistance left to recover.**

Two days after making that gloomy prediction, she fell into a drainage ditch while avoiding a buffalo that charged through camp. She heard a bone in her ankle snap and felt a sickening jolt of pain. By the time she struggled back to her cabin, the agony had become unbearable. During the next few days she treated herself with Darvon capsules and her most powerful sleeping pills; but she remained alert to what was going on.

**Both Kelly and Sandy stayed in Kelly's house last night. . . . She is two days behind with her field notes. Am bloody fed up with this place. I know now I've broke a bone. . . . It is getting very puffy and black and all swollen—pain decreased unless I crunch the bones or ligaments the wrong way.**

By the time Kelly showed up with her delayed reports, Dian was in a savage mood. "You can screw away as long as you like," she barked at Kelly, "but remember, the paperwork has got to be done first!"

Kelly wept and ran.

Two days later Dian was bitten on the knee by one of the venomous spiders that lurked in the underbrush around the clearing.

**It's a big bite and a bad one, which screws up my other leg. Guess this isn't my week, to say the least. Got a note from Sandy trying to make up. He offered to help me out to see Group 4, which is quite close to camp. We went, and I had a great visit with Digit, who seemed to know I was sick and kept looking me right in the eyes. It was really great—a good smell too. I was happy though hurting. Home late, and really wasted, but Sandy was fine all afternoon.**

Contact with the gorillas proved the best medicine, and although Dian's ankle continued to be very painful and the spider bite infection spread, her spirits revived enough for her to appreciate life around her.

**One of the most memorable bushbuck incidents around camp brought to my mind Jody's words from *The Yearling*: "Pa, I done seen me something today!" As usual upon awakening, I looked out of the cabin windows and observed a sight more credible to a Walt Disney movie than to real life. All the hens, led by Walter, were tiptoeing awkwardly toward a young male bushbuck. The chickens' heads bobbed like yo-yos from their stringy necks. The curious antelope minced toward them with a metronomically twitching tail and quivering nose. Each chicken then**

made a beak-to-nose contact with the bushbuck as both species satisfied their undisguised interest in each other. Just about this time Cindy innocently came trotting up the path and froze, one foreleg suspended in the air, as she gazed at the weird spectacle before her. Her presence was too much for the young buck, who bounded off with a bark, his white flag-tail held high.*

During succeeding weeks Dian had to rely on her two students to be her eyes and ears with the gorillas, and her legs and lungs on the mountain slopes, and she insisted they be at least as conscientious as she was.

By June 17 it had become apparent that her ankle was not going to heal properly on its own, so Dian reluctantly descended to the Ruhengeri hospital. It took five agonizing hours for her to stumble and slide down the muddy trail through a steady rain. X rays showed she had snapped her fibula just above the ankle as cleanly as if it had been cut by a panga.

She remained in hospital just long enough to have her leg taped, then hurried to the airport to meet a plane bringing a new student from the States, a dark, shy, and serious young man named Richard Rombach.

Although Dian was initially cool to him, she soon developed an affection for Rombach. The somewhat solitary student established an excellent rapport not only with gorillas but with the mischievous Kima and with Cindy. Dian was pleased to notice that he put the needs of the gorillas ahead of his own, never pushing them beyond the limits of their tolerance.

Kelly and Sandy, however, seemed to view Rombach as an interloper wanting trackers' time and access to the gorilla groups they were studying, and thus a competitor for opportunities in which they felt they had a proprietary interest. Consequently, he got the cold shoulder and was ridiculed for his ineptitude at bushcraft and tracking.

Less than two weeks after he arrived, he left camp one morning to visit the gorillas. As a novice, he would normally have been accompanied either by one of the trackers or one of the experienced students. But he was by then keenly aware of the resentment against him and so chose to go alone in search of Group 5—and promptly got lost.

When he was reported missing at dinnertime that evening, Dian demanded to know why he had not been accompanied by Rwelekana.

*From *Gorillas in the Mist*.

Kelly replied that he didn't *like* to go with Rwelekana, who was too slow for him, so Sandy had taken Rwelekana. I said that was nonsense, then Sandy said, "It's his own fault if he got lost. Visoke was clearly visible all day—he shouldn't have *gotten* lost!" Finally Sandy said it was *my* fault for using up too much of the trackers' time getting them to build new cupboards.

A search party was organized, but when after five tense hours there was no report of the missing youth, Dian became seriously worried.

If the boy is dead, it is Sandy's fault *totally* for being so greedy for trackers, Kelly's fault partially for not wanting the boy to go out with her. They have both mocked him and made fun of him. This I can't tolerate even though I see no great future for the child. At least he is here honestly.

To everyone's great relief, the trackers eventually found Rombach and brought him back to camp hungry and exhausted but otherwise undamaged. Thereafter he was treated more generously for a few weeks by Kelly and Sandy. But when Dian departed to attend a conference in Austria and make a quick trip to California, Harcourt lost no time putting Rombach in his place.

"Richard, much as you may dislike the fact, in any research center you will find that a Ph.D. student's research takes precedence over everybody else's. . . .

"I regret that I have annoyed you, but the fact remains that if you continue to contact Group 4 and 5 as often and for as long as you have done up to now, your work will interfere with Kelly's and mine. We have been accepted as Ph.D. students by Cambridge and Dian; we are obliged to produce a thesis. A thesis requires a large amount of data; and we won't get it if you continue to interpret your topic as you have done up to now. Having read this, I hope you will see that your research must take second place to ours and Dian's."

The trip that had taken Dian away from Karisoke was one to which she had been eagerly looking forward—a visit to Vienna for a week-long conclave of the International Primatological Society, a worldwide fraternity of specialists in primate research. She knew she would be one of the stars and looked forward to delivering her paper before a packed and attentive audience. Nor was she too old to wonder what other adventures might await an attractive woman at such a gathering.

On her first morning in Vienna she awoke with severe pain in her ankle. She went to the American embassy for help and soon found herself in the X-ray department at the city's foremost accident and trauma hospital. After examining the X rays, the doctors were astonished to learn that Dian had been walking on the leg for more than five weeks. "How could you stand the pain?" she was asked.

I said I didn't have much choice at Karisoke. They put me on a stretcher in the hall and put my foot up with wet compresses and tell me to lie there for an hour. One really attractive doctor goes by and asks if it's still hurting. He said it would have healed in a month if I'd stayed in bed with my foot up. Then a young intern, Anton, begins to talk to me about gorillas. He is well read. He stays on when I go to the drying tank to get my cast dried. He takes over. . . . He gets in a cab with me and we go downtown, of all places, and walk! Then to a coffee shop. He is really very, very much too young, but interesting. It is then pouring rain. We walk more, then cab back to my hotel and to my room.

The next day she worked on the paper she was to deliver to the conference until Anton arrived to take her to a performance at the Vienna Opera House and from there to dinner, then back to her room in the Hotel Astoria for a second, disappointing encounter, which reinforced her preference for older men.

The conference began the next day, and Dian was busy attending sessions, renewing acquaintances, and generally enjoying herself.

Robert Hinde leads off the talks—I don't think he was at his best. Jane Goodall was next. A Dutchman gave a talk and was boring as hell—he was the only person worse than I.

For some reason I sure had the blues. At the dinner afterward they didn't give us much time for booze at the bar, but instead pushed lots of wine on us at the meal. That didn't do it for me! I was actually crying at the table!

Then two singers appeared—one of them yodeled for me. I yodeled back and felt a whole lot better. Everyone danced and I SAT with my leg in the cast, but then Robert asked me to dance. He held me under the arms—it was like dancing with a statue, I guess, but he sure did his best.

Things got better and better after that. Jane Goodall pulled off her hair band and went wild. She also "presented" to her partner, which was gross but made us giggle. I've never seen her quite like this. . . . I stayed up till four. Another hangover in the morning.

Dian learned how widespread her notoriety had become when she caught a ride back to her hotel the next day with a group of Japanese primatologists, who told her they had heard she had trained an

117

army of gorillas, which she led in armed attacks against poachers. Still giggling at that as she stepped out of the cab at her hotel, she was further amused when one of the Japanese gentlemen tipped his hat in a polite good-bye and offered, in his less than idiomatic English, "I hope you make out here."

From Vienna, Dian flew to London where she spent several days in a recording studio doing the voice-over narration for a forthcoming National Geographic TV special on primates. She had a surprisingly small voice for a woman of her commanding stature and sounded rather shy when reading the narration.

From London she took the train to Cambridge for a pleasant week of visiting climaxed by an idyllic afternoon boating along the banks of Trinity and St. John's colleges with her thesis adviser, Robert Hinde. Her international stature was now solidly established even at Cambridge, and she found the atmosphere at the Maddingley research lab subtly changed. **Everyone very friendly,** she noted with some surprise. **In fact very nice**.

At the end of the week she flew to San Francisco for a brief visit with the Prices and to formally offer her condolences to her Uncle Bert on the death earlier that month of his wife, Flossie. It was not a pleasant trip. She was full of sadness for her uncle and suffering the distress she so often felt when with the Prices for more than a day or two. She did find time for lunch with her "beloved Ralph," Dr. Ralph Spiegl, for whom she had carried a torch for more than twenty years, and who had been the Prices' family physician for even longer than that. Unfortunately Spiegl, who was usually tender and solicitous, even romantic, seemed to her to be in the throes of a midlife crisis, so even that reunion proved disappointing.

When she arrived in Nairobi a week later, it was as if the whirlwind trip had never happened.

**The sky over Kenya is ever so much brighter blue and the sun in the morning seems so much higher than in England. It is so good to be almost home.**

Now that she had become a major celebrity, Dian's trips in and out of Africa usually involved a courtesy call at the American embassy in Nairobi. While waiting for the twice-weekly plane to Rwanda, Dian lunched with the well-connected ambassador, Robinson McIlvaine, and his wife, who told her the latest gossip from Washington and East Africa. For Dian, whose main source of information on world events was her subscription to *Time* magazine, issues of which invariably arrived at Karisoke a month late when they arrived at all, such conversation had a special fascination.

Back in Rwanda, Dian was met at the airport by an aide to the American ambassador in Kigali, who conveyed an official request for her to appear at the embassy that evening with her National Geographic film and show it to a gathering of diplomats and dignitaries from Rwanda, Zaire, and Uganda.

Well, I was so tired I couldn't believe it. But the evening was a smashing success—I narrated the film, all seventy-three minutes of it, in French, Swahili, and Kinyarwanda. Somehow it clicked and they were rolling in the aisles with mirth. In fact, it was so successful that the president of Rwanda *ordered* me to return to Kigali in ten days' time to show the film to him and his private ruling committee and top-ranking military personnel.

I wore my Greek dress to the palace and went through the same language problems. The president seemed vastly amused—I was nervous. The ambassador was relieved when it was all over, but very pleased with how it went. We were the first white people, except for some king and queen, to be allowed in the palace since the military coup last year.

Then the final straw—last week I was ordered by the president of Zaire, Mobutu, to fly to Kinshasa and show it to *him*. That was another story. His palace was full of drunken wogs and their fat wives. I was glad to get out of there, but I must say that Mobutu seemed to care about the gorillas and that made the trip worthwhile.

That leaves only the presidents of Tanzania and Uganda to give orders, but I doubt that I will obey Big Daddy Amin!

Her ankle was now out of its cast but continuing to cause her a great deal of pain, so she had to keep her contacts with the gorillas to a minimum. Work on her thesis and innumerable reports took an ever-increasing toll on her time, as did her burgeoning correspondence with friends, colleagues, and well-wishers around the world. There was also a steady trickle of VIPs, diplomats, and others to be dealt with. These visitors would arrive for a look at the gorillas, planning on an overnight stay, during which Dian would have to do the cooking as well as entertain as graciously as she could manage. So the summer of 1974 slipped away.

By mid-September, Sandy Harcourt and Kelly Stewart had begun making preparations for leaving Karisoke—Sandy to do eighteen months of paperwork on his doctoral thesis, and Kelly for three months of course work at Cambridge. On September 24, while Kelly was packing and organizing her field notes in her cabin, Sandy decided to pay one last visit to the gorillas.

On his way out to Group 5 he was attacked and badly gored by a buffalo.

About 9:30 in the morning I was typing at my desk by the window and looked up to see him staggering to my door. His face was full of blood and there was blood pouring from his nose. I opened the door and he collapsed in my arms. I then saw blood all over his pants. I asked if it was a dog. He said no, and then went into shock.

I called my houseman, who nearly fainted on the spot! I covered Sandy with blankets, elevated his left leg, put a pillow under his head, and took off his trousers to find all of his leg, the upper, inner thigh, with muscles hanging out like so much hamburger. He was within inches of having to be renamed Sandra! It took me three hours to clean everything properly, put it all back together again, and finally stop the bleeding. When he was conscious, he was screaming, hissing, and groaning—it was unbearable and I had only Darvon to give him, which, thank God, I had got a big supply of from Dr. Spiegl before leaving California. I wouldn't have given him anything stronger anyway because of his condition of shock—his pulse was weak, his face was green, he was cold and clammy, and his respiration was bad.

After three hours of closing the wound with butterfly bandages topped with tons of gauze, and stopping for tourniquets every ten minutes, my houseman helped me put him to bed. I stayed awake with him for three days and nights before having him carried down the mountain on a stretcher.

Dian could not resist a little crowing.

Kelly was a lot of help. She cried for three days and nights and ended up absolutely insanely jealous of me because there was nothing she could do at all, and Sandy ended up so immensely grateful, to say the least.

She then went down the mountain with him to the Ruhengeri hospital for tetanus and penicillin shots, and to Gisenyi to get a plane to fly them both to Kigali and off to England.

Apparently he had looked up and seen the buffalo at about a five-foot distance—it was simply standing there. He just lost his cool and charged at it, hoping to frighten it away. Naturally the reverse happened and the buffalo went for him. She got him in the groin with her horns, threw him, and then rolled on him before standing up to repeatedly gore him before running off. How he made it back to camp I'll never know. His body was in tatters, and you wouldn't believe what she did to his knapsack and clothing!

Although Dian and Richard Rombach took no pleasure in the manner of their going, they were both relieved to see Kelly and Sandy depart.

Sandy will be writing up his thesis for some eighteen months at least and is likely gone for good. Though Kelly is due to return here in January, I wouldn't mind if she didn't come back. The little boy from New York was in tears when I returned from California. I'm allowing him to stay on for another month's trial, and he is working ever so much better since Sandy and Kelly have gone. In fact, the entire atmosphere around camp is very much improved.

ichard Rombach's field observations may have improved, but his navigational skills had not. On October 13, 1974, he got lost again.

**What a night. Basili and Nemeye were out to begin a search at 5:40 P.M. I follow in ten minutes and we climb up elephant trail. They go on to edge of crater and I stay behind and try to make fire—impossible. We get home by 11:00, tired and cold and wet. Basili and woodman go down the mountain to get ten extra men, and Nemeye and I plan for next day.**

**Wogs not up the mountain till 5:45 or nearly 6:00, which makes me mad. Ten of them start out to search, and I establish a central place in the alpine meadow with litter, blankets, fire, water, and some food. I go out of my mind just waiting. It begins to rain at 2:20. . . . We sit in fog and rain until first batch of men return. They have had no luck—had tried all around crater and tourist trail. Then about twenty minutes later, Bambari comes and says they have him. Basili found him just as it started to rain, around the other side of the mountain. We go with a stretcher and find him walking. . . . I ask him if anything is broken or bleeding—he says no.**

Dian was now in full maternal flight and not about to allow her meticulous preparations to be wasted. Rombach, who had fallen into a ravine but had not suffered anything worse than a bruising, was ordered to lie down on the stretcher and was carried back to camp, where Dian changed him into dry clothes before accompanying him (still on a stretcher) to Ruhengeri and the home of Dr. Weiss, who was on emergency call that night.

Until this hour Dr. Peter Weiss, the imposing and compelling fifty-eight-year-old French surgeon at the Ruhengeri hospital, had not been an admirer of Dian, nor she of him. Now quite inexplicably, something dramatic and explosive occurred between them.

**Dr. Weiss and a second doctor examine Richard, and Weiss holds my hand strongly. I am teary since all is over at last. Dr. Weiss is so kind and good to me this time. Not like before at all.**

While Rombach was sent to the hospital for observation, Dian was invited to have dinner with Weiss and his odd family, which consisted of a black "wife," one black child, two white, and two colored ones.

**During dinner he asks, "You are not afraid of me?" We also discussed his "moral obligations" and my "mental" ones. He asked if I really believed I was as obligated to my way of life as he was to his. I said yes, and he said he could respect me better now.**

**He wouldn't let his wife go to the hospital with us—she was mad—but his daughter tagged along. . . . Rombach took a sleeping pill.**

Dian tried to sleep in the hospital ward to keep an eye on her student but finally gave up and walked to the nearby hotel to get a room. But next morning she was at Rombach's bedside in time for early-morning "rounds."

**Dr. Weiss comes on rounds at 8:20. Also a very handsome, well-built young doctor, also a surgeon. But the die is cast, I see only Weiss.**

**Rombach and I must go to the X-ray department—the results are normal and I put him back to bed. Then I leave him and go to Weiss who is in surgery—so I have a long wait.**

**When he's finished, he *demands* that I go to his house at noon for lunch. When I say no, he gets really mad. Really MAD. He says I must never come to him again. "You do not like me. You do not want to be around an old silverback."**

**I get teary and plead work, and he screams, *"Go then!"* I can't say what I want to because the nurse is standing there and I don't know what to do about the way I feel.**

Thoroughly shaken, Dian stopped at the hotel bar for a quick one before driving back to the base of the mountain and climbing to Karisoke. That evening she engaged in a peculiar ritual that she sometimes employed when about to embark on something of great moment. She burned some money—several thousand francs—which was quite a substantial sum considering the perennially precarious state of her finances. Perhaps she was trying to buy the goodwill of the gods.

Next morning she sent a note down to Weiss, along with a photo of a silverback gorilla. "Silverbacks are what I like best. They are fine and noble—even if they do have uncertain tempers."

A day passed during which she accomplished little but spent much time dreamily watching two ringed doves courting in front of her cabin.

**I kind of goof off, it seems. Don't know what is going on. The strangest feeling . . .**

The following day it all hit home.

**A real love letter from Dr. Weiss! Wow, what a letter! I spent the whole day trying to answer it—what a great feeling! I get X in P.M.—no dinner. I am smitten. Who would have thought it!**

Getting "X" was Dian's private code for drinking.

Within a week Weiss had begun trekking up the mountain to spend nights with Dian. Sometimes he came alone and at other times brought some of his children. Dian eagerly anticipated those visits.

**I washed my hair and await my love. . . . God, I want Peter. I ache for him. . . . Oh, Peter, I need you.**

Her life was suddenly full of joy.

November 6: **Wonderful contact with Group 4 in saddle area after they had crossed the meadow in the open going along Camp Trail. Fantastic, and all the more so because I was below, and somehow the weather cleared and it was just like Kabara, going through the saddle richness. . . . Followed fresh buffalo trail too. Contact great except I didn't see Old Goat and her baby . . . super because of Macho and Uncle Bert having a flirtation. I did catch wind of another silverback and found a fresh trail of Peanuts going into the saddle. Also dung, hopefully Amok's, deposited within the last month. Really enjoyed the day. Come home and get Kima in for the night, and Richard Rombach came over to tell me about his day with Group 5.**

**It was all perfect, as I live in love once again.**

But almost in the same breath she betrayed her dread that this, too, would be evanescent.

**I became afraid in the P.M. that I was taking this love too deeply and would lose him, only to be alone again, as always.**

November 8: **Another love letter from Peter. I know he**

doesn't have time to compose them, but I can't believe he can love me as much as he says he does. Anyway, I have hope for tomorrow and Sunday. Oh, Peter, I need you.

Next day Dian received word that Weiss would have to postpone this visit for a week.

I received two letters from Peter. He says he is on duty at the hospital this weekend. Meanwhile I have gotten everything ready for him and the children. I think this is the thing that has finally broken me. He is not coming and all was so ready. He is like all men—talk is cheap. . . . I will not write to him now. He bloody well knew he would have duty this weekend, and he says he is going to Kigali on Monday at 5:00. . . . Love can hurt and I'm so lonely.

As she so often did when she fancied herself rejected by one of her own kind, she went looking for solace amongst the gorillas. This time even they failed her.

Rwelekana and I start searching for Old Goat and her baby. I go onto Cattle Trail, which is quite overgrown since I last saw it—go all the way down to the big meadow with the fallen hagenia trees, then "instinct" tells me to turn into the nettle area—but no trail. I nearly got it from a buffalo at that point. I was tracking through dirt when I heard a snort. I thought it was in the distance, but I looked up to see him ten feet off. He gave a head toss and took a step in my direction. I reckon that if they can see you walking in the opposite direction they will flee—I did, and he did. Hacked my way through nettles and made gorilla noises, to be answered only by Rwelekana's whistle. I joined him, then looked behind and saw another buffalo bringing up the rear! . . . We spend hours mucking around but see nothing, so hack our way home through the nettles. It rains and is horrid on the way.

As the next promised visit from Peter Weiss neared, her spirits began to soar once again.

The air smells like the lobelia tastes—tangy—full of the promise of elephant and buffalo and gorilla behind every bush. It's getting clear—you can see the stars, though there is no moon. Edith Piaf is playing loudly on the tape recorder. I don't think he would like the record but he would like the night—so fresh. . . . All I can live for is tomorrow. . . . God, I love him and I am so happy.

On Saturday, Dian busied herself cooking "lots of good food," cleaning her cabin, braiding her hair, and making herself look her best. She gave her woodman the day off and dismissed her houseman early. Then she waited impatiently.

**I am cranky before they come, as it was so late I had given them up.**

Just at nightfall she saw Weiss and two of his older children, Mimish and Pierre, crossing the meadow toward her cabin, and she immediately forgot her anger.

Dian and Peter Weiss made love and talked late into the night. She learned about his family—mother and father both dead, sister and brother living in France—and something of his career as a doctor. He had graduated from medical school in '39, then fought in World War II, but would not talk about that because it was "too horrible."

He told her his African wife, Fina, had many local friends and was ready to "kill" Dian; that she wanted a settlement of twenty thousand Rwandan francs before she would agree to leave him. Although he claimed they were now estranged, he admitted that Fina continued to live at his house in Ruhengeri, "but just to care for the children."

During subsequent visits Weiss would also admit that he was not, in fact, married to Fina, although she was the mother of three of his five children. He explained that he had married in France in 1949, separated in 1961, but, being Catholic, had not been free until the death of his legal wife early in 1974.

However, nothing he could say or do seemed able to dampen her ardor—or lessen the terrible anxiety that was the other side of the coin.

**I am so old and wrinkled and ugly, it is alarming. I am trying to begin to look decent for Peter, but what's the use.**

By December 15 they had begun discussing marriage, and at this juncture an event took place that would normally have commanded at least a full page of her diary. Now it received only the briefest mention.

**On Christmas Day a poacher patrol brought me one poacher, Hategeka, whom I beat with nettle stalks and used my own sumu magic on. The three guards who took him down were afraid of my sumu.**

The following day she held what had by now become a traditional Christmas party for her camp workers and their families.

**We worked in a frenzy to get everything done. The people all came at eleven o'clock but had to wait while Rwelekana and**

126

Burumbe finished up the food. I think there were thirty-one people in all—I gave up counting. They seemed to really have a good time and drank a lot of beer. Then they slowed down on it and ate tons of food. I couldn't believe the size of their plates! Then I gave out the presents. . . . I really liked Burumbe's baby and wife. They surely enjoyed themselves. The woodman brought his mother and father—nice old people, especially the father.

About 2:30 they all said they wanted to dance and sing for happiness—WOW, what a show, and about an hour of it! Mukera was fabulous as a dancer. He really has rhythm. Never saw anything like it in my life. Bagalo played the drum, and first the two woodmen danced and then Kanyaragana and a woodman's wife. Sexy as hell, all the dances. Then the men began their individual chants, ending up with one about Mlle. Dian Fossey. The dust was flying—they danced the worms out of the woodwork. Everyone went down happy and I was ecstatic.

Kima had to stay inside her cage all day, screaming, but at least no one was bitten. After they left, Burumbe and Rwelekana were really fussy about cleaning up and did so straightaway. I took a two-hour nap, ate a huge dinner, then went for a long walk. The moon was beautiful and it was so clear. I didn't see one animal, but an owl followed me above in the trees. It was gorgeous and magical. I wish Peter had been there.

As 1975 began, Dian's passionate preoccupation with Weiss continued. Nothing else seemed to have much significance for her, including the comings and goings of students and researchers. Kelly Stewart's return in early January got no more attention in Dian's journal than a rather snide remark about the amount of luggage she had brought with her. And the departure of the unlucky Richard Rombach did not even rate a mention.

At the end of January a botanist newly arrived at Karisoke to study the plant life on Mt. Karisimbi burned his cabin as a result of carelessly placing his drying racks too close to his stove while he was out collecting. Dian and three of her Africans fought the blaze with pails of water from Camp Creek, but the building with all its contents, including many of Dian's own books, was a complete loss. Dian had worked herself into exhaustion—"Get so sick I can't stand it." That night she collapsed while carrying a valuable gorilla skull, which dropped from her hands and shattered. This was one of the worst days she had experienced in many months, yet the very next day she was in ecstasy.

Peter brings up a French mail-order catalog full of wedding ring pictures. I was so pleased when he ordered an engagement ring and a wristwatch for me.

The betrothal gifts were a long time in transit and their arrival late in April was an anticlimax.

The ring and watch have come, but he won't pick them up from customs. He says the duty is too high because they contain gold. He has told the customs to send them back to France. I am so hurt by this, but he will never know.

The incident was enough to propel her into a downward spiral of depression and anxiety.

April 29: Yesterday he asked if we couldn't get married in three weeks in the embassy office and send out announcements afterward. Later he said, "I will marry you in your third month of pregnancy." I know he is backing out.

May 4: I was really desolated that Peter didn't come up last night or at least send a note. I guess it's all over. He doesn't want me if I can't have a baby and I guess I never can.

May 17: I wrote to Peter saying if he wants Fina back to take her. Now I feel terrible about it. . . . I spent nearly the entire day thinking only of him and got nothing done. If he does not climb this weekend, then I will no longer write to him.

As ever when in distress, Dian turned to the friends who seldom failed her.

I go to Group 4 this morning and find them close to camp, almost as if they were coming to see me. A lovely, sunny day, and I stayed for hours, mainly with Uncle Bert and Digit. All of us just relaxed in the sun. I even slept and woke to find Flossie looking down at me with a worried face as if she thought I wasn't well. Came home then to catch up on field notes, but was so tired. Had a bath in my new tin tub and sorted out the botanist's crap. Notes took one hell of a long time. I'm still taking sleeping pills because of Peter. He is about all I am thinking of now and I find work literally impossible.

The next day broke cold and rainy and Dian stayed in. The wood was damp and her fireplace smoked, and in the evening Kima broke one of her precious kerosene pressure lamps. Depressed and miserable, Dian went to bed at 10:30. At 11:00 she heard a tapping on her cabin door, and there, wet and shivering, stood Peter Weiss, come to make amends.

He had brought up a locally purchased watch and a ring in lieu of the ones they had chosen from the catalog. They opened the box, lying in her big double bed together.

**The watch is a man's—it says on the guarantee. And the ring also looks like a man's. The stone is lovely but the setting is so very ugly and gross. I know he meant the watch for himself but gave it to me out of generosity.**

Peter departed at 5:00 A.M. in order to get to the hospital in time for his rounds. He left Dian feeling exceedingly confused.

**He says we will never learn to adjust to one another, which I reckon is like saying good-bye. He was so gloomy, saying that I was going to die before he did! When I said nothing because I was starting to cry, he changed his mind and said, "No, you won't die first. I will. But you are wasting both our lives staying up here."**

She spent the next month vacillating between hope and despair, trying to lose herself in her work but living for the occasional notes from Peter. They had reached an impasse. He refused to come up the mountain, demanding that she must come to him.

**He says I must come down, but if I do, I'm finished and he has won. He knows this. If I want him I have to give up living at Karisoke, but how can I do that?**

Late in June, Peter weakened and climbed to Karisoke, where they had a passionate reconciliation. Dian went to Ruhengeri the next weekend.

*Go down to see my Peter and hold him and be held in his arms!* . . . Well, I went, but he was surly and morose. Wouldn't talk and when he did we ended up fighting again because I wouldn't agree to move into his house with him and the kids. Had enough of his abuse, so went to the hotel and spent the night alone.

Dian had suggested several compromises. She offered to spend every weekend with Peter in Ruhengeri or to alternate two weeks in camp and a week in town.

**When I get some new students properly trained to keep the poaching under control and to supervise the long-range studies of the groups, I can take off. Perhaps we could go to France together for a month or so?**

None of these suggestions was agreeable to Peter, but his desire for Dian was so great that he continued to climb to Karisoke, and his visits were sometimes happy ones.

July 12: **Peter up at 7:30 P.M. I couldn't believe it! It was one of the most beautiful nights we've ever spent together. . . . He re-**

ally swore his love to me even on bended knee, saying, "I love only you—there is no other—you are all to me." He could not playact like this. He must mean it.

At this juncture Dian badly needed a friend in camp with whom to talk. For a time after Kelly Stewart's return she had confided in her, if somewhat uneasily. However, even that tentative relationship had been damaged almost beyond repair when, during this period of wild mood swings, Dian opened and read some of the letters flowing between Kelly and Sandy Harcourt. The contents of Harcourt's letters had shocked Dian by the vehemence of his dislike, which she characterized as "real hatred." Since she could find no obvious explanation for this enmity, she concluded that Kelly might have been fostering it, perhaps out of jealousy.

She stopped opening the mail only when it became obvious that the younger woman knew what she was doing. Rather than confront Dian and risk a fight, Kelly drew a padlock on the back of a letter to Sandy before she sent it up to Dian's cabin to await the biweekly mail porter.

This was sufficient to shame Dian into leaving the mail alone; but for weeks thereafter the two women kept their distance, communicating solely by means of notes, and then only when strictly necessary. However, as the summer wore on, Dian was driven to seek Kelly's company again, if only for the relief of being able to unburden herself of her confused feelings and desperate doubts about Weiss. Kelly seemed to be a sympathetic listener, although Dian would unfailingly note in her diary after these confessionals, "I talked too much."

The strains and stresses of the affair were beginning to tell on her in other ways. She had trouble keeping track of the date and at one point discovered she was in the wrong week in her diary.

**I'm really mixed up. My head isn't worth shooting.**

She found she was continually losing things—she misplaced her pistol and spent the better part of a week searching for it, only to discover it "in drawer with all my papers—kind of where I thought I'd put it."

On a hazy, portentous mid-September day Dian descended the mountain and drove in her combi to Kigali airport to pick up Peter, who had been to France for a month's vacation. They drove back to Ruhengeri to find Fina waiting outside Peter's house, hysterical and determined to have a showdown.

**She had all the kids with her, except Joseph, who was with us, because she'd been living in the house looking after them.**

130

While they and the neighbors all watched, she came after me with a club, then Peter went for her. I'll never get over it. She was screaming and so was he. I retreated and yelled at his men to stop her and help him. She was a crazy woman. He really must have suffered because she nearly killed him before his men drove her off. We went into the house. I asked who was going to guard my car. He said not to worry, but then she took her club and broke all the glass in the windshield, while holding Sophie in her other arm. Then I don't remember much. He went out to lock her in the storeroom and get the police. While he was gone she broke all the storeroom windows and tried to climb out. I was watching her and also trying to hide in the house. Sophie was running around after me, crying and screaming. The other kids hid in the bedrooms. Peter came back with two police and they took her off. All the neighbors were watching but no one helped him.

About 3 P.M. he went to the prison and let her go, saying she had to leave town. I couldn't believe he would let her go like that. I took the car to the garage and had a new window put in.

Guamhogazi, Dian's chief porter at the time, was posted along with a *zamu* or watchman to protect the car. Dian spent the night with Peter.

I had a horrible nightmare and woke up screaming. Next day we climbed the mountain together. I took only one and a half hours, which isn't bad for me, but he was angry at me for being so slow. Even Saturday night he wasn't any good—we only did it once in the morning. He acted as if I was the problem. I remember Fina's big boobs and nipples in the yellow T-shirt and yellow pants and her beating him, and little Pierre shoving me away when I tried to stop him from watching. Yves just disappeared and didn't come back.

I couldn't get Peter to talk or smile or anything. I know something is on his mind other than not being able to make love, but what it could be I don't know. . . . He says we'll get married if I insist on it and also repeated that he only wanted to get married before if I got pregnant. Now he doesn't think I can and doesn't seem interested. I'm really sure he doesn't love me anymore.

I know now I will never get married.

On November 2, Dian and Kelly Stewart were chatting outside Dian's cabin when they heard what sounded like a yell. "It's only an owl," Kelly said. They listened and heard it again. Clearly it was someone screaming. Several possibilities flashed through Dian's mind: it could be Fina on the rampage or it could be an avenging poacher. Anything seemed possible since several American students working at Jane Goodall's research center in Tanzania that summer had been kidnapped and held for ransom by political outlaws.

Taking no chances, Dian pushed Kelly into the cabin storeroom, locked the door for safety's sake, and ran for her gun. Just then Basili came pounding across the meadow, shouting his lungs out. There was another fire. Some outdoor clothing Kelly had hung up too near the stove in her cabin had ignited, and the blaze had already spread to the cabin walls and roof.

**I let Kelly out, then I go but can't help much with hauling water, so go into house and dump it on fire. The place had too much of a head start and the wogs had panicked, wasting precious time doing nothing. We stay up until 3—me until 4:50 A.M., trying to save her stuff. I'm finished.**

So was the cabin. But the greatest loss was Kelly's accumulated gorilla data—months of it gone up in flames.

**Very shaky A.M. I could hardly move. Kelly really stunned. Had her for breakfast and told her to take a check and go down with it and start buying materials to rebuild cabin. I don't recall the day clearly. . . . I'm sick in P.M. I really X and collapse. Very bad. No letter from Peter at all.**

That night Dian awoke from a nightmare to find herself beating Kima, who had been sleeping on the bed with her.

**She was shaking with fear. I feel so badly, and worried about what is happening to me.**

So the year lurched ominously toward its conclusion. In December, Kelly Stewart departed for another term at Cambridge, where she would rejoin Sandy Harcourt. Dian was alone at Karisoke with her native staff.

As 1976 began she was trying hard to complete the final revisions on her doctoral thesis, but her personal distress was so great she could not concentrate.

**I work all day, little stopping, on Hinde's suggestions but can't get it right. There is no end to it. . . . Kima acting rather lonely. . . . I've never felt so alone in my life.**

She found herself crying over small irritations or just from fatigue. She began drinking more. Her diary entries became erratic, sometimes just a scribbled word or two, sometimes nothing at all. She was slipping more deeply into the slough of depression.

January 23: **I write a horrid letter to Peter. I am so fed up with everything.**

By early February her diary had degenerated into indecipherable scratchings made with such violence the pen all but pushed through the paper. She had somehow injured her arm, and the pain was keeping her from sleeping.

**Arm so Bad. Can't sleep. Awake all night. Fuck the world. No Peter.**

Gradually the writing began to improve, although the entries remained terse.

February 10: **No good—can't sleep anymore at all—arm is much much worse.**

February 11: **Not well. Reading for thesis discussion.**

February 12: **Have Nemeye spend night up here tending fire so can stay awake to complete thesis.**

A few days later her handwriting began to return to normal, although her frame of mind seemed only marginally improved.

**Bad hail storm. Kima so sick. I go down. My arm so bad decided must go to Ruhengeri. First time off mountain for months, but Peter was in Gisenyi and didn't return till 6:30 so I just had to sit and wait in his office. He seemed glad to see me and was very gentle. Gave me a bath. I cried most of the night.**

The following day Dian had her arm x-rayed at the Ruhengeri hospital and found she was suffering from an acute case of tendonitis.

**I went to pick up X rays and then to Peter's office, where everyone was after him—everyone. A nurse from Uganda was there with a girl with bilharzia and a little baby dying from a cracked skull. I started crying again when I saw the baby. Peter is so respected—beloved—I was so proud of him and ashamed of myself.**

Slowly she pulled herself together and got back into the routine of the camp, once again trying to compensate for her aloneness by seeking contact with the gorillas.

**Out to Group 5—fantastic contact. All silverbacks came near us. Puck takes camera lens after I take pictures. . . . I took *National Geographic* magazine with me and Puck was really funny looking at gorilla pictures in it—but got *too* funny at end of contact, acting the big fool and beating the hell out of me. He must**

**think I'm as tough as he is. For the first time I wondered about their getting overhabituated.**

In May 1976, Dian returned to Cambridge. Her thesis had been accepted and she now only had to pass an oral examination. Although she had never earned a master's degree, and even her B.A. in occupational therapy had no bearing on zoology, her study of the mountain gorillas of the Virungas contained such an enormous amount of new information on so many varied aspects of their lives that the examiners were pleased to confirm her doctorate.

At long last she was *Dr*. Fossey.

From Cambridge, Dian traveled to California to take part in a National Geographic Society–sponsored symposium featuring herself, Dr. Jane Goodall, and the as-yet-undoctored Biruté Galdikas—Leakey's three primate ladies, or the "trimates" as they were sometimes called. This was a rare treat for the audience but a harrowing experience for Dian, who was suffering from dysentery.

There was the usual obligatory visit to the Prices, after which Dian flew to Washington where she cataloged film and photos for her National Geographic sponsors and brought the Research Committee up-to-date on Karisoke's operations. She returned to Karisoke late in June with her emotional equilibrium much improved.

Her first concern was for her gorillas. The day after her return, she and Rwelekana made a twelve-kilometer sweep through the highlands, searching—unsuccessfully, she was happy to note—for traps and other evidence of poachers. A week later she trekked across the mountains to Kabara in Zaire (as the Congo was now called) to satisfy herself that all was well with the gorillas in that region.

Several students worked at Karisoke through the summer of 1976, and Dian kept close rein on them. There were confrontations with certain individuals who resented her "interference" in their work, an attitude that exasperated her.

**Who gave them their work? Who showed them how to do it? The arrogance of some of these know-it-alls is not to be believed. One little shit from New York with a master's had the nerve to ask me where I got mine. I told him to call me DOCTOR Fossey from now on.**

In August she had trouble with a group of French students.

**I went to their cabin to tell them their field notes were overdue, and one of the bastards pushed me out the door and down the steps to the ground. I do believe he would have hit me to death if my Africans hadn't been present. He screamed, "You treat us like monkeys." I believe he is cracking up. At any rate, I'll**

keep my cabin locked until next Wednesday when they leave.

The "student" she liked best during that period was not a student at all. She had found Tim White hitchhiking along the road near Ruhengeri. He was a young Virginian who had been seeing the world on the proverbial shoestring. Finding himself in central Africa, he had gravitated toward the Virungas after hearing about the gorillas. Although he had no academic training, he proved to be an excellent field worker, selflessly devoted to the interests of the gorillas. More than that, he was a genuine handyman, which was something the average Stanford or Cambridge Ph.D. student seldom was. Among other things, he soon had every Aladdin lamp and spirit stove in camp repaired and functioning perfectly.

Dian rarely saw Peter Weiss during the summer of 1976, although she continued to receive regular intelligence reports on Fina's activities.

**Fina seen in Ruhengeri by Guamhogazi with kids, at the Indian store. If she is shopping in town she must be living with Peter.**

October 12: **Guamhogazi said Fina was seen in the car with Weiss in the afternoon along with the kids. BUT he was seen alone in the car in the A.M. and she alone walking on the road beyond the hospital.**

Early in October, Kelly Stewart returned to Karisoke to continue her studies. Dian welcomed her back, but there was an element of constraint between them.

**I go down to Kelly's, find she has dyed her hair but is still fat. She started to say, "I'm so happy to see . . ." then just let it trail off. She had pinned a sketch of a gorilla done by Sandy Harcourt on her wall, and she showed me a fertility charm given to her by his sister, so I guess they will get married when she finishes here. I wish her lots of luck. . . .**

On the morning of October 24, Dian unexpectedly received a "passionate letter" from Peter. This was the first she had heard from him in months, and despite her resolution to put him out of mind, she immediately decided to go down the mountain.

**He was home when I got there and wanted me at once, but not ten minutes later the phone rings—a cesarean at the hospital and he is gone for an hour and a half. Then the kids come home—hell. Then we start again and some bastard comes over for a beer and I have to stay in the bedroom—and then dinner. He said little about Fina, just that she'd been there three times for lunch.**

The visit had been less than satisfactory, and when Dian gloomily returned to Karisoke the next day, she learned that Cindy had tried to follow her to Ruhengeri, with near-disastrous results.

**She ran down the road after the combi, and two wogs, full of pombe, both poachers, came out of a bar and stoned her. They hit her and Semitoa, who was trying to catch her. My watchman caught her as she was fleeing from the wogs and brought her back to camp. No bones broken, but she was badly bruised. Nemeye said I should charge them, so I did.**

One of the two men who had stoned the dog served two months in jail for his offense. The other could not be found.

Nearly two months later a group of park guards arrived at Karisoke with a prisoner in tow. He was identified to Dian as being the second man in the Cindy stoning incident.

**He had been hiding in Zaire, they said. He was drunk. I played "let's stone Cindy" and nearly knocked him out.**

Dian's helpful hitchhiker, Tim White, left Karisoke early in December to continue his world travels. It was a sad day for Dian. However, his replacement had already arrived. This was Ian Redmond, a fair-haired, boyish young Englishman who would prove to be everything Tim White had been and more. Dian considered him the finest student ever to set foot in the park, although this opinion may have rested more on his devotion to the welfare of the animals than on his academic prowess.

Her initial impression of Ian Redmond was, however, anything but favorable.

November 7: **Ian character arrives at 7:30 or so wearing shorts and no shoes—crazy. For sure this kid is not going to work out.**

November 8: **Redmond kid still hasn't fixed breakfast by 9:30—wants to do cine and stills and everything else he can think of. A real mess. He got from England to Mombasa on £9! That's impossible!**

Although she thought him feckless, she could not help liking him. She began referring to him half derisively, half affectionately, as "the boy," "the kid," sometimes "the child."

In a continuing effort to patch things up with Dian, Peter Weiss invited her to spend Christmas with him and the children. Ever hopeful, she descended the mountain.

**Peter gave me a tape recorder and seemed very proud of it. We have champagne and cake for dinner—not much else. . . . We have breakfast alone and then he goes out to fiddle with car. I am so bored. I work on slides.**

Very good fillet for lunch and then he naps. I return to slides and in comes Fina. I was scared—she didn't talk to me. I gathered up slides and returned to the bedroom. We waited for her to leave.

In evening we start game of Master Mind and I win. We play more after dinner and he loses all.

On Boxing Day she returned, dispirited, to Karisoke, convinced at last that no possibility of a life with Peter Weiss existed. Since this was the case, she continued to make the best of what she had.

Climb up mountain cold and wet. Change clothes and fix Christmas for the two kids, who were feeling sorry for selves. Ian brought me a mobile he'd made out of tin can lids, and Kelly gave me some neat sketches. I gave them each a pile of stuff. It was really pleasant, and I cooked a good dinner for a change, and we all had some fun while the hail banged down on the roof like fury. They didn't leave until long after midnight. I couldn't sleep and feel so tired of it all.

Next day in P.M. Kelly said the boy told her he had never had a nicer Christmas and never gotten so many presents.

Christmas 1976 at Karisoke had been relatively pleasant. Dian's friendship with Kelly had regained some of its warmth, and she was becoming fond of Ian, who was developing into a gorilla enthusiast after her own heart. The African staff was functioning well; the poachers seemed to have been at least temporarily subdued; and the gorillas were free of undue interference from mankind.

However, not all was sweetness and light. Dian's health was worsening and she found it increasingly difficult to join the gorillas on their rain-chilled daily rounds. Trapped more and more in her cabin by an ailing body, she was also bogged down in the never-ending demands of scientific record-keeping and of preparing the monthly reports to her sponsors in the United States, upon whom the survival of Karisoke depended. An avalanche of paper was becoming the bane of her existence. Now that she had her Ph.D., she was also under increasing pressure to publish her scientific findings. And she was making her first tentative attempt to write a popular book about her life with the gorillas.

During early January 1977, she had a visit from Barbara and Richard Wrangham, friends from her Cambridge days. When the Wranghams left on January 12, Dian accompanied them to Kigali, nominally as an act of courtesy but in fact as an excuse for an unheralded and hopeful visit to Peter. It was an ill-omened venture. Torrential rains had turned the roads into wallows, and having mired her car a mile outside of Ruhengeri, Dian appeared at Peter's door soaked and covered with red mud.

To her relief there was no sign of Fina. Although Peter took her in and somewhat reluctantly made love to her, it was a passive gesture devoid of real affection. Nevertheless, Dian tried to evade the obvious conclusion.

**I guess he was bothered at trying to hide his deceit with Fina, or perhaps he was feeling guilty, which I can understand.**

Early next morning she slogged her way back up the greasy trail to Karisoke, wrestling with the onset of another attack of pneumonia. Dosing herself with antibiotics, she crawled into bed but could not sleep. All night long she lay listening to the rain beating on the cabin roof, thinking about Peter. Was he really lost to her for good? She would not yet believe that this was so. With the morning she decided that the matter had to be resolved. Once more she descended the mountain. Realizing that she was ill, Basili offered to accompany her to the car park but was brusquely refused and told to go about his business.

Peter had just returned home from the hospital when Dian burst in upon him, full of angry accusations alternating with pathetic demands for reassurance. Goaded beyond endurance, Weiss admitted that he had indeed been sleeping with Fina—the last occasion only four days earlier.

**He couldn't lie to me when I asked him directly. Now I'm sure she must be pregnant again and that he will marry her.**

"Do you really love her, Peter?" Dian pleaded, putting all to the test.

"I love many people," was his cold response.

Alternating between concern for her and self-justifying anger, Weiss poured her a drink of rum and put her to bed. It was not the bed of reconciliation. Dian swallowed three sleeping pills and finally slept.

He left the house at an early hour and Dian awakened to the bleak certainty that she had once more been cast out from the solace and sanctuary of a human heart.

**I lay on his bed for a long time and cried and cried. I held Sophie in my arms, but I knew I had lost her too.**

Leaving Peter Weiss's house for the last time, Dian fled to Rosamond Carr. By the time she had bounced her combi over the rock-strewn track to the plantation, she was so ill she had to be helped from the vehicle by Sembrugari, Rosamond's headman.

As she had done so often, Rosamond took Dian in and comforted her.

**She was so nice to me. She made me a lovely lunch, gave me a hot bath, a brief dinner and put me to bed, for sleep.**

Despite Rosamond's remonstrances, Dian insisted on returning to camp a few days later, to be cared for by her "wogs" until the pneumonia had run its course.

While Ian, Kelly, and the trackers continued to slog through the saturated forests and nettle patches, collecting infinitesimal facts to add to the scientific chronicle of gorilla lore, Dian fought her way back to a semblance of normality.

On January 24 she and Nemeye set off in pelting rain to visit Group 4 on Honeyman Hill. Dian's scientific notes for this day are so sparse it seems obvious that her real motive was not the requirements of science but the needs of self. Through five long hours she crouched in the sodden vegetation communing with living beings who she knew would not reject her.

**Uncle Bert was so super—he rested next to me in his day nest and all of them stayed close by. Little Kweli, Uncle Bert's year-old baby, came and sat on my foot while his mother, Macho, groomed herself, eyeing me once in a while to make sure I was doing a good job as a baby-sitter.**

Late in the day a singularly heavy downpour roared through the clearing where the band was feeding. Visibility had dropped to almost nothing when out of the murk Dian's favorite, Digit, appeared. He stood erect for several seconds, staring down at her recumbent form while the rain streamed off his gleaming pelt. Then, with what must have seemed to her like a calculated gesture of empathy, he pulled up a stalk of wild celery, stripped away the tough outer leaves with one strong hand, dropped the peeled stalk close to her feet, and slipped away into the gathering gloom.


Although the poaching lull continued throughout February, its end had been foreshadowed in late January by Seregera, a guide-turned-poacher who had worked for her in the early years and whom she had fired in 1972, was released from a spell in prison. Seregera not only considered the Karisoke study area his own personal hunting ground, but his resentment of the camp and all it stood for guaranteed that he would return to plague it.

Trouble began on March 7. Nemeye and Ian were visiting Group 5 on the distant western slope of Mt. Visoke when the gorillas were spooked by some unseen presence and fled panic-stricken. Leaving Ian to follow the gorilla's flight trail, Nemeye climbed upward through the sopping tangle to emerge upon a path above the place where the gorillas had been feeding. Here in the soft ooze he found several sets of naked human footprints—so fresh that they had not yet filled with rain. Nemeye could not muster the courage to pursue that many poachers single-handedly, but when he tried to rejoin his *bazunga,* he found that Ian had returned to camp without him.

That evening Dian called a council of war, at which she chewed Redmond out for failing to pursue the poachers.

"Why the hell didn't you follow through? You could have caught them if you'd really tried!"

Ian knew better than to defend himself. He listened quietly until Dian was done, then volunteered to lead a counterattack next day.

This was the kind of reaction Dian admired. Together they planned a sweep right through the study area and deep into Zaire, where poachers were in the habit of establishing temporary camps.

If he had made a bit of a muck-up the day before, Ian redeemed himself on March 8. Shoeless because his companions had no shoes, and clad only in a T-shirt and tattered shorts, he led the three trackers out of camp at dawn on a cold, glum day. When the little posse returned at nightfall, they were exhausted but triumphant. Scouring the saddle area right to Mt. Mikeno, they had found and destroyed three poachers' shelters and twenty-one recently set snares.

Ten days went by before the poachers struck back. On March 18 at least two groups infiltrated the distant northwestern portion of the study area and saturated it with traps. Although Ian and Nemeye found and destroyed thirty-five of these in two days, Dian remained extremely concerned for the safety of the Group 5 gorillas, who were then roaming this distant region.

**They are too far away. We can't find all the traps. Sooner or later one of them will get caught.**

Very reluctantly, for she hated to interfere with their ordered ways, she decreed that Group 5 must be herded back into safer territory.

This was a traumatic business for all concerned. Ian and four other men made a circuit to the north of Group 5, then cautiously closed in on the gorillas while at the same time ringing poacher dogbells and making poacher whistle signals.

Pandemonium ensued. The chill air quickly grew rank with the stench of fear. The young male, Icarus, roared furious challenges as he became the vanguard of what soon turned into a rout. The females and younger animals crashed through the undergrowth hard on the heels of Beethoven, who was leading the escape. Implacably the bells and whistles followed. Several times Icarus charged the unseen persecutors. The flight trail of smashed and shattered vegetation was awash with diarrheic dung in which the herders slipped and fell. The forest echoed and reechoed to the screams of terror-stricken animals.

Dian took no part in any of this.

**I stay in and make sure I won't hear anything. It is HORRID, but it must be done.**

Her fury against the poachers who had forced her to inflict this indignity on her friends was mounting to white heat.

On April 1 Kelly Stewart said her farewells and departed to rejoin Sandy Harcourt in England, there to prepare for her marriage to him in early June. Although Dian and Kelly had often been at odds in recent months, Dian's affection for the younger woman had survived all their tribulations, and she wept unabashedly at the parting. Perhaps some of her tears were shed because Kelly was traveling to her love, leaving Dian behind to mourn the loss of hers.

On April 3 a party of six poachers struck again. This time they set their dogs on Wageni's Group, pursuing its members for several hundred yards. Ian and Vatiri happened on the scene in time to prevent what might well have been a gorilla murder. They chased the poachers right across the crest of Mt. Visoke at an altitude of nearly thirteen thousand feet, with the temperature only a few degrees above freezing, but they failed to catch them.

Dian was convinced that the poachers were again hunting gorillas for their heads and hands, so next morning she and the entire camp staff mounted a counterraid. It hailed off and on all that day, and when it was not hailing, it was raining and bitter cold. Dian plodded as far as Group 5 but was by then so exhausted she had to return to camp where she collapsed. Vatiri, Nemeye, Rwelekana, Ian, and two other men patrolled all the way around Mt. Visoke but found no poachers and only a handful of snares.

It was at this tense juncture that a new student arrived upon the scene. Leonard was a young American biologist whose ideas of Africa and gorilla-watching seem to have been more than usually romanticized. The reality of what was to be required of him struck home the day after his arrival when Ian hauled him off on an antipoaching patrol that lasted for five drenching hours and entailed a lung-straining climb almost to the crest of Mt. Visoke. Instead of a leisurely life viewing gorillas in a tropical jungle, Leonard found himself involved in a forest war against unseen pygmies armed with spears, bows, and arrows, all in a dank and frigid world inhabited by testy elephants, invisible leopards, and pugnacious buffalo.

A week after Leonard's arrival, Nemeye was treed by a charging buffalo that kept him shivering in a hagenia tree until long after dark. When Dian went to inspect the scene next day, the buffalo thundered out of a nearby thicket and sent *her* up a tree.

It was all too much for Leonard. The last straw seems to have been Dian's request that he spend part of his time dissecting gorilla dung in search of parasites. Early on the morning of April 15 he packed it in. It was probably as well that he left when he did for the events of the rest of that day would have appalled him.

In midmorning Basili joyfully called Dian out of her cabin to savor the spectacle of five park guards frog-marching a diminutive prisoner into camp. Dian recognized the ragged, barefooted Batwa as Munyarukiko, the leading poacher of the Virungas who had for so long been a thorn in her side. When he stood, downcast, in front of her, she was so ecstatic that her native shrewdness deserted her.

The guards had quite a story to tell, and despite all the years I'd dealt with these men, who had the habit of losing poacher prisoners while on the way down to park headquarters after collecting a reward from me, I swallowed it this time with all the gullibility of a tadpole.

They claimed to have spent two long days and nights in the alpine meadows of Karisimbi trailing Munyarukiko and his hunting party before finally closing in on him while he and friends were digging a buffalo pit trap. They bemoaned the escape of the others, but at least they had caught the prize poacher of all, so they brought him straight to me to display the efforts of their labors and, more to the point, to collect reward money.

I was surprised when they refused to persuade him to tell who his companions were, with the usual nettle-lashing routine. In fact, they wouldn't go near him, and I foolishly thought they must be afraid of him because he had some new sumu.

I asked them why they hadn't brought back Munyarukiko's bow and arrows, spear, panga, and other paraphernalia always carried by poachers. They replied that the other men had fled with them. Well, that seemed peculiar too because the last things a poacher parts with, even when being chased, are the tools of his trade. The situation seemed even more puzzling when all I could find in his pockets were a comb, broken fragments of a mirror, a razor blade, and a bit of soap—none of which would be much use in a successful buffalo hunt!

When all the formalities had been carried out, including

paying the guards the equivalent of a $120 reward, I decided I would go down with them and the prisoner and drive them to Ruhengeri to the parquet where Mr. Nkubili, the *chef des brigades*, would pop him into jail.

This met with strong resistance, the guards insisting their orders now were that poachers had to go first to the conservator's office near the park for questioning. There was nothing to do but let them go off alone, which I thought they did a bit too merrily.

That was all right, but later that afternoon our woodman came into camp after spending his day off below and told my other men that the park guards had actually met Munyarukiko in the village bar that morning and had planned the entire ruse! They arranged that he would go with them to Karisoke, pretend he'd been caught, and later get his share of the reward, about twenty dollars, which was a small fortune.

I could have endured being made a fool of once more (it wasn't the first time) for the capture of Mun, but it happened that an hour or two later Nemeye and Ian came into camp to report another bunch of poachers harassing the gorillas of Group 5. This combination of events ticked me off more than I could say and I went on the warpath.

I slid down the mountain in the rain along with Basili and Nemeye. The combi wouldn't start and I was furious. Finally it went, and we drove to the Twa village of Mukingo and parked. Basili stayed to guard the car while Nemeye and I walked along a narrow track to Mun's shamba. He had gotten home by that time, after he and the guards had spent part of their reward money filling up on pombe at the bar.

When we appeared on the scene, it was already dark and there was lots of confusion because Mun had several houses—just grass huts—five wives, and I don't know how many children. By the time we located the house where he lived with his eldest wife, he had fled along with his partner in crime, Gashabizi. All of the poacher's dogs could be heard barking and yelping as they were run off before I could get to them. Since I couldn't catch them, I grabbed one of Mun's almost-naked kids instead.

Nemeye and I couldn't handle *all* the wives and children so I told him to hang on to this one youngster (which wasn't easy) while I took out of Mun's hut about fifteen dollars worth of matting, baskets, cobs of corn, and old clothing. I took all this stuff about twenty feet from his hut, then threatened to set fire to it,

144

but only after I had told his wives to yell for him to come back and give me the reward money if he didn't want it burned.

When he didn't come back, I set fire to his stuff. It made a big blaze and looked scary with all the shining eyes of the Batwa in the background. I decided it was time to go, so we took the kid, who was about four, and headed back to Karisoke. I was so beat I had to crawl up the mountain on my hands and knees. It was still raining and I have never been so cold and muddy in my life. I slipped twice on the trail, but the two men, taking turns carrying the boy, wouldn't leave me. When we finally got to camp, the child was so happy just to get good food and toys that he set up a squall next day when he knew he was going home. But I had to return him instead of keeping him until I could get the money back from Munyarukiko because the Europeans down at the park made so much yak.

During the next ten days Dian worried about possible repercussions from what she would later call her "worst no-no." The camp staff brought back vague rumors that she was going to be expelled from Rwanda, and for a time she feared that Munyarukiko and his friends might try to fire some of the Karisoke cabins. The wily poacher chose another form of retaliation. He obtained a legal judgment against Dian, under the terms of which she was fined the princely sum of six hundred dollars, much of which went to him in compensation for the material damages he claimed to have suffered at her hands. Dian paid up without demur, ruefully acknowledging that Munyarukiko had got the best of her.

Rwandans viewed this incident with amusement. The account of how Dian had been outwitted, not once but twice, brought uproarious laughter in the pombe bars of the villages lying at the foot of the volcanoes. However, maliciously exaggerated versions of the story portraying her as a racist, sadist, and even worse were later circulated by some of her fellow whites.

With the approach of spring Dian took to spending two or three days a week in her cabin dealing with her voluminous correspondence and the dreary monthly reports. However, she went to the gorillas as often as she could, spending much of her time with her special friends in Group 4. In the evenings she took Cindy for walks and attended to Kima's insistent demands for attention. During odd moments she drew never-ending pleasure from watching and listening to the many creatures for whom the meadows and woods surrounding Karisoke had become a sanctuary where human beings were not dire enemies. Their numbers included a score of duikers, many bush-bucks, ravens, hyraxes, parrots, and even bats. Dian knew most indi-viduals of the larger species by name.

The Africans had their own well-established patterns. Twice a week Gwehandagoza, now the head porter, drove his little Honda motorbike into the parking lot, climbed the mountain path with mail and supplies, and descended again with outgoing mail and shopping lists, which he filled at stores in Ruhengeri and Gisenyi.

Basili busied himself with houseman's chores, cooking for Dian when she required it, washing dishes and clothing for her and Ian, and generally keeping the camp and cabins shipshape.

At dawn each day the woodman appeared from his village far below to spend long hours collecting dry fuel for the camp stoves. Dian had strictly forbidden the cutting of live trees of whatever size and would not even permit the felling of dead ones in the vicinity of camp for fear this might disturb the birds and other animals. A woodman's lot at Karisoke was not an easy one.

One or more of the three principal trackers—Vatiri, Nemeye, and Rwelekana—would set out at seven-thirty every morning to visit the gorilla groups, sometimes accompanied by Dian or Ian but often on their own. They were charged with reporting the daily movements of the great apes and with keeping a sharp eye peeled for signs of poachers or their snares. They also had to bring back plastic bags full of gorilla dung that they had collected from the previous night's nests.

This odoriferous material went to Ian Redmond, who, at Dian's request, had undertaken a study of the internal parasites that plague gorillas. It was his unsavory task to examine minutely each day's dung collection, with the aid of an ancient microscope he had scrounged at the Ruhengeri hospital, and make meticulous drawings of the pecul-iar creatures that inhabit the guts of gorillas. Ian's dedication to this arcane project baffled the Africans, but in recognition of the peculiar-ities of *bazungas,* they gave him a new name. He became known far and wide as The Worm Boy.

Each evening Ian was expected to send Dian a written report of the day's observations, delivered by Basili or some other member of the staff, to which she would respond with instructions, suggestions, and sometimes peremptory demands for more data. Although sepa-rated by no more than a couple hundred yards, the two whites sometimes did not see each other for days on end. About once a week Dian would invite him for dinner and occasionally would visit him to register some particularly vehement complaint about his slowness in writing up reports. She deliberately left little room for intimacy between them.

Nevertheless, his presence put an enormous strain upon her determination to remain aloof. If ever there had been a man after her own mold, this was the one. Although trained as a biologist, Ian did not accept science as an all-consuming vocation. As his time at Karisoke lengthened, he became increasingly preoccupied with the vital question of how to help the gorillas to survive and far less interested in them as subject matter to advance a professional career. He saw them as Dian did—living entities to be understood and cherished on the emotional level as well as with the intellect.

Even-tempered, witty in the understated English manner, tolerant of the foibles and frailties of others, and irrepressibly enthusiastic, he had little difficulty dealing with Dian's prickly side. "Her outbursts," he told a new student, "are like the charge of an old silverback guarding his group—ninety-nine percent bluff. If you stand your ground the same way you do to a charging gorilla, she is no problem at all."

As her affection for Ian grew, Dian experienced increasing difficulty maintaining her distance. Although she suppressed any sexual manifestations of it, she could not deny the growing warmth she felt for him. Making the most of the twenty-year age difference, she sublimated her feelings into a kind of maternal relationship in which he was cast in the role of a charming but feckless adolescent who needed to be treated with a firm but kindly hand.

The relatively even tenor of life at Karisoke was briefly interrupted on May 1 when Dian went off to Kigali to collect a new student arriving by air from the United States. Daniel was yet another pleasant but callow youth, quite unprepared for the African realities. Nevertheless, Dian was astounded when, just four days later, he told her he wished to leave.

**I couldn't believe it! But he is, according to Ian, a conscientious objector and dislikes my antipoaching activities. . . . I talked to him for an hour but he didn't give any conclusive reason why he wanted to leave . . . he just said I had a colonialistic attitude, but we settled on a week's stay as a trial.**

When Dian awakened late next morning it was to find that—trial or no trial—Daniel had departed. She was philosophical about it.

He came and went so fast we weren't sure he'd even been here. I guess he'll go into the history of Karisoke as the Four-Day Wonder.

A few days later one of the park guards reported that a party of gorillas at the foot of the mountain near the cultivated fields had the farmers in an uproar. Dian hastened to intervene. The animals turned out to be members of Group 5 meandering about on the park boundary at a rocky outcrop called Jambo Bluff.

The group seems to like this ledge since it allows them, from a position of relative safety, to look down over the open fields at their toiling primate relations as if to say, "Still at it, eh?" Simultaneously the natives gather to shriek "Ngagi! Ngagi!" Gorilla! Gorilla! Neither these Hutu people nor the gorillas are really afraid of one another in this particular area, which is far from the Twa poachers' village. A respectful distance is maintained between the two species since there is nothing to interest the gorillas in the denuded pyrethrum fields. It isn't possible to decide who is the onlooker and who the viewer.

The gorillas, their curiosity satisfied, finally leave the ledge to go on with their feeding and the Africans go back to their never-ending toil of hoeing the fields.

On this occasion I simply couldn't resist the impulse to mingle with the gorillas as they climbed out onto the ledge as though to acknowledge the greetings of their subjects. When my head suddenly sprang into view between those of Puck and Tuck while we all crawled slowly to the lip of the ledge, the outburst of human screams and shouts seemed to triple. "Nyiramacheballi! Nyiramachabelli!"—that not-so-adorable nickname they have given me—The Lone Woman of the Forest!

People came running by the dozens from the lower fields. Huts emptied; children hid behind their mothers' skirts shrieking; men and women were pointing and making such a clamor one would have thought it was the Second Coming. The gorillas seemed only mildly discombobulated by the uproar and filed off the ledge in a far more dignified manner than I; but it took the people a long time to settle down.

At the end of May filmmakers Genny and Warren Garst climbed to Karisoke to make a documentary about Dian and the gorillas for the television series *Wild Kingdom*.

An easygoing pair of professionals, the Garsts and an accompanying couple who did the sound recordings got on well both with the Karisoke people and with the gorillas, showing respect for both.

The newcomers had a spectacularly invigorating effect on Dian.

**Warren Garst and I had a *fantastic* day with Group 5—he shot twelve hundred feet of cine of the silverbacks and of the females, Effie, Marchesa, Tuck, and Puck. Icarus, the number two silverback, was great and made three charges! Then we went on to Group 6, where Garst ran out of film. It was a marvelous contact, with every one of the gorillas doing something. The day was sunny and perfect. I was in a joyous mood when we came home and went down to their cabin for dinner. First time I've been happy in ages—really happy!**

Even the loss of her precious asthma inhalator while out tracking a gorilla group with Garst did not upset her.

**I'm in such a good mood for a change nothing seems to bother me, but I don't know how long it will last.**

In the company of these new people, her sense of the ridiculous flowered once again.

**During the Garsts' stay, camp acquired a new inhabitant never seen before over a ten-year period, a member of the Giant Rat species. He took up residence near my cabin, and I named him Rufus and set about making friends.**

**I wondered where Rufus could have come from. Although the Africans said they were common in the villages below, I thought this was an awfully long hike to make just on the off chance of a few grains of corn being left over by my chickens. As soon as Rufus became tame, I experimented with various foods and found he would eat anything except meat. He obviously belonged to the new vegie wave!**

**He became completely accustomed to flashlights and pressure lamps, and I would force my reluctant guests to go out at night and marvel over Rufus—all forty inches of him! Then sometime later he was joined by a lady rat I called Rebecca; and a few days later by Rhoda; then in rapid succession out of nowhere came Batrat, Robin, Russ, Rufus, Rascal—and on and on it went.**

**Individuals could be identified by variations in tail coloring, and there was a definite pecking order amongst them when the food was set out. Rather than risk being trampled by the mob, I took to simply tossing the food and then running back into the house while they poured out of the forest and from under the cabin itself.**

**About then I chanced to read a *National Geographic* article that explained in vivid detail why rats are the most successful mammalian species in the world. It gave nightmarish figures on**

their reproductive rates. This, plus the fact that it was getting a bit squishy underfoot outside the cabin at night, convinced me that I had to either learn to play a flute or cut off their food supply.

First, though, I wanted to get some pictures of them. One night I surrounded the feeding area with pressure lamps and took a precarious position myself on the wood basket inside my cabin below an open window, with flash in one hand and camera in the other.

Before you could say "rat fink" the area filled up with slithering bodies and writhing tails reminiscent of a snake pit. In my eagerness to get as many rats as possible into the picture, I leaned out a little bit too far and fell crashing to the ground. Unable to break my fall while trying to save the camera, I felt a pain in my ribs that was not to be believed. I'd gone and done it again, I thought, broken a rib for a totally ignoble cause.

Although the rats brought some light relief, dark times were returning to Karisoke. One day while in Ruhengeri for supplies, Dian encountered Lolly Prescada, a Spanish surgeon and old friend who worked in a leper hospital.

She told me about Peter—the banns have now been posted for his marriage. He's been given only ten more months' extension on his visa, but if he marries Fina he can get permission to stay in Rwanda permanently.

This news was closely followed by the event itself. On July 1, Dian penciled one brief, furious entry in her journal to mark the end of the affair.

Today Peter married to black bitch.

The spell of bright and sunny weather that had made June remarkable now ended. Heavy clouds overflowed the skies and the rains again beat down. The energy Dian was investing in the film left her in a chronic state of fatigue. Sciatica in her right hip had become so severe she could barely endure accompanying Warren Garst out to the gorillas. More worrisome still, a fierce pain in her chest, which she did not associate with her fall from the window, was keeping her awake at night unless she was drugged by sleeping pills.

Her mood became darker with the delivery of a letter from Debi Hamburger, a young friend and ardent admirer in California. It had been arranged that Debi would come to Karisoke in 1976 as a student, but just before her departure it was discovered that she had cancer of the breast. An operation followed. Now Debi wrote to say that the prognosis was bad. "But I am *going* to get well, Dian, you can rely on that! What I want most in all my life is to stay with you and the wonderful gorillas at Karisoke. I'll make it, don't you worry!"

Although Dian liked the Garsts, it was with relief that, after almost two months, she saw them off the mountain. She had become disillusioned with the way films are made.

**Bullshit film finally finished. It is not to be believed how much time and energy gets wasted. And everybody has to play a part, including the gorillas. Simply to cine the *real* thing would be too dull!**

She was again reliving the nightmares of her childhood when it had been mistakenly thought she had tuberculosis. In her middle-class milieu, the disease had been—and still was—viewed as a shameful affliction denoting poverty, filth, and fecklessness. Dian's phobic horror of it, exacerbated by her contact with tubercular patients at the city of Hope Hospital during her internship as a physical therapist, was beyond reason. And this time there was no Louis Leakey to banish the phantom. She was now convinced that the disease was real. Shortly before the Garsts departed, she declared in her journal in a still, small voice.

**I am not well in lungs—TB.**

As summer drew on and her fear mounted, she became consumed by a passion for housekeeping. She drove the Africans into a frenzy of cleaning, painting, and repairing. She even had Nemeye abandon his normal tracking duties and devote his time to picking up the bits of litter that had accumulated on the porters' path as a result of the steadily increasing tourist traffic. Not even Redmond was exempt. Dian harried him mercilessly to bring his reports and records up-to-date.

During the first week of August she started sorting through the documents that had accumulated in camp over the past several years and then began systematically burning her private papers. She was ruthless about this. Only her journals and a scattering of other writings survive from the period between 1974 and the latter part of 1977. A sense of impending doom lay over her.

**Today I finish burning last boxes of letters nobody should see and tomorrow begin contents of suitcases and start on green box that contains much of my thesis and Peter's letters, which will all go into the fire.**

Among the few letters to escape the flames was one from Walter Baumgartel of the Traveler's Rest. Baumgartel had returned to Germany and had written a memoir about his years in the eastern

Virungas. He had taken some minor liberties with Dian's own story, and an indignant American friend sent her a copy. Instead of being annoyed, Dian wrote a glowing letter to Baumgartel, to which he replied:

"I have not the right words to express what I felt on receiving your long, warm-hearted letter. It is such a relief to know you are still my friend. Thank you, dear Dian . . . now Doctor Fossey! Congratulations on your Ph.D. You earned it the hard way, having collected your material over years under strenuous and risky circumstances. But I am not happy about your state of health, particularly about your lungs. You are still young and pretty tough, but there are limits to what a body can take. Living ten years like a mountain gorilla and at that high altitude is enough, I should say. . . . I also fear for your life—not that a gorilla might do you any harm, but that the herdsmen and poachers will try to get rid of you. It is amazing that they have tolerated you all these years."

On August 17, Dian entered the French hospital at Ruhengeri. Her friend, Dr. Pat Desseaux, x-rayed her hips and lungs. The hip pictures showed severe inflammation of the right joint. The chest photographs revealed a dense pattern of lung lesions that Desseaux feared were indicative of advanced tuberculosis. Deeply perturbed, he told Dian to return immediately to the United States and put herself into the hands of a specialist there.

The prospect of undergoing a major operation did not in itself deter Dian. Anything would have been better than having to endure the torment that was now her lot. She was, however, appalled at the prospect of having the nature of her disease become public knowledge, something she believed was sure to happen if she returned to the United States.

**Pat wants me to go home. Home? I don't have any unless it is here. My God, to end up in a place like the ward in Hope!**

Where Dr. Desseaux failed to persuade her, the Spanish surgeon, Lolly Prescada, succeeded.

August 26: **Lolly climbed this A.M. Had heard from Pat I was dying. She came up with three porters and tons of medicine, and then she gave me shit!**

In Dian's little living room, Lolly listened as her friend tried to explain her obduracy.

"I've likely had it for years. Maybe since I was a kid. I doubt there's much to do about it now. And there is no way I'm going into a TB san at home. God, they are awful places! Even some of the nurses act as if the patients are untouchables. You must know what I mean—you work with lepers!"

The slight, still-young Spanish doctor proposed an alternative; and she was persuasive. She reminded Dian that a mutual friend, Dr. Jean Gespar, a Belgian cancer specialist who had spent several months in Rwanda, was now back in Brussels.

"Jean will arrange everything for you there, Dian. He is so discreet and so very kind. I shall cable him at once. Nobody need know anything about it. But you *must* go. What would happen to the gorillas if you were to die?"

In the end, perhaps as much to please her friends as from any belief that good would come of it, Dian gave in. It was agreed that she would accept an expense-paid invitation to attend an anthropological conference in Germany in mid-September and would then go on to Brussels.

During the first part of September smoke continued to curl from her chimney as stacks of paper fed the flames. She avoided human contact even more than usual. As the months drew on she packed in desultory fashion but spent much of her time communing with her attendant animals—Cindy and Kima, a duiker named Prime, the giant rats, and, on better days, with her gorilla friends.

At nine-thirty on the morning of September 16 she descended the mountain for what she feared might be the last time.

A Peugeot half-ton "taxi" was waiting to carry her to Ruhengeri airport.

**Just as the taxi pulls into the airport the plane comes in from Kigali with Peter, Fina, and two kids, all dressed up. The pilot wants me to go on board, but I stay in the Peugeot and hide so I barely got a glimpse of Peter. Got on the plane only when they were gone—it smelled of Fina's perfume, or of his.**

At 5:00 A.M. on September 17 the Sabena flight from Kigali touched down at Brussels. For Dian it had been "a long, long, long trip with little sleep and lots of pain"—lots of time to dwell, too, on what was behind her and on what lay ahead. However, the arrival at Brussels, where she was to transfer to a Frankfurt flight, was not as grim as it might have been. While slumped in the transit lounge, Dian heard herself being paged. When she went to the gate she was greeted warmly by Jean Gespar and his wife, who, alerted by Lolly Prescada, had driven to the airport at that ungodly hour to reassure Dian that she would be in the hands of caring friends when she returned from Germany. Indeed they pleaded with her to cancel the onward flight and to go home with them to rest until her first appointments with the doctors. Dian refused. For her, it was virtually impossible to welsh on a commitment.

An hour later she flew on to Frankfurt, then to Hamburg, where the conference was being held. Here were no friendly faces to greet her, so she found her way to a "horrid room in a horrid hotel" and collapsed. She spent the following day mostly in bed, pain-racked and depressed.

On the morning of September 19 she rose and went out into the busy streets.

**I had the morning to kill and hated it. So I went to the Hermes shop across the street from the hotel and for the hell of it bought a $750 dress! It really is made for me. . . . Then went to register at the conference where everything went wrong. No one spoke English and I began to be very confused. . . . I tried to walk home but got lost and had to take a cab.**

The purchase of the dress did what perhaps nothing else could have done—it lit a little flame in her heart. Next morning she returned to the conference, still without having established any meaningful human contact. She sat alone through several scientific dissertations that she would probably have found inordinately boring even if they had not been in German. Near the end of that ponderous afternoon she delivered her own paper on gorilla behavior.

**I guess I gave my talk, but I didn't give a damn what I said. I was just happy to get the hell out of there.**

She decided that for the duration of her stay in Hamburg she wouldn't think about serious matters at all. She had her hair set, then wearing her new dress, went out to set the town on fire.

She encountered two young men, an English anthropologist and a German student. There followed one of the more memorable nights of her life. Her journal notes are succinct, but they give the flavor of what followed.

**Oh, what an evening. We bought a big balloon dog from a man on the street—just because it had such a beautiful tail! Had beer and schnapps in a dozen cafés, then went with them into a whorehouse just for fun, and the girls got mad and went after me . . . met a Great Dane and tried to take him with us into a bar and got chased out . . . one of the boys got pretty sick. . . . I was very funny dancing at a beer house . . . finally took one to his hotel, and the German student took me to mine . . . into a trance with him, he was so gentle.**

Dian was probably still in a trance of sorts when she left Hamburg the following morning.

**To Brussels—I think so. . . . Left hotel in very early hours, after almost two hours sleep, and for first time I am feeling no pain!**

She spent the succeeding five days under the aegis of the Gespars, who took her on a seemingly endless round of examinations and consultations and entertained her at small dinner parties. Her lifelong predilection for doctors and for older men sharpened her interest in Jean Gespar, an ebullient and effervescent fellow in his early fifties who radiated empathy and competence. He responded to her admiration, taking her on excursions through the city and into the nearby countryside to show her his favorite places and to drink wine at his favorite bars.

By September 27 medical specialists had decided that although both lungs were scarred by lesions, there was no indication of active tuberculosis or of cancer. More X rays were taken and it was finally concluded that Dian had splintered her seventh thoracic rib so badly (when she fell from her window while photographing the giant rats) that a number of bone splinters had been set adrift in the pleural cavity. The doctors proposed surgery . . .

**to sever the main nerve in that region and relieve the pain, and to find out how much more is broken up. When they told me this I cried.**

Dian cried from relief.

**That afternoon, Jean and his wife and I went down to the big square for tea, beer, and wine. I was wearing my gorgeous new Hermes dress, and we did have fun. It was a lovely afternoon and we spoofed Americans walking up and down the square.**

Next morning, after gaily buying yet another new dress, this time a silk creation from Jaegars, Dian entered the hospital in an almost ebullient mood. On the following day surgery was performed.

**Jean came in—was I glad to see him, but I was too weak to raise my hand to touch his . . . he was so kind. I slept most of the next day and again Jean came alone—I held his hand for the first time—he says such nice things. I could dream about him forever.**

On October 2, **I was lonely in A.M., then Jean came alone and we held hands and talked and talked and talked with no concept of time passing. Very special good-bye from him that left me glowing.**

She had become so engrossed with Jean Gespar, and he with her, that she seemed relatively uninterested in what had been done to her body. She was unconcerned when further X rays showed a buildup of fluids in her left lung and a lab report indicated that she had hepatitis. She was alive. She had a new love.

On October 2 her doctors told her she could leave the hospital in two days' time but must spend the next two weeks resting and recuperating. They also assured her that she would be able to return to Karisoke, though not for a month or more.

This was good news, but it posed a problem. She could not return immediately to Karisoke, but she was too poor to stay on in Brussels. The alternative was to take a cheap, standby flight to the United States, where she could visit friends while recovering and try to arrange for some badly needed funding for Karisoke.

The day before her departure, Jean brought her a special pair of Zeiss binoculars—for gorilla watching—and the two made tentative plans for the future. Dian suggested they might meet in Nairobi, whither Jean was bound in a few months' time on a research project.

On October 6, Dian flew to New York, then on to Washington. She was in a cocky and exuberant mood. Although the incision in her chest was by no means healed and she was still in considerable pain—**I was a basket case by the time I arrived**—she was not about to obey the injunctions of her Belgian doctors.

More urgent matters required her attention. Delivered from the valley of death, as she now believed herself to be, she was brimming with new plans for Karisoke, but in order to implement these she had to ensure support from her major sponsor, the National Geographic Society. To this end she spent her first week in the United States haunting the society's offices in Washington and reestablishing relationships with such key figures as Dr. Edward Snider, secretary of the Committee for Research and Exploration. Only after Snider had agreed to arrange a funding meeting early in November, and after a Washington doctor had warned her that rest was imperative for her recovery, did she leave Washington to seek the care and comfort of the Henry family in Louisville.

This was a healing time during which she saw old friends; revisited the Korsair Children's Hospital; had a picnic on the grounds of her old cottage; and stocked up on her favorite junk foods in the local supermarkets. On one of these shopping expeditions she found and bought a small, plush gorilla—which she named Jean.

Rested and invigorated, she flew on to San Francisco for the usual obligatory stay with the Prices. Her record of this visit is notable for its brevity. It was clearly an ordeal during which Dian had to fend off further attempts to persuade her to abandon Africa and return to a sane and normal way of life.

She fled to Chicago for a few day's postproduction work with Warren and Genny Garst on the *Wild Kingdom* film. While there, Dian interviewed three applicants for research work at Karisoke— David Watts, Bill Weber and Amy Vedder—all of whom would have a considerable impact on her future life.

By November 6 she was back in Washington to present herself before the august Research Committee of the National Geographic, presided over by the Olympian figures of the president, Dr. Melvin

M. Payne, and the vice-president, Dr. Gilbert M. Grosvenor. Dian found these two patriarchal gentlemen sympathetic. When she left Washington a few days later, she carried with her the assurance that the society would continue to support her work.

As she boarded her plane for the long and weary flight back to Rwanda, she was content. The gorillas awaited her, and in her hand-bag rode a furry little toy that was the token and assurance that the times ahead would not be devoid of human passion.

One of the first things Dian did on her return to camp was draw up a "plan for the future." It committed her to a concentrated effort to finish what she had now begun to refer to as The Book, a determination to shake Karisoke out of its current doldrums by bringing in new students, and a decision to put "X" out of her working life.

Warmly greeted by Ian Redmond and the staff, she was soon hard at work. There was also time for pleasure. One day near the end of November she took advantage of a rare burst of sunshine and accompanied by Rwelekana, climbed to Group 4.

**I had a wonderful contact, especially with Uncle Bert, who was an angel and led the whole group over to my side of a steep ravine I couldn't cross to get to them. Digit came over last, taking his time as if he couldn't have cared less. Then he finally came right to me and gently touched my hair. . . . I wish I could have given them all something in return.**

On the way back to camp Dian was startled by a Batwa bursting from cover at the edge of a meadow. He went racing across the open-ing, arrogantly brandishing a bow and arrows over his head. She took this as a flagrant challenge and set off in hot pursuit, but was in no shape to outrun an agile hunter. Gasping as much with anger as fa-tigue, she ordered Rwelekana to hasten back to camp and fetch Ian—with a gun.

Meantime, she backtracked the Batwa and soon found a blood-stained clearing where several men had slaughtered a duiker and had been butchering it when she happened near the spot. She realized that the Batwa had deliberately flaunted his presence in a successful ploy to draw her off.

By the time Ian and Rwelekana reached her, she was raging. "I want those bastards caught at any cost."

By then it was early evening and hardly the time to enter the darkening forest in pursuit of a gang of well-armed hunters. But Ian was game, and Rwelekana so cowed by Dian's fury that he preferred to face the poachers rather than his boss. The two loped off on the poachers' trail, leaving a fuming Dian to make her way back to camp.

As it turned out, the lateness of the hour worked to the advantage of the pursuers. Thinking themselves safe as darkness fell, the Batwas circled back to a crude hut they had built near Fifth Hill on the saddle between Visoke and Karisimbi. Here they lit a fire, loaded their hashish pipes, and began cooking some of the antelope meat. Being in a happy mood, they laughed a lot; and as the hashish took effect, some of them began to sing.

Darkness comes swiftly and suddenly in the tropics. So did Ian and Rwelekana as they homed in on the sound of voices and the glint of flames. Screaming like a veritable banshee, Ian leapt out of the dense bush into the center of the poachers' circle while Rwelekana thrashed noisily about in the underbrush attempting to sound like ten instead of one.

Abandoning most of their belongings, the pygmies dived head-long into the blackness of the surrounding forest with such celerity that neither Ian or Rwelekana managed to catch one. To discourage any thoughts of a counterattack, Ian fired a few pistol shots after them, though aiming high enough to miss.

Having smashed the hut, the victors loaded themselves with the meat of four duikers and a baby bushbuck, three spears, three bows with about thirty arrows, and two hashish pipes. Then they beat a hurried retreat, not without some apprehensive backward glances.

They reached home at about 9:00 P.M. to find a contrite Dian pacing back and forth by the camp cooking fire, fearful that she had sent them to their deaths. Her relief at seeing them was so great that she gave them both a tongue-lashing for "taking silly risks."

Most winter days at the tag end of the year were less exciting. As the weather worsened, it became a misery to go anywhere. Torrential rains and stinging hailstorms became the daily norm. Dian typed away at the book and did other paperwork, while Ian squinted down the barrel of his microscope at worms and yet more worms. In mid-December he sallied off the mountain to fetch a Christmas tree as the centerpiece for the "Wog's Christmas Party"; and thereafter Dian busied herself for days, wrapping innumerable presents for the men and their enormous families.

The party was held on December 23 and was attended by some fifty people ranging from suckling babes to an old crone who, much to everyone's merriment, claimed to be Basili's abandoned wife. Despite a persistent drizzle, the party went on far into the night, with dancing, miming, and singing around a roaring bonfire. Dancing with the best of them, Dian was in her element.

**Carried on like crazy. . . . I got a little X but no one noticed. Really had a good time . . . was very happy. . . . There have been**

some rough spots but this year on the whole was pretty good. . . .
I've got two or three new students coming in January, and if they
are any use, things should look up around here. . . . I'm working
well on my book. The poachers seem to have crawled back into
their holes and the gorillas are fine. Digit has become a "big
man" now, and you'd be proud of the way he helps Uncle Bert
look after the group. So I guess it's safe to say things look pretty
good for 1978.

Dian Fossey was looking into a clouded glass.

**15**

Sunday, January 1, 1978, broke warm and sunny. Dian wanted to visit the gorillas, but was preoccupied with the imminent arrival of a BBC film unit for the television series *Life on Earth*. The star of the show, David Attenborough, would be on hand, and Dian was anxious that Karisoke make a good impression.

Only Nemeye could be spared from sprucing up the camp. Dian sent him to locate Group 4, which had not been visited since December 28. Happy to avoid the fuss, he set off early, but the animals were missing from their usual haunts on the southwestern slopes of Mt. Visoke. After a search lasting several hours he finally came on their travel trail leading across the saddle toward Mt. Mikeno. At the same time he encountered an obstreperous herd of elephants and prudently turned back.

The weather next day remained so lovely that Dian could not stay in camp. Having dispatched Ian and Nemeye to locate Uncle Bert's errant family, she set out nominally to look for poachers' traps, but actually to revel in the welcome heat of a blazing sun and to enjoy the rich smells and sounds of the steaming forest.

Lithe and limber as a duiker, Nemeye led Ian at a brisk pace toward the saddle. A mile from camp they crossed the unmarked border into Zaire. An hour later the two men came across a wide swath of crushed and flattened vegetation sprayed with liquid dung, testifying to the headlong flight of a dozen or more gorillas. Telling Nemeye to stay put, Ian backtracked to see if he could find out what had frightened them. A hundred yards along the flight trail he entered a little glade and almost stumbled over the crushed body of a native dog.

A few paces beyond loomed a black and shapeless mound hazed with an aura of blowflies—the huge corpse of a gorilla, mutilated almost beyond recognition. The head was missing and the arms terminated in blood-encrusted stumps from which shattered slivers of bone protruded. Belly and chest had been deeply ripped and gashed. Everywhere the once-sleek black hair was matted and spiked with coagulated blood and fouled with body fluids.

Shortly before noon Dian was making her way back to camp after what had amounted to a languid stroll under the hagenia trees. With shirt unbuttoned and hair swinging loose, she was delighting in the warmth, in birdsong, and in the feeling that strength was returning to her body.

She had reached the camp meadow when she saw Ian jogging along the trail toward her, Nemeye following well behind. She paused and waited. As Ian came to her, he blurted out, "Oh, God, Dian! I hate to tell you this. Digit's been murdered."

**There are times when one cannot accept facts for fear of shattering one's being. As I listened to Ian's terrible words, all of Digit's life since my first meeting with him as a playful little ball of black fluff ten years earlier, poured through my mind. From that dreadful moment on, I came to live within an insulated part of myself.**

During the final two days of December, Group 4 had been chivied by six poachers and their dogs away from the relative safety of the Visoke slopes, onto the saddle and into Zaire where there would be small likelihood of anyone's interfering with what was intended. There, on December 31, the exhausted and terrified animals had been brought to bay.

True to his task as the rearguard defender of the family, Digit had charged to cover the retreat of the rest—to be met by a phalanx of men with upraised spears. During the melee that followed, Digit killed one of the dogs but was himself speared to death. The effect on Dian of Digit's killing was catastrophic. No previous experience, not even her own botched abortion, had ever dealt her so savage a blow or imposed worse mental anguish. And no other conceivable disaster could have fired her to such a pitch of passion as did this bloody butchery.

At first she managed to keep her grief and fury moderately in check. While several of the men were bringing Digit's body back to camp lashed to a bamboo carrying pole, Dian was writing letters. One was to Major General Juvenal Habyarimana, president of the Republic of Rwanda. Considering the circumstances, it is remarkable for its control:

"You have had the kindness to show interest in the gorillas of the Parc des Volcans. . . . I'm sure you remember the gorilla who took my notebook and pen in the National Geographic movie and then returned them to me very gently before rolling over and going to sleep at my side. That same gorilla, named Digit, is also pictured on a big poster for Rwandan tourism saying 'Come and see me in Rwanda.' . . . On December 31, Digit was speared to death by Rwandan poachers. They killed him, then cut off his head and hands and fled with them. . . . These killers are all of the Commune of Mukingo. . . . I would like to ask that they receive full punishment for their crimes. . . . I would have given my life to have saved Digit's life, but it is too late for that now."

Writing to Dr. Snider at the National Geographic she was less restrained. "Poachers have never before dared attack any of my working groups, and I am now wondering if this is the beginning of the end . . . for if they get away with this killing, how much longer are the others going to last? I feel . . . that probably most of the gorillas on the other mountains, barring Mikeno, have been killed off by now for heads and hands. . . . I can assure you I've done nothing illegal in retribution for Digit's death, but I am not allowing myself to think about how he must have suffered. . . . My plan of action is to publicize the affair as strongly and graphically as possible to every conservation society I can reach to ask them to apply pressure onto the Rwanda government to threaten to cut the vast amounts of money coming in to the Parc des Volcans for guards and a conservateur who do NOT work at protection of the park—that work is done by this camp—and to put pressure on the government to enforce extreme penalties for poachers—either prolonged imprisonment or death, and to allow guards to kill poachers within the park."

Now she was beginning to hit her stride. Through January third and into the early hours of the fourth, she and Ian drew up battle plans. She described these to Richard Wrangham in England.

"First, I'm paying cash to anyone who can yield information on the whereabouts of his killers. Second, I'm going to make a new set of posters saying 'Come and Visit Me in Rwanda' with Digit's body, headless and handless in as near as possible the same position as the original poster picture. I know it sounds ghoulish, but it might have some effect on the people who buy heads and hands. Third, we will make a thirty-minute documentary entitled *Digit in Life and Death*. Fourth, we will sell every conservation magazine I can reach the story of Digit with life and death pictures."

Ian Redmond proposed that they launch an international campaign, fueled by Digit's death, to raise money with which to hire, outfit, and train antipoacher patrols to take the battle to the enemy.

Dian agonized briefly over the idea, worried because it would be illegal for the Karisoke Research Center to wage such a war. Finally she concluded there was no other choice. Under her aegis these patrols could do what the park guards were paid for but failed to do. They could fight back on behalf of the gorillas, the duikers, and all the other creatures for which the park was supposedly a sanctuary.

Such was the origin of what would come to be known as the Digit Fund. With this beginning, Dian took her first deliberate step into the limbo reserved for those who, with the best of intentions, trespass against the sanctity of duly constituted authority. She embarked upon a course of action that would eventually cleave an unbridgeable abyss between her and much of the scientific community, of which she was a maverick member, as well as between her and those fund-raising conservation organizations that value respectability at any cost.

Ian spent the next morning filming Digit's corpse. Then he set off for Kigali to collect the BBC party that had just arrived from England. In his absence Dian was visited by the nervous and perspiring park conservateur and some of his armed guards, come on a mission of appeasement. She treated them with such white-hot contempt that they fled the camp.

Although she had no direct evidence as to who had killed her friend, her suspicions amounted to near certainty that the deed had been done by Batwa hunters led by her archantagonist, Munyarukiko. In her mounting frustration and fury she contemplated a retaliatory raid upon his village, which, had it occurred, might well have had disastrous consequences, for by then she was near the limits of her self-control.

The following morning, Dr. Desseaux and a woman lab technician toiled up the trail to camp, responding to an urgent note from Dian requesting an autopsy on what was left of Digit.

Just as we were about to start the autopsy, my woodman, working about fifty feet from my house, began yelling in Swahili, "Poachers! Poachers!" The houseman ran into the cabin scream-

163

ing the same. The woodman had seen a poacher with bow and arrows just on the fringe of the camp area.

No poachers have dared come near my camp for at least three years! But now they've nearly exterminated all of the antelope within the rest of the park and the only place where antelope now flourish is here. If they could get away with killing a gorilla in the study area, why not antelopes at camp?

I yelled to my camp staff to chase the poachers while I grabbed my gun (not legally registered) and ran after them, leaving the two Europeans, who just sat there stunned. I kept running and shooting up in the air to keep him from crossing the main open meadows above camp where he could have disappeared into the forested areas and never have been found. My men, including Vatiri, Nemeye, and Kanyaragana, could then squeeze him up against the slopes of Visoke, which is what they did, and captured him there along with a bloodstained bow and five arrows.

He was a baby-faced little Twa and one of Digit's killers, as he admitted. Both the front and back of his tattered yellow shirt were sprayed with fountains of Digit's dried blood. We were a good hour catching him. I'm really proud of my men, and I haven't run like that myself since I was ten years old!

We brought him back to camp and tied him up, and my Africans began to "question" him while we went on with poor Digit's autopsy. It was a gruesome business in that the spears and pangas had pierced so many of his organs—lung, heart, spleen, intestines, and stomach. When we finished, we three went inside my cabin for a bit of lunch that nobody felt like eating. While this was being prepared, my Africans were outside with the Twa examining him.

We hadn't been in five minutes when all hell broke loose and my men began screaming "poacher" again. I thought the original prisoner had escaped and dashed outside, but in actual fact three of his accomplices had crept up to look for him and were seen by my men. By this time the Europeans were almost basket cases. My Africans and I began another chase, but I had to give up, though they followed the tracks for another two hours without result.

I returned to camp to guard the Twa. By this time the Europeans seemed extraordinarily anxious to depart, so I brought the Twa inside and hogtied him to the beams for a lengthy period of questioning. I did nothing terribly illegal, though my men and I examined him very very very thoroughly. I can't say how difficult it was for me not to kill him when he admitted having been one of Digit's killers. I asked two of my Africans to spend the night sleeping on each side of him. I could not trust myself alone with that thing.

We "interviewed" him until quite late at night, and during the course of our interrogation we obtained the names of *all* Digit's killers. The chief ones were Munyarukiko, Gashabizi, Ntanyungu, Rubanda, and Runyaga, all from Mukingo commune.

What stunned me almost more than anything was the motive for Digit's death. A Hutu merchant had offered to pay the head poacher, Munyarukiko, the equivalent of twenty dollars to get the head and hands of a silverback. Digit was a young silverback. The Hutu hoped to find a tourist who would pay him much more for the souvenirs. This man has succeeded in obtaining a number of gorilla heads and hands previously to sell to tourists. The Twa prisoner told us he knew where Digit's head and hands were buried, near Munyarukiko's house under a clump of bamboo.

Next day I sent down a message to the *chef des brigades*, Paulin Nkubili, saying we'd caught one of Digit's killers and that I would *not* release him to the park guards, who have a way of "losing" their prisoners. Therefore on the seventh, Nkubili climbed to camp, accompanied by three commandos. They repeated the interrogation, but didn't learn anything my men and I hadn't already gathered.

Finally I allowed them to take the Twa down to a military security compound, where he is being held awaiting presidential decree as to the extent of his punishment. Nkubili seemed somewhat afraid of me. I can't imagine why.

I can say that to let the Twa go was one of the most difficult things I've ever done in my life. It was only in respect to Digit's memory that the bastard left here untouched.

It now appears that many of the Virunga gorillas have recently been killed off by poachers. The only abundant population remaining consists of my study groups. This could be the beginning of the end of the remaining two hundred or so mountain gorillas. Only if I can elicit enough interest and support can their total decimation be prevented.

Most of this was written well after the event, by which time Dian had somewhat recovered from the initial shock. However, as the first week following the discovery of Digit's corpse drew to its close, she was not only in a perilous mental state but was again verging on physical collapse. Nevertheless she insisted on leading three of her men on an antipoaching patrol to Nelele Hill, where the survivors of Digit's family had regrouped. That night she had a temperature of 104°, as well as other symptoms of pneumonia.

Her journal recorded that she was hardly able to get out of bed to greet the five BBC men when they climbed the mountain with Ian Redmond. They had arrived just too late to film the burial of Digit's corpse in the plot of ground near Dian's cabin reserved for her gorilla friends.

Sick as she was, Dian spent long hours in the company of Attenborough and his crew during the following week, assisting in the filming of "her" gorillas in the hope that the ensuing publicity might help to save them from a fate like Digit's.

On January 11 she was coughing blood but was still able to respond to a new provocation. Ian and the cine crew were filming Group 5 when they encountered an armed park guard escorting four Belgian tourists to see gorillas. A set-to ensued. The guard pushed Ian off the path and prevented the crew from further filming. That evening, by the hissing light of her pressure lantern, Dian ripped off a scathing letter to the conservateur, and an equally vitriolic one to Alain Monfort, the chief Belgian adviser to ORTPN, the Department of Tourism and National Parks. The letters were so inflammatory that even Dian herself suspected she might have overdone it.

Monfort, a senior member of the Belgian Aid to Rwanda project, was the man directly responsible for the scheme to exploit the mountain gorillas as a prime tourist attraction. He had already had a number of brushes with Dian about this touchy business, but had agreed to keep tourists away from the Karisoke study groups, of which Group 5 was one.

The smoldering conflict between Dian and this somewhat officious Belgian ten years her junior now burst into open flame. Monfort decided it was time to teach the "crazy American" a much-needed lesson.

Afraid to tackle her directly, he opted to strike at her through the BBC team. He intended to climb to camp and arrest the crew for being in the park without official permission, having first decoyed Dian off the mountain by demanding that she attend an ORTPN conference at park headquarters on January 14.

Apparently it never crossed his autocratic mind that she might not comply. At noon on the fourteenth he set off up the Karisoke trail, accompanied by six armed park guards. Partway up he was considerably discomfited to meet one of Dian's camp staff who told him that not only was Nyiramachabelli still at camp, she was in a distinctly foul mood. Fuming, but unwilling to face her in her lair, Monfort ignominiously climbed back down.

Attenborough and his people departed in midafternoon of the sixteenth—Dian's forty-sixth birthday. A string of porters carried their gear down the long trail to a truck waiting to ferry them to Ruhengeri airport. The old vehicle bounced off down the rough lava roadbed. As it came abreast of the park entrance, a guard tried to flag it down.

Thinking the man was looking for a lift, the driver kept on going, shouting that he was already overloaded. Those riding in the back were appalled to see the guard swing up his rifle and send a bullet whistling close over their heads. The driver floored the accelerator. A few minutes later, traveling at full speed, the truck rounded a curve to find a Land Rover parked squarely across the road. The driver jammed on his brakes and came to a squealing halt.

**That bloody useless Belgian had found out from the porters when the BBC team was leaving and laid an ambush for them. When the truck stopped, there was Monfort with armed guards and police, just like a posse in the movies!**

Monfort informed the thoroughly frightened truck driver that the *bazungas* he was carrying were under arrest, suspected of being mercenaries engaged in smuggling arms into Uganda. He then put two policemen aboard the truck and sent the bewildered and apprehensive Englishmen to the Ruhengeri military compound. Here they were ordered out of the vehicle and forced to open all of their cases and submit them to a thorough ransacking.

It is impossible to know how far Monfort might have pushed this exercise in intimidation.

**Fortunately someone tipped off the *chef des brigades*, Paulin Nkubili, a *real* Rwandan and head of the judiciary for the region. He went to the military camp and demanded to know what was going on. Very meek and mild, M. didn't mention mercenaries but just said the BBC crew had no papers to enter the park. The chef blasted him for treating visitors that way and told him he'd have to pay the cost of an air charter to Kigali if he made them miss their flight. So M. backed off, but not before he had kept them in the open under armed guard for several hours.**

Dian's problems with ORTPN were not yet at an end. On January 23 she received an urgent cable from Dr. Payne of the National Geographic:

WE ARE GREATLY DISTURBED BY OFFICIAL REPORT RE-
CENT INCIDENT INVOLVING YOURSELF AND POACHERS
STOP FULLY UNDERSTAND YOUR POSITION BUT URGE
UTMOST RESTRAINT IN VIEW YOUR STATUS AS ALIEN
RWANDA TOTALLY DEPENDENT UPON GOVERNMENT
GOODWILL FOR CONTINUATION YOUR RESEARCH.

This was followed by a worried letter from Frank Crigler, United States ambassador to Rwanda, telling Dian that the U.S. State Department had received a complaint about her "illegal actions in Rwanda." The source was not identified, but Dian believed she knew who it was. Her suspicions seemed to be confirmed by a letter she received from General Dismas Nsabimana, director of ORTPN:

> Mademoiselle,
>     We sincerely regret the acts of poaching that were di-rected against the gorilla DIGIT, on December 31, 1977.
>     You know that park guards have carried the dog, killed by the gorilla, in front of the people in order to try to identify its owner Munyarukiko, a presumed poacher, but he still managed to escape. L'ORTPN was outraged by the poaching of this gorilla, perhaps more than you, for this act constituted a grave injustice against the heritage of Rwanda.
>     However, that you should have invited an English tele-vision crew to make a film about the Park des Volcans, just at the moment when the gorilla had been killed, is not in the spirit of a true collaboration between the Office and yourself.
>     We know that you had readily allowed the filming of the dead gorilla in order to get the kind of publicity that would discredit Rwanda and Rwandan parks.
>     Because it apparently didn't concern you that no one from L'ORTPN authorized these photographers, we have concluded that you asked them immediately after the death of the gorilla, pretending that it was pure coincidence.

The repercussions of the BBC affair took weeks to die away, and the antagonism between Monfort and Dian worsened as he contin-ued to urge Rwandan tourist officials to ever greater exploitation of the park gorillas, and as Dian resisted what she saw as yet another potentially disastrous disruption of the lives of her already belea-guered friends.

Although January had brought personal tragedy to Dian, she remained capable of extraordinary thoughtfulness toward others in distress. During the latter part of 1977, she had come to know the staff of the American embassy and had become especially friendly with Ambassador Crigler's wife. Bettie Crigler frequently lamented her separation from her youngest son, fourteen-year-old Nacho, who was at boarding school in the United States and who, because the family could not afford it, had been unable to visit his parents over the Christmas holidays. Toward the end of January Bettie's distress had deepened into despondency, so Dian proceeded in her forthright way to do something about it.

Although, as always, she was short of funds, she wrote to Nacho's elder brother in the United States, enclosing a check with which to pay the younger lad's return airfare so that he could spend the Easter break in Kigali with his parents.

When the elder Criglers heard about this magnanimous gesture they were stunned, especially since they knew what Dian herself was enduring at the time.

"Dian," Bettie Crigler wrote, "I am so overcome by the generosity and kindness of your offer—I'm completely at a loss to know how to express our gratitude at having you for a friend. It's the most wonderful thing anyone ever offered to do for me in all my life. . . . Today is my birthday, but no present ever given to me means more than this. At the risk of sounding perhaps corny or trite—if I could have had a sister I would have been lucky to have had you."

To which Frank Crigler added, "You have got to be one of the craziest, loveliest people I've ever met. I was dumbfounded. It was particularly poignant because Bettie had been weeping over not knowing how Nacho would be spending his spring vacation. She was awfully upset and anxious . . . then the very next day came letters from both Nacho and Jeff, telling the whole story. She was so amazed and so very grateful to you for your incredible generosity, just as I was."

The Criglers may have been astounded, but the many other people who over the years had been recipients of similar acts of kindness from Dian would not have been surprised.

On January 28, Dian came down from the mountain for the first time since her return from the United States. "She looked like death warmed over," wrote one of her Kigali friends. "But she was in fighting trim."

Two more of Digit's killers had been captured, and one of Dian's reasons for coming to Kigali was to exert pressure on the

Rwandan authorities to ensure a fitting punishment. She pressed for life imprisonment; they were each sentenced to three to five years.

She also attended a meeting at the American embassy called at the behest of J. P. Harroy, a Belgian who had been governor of Rwanda prior to independence and who still claimed considerable influence in the country. Harroy was a strong supporter of the Belgian plan to exploit the gorillas for the benefit of tourism. Now he took it upon himself to reprimand Dian in front of her own ambassador.

He had the nerve to say that Digit had been killed because of me! If I had to live with that kind of accusation I would put a bullet through my head right now. He said the poachers wanted revenge because I've stopped their activities. He is a senile old man! If they had wanted revenge they would have done something long before now, and they would have burned up a cabin or something connected with the camp. Harroy also had the audacity to tell me that it was wrong for me to catch one of Digit's killers!

Steaming, she emerged from this confrontation to descend on two Rwandan officials whom she identified only as "the president's no. 2 and 3 men."

I really liked them. The president himself called to say he would really like to see me, but this week was badly timed because there were rumors of a coup. I am insisting on the death penalty for Munyarukiko at least, if he is ever caught. Both the no. 2 and the no. 3 men agreed that he should be killed—oddly, they prefer hanging to military execution.

She also demanded, and got, an interview with the director of ORTPN, General Dismas Nsabimana.

He is typical of an African Big Man, pompous and overbearing, but he ended up being very straight with me, although initially he was a bit terse because of the BBC team. One reason I think we finally hit it off is that he was very very enthusiastic over my "no-no" of last year when I burned some of the belongings of Munyarukiko's house. He said I should have burned down the whole house and was amazed to know I had had to pay six hundred dollars for my activities. He considered it an accomplishment, not a misdemeanor.

One can imagine an audible sigh of relief from the official in Kigali when Dian finally rounded up two new research students who had just arrived by air from the United States and shepherded them up the mountain.

The newcomers appeared rather unlikely candidates for life as it was lived at Karisoke. In her mid-twenties, Amy Vedder was "pretty as a china doll." She seemed much in love with her companion, Bill Weber. Both had spent time in the Peace Corps, but Dian's initial evaluation of them was not overly optimistic.

**I believe Bill is slightly helpless—for sure he will never take up a gun nor will I ask him to. I wish he was stronger stuff. I think the girl is the real engine in that bus, but there is a hard gleam in her eye.**

Dian's most pressing concern was to establish the antipoaching patrols she and Ian had envisaged. First she had to find the money to pay and outfit the men. The Digit Fund was to be the financial instrument; but being isolated on a mountain in equatorial Africa, there was no way Dian could organize the fund herself. In this extremity she was forced to turn to others for assistance.

Her choice in the United States was her legal adviser, Fulton Brylawski, in Washington, D.C. She wrote to him on January 17 about her difficulties:

"I am writing for help to everyone I can think of concerned with mountain gorillas. If they decide to give money to the Digit Fund, can I use you as a recipient? . . . I believe I could get five thousand dollars within the next months but I don't want to handle the money, and I don't want this to be just another vague conservation plan that spends half of its money on so-called overhead.

"I do not want Digit to have died in vain, thus the reason for this fund. Many, many other gorillas have suffered a death similar to his . . . he cannot be a lost cause; he must not be a lost cause. Digit typifies all that may happen to the rest of the mountain gorillas. It is a chance to save the entire subspecies, or turn our backs and let them all be killed off for their skulls. The Parc des Volcans was established by international treaty in 1929 for the protection of gorillas and other wildlife—I want to push this law and enforce it as it has never been enforced before."

Because of the slowness of the mails, Brylawski's acceptance did not reach Dian until early in March. Meantime, she had been concentrating her efforts on another front, from which she hoped for quick results. On January 16 she had sent her Cambridge friend Richard Wrangham a long description of Digit's death and of her plans to turn that act of butchery to the account of the surviving gorillas. She concluded with a plea for assistance in getting her message to the British public.

Wrangham did not disappoint her. Despite his own teaching commitments, he set about rousing the well-known English sympathy for animals in distress and recruiting assistance from conservation organizations. He acted with such dispatch that by the twenty-seventh he was able to report to Dian that public horror about Digit's death was already mounting in the United Kingdom. "I met with the Fauna Preservation Society two days ago . . . they are acting as quickly as possible and hope to have five hundred pounds sent to you by mid–next week. They are setting up a Digit Fund at once. However, they are calling it 'Mountain Gorilla Fund, U.K.' because, they advised, the name Digit Fund simply wouldn't raise the money."

To which Dian enthusiastically replied: "It was very fine of FPS to offer the five hundred pounds. That's great news as it means I can start the extra mobile patrols that even my own Africans wish to increase—they've been working their guts out."

The next news from Wrangham was less palatable. The International Union for the Conservation of Nature had concluded it could do nothing directly to assist her work. Instead, "there was considerable support for the idea of a group of gorillas being habituated for the use of tourists as the best means of encouraging Rwanda to protect the animals." The implication seemed to be that the chosen group should be one of Dian's. Wrangham also reported that Sandy Harcourt—now Dr. Harcourt—who had initially responded to Dian's and Wrangham's SOS with some alacrity, was supporting the tourism approach.

That was not all. Very apologetically Wrangham told her that the bulk of any monies accruing to FPS's Mountain Gorilla Fund would probably go to ORTPN, not to Karisoke. Dian's reaction was predictable.

"If any monies are sent directly to the Rwandan government or, as you have put it, 'routed through the national parks,' then I disavow it. It is not my responsibility to keep the Rwandan park guards in pombe. To support the current people directly in charge of the park is only to continue the decimation of the mountain gorillas. . . . I hope you know that the more cash the FPS gives to the Rwandan government, the more you are encouraging the killing of individuals in the study groups."

She was equally vehement about the suggestion that the best way to aid the gorillas was through tourism.

"I don't see how it is possible to talk about tourism when the park is overloaded with gorilla killers. You and others, Richard, sit on distant perches across the ocean and talk about tourism while ignoring Digit, poachers, and the killing of game within the park. His killers have to be apprehended. There is another bit of really bad news. Seven gorillas from one group in the northeast sector of the park have been killed since Digit died, but this is apparently not important to people who want to concern themselves about tourism."

Wrangham replied in a letter charged with gloom. He told Dian that even payments for her *own* articles on Digit's death had somehow gone into the Mountain Gorilla Fund, which now amounted to nearly three thousand pounds. Worse still, he reported that the FPS would not send any of this money either to Dian or to her Digit Fund in Washington.

"I will remind them," Wrangham wrote, "that the FPS fund was initiated as a holding fund for money coming from public subscription and that it was your initiative in the first place. . . . The FPS wrote to General Dismas [Nsabimana], head of ORTPN, asking what he would like done with the money. Dismas [Nsabimana] replied, copy to World Wildlife Fund, that he'd like to see the International Union for the Conservation of Nature/World Wildlife Fund education/tourism approach to primate preservation supported. So WWF is expecting it, and Dismas [Nsabimana] is expecting it . . . but it will all be very tragic if the public response to the Digit Fund doesn't get used properly."

To call the situation merely tragic was an understatement. Since Digit's death Dian had been investigating the gorilla trophy trade, with bleak results.

All but eight of the gorillas living on Karisimbi have been killed for heads and hands. In 1976 a doctor in Ruhengeri swears thirty-six heads were brought into town during that one year. Eight of these came from Mt. Sabyinyo, that I know. I guess that four of them came from Mt. Muhaburu, some from the northern slope of Visoke, and all remaining from Karisimbi. The Belgians have a huge Technical Aid Assistance program going for the Parc des Volcans, getting more money in one year than I get in four, but the park guards are now paid less than my men and they are lazier than ever. They will no longer even enter the forest.

I am out of funds but am continuing with my plans, in memory of Digit. Daily we keep up the patrols. Although I have four students I need many more Africans. . . . Today I sent two of the student kids out with Rwelekana after poachers whose dogs we could hear in the saddle, but they didn't move fast enough and only collected one spear, three hats, three hashish pipes, and one freshly killed duiker. One of the poachers was Munyarukiko, a second was Gashabizi, and they had five dogs with them. Today was a perfect example of our not getting the English Digit Fund money. If I was able to hire two or three more Africans, they'd have caught the lot. Every day that the conservation groups procrastinate means more and more animals are killed. Tomorrow it will be the same, and my personal savings can only go so far.

By the end of March Dian still had received none of the money raised in England on behalf of the gorillas. She wrote to Bettie Crigler with growing bitterness. "The Digit Fund in England has accumulated four thousand pounds as of Tuesday's mail. I've been told I *may* get five hundred pounds out of it. The rest will go to General Dismas for a new Toyota."

In early April, Richard Fitter, secretary of the Fauna Preservation Society, wrote Dian:

"I am sure you will agree it is essential for any project to have the full cooperation and blessing of the Rwandan wildlife and tourism authorities. . . . In order to coordinate fund raising and publicity of this we have persuaded Sandy Harcourt to work for FPS as project coordinator of the Mountain Gorilla Fund."

This was followed by a letter from Harcourt himself, in which he confirmed that he had become coordinator of a major FPS fund-raising project. He stated his opinion that if as much money was to be raised, a major emphasis would have to be made to encourage gorilla "tourism," and he asked Dian for any thoughts she might have on this. He also told her that he had arranged for a veterinary student, Paul Watkins, to come to Karisoke that summer, funded by the FPS, "as a way of getting a larger share of the £4,000 Mountain Gorilla Fund to you."

Figuratively grinding her teeth, Dian replied that she had no need of another student—and if she did, she would choose her own. "What I need is funding for the patrols," she told Harcourt. As for the question of tourism:

"Two guides were trained here by ourselves in 1975 for the Rwandan park branch, specifically for guiding tourists to the gorillas . . . of the Sabyinyo area. Many Land Rovers and Toyotas donated by the World Wildlife Fund were to be used in this program. Until two years ago tourists were being taken to the Sabyinyo gorillas on a regular basis. Then Alain Monfort took over and claimed the gorillas there were far too aggressive to expose tourists to and there were far too many 'man-killing' elephants constantly posing dangers to tourists. As a result, all tourists have been sent to our Group 5 for the past year. You can imagine what this is doing to the research program. How would you have felt if eighty percent of your contacts with Group 5 had been interrupted by a horde of loudmouthed Europeans? This is the case now despite the fact that Dismas, the Director of Tourism of Kigali, has stated that Group 5 be left alone as a research group. . . .

"I am only *one* person, but one person on the spot. I know what needs to be done for the protection of the gorillas—long, tiring, strenuous roving patrols over the entirety of the Virungas using Rwandans who can prove themselves. This is *actual* conservation, not *theoretical* conservation."

Harcourt's response offered scant comfort. He pointed out that the FPS rules, which stipulated that before more than £500 could be allocated to a project, the society would have to evaluate a proposal from the applicant—one, moreover, which had been approved by the proper authorities in the country concerned. He suggested she send an outline of her training scheme, drawn up jointly between herself and the Parc Conservateur of Dismas Nsabimana; if she did this, he said, there would be no reason why the society would not agree to send her an additional £1,000.

He also explained that, since the FPS had already told Nsabimana about the fund and how much was in it, it would be "tactless" not to contribute the £2,000 toward the construction of guard huts near the park, a project near to Nsabimana's heart.

"Therefore, Fauna Preservation plans, at the moment, to contribute about two thousand pounds from the fund toward construction of huts near the park for the guards, following a direct request from Mr. Nsabimana."

As far as Dian was concerned, this was meaningless double-talk. She was furious with Sandy Harcourt.

**He knows damn well that Dismas won't endorse any antipoaching proposal of mine. That "Big Man" has got other fish to fry with the help of the Mountain Gorilla Project and Digit's blood money. I never thought Sandy would turn out like this.**

She was now face-to-face with the cruel realization that not only would contributions made by British well-wishers in the memory of Digit be withheld from her, they were earmarked for projects she considered either nonessential or downright trivial.

**Digit has died in vain!**

She scrawled the bitter phrase in heavy letters across a page of her diary, and there are stains on the page that may have been left by tears of anger and frustration.

In May the five hundred pounds promised her by the FPS almost four months earlier finally reached Karisoke. It did not suffice to cover the patrol expenses she had already incurred since Digit's death, and she was once again forced to fall back on her own savings in the never-ending battle to keep the poachers at bay.

She may or may not have appreciated a mea culpa from Richard Wrangham received in early June.

"John Burton, Secretary of the FPS . . . assured me that the FPS would receive money as a holding station for you, but then later turned around and said that its disposal was entirely the responsibility of FPS. . . . It leaves a very bad taste in the mouth that they didn't state clearly what would happen to the money once in their hands."

She certainly did *not* appreciate a second letter from Sandy Harcourt.

"Paul Watkins has got his visa and I arranged at FPS yesterday that they would give him five hundred pounds from project funds for his costs in getting to and from Karisoke and for his maintenance while there."

Harcourt also informed Dian that he and FPS vice-president, Dr. Kai Curry-Lindahl, would visit Rwanda that summer "to discuss and report on everything concerned with conservation of the Parc des Volcans."

Somewhat later Dian wrote to Bettie Crigler: "I have received only five hundred pounds of the sum collected in England. The rest is to be used for huts for 'guards' and for air fare for 'conservationists' to fly to Rwanda to assure the safety of the gorillas. . . . An additional five hundred pounds was used—I call it Digit's blood money—by Sandy Harcourt to send a twenty-one-year-old English boy here after I had asked him not to come. . . . He was another 'four-day wonder.' Has now left for home, but knew he'd been used at the other end since he didn't want to come here all that badly. . . . I am more than a little angry. Surely Digit didn't die to pay the air fare of Englishmen."

Amy Vedder and Bill Weber, whom Dian soon came to refer to as the V-W couple, were soon followed to Karisoke by another American, a studious-looking youth by the name of David Watts, who was given to wearing granny spectacles and playing the violin. While Vedder and Watts immersed themselves in gorilla research for their doctoral degrees, Weber was gathering material on socio-ecology for his master's. Ian Redmond, now the veteran in camp, continued to spend most of his time on antipoaching work.

Ever since Digit's death, Dian had been apprehensive that another disaster would be visited on the gorillas. In early March she heard that a Rwandan poacher had been arrested while crossing into Zaire with a captive baby gorilla. According to rumor, the young animal had been confiscated by the Zairean authorities and was being kept at the headquarters of the Parc des Virungas, which abuts on the Parc des Volcans.

Dian alerted her intelligence network and by mid-March had confirmation of the rumor, together with the information that the young gorilla was very sick.

She decided to mount a rescue mission. On March 18, accompanied by the V-Ws, she drove to Gisenyi, close to the Zairean border, where she had many friends, both native and European.

By means that still remain somewhat murky she established contact with an assistant conservateur at the headquarters of the Parc des Virungas in Rumangabo—a young man whose real identity she protected behind the nom de plume of Faustin. Faustin managed to spirit Dian's party across the border and into the unpleasantly familiar "castle" where Dian had languished during the Tshombe rebellion. Here they were shown a four-year-old juvenile gorilla in a near-terminal state of illness and emaciation.

The park people had a problem. They had strong orders from Kinshasa, the capital of Zaire, a thousand miles to the east, to keep it alive at any costs, but when we got there it was nearly dead. I told the worried conservateur if he would let me have it, I would try to save its life and would give it back to them if I succeeded.

After a considerable period of deliberation, he concurred, but there was no mistaking his fear of Kinshasa. He told us the gorilla couldn't be moved until the capital was contacted by radio for authorization. It was too late to do it that day, so in the meantime we were given a guard's room where I asked Amy to stay with the baby for the night, to hold it and give it the love it so desperately needed. I didn't dare stay since I was illegally in Zaire and had to drive back across the border before dark.

I sneaked back again next morning with Faustin. We drove to Goma, where there was a radio that would reach the capital.

We were given one hour to complete the call. It took fifty minutes to reach the proper person to hear our request; but he said the president of Zaire would have to rule on it, and the reply might come late that afternoon via a series of local radio links. So we went back to park headquarters to wait.

Finally at 4:00 P.M. a garbled message came through giving the President's permission to take the baby back to camp. For reasons not disclosed, the conservateur wouldn't let the youngster be taken across the border by car, so Bill and Amy agreed to take it to Karisoke over the mountains, taking turns carrying it in a sling, accompanied by armed Zairean guards.

It was then after 5:00 P.M., when the Rwandan border closed until morning, so I had to sit in the car between the customs posts all night, scared that the Zairean military might come and arrest me. But at dawn I got across to Gisenyi and then back up the mountain where the baby had just arrived.

It is near death, anemic, totally dehydrated, emaciated, diarrheic, blood and mucus in the dung, filled with oozing sores, lice and fleas, with wire scars around its wrists, and—the one thing above all that will likely kill it—his left foot is only a swollen, gangrenous stump with the wire snare that caught it deeply embedded above where the foot should be. I never saw anything like this; the toes we only found today, bent under the foot and embedded in the layers of pus and skin flaps on the sole of what was once the foot.

We've had it five days now, giving it twenty-four-hour-a-day care. But yesterday I made the decision the foot has to come off, despite its general physical condition, or it will die for sure. Have asked a leper surgeon, highly qualified, to come to camp to perform this as soon as possible. At least we can get the snare off and, from there, see if it can be saved. I am becoming more and more depressed about the chances of any miracles keeping it going, and the surgery is the last resort. This, on top of Digit, is so frustrating it leaves nothing left to be believed in.

Lolly Prescada, the surgeon referred to, sent an apologetic note to the effect that she could not climb to Karisoke for a day or two, which Dian felt would be too late. This message arrived along with mail from England containing more bad news about the Digit Fund. Combined with other recent events, the effect of these several disappointments was to sink Dian into deep depression.

Pending her arrival, Lolly had recommended giving the sick gorilla a saline solution orally to counteract its dehydration. Late in the evening Dian went to the cabin shared by the V-Ws, in a spare room of which the animal was temporarily housed.

**I went down and made Bill and Amy angry. I did make them give the medicine and the baby choked. Later that night got note from Amy saying baby was dying. Artificial respiration. She did—he didn't. I tried and failed. Amy cried. Terrible. He said I wanted baby to die. I carried body back to my house. I stay awake all night.**

Next morning Dian took the corpse to Ruhengeri hospital. An autopsy confirmed a massive gangrene infection in the injured foot, and pneumonia of such long duration that both lungs had become little more than pus- and mucus-filled sacs. The doctors concluded that the animal had been doomed long before it reached Karisoke.

It is not clear whether Dian fully accepted this verdict. There is no doubt but that the episode would haunt her for years to come. There is also no question but that accusations to the effect that she had been the proximate cause of the baby's death would be used against her by ill-wishers with telling effect. The pain of Digit's death had been almost unbearable—it had now been agonizingly intensified by her failure to save the kidnapped infant.

In her extremity she could not immediately face returning to Karisoke, so she drove to Gisenyi, hoping to be able to unburden herself to Rosamond Carr. Unfortunately, Rosamond had just left home for a trip to the United States. Although by then it was late in the evening, Dian retraced the rough route to Ruhengeri, then turned southeastward to make the three-hour drive to Kigali.

Although she was aware that Bettie Crigler was also away in the United States, she nevertheless went to the embassy. Here she found a comforter in the ambassador, who gave her food and drink, listened patiently to her outpouring, and provided her with a room and bed. Her gratitude was heartfelt, if somewhat enigmatic.

**Everything came true, just as I knew it would.**

On April 7 the parents of Debi Hamburger, the young woman who had so wanted to work with Dian, came to Karisoke. They bore her ashes and a bronze memorial plaque. Although their arrival at this particular time might have been expected to produce an unbearable emotional overload on a woman already stressed to the breaking point, it had the opposite effect.

**Simba, the female who was carrying Digit's child, had her baby on the night of the sixth—a bit of badly needed good news. The baby's name is Mwelu, which in Swahili means Bright and**

179

Shining Light. This little bit of Digit was given this name that we had earlier chosen for the American girl, Debi Hamburger, who was due to come up here two years ago, until she was found to have cancer of the breast. Once that was operated on, she was determined to come up last year; but it was too late.

I'd previously told the students that the next baby born would be called Mwelu, in honor of Debi—a super girl. Simba timed her birth rather well so that on the eighth I was able to take the Hamburgers to see Group 4 and listen to Mwelu scream her head off because she was in a nettle patch. Debi's parents were so happy.

Next day, with Group 5, Debi's mom and pop were covered with gorillas and their happiness made me ever so happy too. But of course they had to leave. I will hire a plane before the end of the month to scatter Debi's ashes over the Virungas, as this is what she wanted.

Meanwhile, still brooding over the grim night of the baby gorilla's death, the V-W couple decided to go to Kigali and tell ambassador Crigler their version of what had happened. "Because he was a very good friend of hers, we thought somebody should know how low she was sinking . . . we weren't about to drag her through the mud or anything. We thought . . . that the best thing to do would be to try to convince her to leave the country."

Perhaps their stint in the Peace Corps had persuaded them that they were competent to judge a woman like Dian Fossey. Unfortunately, the story—which lost nothing in the telling—reached Monfort and the other Europeans, with the result that within a very brief span of time it gained common and contorted currency. Drunk and incompetent, Dian Fossey had been responsible for a gorilla's death! The woman who pretended to be the mountain gorillas' most dedicated champion was hardly better than the poachers she persecuted! Crigler himself wrote off the ugly gossip for what it was, but those who disliked Dian made the most of it.

For some time she was unaware of what was being said about her. She was, in fact, enjoying the only happy weeks the year would bring. On May 8 a dream she had been nurturing through eight long and lonely months became a reality. Dr. Jean Gespar arrived to spend the best part of a month with her at Karisoke.

The interlude with him was not entirely idyllic, but it was close enough. Jean was almost as fascinated by the lives of the gorillas as she was, and the couple spent endless daylight hours with Groups 4 and 5. In the evenings after dinner, which Dian cooked in the little

Dian with her gorilla friends sharing the intimacy of touch,
the closeness she spent long, lonely years developing.
(Peter G. Veit/DRK Photo)

Preserving and classifying skulls and skeletons of the rare mountain gorillas
was part of the work at Karisoke. The bones were cleaned and shipped to the U.S.
for further study. (Photo by BOB CAMPBELL)

Dian beginning the long hike up the porters' trail to Karisoke. In later years, as her emphysema grew worse, she needed an oxygen bottle to make it. (Photo by BOB CAMPBELL)

Dian with her beloved Digit. Such close-quarters observation came only after years of patient effort in habituating the gorillas to humans. (Fossey archive)

Dian's gorilla friend Digit, who became the symbol of her fight to preserve his species and in whose memory the Digit Fund, Inc., was established. (Dian Fossey, © 1981 National Geographic Society)

An unidentified poacher awaits delivery to the police. (Fossey archive)

Ian Redmond, more than any other student at Karisoke, took an active role in anti-poaching activities. He brought Dian the traumatic news of Digit's slaughter. (Fossey archive)

Anti-poacher patrols organized and financed by Dian led to the confiscation and destruction of thousands of snares and traps and the capture of hundreds of spears, bows, and other weapons. Dian estimated that two-thirds of gorilla deaths in her study area were caused by poaching. (Photo by BOB CAMPBELL)

Karisoke and Dian's cabin at dusk. This photo captures the atmosphere at the often cool and misty 12,000-foot Mt. Visoke. (Photo by BOB CAMPBELL/© 1971 National Geographic Society)

The mutilated corpse of Uncle Bert, slaughtered by poachers. (Fossey archive)

Lee is buried in the gorilla cemetery outside Dian's cabin at Karisoke. This young animal contracted gangrene after being caught in an antelope snare set by poachers. (Dian Fossey, © 1981 National Geographic Society)

The funeral service. Wayne McGuire is third from left; Rosamond Carr fifth from left. The eulogy was delivered by the Rev. Wallace of the Seventh Day Adventist Church. (Brenton Kelly/*Life* magazine)

Dian's body awaits interment next to Digit in the gorilla cemetery at Karisoke. (Brenton Kelly)

After the funeral: Dian's flower-strewn grave, marked by the wooden post bearing her photograph. Grave sites of gorillas who fell victim to poachers stretch into the background. (Brenton Kelly)

Peanuts has just touched Dian's hand. The photo captures a momentous event — the first photo record of physical contact between gorilla and researcher. Dian is using the technique of imitation of gorillas gestures that won her the confidence of the animals. (Photo by BOB CAMPBELL/© 1971 National Geographic Society)

kitchen of her cabin, they walked hand-in-hand on the meadow under the looming old volcanoes, listening to the eerie cries of the hyrax and the barking of the bushbucks.

On May 10, Ian Redmond returned to England, having prolonged his stay at Karisoke for three months in order to organize the antipoaching patrol program. He had done incomparably well; but the failure of the Fauna Preservation Society to provide the funds needed to hire and train new men meant that the burden of patrol work had fallen mostly on him and the camp trackers. This had resulted in increasing friction between Dian and the three research students, who were not particularly interested in fighting poaching, but did want the services of the trackers in order to further their own projects.

Ian's efforts had been effective in keeping poachers under control in the home territory, but beyond that they did as much as they pleased. On his last patrol, two days before leaving Karisoke, Ian had found and cut some forty snares in the saddle region where Digit had been killed—ominous evidence that the poachers were still ranging in force on the periphery of the study area.

Jean Gespar left Karisoke on May 26, having made it clear to Dian that he considered his visit to have been a pleasant interlude but that the affair was something he did not intend to pursue.

With his departure Dian was alone in a camp whose other white occupants were either neutral or hostile toward her. Surrounded by poachers against whose depredations she could do very little, she was deeply apprehensive about what might happen next.

After Digit's death the entire responsibility for the security of the Group 4 family settled back on Uncle Bert. Given a few more years, the two cocky young blackback males, Tiger and Beetsme, would have been able to give useful support to their leader, but they were not yet interested in adult duties. To make Uncle Bert's load even heavier, all three of his mature females were nurturing young. Macho had three-year-old Kweli; Simba was nursing Digit's daughter, three-month-old Mwelu. Flossie not only had her newly born baby, Frito, but was also rearing her four-year-old son, Titus, while at the same time keeping an eye on Cleo, her seven-year-old daughter. Another young female, eight-year-old Augustus, was the eleventh member of Uncle Bert's family.

On July 18 a large "fringe group" of gorillas from the northern slopes of Visoke intruded into Uncle Bert's home territory and a violent confrontation took place. Without Digit's support, and with so many females and younger animals to encumber him, Uncle Bert elected to yield ground. He withdrew along the saddle into Zaire. When David Watts caught up with the group at noon next day, he found the animals contentedly relaxing in their day nests in a sunlit glade not far from where Digit had been killed.

Poachers were again ranging freely through this region far removed from Karisoke, and when Watts reported the move to Dian, she was deeply alarmed. During the next few days she debated with herself whether or not to try to herd Group 4 back to the relatively secure slopes of Visoke. However, the turmoil this would have entailed for the gorillas made her hesitant. In the end, she concluded that so long as Watts could be with them during most of the daylight hours, they would be safe enough until they decided to return to Visoke of their own volition.

A week later, at ten-thirty on the morning of July 24, Dian was sitting at her typewriter when there came a hesitant knock on her door. Since everyone in camp had good reason to know how deeply she resented being interrupted when at work, she supposed the intruder to be a tourist, more and more of whom were invading Karisoke uninvited and unannounced. She ignored the knock. When it came again and yet again, she sprang up impatiently and flung the door wide.

David Watts stood before her, his face running with sweat.

One glance told Dian that another disaster had overtaken the gorillas.

"*Poachers!*" It was a statement, not a question.

Watts took hold of the doorjamb to steady himself.

"Uncle Bert's been shot—and his head cut off."

Half an hour later Nemeye was trotting swiftly down the mountain with a somewhat incoherent note from Dian to Bill Weber, who was "below," where he had taken to spending much of his time:

"Bill—David just came back from Group 4 with terrible news—please brace yourself for it. Uncle Bert has been killed by poachers.

"Poor David found no sign of the rest of the Group. I'm afraid they've all been killed without Uncle Bert. David's gone out with Vatiri, Rwelekana, and Mukera now to find them. Uncle Bert was probably killed this morning, meaning that Munyarukiko and the other poachers haven't yet gotten to Mukingo or wherever it is they hide out after a killing. I gave David the guns, but of first importance now is whether or not any of the group remain alive and if we can help them.

"I am asking you to come up with Nemeye to do a roving patrol to Karisimbi to attempt to capture Munyarukiko, Gashabizi, and Runyagu.

"I am not sure of what I can do that is most functionally right now except kill. . . . I would like to fly to Kigali and insist on a commando unit for the takeover of Mukingo and then use the soldiers for patrol. I must see President Habyarimana. No more placation or lack of action. Will need people to safeguard anything that possibly remains of Group 4.

"I don't know what I'm going to do."

Dian knew well enough what she was going to do about the gorilla killers, if she could catch them—but did not know what to do about herself, how to absorb and survive the grief that welled within.

Armed with pistols, Watts and the three Africans returned to the saddle. Uncle Bert's body lay where it had fallen with a bullet through the heart. The old silverback's head had been hacked off and was missing. His right side had been ripped open, doubtless for the gall bladder, but his hands were intact. The body was still warm, indicating that Watts must have surprised the poachers at their grisly work.

Cautiously, with pistols cocked, the four men searched the surrounding hagenia woods and nettle patches. They found no other members of Group 4, but a trail of crushed vegetation showed that the survivors had fled back toward Visoke's slopes. The search party tracked the gorillas for an hour, until halted by a tremendous outburst of shrieks and chest thumping some way ahead.

The fleeing survivors of Group 4 had collided with the fringe group that had dispossessed them a few days earlier. There was pandemonium as three alien silverbacks charged into the panic-stricken fugitives.

Group 4 might well have disintegrated then and there had it not been for David Watts, who led his party to the rescue. The sudden appearance of human beings sent the fringe group off in screaming flight, leaving the now frantically overwrought members of Group 4 to settle down as best they might. Afraid to press on and afraid to turn back, the frightened animals gathered around the nearest approximation of a leader remaining to them—ten-year-old Tiger.

Peering through the foliage, Watts anxiously counted the survivors. Only Uncle Bert and his premier mate, Macho, seemed to be missing. Macho's young son, Kweli, was present, but whining pitifully. When Watts got back to camp with his report, he and Dian concluded hopefully that Macho had been swept away with the fringe group.

It was now early afternoon. Bill Weber had not yet appeared and Dian would wait no longer.

**All the horror and shock of Digit's murder had returned and I felt I was going to go mad.**

Only violent action could bring relief. Raging, she went down the mountain to the office of Paulin Nkubili—"Uncle Billy," as she called him to herself—the one Rwandan official she felt she could count on to assist with what she had in mind.

Nkubili did not disappoint her. Outraged himself by what had happened, he agreed to stage a raid on Munyarukiko's village. He summoned a platoon of commandos from the military camp, and at dusk Dian and the well-armed force carried out an assault on the

Batwa village. It was a scene of great confusion, yells of fear and fleeing people—a scene comparable perhaps to what had ensued when Group 4's survivors had been assaulted by the fringe group.

The soldiers found and confiscated a quantity of spears, bows and arrows, and hashish pipes, but did not find Munyarukiko, who, it was later learned, had fled into Zaire. However, they *did* discover his boon companion, Gashabizi, huddling under a bed. Terrified by the presence of that avenging Valkyrie, the Lone Woman of the Forests, no less than by Nkubili and the commandos, the man confessed his complicity in Digit's death and to having taken part in this latest atrocity as well.

**Gashabizi's capture made that long night worthwhile. Maybe it was best that Munyarukiko wasn't there. I might have killed him myself. Uncle Billy asked if we had done enough, but I said "No!" He just looked at me and nodded.**

Next morning she accompanied the soldiers and Nkubili in a raid on the village where another notorious poacher, Sebahutu, lived with his seven wives and families.

**We caught him outside his compound as he tried to flee. Then we found his jacket, sodden with blood, and a blood-sticky spear and panga that one of his wives tried to hide from us.**

Sebahutu, it was revealed, had fired the shot that killed Uncle Bert.

Exhausted physically and emotionally, Dian slowly drove her Volkswagen combi back to the foot of the mountain. Before she could begin the long climb to camp, a porter intercepted her with a message from Amy Vedder:

"We hate to have to tell you this. Macho is dead. Vatiri found her body only a hundred feet from Uncle Bert's. Both the bodies are now back at camp. She was also shot. Her side was slashed open, but they did not take her head. . . ."

The passions this note aroused were so intense that nowhere, not in her journal nor in her letters, was Dian able to commit them to paper at the time, but in her book, written many years later, she tells us something of how she felt.

**Dazed, disbelieving, I drove back to Ruhengeri thinking of the day Macho had walked up to my side to gaze into my face with her wide, trusting eyes, and the tenderness she had always lavished on Kweli. How would the three-year-old survive without his mother or father?**

**Nkubili's reaction upon hearing of yet another killing was intense anger. He immediately planned a third patrol and ordered**

*all* suspected poachers brought in for questioning. The next day I drove my combi filled with armed soldiers and a police inspector to a village adjacent to the Parc des Volcans. I parked out of sight of the village and the soldiers poured from the car. Carrying their guns high over their heads and moving as if they were marines making a beach landing, the men quickly surrounded the market-place to confine several hundred people inside the square. . . . One Hutu man wouldn't stay in the hut where we told him to go. Urgently he pleaded in Kinyarwandan to stay out while I replied in Swahili for him to return inside, neither of us understanding what the other was saying. After several minutes, with as much dignity as he could muster, he walked about a dozen yards away, turned his back and tended to the call of nature to the delighted cheers of the nearby people. . . . From the market we hurried to a nearby, secreted little Twa village where three of the smallest Twas I've seen yet were captured. One was Gashabizi's brother-in-law and has a long poaching record. We then went to a distant settlement to capture Munyarububga, whom the military were particularly pleased to capture as he had escaped from them several times in the past. Munyarububga was an evil man whose situation was not helped by the fact that he'd been drinking heavily. I could feel his eyes boring into the back of my head as we drove back to the Ruhengeri prison . . . these were some of the five surprise raids made that day on villages around the park. The raids resulted in the capture of fourteen poachers, all of whom were detained in the Ruhengeri prison to await trial.*

Any sense of satisfaction Dian may have felt at the conclusion of these raids, and any belief she may have held that all the principal perpetrators of Uncle Bert's and Macho's slaughters would soon be apprehended, were of short duration.

After the final raid, as she was driving toward Ruhengeri accompanied by Gwehandagoza, six captured poachers, some soldiers and policemen, she overtook the park conservateur walking along the road. Dian offered him a lift to park headquarters. He climbed into the combi, where he burst into an incomprehensible tirade in Kinyarwandan.

After she had let him off, with no more thanks than an angry glare, she asked Gwehandagoza what he had been saying.

The conservateur had told the officials with me not to continue the pursuit of poachers because the killings had occurred in

*From *Gorillas in the Mist*.

186

Zaire and were not, he stressed, the concern of the Rwandans.

He also told them that he was then returning from Gisenyi where he had gone to take "protective" custody of a young gorilla. He was angry because something had gone wrong and the baby gorilla wasn't delivered to him, and he gave the impression I was involved in this.

Until late that night Dian mulled over her dark memories of 1969 when the young gorillas Pucker and Coco had been captured on the orders of an earlier conservateur. The black conviction was forming that the deaths of Uncle Bert and Macho had been part of a new zoo kidnap plot.

As soon as it was light next morning, she sent the trackers out to determine if Kweli was still with Group 4.

Although the animals were too disturbed to tolerate a close approach, binoculars revealed that Kweli was with the group—but seemed to have lost the use of his right arm.

Dian was able to piece together the story of what had happened to Group 4.

The latest news is tragic beyond belief. On July 24, Uncle Bert, the majestic silverback, was killed by a bullet in his heart. The sixteen/seventeen-year-old female, Macho, mother of three-year-old infant, Kweli, was shot and killed in the same raid by a bullet that went through her right arm, directly through her heart, smashing the ribs and exiting from her body. Her son, Kweli, was wounded through the right upper arm, probably by the same bullet, but he lives.

By tracking we found that the poachers had spent the night in the park in a distant area of Mt. Karisimbi before descending into the saddle area of Zaire where Group 4 had been for several days. They met the Group in what was evidently a planned event shortly after they'd arisen from the night nests, chased them for roughly ninety meters, and first killed Macho, who was probably carrying Kweli.

Trail evidence suggests Uncle Bert was fleeing in the lead of the Group as he had when Digit was killed, trying to lead them back to the safety of the mountain slopes. When Macho was shot, he turned back in an attempt to go to her assistance and was shot head-on.

Although the poachers took Uncle Bert's head, they were really after Kweli. They would probably have got him if Uncle Bert had not come back and given his life for him so he had time to escape with the others. The conservateur knew there would be killings the day *before* they occurred, and he went off to collect Kweli, not known to him by name of course, the morning of the killings.

Any remaining doubts Dian might have had that the double murder had been part of another attempted kidnapping were dissipated when a friend who worked as an adviser to the conservateur of the Zairean Parc des Virungas visited her soon afterward at Karisoke. He had seen a letter from the Rwandan conservateur to his opposite number in Zaire that expressly stated that two gorillas "from one of Fossey's groups" had been killed so that an infant could be captured. The Rwandan conservateur regretted that the attempt had failed!

This information drew a cry of bitter outrage from Dian to ambassador Crigler:

"Frank, it is very similar to the case of Coco and Pucker from Karisimbi, who were ordered for capture by the Cologne zoo, and the conservateur at that time killed off two groups to ensure that the babies were given. The entire affair begins and ends in the same way—someone had proposed money for a youngster's capture."

Worse was to follow. A few days later Dian learned from a knowledgeable friend in Kigali that the selection of one of *her* groups as the source of a young gorilla had been no accident.

Reports circulating in Kigali had reached the Zairean authorities to the effect that Dian had been *personally responsible* for the death of the infant gorilla that had been placed in her care in March.

"You see, Dian," it was explained to her, "either Zaire had a buyer for that baby, or what is more likely, it was intended as a present for the zoo of some important foreign government. If, as it appears, they believed you killed it, it would probably seem only right to them to replace it with one of 'yours.'"

Now, indeed, the iron was biting deep into her soul.

At this juncture she received a letter from Sandy Harcourt on the impressive new letterhead of the *Mountain Gorilla Project— Project Coordinator: Dr. A. Harcourt, Ph.D.* In it he again pressed her to cooperate with Rwandan park authorities in the best interests of the mountain gorillas.

Dian saw red.

**If they had only sent *me* the money people in England gave for the Digit Fund, I would have hired enough patrols to drive the poachers off the mountain months ago. Uncle Bert and Macho died because of that! Digit *did* die in vain!**

Just two days after Uncle Bert and Macho were killed and Kweli wounded, the promised delegation from the Fauna Preservation Society arrived in Rwanda to determine how best to protect the mountain gorillas. It consisted of Harcourt, Dr. Kai Curry-Lindahl, vice-president of the FPS, and Brian Jackman, a reporter from the London *Sunday Times*. In her book Dian described what ensued.

Their long-planned visit had been greatly anticipated by park officials who were to receive additional financial assistance, equipment, and supplies from the consortium of gorilla-preservation agencies that had sprung up following Digit's much-publicized killing. The conservationists were met at Kigali airport by the park director, his assistants, and a Belgian aide [Monfort]. Immediately, of course, they were informed of the latest gorilla slaughters. The reporter was able to telephone his story to London, datelined Kigali.

The [FPS] team spent two more days in Kigali before going on to Ruhengeri, where I encountered them while organizing legally conducted village searches for poachers. I was muddy, hungry, and more depressed than I had ever been at any point of the eleven-year research. . . . The reporter nimbly jumped out, tape recorder in hand, wanting an on-the-spot interview about the happenings of the past few days. My mind flashed back to the long deliberation between Ian Redmond and myself the night . . . following the killing of Digit. Since Digit's killing had proved so profitable to the Rwandan park officials, could there possibly be a connection between the first tragedy and the latest timely slaughters? . . .

The next day . . . the European conservation mission left Rwanda. From an article subsequently published in a British conservation journal, I read that the group had been extremely gratified at the timeliness of their visit, the financial assistance they had given and pledged to the Park des Volcans, and the wide attention that the reporter's news-breaking articles had received from a sympathetic public.*

This was a measured account written after a considerable lapse of time. In a letter shortly after the incident, Dian was much less circumspect. Although she expected to be labeled paranoid for her views, she was convinced that the timing of the second raid on Group 4 had been planned to coincide with the arrival of the FPS delegation, in order to further stimulate the flow of funds into the hands of park officials. Her opinions of the Mountain Gorilla Project were hardly polite. Suffice it to say that she did not show a high regard for the "conservation mission"; and her comments as to the value of the

*From *Gorillas in the Mist*.

189

methods proposed to protect the gorillas and to ensure their ongoing survival are worthy of a Marine sergeant. When there was need, Dian Fossey could command a vocabulary to make a strong man pale.

Once returned to Karisoke, Dian began putting her life together again as best she could. Macho and Uncle Bert were buried in the rapidly expanding graveyard close to her cabin, and she tried to bury with them, as much as possible, the agonies their deaths had inflicted on her.

The focus of her life had already been narrowed by the tragedies of Digit and the Zairean gorilla baby. With the loss of Uncle Bert and Macho, she began directing almost the whole of her energies to defending and preserving what remained of the Virunga gorilla population. Everything else seemed relatively unimportant. The accumulation of scientific data now seemed irrelevant to her. Even the writing of her book became a distraction.

On August 4 she wrote to her lawyer in Washington, Fulton Brylawski:

"With no silverback to lead them, the prospects of Group 4 are relatively nil as they have only ten-year-old Tiger and one older female, Flossie, who've been trying to lead and protect them. So far they've rejected the attempts of another group to split them up and yesterday were fleeing from the advances of what appeared to be a lone silverback. Such interactions are bound to cause serious injuries. I also feel poachers will strike again, knowing the group is now without a leader.

"The entire situation is almost too much to bear. Ever since Digit's death I've been continuing, on a small basis, regular poacher patrols, especially with Ian Redmond, who excelled at same. He had to go home in May but has just cabled that he will get back here some way soon so we can escalate the patrols. We must catch or kill Munyarukiko. It is as though all our efforts over the years have been wasted with these new deaths."

One of the canards circulated about Dian is that she was an alcoholic. In truth she enjoyed a drink, preferably Scotch. The testimony of people who knew her best, including her doctors, shows she was neither a drunk nor an alcoholic. She drank to excess upon occasion, but as an anodyne for acute physical distress or when severely depressed.

Following the deaths of Uncle Bert and Macho, she drank more heavily than usual. Suffering from chronic emphysema and sciatica, debilitated by the strain of living at a high altitude, plagued by a severe calcium deficiency, insomnia, and other ailments, she was also enduring the brutal loss of several of her closest animal friends and the prospect of the total dissolution of her favorite gorilla family. Also weighing heavily upon her was the belief that she had been and was being betrayed by some of the whites at Karisoke and that her cause was being perverted by ambitious and self-serving individuals and organizations in Rwanda and abroad. The wonder is that, in this extremity, she did not seek oblivion in alcohol.

What she sought instead was the solace and support of friends like Rosamond Carr; the Criglers; a French Canadian girl, Noella de Walque; Dr. Lolly Prescada and several other women living in Rwanda; together with a score or more of intimates abroad whom she could only reach by letter.

She could count few men among her close confidants, which is perhaps not surprising since most male primatologists thought of her as a competitor; male professionals in the conservation business saw her as an interloper; and male bureaucrats generally viewed her as a mischief-maker. She impinged too heavily on male preserves to be acceptable to many men other than in sexual terms. Nevertheless, and it was a measure of her enduring naïveté, she continued to place a remarkably uncritical degree of trust in any man who showed sympathy for her or who professed to an understanding of her problems.

One of the very few men to prove worthy of her trust was Ian Redmond.

He was in England working toward his master's degree when he heard of the new slaughter. No matter. He abandoned his own plans and began scratching for funds to get him back to camp.

In the meantime, relationships between the four whites at Karisoke were steadily deteriorating, with Dian and the V-W couple pitted against each other while David Watts attempted to remain aloof.

Dian took what comfort she could from the companionship of Kima and Cindy, and from the visits of the bushbucks, duikers, giant rats, and birds. She was reluctant to seek human companionship below, for fear the poachers would strike again if she abandoned her vigil on the mountain even for a day or two.

The poachers had doomed Group 4. Deprived of any males old enough and experienced enough to take over the leadership, that family was fast disintegrating. On August 15 the young blackback, Beetsme, killed Flossie's and Uncle Bert's two-month-old baby, Frito, doubtless because by so doing he could expect to bring Flossie back

191

into estrus and available for mating. However, a week after the infanticide, Flossie and her remaining daughter, Cleo, accompanied by the young female, Augustus, fled from Beetsme's advances to take refuge with Nunkie's Group.

Dian's anguish at the collapse of the family was intensified when she realized that Kweli, the intended victim of the kidnappers, was not recovering from his wound. Although Tiger tried to be mother and father to the orphan, protecting him from the increasingly aggressive Beetsme, and even sharing his night nest with the youngster, Kweli became ever more lethargic. Torn between the choice of leaving him to nature or trying to capture him for treatment, Dian reluctantly concluded that she could not intervene.

**Decided not to use dart gun, first because our old tranquilizer drugs are probably ineffective, second because would have to dart Tiger and probably Beetsme too, and even if this worked, the trauma would split the group into fragments.**

Dian's apprehension over possible reprisals by the poachers or their sponsors may not have been unfounded. On September 3, several unseen men circled Karisoke, keeping to the cover of the woods while screaming obscenities. Dian responded by firing a pistol into the forest. Three days later Gwehandagoza, who had been trying to obtain more evidence against the park conservateur, told Dian he believed someone was trying to poison him.

Two days after that the tracker Semitoa staggered back to camp suffering from a broken nose and concussion. He said he had been ambushed and forced to leap into one of the dangerous chasms that radiate from Visoke's peak. With her usual solicitude, Dian nursed him night and day.

**Codeine—ice packs; iodine and medicinal spray, blankets, etc.—moved him to bed in my cabin at 10:20; codeine at 2:00 A.M. after soup and coke—sweating now. By 3:00 P.M. next day temperature finally normal.**

Although she had been able to contribute only a small sum from her nearly exhausted resources toward Ian Redmond's airfare, friends in Kigali raised two hundred and fifty dollars and Ian himself did the rest. On September 10 he briskly climbed the familiar trail, returning to the scattering of green-clad cabins in Karisoke's meadow. Reinforcements had arrived.

Dian was overjoyed.

**Ian's return was super! Unlike the current students, who hadn't shown the slightest interest in patrols, Ian knew that work at this camp involves far more than daily recordings of one's own**

data and that there is an obligation to the security of the gorillas as well.

With his arrival active patrols were resumed at once. After 120 hours on 15 patrols, 362 traps had been found and cut down, and three trapped duikers released unharmed. Most of the traps and snares were in Zaire on the western side of Visoke and in the saddle terrain where the killings had taken place. But Rwandan and Zairean poachers were equally responsible for setting them.

Ian and one of the trackers succeeded in capturing a specially active trap setter and brought him back to camp. I think he would have sold his soul to escape the "sorcery" he was exposed to in my cabin, in the form of plastic Halloween skulls that rattle when shaken, rubber snakes and masks, whispers coming from all directions, and lastly, most virulent of all, American *sumu*—slimy jelly stuff you can buy at any local drugstore in America in a variety of colors. It sure was effective. This man talked for almost two hours about the poaching business, naming many of them and providing us with invaluable information.

The patrols did not always have things their own way. On October 15, Ian Redmond and Vatiri set off to do a sweep on the northwestern slopes of Visoke through the home territory of a gorilla family known as Group 13.

This is an area of narrow ridges preferred by poachers, who know the antelope don't have much alternative but to travel along these confined strips. Ian and Vatiri soon encountered three new, wire duiker traps and were breaking the poles and removing the snares when they heard the sound of chopping about fifty meters from them. They quickly ducked out of sight behind a small knoll, hoping to wait quietly until the trap setters had left before destroying these traps too.

After a while things became quiet and Ian was standing up to take a look around when three spearheads came bouncing into view, held vertically against the sky.

He immediately ducked, but as fate would have it, the poachers elected to climb onto the top of the knoll where they could look right down on the *bazunga* and Vatiri.

Ian was unarmed but immediately jumped to his feet and found himself eyeball to eyeball with the middleman of three spear-carrying poachers. Those on either side promptly fled, but the middleman dropped his panga, and using both hands on the spear shaft, tried to stab Ian to the heart before fleeing himself.

Ian remembered an old Bruce Lee film showing how to

thwart a spear thrust, so he flung up his left arm and dropped into a crouch. This protected his vulnerable parts, but the spear caught him in the wrist and made a long cut right to the bone.

It was typical of Ian that, after getting Vatiri to bind his arm, he insisted on searching for and destroying the other traps the men had set because they were in the Group 13 territory and a danger to the gorillas.

On their way home Ian whistled our SOS signal to the student working with Group 4, hoping to get some help, because he had lost a lot of blood. This student later said he heard the whistle but thought it was poachers so he hid.

Later that night Ian went into the Ruhengeri hospital where his wound was cleaned and sutured, and he was back patrolling within a week.

Although the wound appeared to heal, Ian did not recover normal use of his hand. Major nerves had been severed, and during succeeding weeks control of the hand deteriorated until he was reluctantly forced to return to England for specialist treatment.

Since little assistance was forthcoming, financial or otherwise, from the British-based conservation organizations that had taken unto themselves the mantle of the saviors of the mountain gorillas, Dian had to turn elsewhere for help. Her American lawyer, Brylawski, had agreed to handle any funds that might be raised in the United States. On August 7 she sent him a budget: the cost to train, equip, and pay six men to carry out antipoaching patrols for a year would be slightly less than ten thousand dollars—a piddling sum compared to the amounts the FPS and other conservation groups considered necessary.

Although Brylawski had agreed to be the repository for the money, the question remained, who was going to raise it? Dian had written to the Leakey Foundation, which was sympathetic but could not legally act as a public fund-raising agency. Her other major sponsor, the National Geographic Society, could not undertake this role either.

At this juncture, Ambassador Frank Crigler volunteered a plan of his own. The first Dian heard of it was on August 31, when she received a telegram from the embassy.

HAVE TAKEN LIBERTY USING YOUR NAME IN APPEAL-
ING TO U.S. CONSERVATION LEADERS TO PUT TO-
GETHER COMPREHENSIVE ASSISTANCE PACKAGE FOR
PARC DES VOLCANS MANAGEMENT AND GORILLA PRES-
ERVATION UNDER OVERALL MANAGEMENT OF COMPE-
TENT CONSERVATIONIST . . . HOPE YOU APPROVE.

Influenced by political considerations—he was, after all, his country's representative in Rwanda—Crigler had in mind to enlist the aid of organizations such as the World Wildlife Fund under the American banner, then raise really impressive sums of money that would be dispersed according to the wishes of the Rwandan government. Realizing that this would be a pill Dian would find hard to swallow, he sought to sugarcoat it:

"I know there are aspects of my campaign that will give you indigestion, but I'm really aiming at nothing more than what you and I have discussed so often: guard training, basic equipment, housing, and expertise to enable the Rwandans themselves to preserve the gorillas and their habitat."

Crigler asked the director of ORTPN to submit a budget for the protection of the remaining gorillas, and General Dismas Nsabimana was happy to oblige.

His estimate for one year included $100,000 for new roads to facilitate the movement of guards in all-terrain vehicles; $45,000 for new buildings; $42,000 as an initial sum only for new vehicles; $10,000 for educational activities; and various sundries, for a total of $208,000.

Crigler at least had the grace to ask Dian to comment on this proposal. Although it sent her blood pressure rocketing, she nevertheless returned a reasoned assessment.

**I told him that any part of the park that could *ever* be reached by road without multimillion dollars being spent was already accessible to ordinary combis and to the park pickup trucks. As for buildings, the twelve sheet-metal guard huts already built with U.S. funds around the boundaries for the guards have been so totally neglected that only three are still livable, but are seldom used by the guards in any case.**

"Sure," she wrote Crigler, "I can visualize Dismas's ultimate dream come true. All the mountains surrounded by a strip of tarmac. A big entrance gate and lots of facilities for the tourists. New vehicles for the park officials and the foreign advisers. But how is that going to serve to cut traps and capture the Munyarukikos of the park? What good is it to have all that down below when the park is being destroyed from within? I am sorry—am afraid I've hurt your feelings, which distresses me. I'd be a lot happier about it all if I knew that poachers were being caught and traps were being cut."

To Brylawski she lamented: "Even the ambassador seems to have swallowed the bait. Dismas's 'proposal' will now go to all the big conservation organizations, and they will take it up with bands playing. . . . The ORTPN officials will get what they want and nothing else will change. There is *not one cent* in that budget for training antipoacher patrols that will do the job. If it wasn't for the memory of Digit and Uncle Bert and Macho, I would just give up."

The pressure on her to do just that was mounting. On the same day he sent her the letter detailing his new plan, Crigler dispatched a personal note:

"This town is awash in unfriendly 'Fossey stories' right now, all about your heavy drinking, gun slinging, and manic-depression. Some of it, at least, is reaching the Rwandan authorities—one of the latter recently recited a rumor about how you inject urine into poachers' arms with a syringe.

"Dismas told me ten days ago he wanted to come see me to talk about the 'Fossey problem,' and I know there are people within ORTPN who are pressing to have you expelled. . . .

"There's a real danger that even well-meaning people could become convinced that Fossey is more of a liability than an asset to faunal preservation now. And those outraged letters to the Rwandan government from American conservationists, all of them citing your name, aren't helping matters either."

This last was a reference to people in the United States who, having heard about Digit and then about Uncle Bert and Macho, had been writing indignant letters to Kigali demanding that the gorillas be given meaningful protection.

In another note Crigler tried to drive the point home:

"It is clear that some people are worrying more and more about the implications of the deaths in Group 4, with people becoming increasingly convinced that they are the results of a vendetta aimed at you personally. I take every opportunity to stress that . . . the government must crack down on the persons behind this vendetta. But there is nevertheless a tendency for some to want to take the easier way out, i.e., to remove the target of the vendetta."

These were by no means the only malicious rumors being fomented about Dian. Her old friend Bob Campbell, with whom she still corresponded at erratic intervals, wrote from Nairobi, "I know that bad reports concerning yourself and your research project are on record in the State Department in Washington, and I have heard that you were obliged to leave the mountains shortly after Digit was killed."

Crigler not only had the first word in this attempt to bring Dian around to his way of thinking, he had the last one too. On September 22 he wrote, "Let me just say one final word and then I'm through: There is no hope for the eventual survival of the gorillas without the full and positive cooperation of the Rwandan government. And in my view the only way that cooperation will be obtained is to engage the world conservation community in a serious, comprehensive program of technical and material aid to the park. It may even go so far as tossing in some unneeded assets—roads, cabins, etc.—in order to get what you want."

Belatedly, Dian now realized that she could never rally effective support for the gorillas so long as she herself remained isolated at Karisoke. There were simply too many people and organizations out there standing ready to jump onto the bandwagon of gorilla conservation, then drive off in directions of their own choosing. She knew too that if things continued as they were, she would soon be unable to keep even the minimal Karisoke patrols going because her own resources were almost at an end. By definition, the National Geographic Society grants could only be used for research purposes, and there was no guarantee that even these would continue into the new year. When she heard that Crigler would soon be visiting the United States, she begged a favor of him.

"Could you please call Ed Snider at the National Geographic, as he is a person one can be absolutely straight with, and ask him if I have any chance at all of a grant next year. I am terrified the answer will be no because of the killings and what is being said about me."

Much as she dreaded leaving her camp when most of her current students were, or so she was convinced, indifferent to the long-term future of the gorillas and hostile to her concept of "active conservation," there was clearly no help for it. She could at least comfort herself that, in her absence, Ian Redmond would carry the shield for the gorillas. At the end of October she arranged to fly to the United States.

There was some good news. It was reported from Zaire that the formidable Munyarukiko had been poisoned, some said by order of a "Big Man" in Goma, and had died a lingering death. Although the report eventually turned out to be false, it brought balm to Dian's soul.

There was also bad news. On October 25 the bullet-crippled youngster Kweli came to the end of his long and painful struggle. He died a ghastly death from gangrene. In *Gorillas in the Mist*, Dian wrote:

**On the morning of his death he was found breathing shallowly in the night nest he shared with Tiger. . . . The gorillas returned to his side repeatedly throughout the day to comfort him . . . every animal seemed to want to help but could do nothing . . . each member of the group went to Kweli individually to stare solemnly in his face for several seconds before silently moving off to feed. It was as if the gorillas knew Kweli's life was nearly over.**

By evening the remnants of the group had moved far enough away to allow David Watts to approach the now-unconscious infant. He picked it up and carried it back to camp in his arms. Dian and Ian tried to revive it with mouth-to-mouth resuscitation and cardiac massage, but Kweli never regained consciousness. The young gorilla's emaciated body joined those of his parents in the graveyard near Dian's cabin.

Kweli's death brought Dian to the verge of collapse.

**I went to bed about 11:00 P.M. and woke at 1:00 A.M. ready to vomit and feeling that I had a plastic bag over my head. I couldn't get my breath. For the first time in my life I was terrified out of my senses. The nightmare that had awakened me was a combination of poachers, bullets, Uncle Bert torn apart by bullets, ditto with Macho and Kweli, the National Geographic board members asking me why *I had killed them*, and on it went.**

**I got up and lit the gas lamp and sat in bed; went into a sweat, then a chill, then threw up and felt I was going berserk. Finally, at about two-thirty I woke one of my men and asked him to get Ian.**

**Honestly, I don't know what I would have done if Ian hadn't been there. My pride wouldn't have allowed me to ask for the V-Ws or Watts. It was difficult enough to ask for Ian. I felt like an exorcist victim!**

**When poor Ian finally awakened and came up here, I made him talk about everything he'd done in England, the movies he'd seen, the books he'd read, etc., so that I could think of anything except the nightmare.**

**Well, Ian had only seen two science fiction movies! But they**

**sure helped, plus stories of his grandmother, sister, mom, etc. I was too terrified to go back to sleep and asked him to spend the night in the bed next to mine, which he kindly did.**

**When I finally fell asleep the dream started again, waking me up screaming; but hearing him snoring away just lulled me back to sleep, this time to dream of spaceships. I have never known this kind of fear before. I am somewhat ashamed of it but am interested in why it happened. Probably because we'd talked so long about what had occurred, that and the suggestions of others that I had been the cause of the killings must have been it. I think I might really have gone bonkers if Ian hadn't been around.**

On October 29, Dian left Karisoke for Kigali, there to spend a couple of days before departing for the United States. She visited ORTPN headquarters to get permission for Craig Sholley, a newly arrived American student, to work in the park. While there she learned that the director, Dismas Nsabimana, had authorized the transfer of two thousand pounds to Karisoke from the grants given to ORTPN by the FPS. She was overjoyed but puzzled.

**I never quite knew why he did that. But he personally did understand the poachers had to be stopped. When I heard he had been fired a few weeks later, I wondered if it was because he gave that money for our antipoacher patrolling.**

Dian left Kigali on a Sabena flight for Brussels after a bittersweet scene with the Criglers.

**Bettie cried, but though Frank kissed me good-bye, he wouldn't come to the airport and wouldn't even play the piano for me.**

It was clear that the special relationship between them had been ruptured.

She was forced to spend a miserable day in Brussels awaiting an ongoing flight. Nobody met her at the airport this time, and there was not even a message from Jean Gespar, from whom she had heard nothing since his visit to Karisoke.

Loneliness enshrouded her during the long flight across the Atlantic. Changing planes again in New York, she continued on to Charleston, South Carolina, where she was to participate in a symposium on conservation.

Also in attendance was Robinson McIlvaine, one-time American ambassador to Kenya, now executive vice-president of the African

Wildlife Leadership Foundation, a prestigious organization that numbered amongst its officers such luminaries as Kermit Roosevelt.

McIlvaine was an urbane, older man, well versed in diplomacy, whom Dian had known briefly in Nairobi. Delighted to meet him again and warmed by his interest in her, she was soon confiding her problems with the Digit Fund. Rob, or Bob, as she called him, was gratifyingly sympathetic. They arranged to meet again in Washington where he promised to help her organize the Digit Fund and to give her the benefit of his own experience in raising money for a cause.

Dian's ninety-five-year-old uncle, Albert Chapin, died in Fresno, California, while she was still in Charleston. Although Albert and Flossie Chapin had been less than pleased when Dian affectionately named two of her gorillas after them, she now learned that she had inherited fifty thousand dollars from Uncle Bert's estate. This was an enormous sum to a woman who had been impoverished all her life. However, she did not see it as money to be personally enjoyed.

**It is a big relief to know that even if the grants don't come through, now I can keep Karisoke going for three years at least.**

The legacy almost failed to materialize. Although Dian's mother had benefited from Uncle Bert's death, it was not to the degree Richard Price thought proper, so he decided that his wife and Dian should challenge the will in favor of an earlier one by which the two women stood to inherit the bulk of the estate. Dian had no wish to do this; indeed, Brylawski warned her not to get involved, but Price brought such pressure to bear that she eventually capitulated. Fortunately she recanted after returning to Karisoke. It was well she did. The will contained a clause to the effect that any beneficiary who dared to challenge it and lost would receive the sum of one dollar and not one cent more. Eventually Dian realized some forty thousand dollars.

On the fifth she arrived in Washington, there to spend the next twelve days striving to turn the nascent Digit Fund into a lusty champion of the gorillas.

The National Geographic Society proved supportive and not only gave the Digit Fund a special five-thousand-dollar grant to be used "in equipping and beefing up your patrols to hold down poaching," but the chairman of the committee, Dr. Melvin Payne, was also reassuring about her application for a 1979 operating grant for Karisoke. "You may be sure I will help to give it a fair wind when it comes before the committee," he told her.

The World Wildlife Fund (U.S.) also donated five thousand dollars, although not without considerable internal conflict. Increasingly malicious reports of Dian's "illegal" activities in Rwanda were now raising the hackles of reactionary scientific colleagues who acted as advisers to organizations such as WWF. One such venerable pundit tried to veto *any* assistance to Dian on the grounds that she would "use the money to equip a police state."

Even the National Geographic was affected by the spate of stories coming out of Kigali and Karisoke. Near the end of her stay in Washington, Dr. Payne had a long, fatherly chat with her, during which he strongly advised that she return to the United States to spend at least a year writing up her scientific studies and finishing her book. In truth this was less a suggestion than an ultimatum, since Dian was given to understand that if she did not follow this sage advice, she could expect no further grants from the society.

Dian believed that an organized conspiracy to get her out of Rwanda came into being during the autumn of 1978. Certain it is that a number of associates thought she was getting "bushed" and ought to be "persuaded" to leave Rwanda. These included Frank Crigler, several senior people at the National Geographic and the Leakey Foundation, and even, although she did not know it at the time, her new and ardent supporter, Robinson McIlvaine.

There were also those who wanted her out because she was causing problems for them. These included the U.S. State Department, the Belgian Aid organization in Rwanda, the executive officers of some prestigious conservation organizations, and last but by no means least, some of the researchers who worked or had worked at Karisoke.

Although Dian's intimate relationships with men were often disastrous, she could develop enduring friendships with professionals such as lawyers, doctors, accountants, and men of God, particularly if they were considerably older than herself. She had a singular need for the supportive and protective qualities such men could supply and that she had not enjoyed either from the one father she had never really known or the one who never really knew her.

Fulton Brylawski, senior partner of the legal firm of Brylawski and Cleary in Washington, D.C., had been recommended to Dian in the early 1970s by mutual friends at the National Geographic. By the spring of 1978, when she wrote asking for help in setting up the Digit Fund, he had proved himself a firm friend and doughty defender who could be relied upon in any eventuality.

While Dian had been losing the Digit Fund in England to the Fauna Preservation Society, Brylawski had established its existence in the United States on such an unshakable basis that it is still very much alive today. When Dian arrived in Washington in November, Brylawski presented her with Digit Fund Incorporated, a registered charitable body with full legal powers to receive and dispense funds and to perform all other necessary corporate functions. Brylawski refused to accept any payment for the work he and his firm did for the fund.

All that was still needed was a board of three trustees and an executive officer. Dr. Snider agreed to serve as a trustee; Brylawski also volunteered; and Dian, as president, became the third. There was still the problem of finding someone to run the show.

Dian believed she knew exactly the right person. Within hours of her arrival in Washington she had been in touch with McIlvaine. After having a long lunch with him on the sixteenth, she wrote a note to Brylawski:

"Had a meeting with Bob and he agrees to be the secretary-treasurer of the Digit Foundation. He prefers that title rather than executive director. I don't think the title is of much importance as long as we have someone of such tremendous integrity and value who is willing to help toward the mountain gorilla aid program.

"I do want to thank you for everything you've done in making the Digit Fund possible. As you said the other day—it is like giving birth to a baby, but quite frankly I feel more as if it is giving birth to three sets of twins of different fathers simultaneously."

McIlvaine had agreed to supervise the work of the fund—said work to consist mainly of raising money for it—until a permanent, salaried manager could be found.

In December 1978, he initiated a direct mail fund-raising campaign sponsored jointly by his own African Wildlife Leadership Foundation, the International Primate Protection League, and the Digit Fund Incorporated. Contributors were told to make their checks payable to the African Wildlife Foundation. According to McIlvaine, five hundred thousand solicitations were mailed. However, the Digit Fund Inc. received none of the proceeds.

Some years later McIlvaine wrote of his association with the Digit Fund, in this wise:

"When Dian Fossey was in the States in the fall of 1978, she asked me to take over management of the Digit Fund. . . . I told her that since I was the full-time operating head of another foundation, there was no way that I could do justice to the Digit Fund in my spare time. I also told her that, in my opinion, the situation in Rwanda required a formal, institutionalized approach in order to involve the government and, in particular, to coordinate activities already in train by World Wildlife International, the Fauna Preservation Society, and perhaps others. I also told her it was politically risky, as well as an interference with her research work, for her to be intimately involved in such an effort.

"I suggested that one solution . . . would be for the African Wildlife Leadership Foundation to take over, seek agreement of all interested conservation organizations on a unified program, and then negotiate an agreement with the government . . . the Digit Fund would eventually be dissolved and its remaining funds transferred to the AWLF-managed project. . . .

"In March 1980 I suggested . . . that perhaps it was time to dissolve Digit and transfer what funds were left to the AWLF project. For reasons of her own, Dr. Fossey decided that she did not want to dissolve Digit at that time. I subsequently concluded that I should resign as secretary-treasurer and did so."

Dr. Shirley McGreal, whose International Primate Protection League had lent its name to the fund-raising campaign solely as a means of assisting Dian's Digit Fund, was not pleased with the outcome. She has gone on record as saying that, while McIlvaine claimed he had an agreement with Dian to merge the Digit Fund into the AWLF, Dian herself denied this—"she said she would *never* have agreed to abolish her own Digit Fund!"

When asked to explain how she thought Dian might have been misled, McGreal replied, "I think the leverage they had on her was that she was very unhappy, insecure, traumatized, and genuinely upset about her gorillas dying. She never saw their deaths as an opportunity for herself. You know, it often happens that the only person who is grieving for dead friends may be exploited by a host of relatives who are looking for opportunities."

But this was still in the future.

Sure now that all was well with the Digit Fund, Dian traveled to Louisville in early November of 1978 for a comfortable visit with Mary White's older sister, Betty Schwartzel, whom she once described as "the mother I wish I'd had."

From there she flew to San Francisco and on to Atherton for a not-so-comfy visit with the Prices. Richard Price insisted she must challenge Uncle Bert's will. He wore her down.

**I am so sick of arguing with him and watching my mother's disintegration that I really don't care one way or the other what happens to the will as long as she can be left in peace.**

Dian escaped by telling the Prices she was booked to fly back to Rwanda via New York on December 10.

In truth, she was not due to leave New York until the fifteenth.

She spent the intervening days there mostly in the company of Robinson McIlvaine. Those were good days. Dian indulged herself with a shopping spree at Saks Fifth Avenue, where, amongst other things, she bought a $175 sweater as a present for Bob.

**We did the carriage ride and the discos—it was so great an evening! I doubt I will ever know another one like it! I danced all night in my new silk dress.**

Arriving in Kigali on the sixteenth, she taxied to the foot of Visoke and climbed the mountain trail in an hour and thirty minutes, as she noted with some pride, following Gwehandagoza and leading a long string of porters loaded with camping gear, clothing, boots, and other equipment bought in the United States for the antipoaching patrols with money from the Digit Fund.

It ought to have been a triumphant homecoming, and so it was as far as the blacks were concerned since Dian brought gifts for everyone. But Ian Redmond was the only white on hand to greet her. The V-W couple were not in evidence, nor was David Watts or the new student, Craig Sholley. In a way, Dian was just as pleased. She was not looking forward to another attempt to coexist with Amy Vedder and Bill Weber.

Ian had mixed news for her. During her absence he, Vatiri, and Rwelekana, occasionally assisted by Craig Sholley, had carried out many patrols but had found only a handful of traps. It seemed that the poachers had abandoned the research area, and Ian believed they would stay away as long as the patrols remained active.

The bad news was that gorilla skulls were "still being hawked around to Europeans" in Gisenyi, and at least one was from a recently killed animal. (When the poacher Sebahutu was captured by Dian's men in 1985, he confessed to the 1978 killing of a young adult female from Nunkie's Group, on Mt. Karisimbi, during another attempt to capture a baby gorilla. The skull of the dead female was sold to a dealer in Ruhengeri and was probably the one referred to here.) The park guards, both in Zaire and Rwanda, were still mostly notable by their absence, and poaching in the regions they were supposed to patrol was at a new high.

Ian also showed Dian a letter he had recently received from Sandy Harcourt in which Sandy complimented him on his antipoaching work, but pointed out that the FPS could not condone "illegal anti-poaching activities in another country's national park. . . . I hope," he wrote, "you can see the distinction between us personally admiring the work you are doing, but the FPS collectively having to disassociate itself from that work."

"Digit's got his fund—so to hell with them!" was Dian's response.

Ian's wounded hand was causing him so much distress that he now felt forced to return to England. On December 23 he drank a farewell Christmas toast with Nyiramachabelli, then set out on a most peculiar odyssey that found him stranded in Moscow on New Year's Eve when the Aeroflot flight to London he had booked out of Nairobi was diverted home.

At that he probably had a better time than did Dian. In the lonely hours of New Year's Eve she had to content herself with the company of Max—an electric dildo she had been given just before leaving New York.

Alas, Max's sojourn in the misty Virungas was to be short-lived, as a letter from Dian written on January 22, 1979, eloquently testifies:

Dear Rob,

I really received some bad news today. A close friend of mine, actually I only really got to know him well on three occasions, died after a lingering illness, as yet not properly diagnosed.

Perhaps you know him, as he was fairly well-known in conservation circuits; his name was Max Standby. Apparently he had some kind of electrical pacemaker, and when that started to fail, there was no place in Rwanda to get it fixed, so he just sweated it out until the end.

I do admire the pluck he showed, but I can't tell you how much I miss him. He was one of those you thought you could always rely on in time of need. I can't understand why all the good guys have to go first.

As ever,

Dian

As 1979 began, Dian found herself threatened with exile, which was paradoxical for she had long since exiled herself from her native land. She felt she was being nudged, inveigled, and pressured into leaving her adopted country—that amorphous patch of hoary old volcanoes, dripping hagenia forests, bamboo, and nettle scrub that was the shrinking world of the Mountain Kings.

During her visit to Washington she had become half convinced that those who were insisting she return home at least long enough to write up her scientific data might have a point. Yet somewhere in her subconscious she sensed the hidden intent. Awareness was slow in surfacing because she found it terribly difficult to believe that some of the people she trusted most were conspiring to divert permanently the vibrant current of her life in the Virungas into a sterile backwater on some American university campus.

The saga of Group 4, the family Dian had cherished for so long, was still echoing to the reverberations of the murderous assault upon it in July of 1978. In mid-December, while Dian was in the United States, the remnants of Group 4 had encountered Nunkie's Group, and in the ensuing conflict the infant, Mwelu—the Bright and Shining Light—Digit's only offspring, had been killed. Although news of this new death devastated Dian, she at least understood the reason for it.

Simba's infant, Mwelu, was killed by Nunkie when he and his group took Simba from Group 4. This was inevitable because the dominant male of any group is dedicated to keeping his own bloodline going and so tries to mate with a new female as soon as possible; but it hurt me so much as I so wanted Digit's only off-spring to live. Simba is much better off with Nunkie, if he keeps his group on Visoke, but he is now testing out Group 4's old range on the saddle. This is all right for the time being since there are no poachers operating within five kilometers of camp, but tomorrow could well bring disaster.

The lone silverback, Peanuts, has now taken over the three males that were all there was left of Group 4. They readily sought his company. Peanuts has at least eight years of maturity over the blackbacks Beetsme and Tiger and is capable of acting as the leader and protector of them and young Titus. But he has never had a female of his own and will probably seek interactions with other groups in search of females, and may not be able to handle the ensuing conflicts, thus subjecting the three young males to se-rious injury. Worst of all, he may take them to the "moon" as he tries to stake out a new territory for "his group." He is now close to Mt. Mikeno and is already five hours away from camp, but thank God, hasn't yet run into poachers or traps.

On January 15, Karisoke was visited by Benda-Lema, the new director of ORTPN, accompanied by a number of his senior officials, including the park conservateur with whom Dian had had so much difficulty. The meeting that followed was long, complex, and some-times incomprehensible since several languages were being spoken, but the upshot was that Dian felt she and Benda-Lema understood each other and would work together to the advantage of the gorillas and of the park.

Although she had done her best to be diplomatic, she had not been able to entirely suppress the Fossey in her. She told Crigler of her indiscretions in a letter written only hours after the delegation had departed in pelting rain down the muddy trail:

"One thing I said that made Benda-Lema furious—which was good by the way because I want him to be honest with me—was that Africans aren't allowed to approach my gorillas to proximity because of their skin color (I can just envisage you beating your head right now). Benda-Lema says, 'What is the park for? *Bazungas* only?' Then I tried slowly to explain about that one split second it might take a gorilla to distinguish between an African he knew and a poacher in-tent to kill him, which could cost him his life. I had Nemeye explain this to him too. I don't know if he grasped the idea or not. I also told him I had said the same thing to his president and his president un-derstood, therefore so should he.

"Might as well tell you one more thing you won't like. I took them all out to the graveyard when they were ready to leave, for pictures. They looked solemnly at the little wooden markers with the names of the gorillas on them, and it seemed to make some of them uncomfortable. Most of them are Catholics, and the idea of a graveyard for animals was pretty strange. The park conservateur was specially uncomfortable, and kind of groveling with his tail between his legs because Benda-Lema had been giving him a hard time. I asked him in Swahili, French, and English to move in a little closer as everyone else was posing. Finally I just said, in what I thought was a whisper, 'Banzubaze, get your ass in the picture!' Wow. Everyone just broke up."

Crigler was not amused. He replied on the nineteenth with his version of what had transpired at an earlier meeting of his own with Benda-Lema:

"He professed the very highest regard for you and your work, and he said he hoped your research would continue indefinitely at Karisoke. However, he said he was concerned that there were a growing number of people inside and outside the park who regarded themselves as 'enemies' due to the firmness of your efforts to protect the gorillas. . . . Benda-Lema observed that those who had personally felt the sting of your anger harbored extremely serious resentments toward you—to the point, he said, that he feared for your personal safety and even your life."

Since neither Benda-Lema nor his staff had said anything of the kind to Dian herself, she did not take this seriously. In her response she pointed out: "He was speaking of the Mukingo village of poachers. He went there recently. Naturally these people don't like me—no poacher in his right mind should. I wouldn't worry about the personal safety bit . . . talk to the Africans in the Kinigi farming commune at the base of the mountain. You won't find a single Fossey enemy there. These people have given me their trust and friendship throughout the years and continue to do so."

Dian was becoming irritated by the dire prophecies of doom and disaster emanating from the embassy. She may have suspected that it might be part of a design to scare her off the mountain and out of Rwanda. If so, it was the wrong tactic to use against Dian Fossey.

There were other indications that the noose was tightening. In early January a letter from the Leakey Foundation intimated that funding for Karisoke from that source would also be in jeopardy if she insisted on remaining in Rwanda. One of the elder trustees, Dr. H. Coolidge, was particularly adamant about this.

This was closely followed by an ominous letter from the National Geographic telling her that the ten-thousand-dollar maintenance grant she was counting on had been delayed for further consideration, and that her book was of such paramount importance that she should return to the United States at once in order to complete it.

Her response was a grim determination to complete the book within three months—at Karisoke. To this end she cut herself off from human intrusions even more than had been her wont. Working at her typewriter night and day, she became so reclusive that even old friends such as Rosamond Carr and Alyette de Munck hardly dared intrude upon her.

Her reaction was volcanic when, on February 6, a French television crew preceded by a long line of heavily laden porters unexpectedly straggled into camp. As Dian watched, unbelieving, their dapper leader, clad in spotless safari clothes, approached and arrogantly informed her that he and his eight men would be her guests for the next six weeks! This invasion had been sanctioned by Benda-Lema, so an almost apoplectic Dian was told. Further, the French told her they not only wanted the camp staff and gorilla study groups made available for filming, but expected her to act as research consultant too!

Drawn up to her full imposing height, eyes flashing and arms akimbo, Dian erupted.

"Holy hell! That's *all* you want? You don't want me to hang by one arm from a tree and beat my chest? I don't give a shit *who* said you could come here! Out of my sight!"

Retreating to her cabin, Dian fired off a furious salvo of letters to Benda-Lema and Crigler, then she cabled Melvin Payne at the National Geographic for help in evicting the interlopers. Since the society claimed exclusive rights to all film made at Karisoke, whether stills or movies, the French invasion was clearly a major transgression on those rights. Dian confidently anticipated Payne's support.

When she attempted to prevent the Karisoke research students from cooperating with the French, she found she had a mutiny on her hands. Far from being perturbed by this interruption of their studies, the V-W couple and Craig Sholley seemed delighted with the prospect of being filmed. Dian exploded yet again.

**There is big trouble now in this camp. The new director of tourism has allowed a French cine team to come here. They came out of the blue. I blew my lid but I was so, so alone. They have put up tents galore and are living in part in the cabin of the Vedder-Weber couple, who make Kelly and Harcourt look like angels!**

They have told me I will be removed from the country within thirty-six hours if I continue to oppose the French invasion. . . . She makes her *merde* with the gorillas and laughs about their reaction to it. Her husband looks like Jesus Christ Superstar, speaks perfect French, and sits around playing his guitar. Ambassador and Mrs. Crigler won't have them in their house because of the stories they have spread about me.

More was soon to come. On February 11 an army of 107 porters poured into camp bearing the parts and pieces of a huge hot-air balloon from which the French team hoped to take aerial shots of the Virungas and of the gorillas too!

Dian struck back in earnest. Within twelve hours most of her African staff had reported sick of a mysterious malady and had gone down the mountain, each to his own village to "recuperate." The French appealed to Benda-Lema for help. He went to Crigler. On the seventeenth the ambassador and his wife climbed to Karisoke, nominally to pay a social visit and go for a ride in the balloon, but primarily to get Dian off the mountain, if only temporarily, and thereby end the war with the French.

On the twentieth Dian noted in her journal: **Balloon going up.**

She could hardly have realized how prophetic that remark would be.

Crigler's bait to get Dian away from Karisoke proved irresistible. Robinson McIlvaine was arriving in Kigali on the twenty-first and would be staying with the Criglers. Putting her feud with the French on hold, Dian hastened to join him there. She spent the next two days enjoying herself, although there were some problems. Crigler and McIlvaine formed a duet, the burden of whose tune was that "for her own good" she must leave Karisoke by May at the very latest for "an extended stay" in the United States. In addition, the V-W couple met McIlvaine by arrangement and according to Dian, **Discussed how horrid I was, and begged the AWLF for funds for themselves.**

Never mind. Candlelit dinners at the embassy, the Sierra Club, and the Mille des Collines hotel lightened the clouds. When McIlvaine departed on the twenty-sixth, the parting was emotional.

"I very nearly cried, saying good-bye," he wrote Dian while he was still airborne between Kigali and Nairobi. "I understand the very real trauma you are suffering. Have faith, and never forget that you have many good friends ready to support you."

Maintaining such faith was easier said than done. When Dian returned to Karisoke next day, she was greeted by a cable from one of those good friends:

OVER LAST WEEKEND RECEIVED SERIOUSLY DIS-
TURBING REPORTS CONCERNING EVENTS YOUR CAMP
STOP SUCH ENCOUNTERS CREATE CONCERN AND EM-
BARRASSMENT NATIONAL GEOGRAPHIC STOP URGENT
REPEAT URGENT REPEAT URGENT PLACE YOURSELF IN
AMBASSADOR CRIGLER'S HANDS AND BE GUIDED TO-
TALLY BY HIS ADVICE AND COUNSEL STOP ESSENTIAL
YOU ATTACH GREATEST IMPORTANCE TO THIS RE-
QUEST FOR CONTINUANCE FUTURE GEOGRAPHIC RELA-
TIONS STOP DO THIS FOR ME AS PERSONAL FRIEND AS
WELL AS RESEARCH ASSOCIATE STOP

This was signed by Melvin Payne, President of the National
Geographic Society.

On this same day Crigler received a long telex from his top boss,
Secretary of State Cyrus Vance.

Under the heading DR. DIAN FOSSEY—KARISOKE'S FU-
TURE, Vance told Crigler that his departmental cables from Rwanda
about Fossey had been copied to the National Geographic, and then:

DR PAYNE CONFIRMED YOUR THINKING RIGHT IN LINE
WITH HIS ... DR PAYNE SHARED WITH US HIS LETTER
TO DR FOSSEY OF NOVEMBER 21, 1978 IN WHICH HE
CONFIRMS THEIR UNDERSTANDING THAT SHE WOULD
RETURN TO RWANDA ONLY FOR A SHORT PERIOD OF
TIME TO ORGANIZE THE MANAGEMENT OF THE CEN-
TER AND COLLECT HER NOTES SUBSEQUENTLY SHE
WAS TO RETURN TO THE U.S. FOR AT LEAST A YEAR OR
SO ... NG PROVIDED FOSSEY WITH $5,000 FOR HER RE-
TURN TO RWANDA TO SET THINGS STRAIGHT AND HAS
EARMARKED BUT NOT RELEASED $10,000 FOR THE OPER-
ATION OF THE CENTER IN HER ABSENCE ... DR PAYNE
AND NG RESEARCH COMMITTEE BELIEVE IT NECESSARY
THAT DR FOSSEY LEAVE RWANDA FOR A WHILE. THIS
WOULD HELP DEFUSE LOCAL TENSIONS ... DR PAYNE IS
ENCOURAGED BY AWLF ANTIPOACHING PROPOSAL ...
DR PAYNE PROMISED TO REVIEW YOUR PROPOSAL RE-
GARDING REGULARIZATION OF KARISOKE CENTER ...

Despite the fact that the five thousand dollars to which Vance
referred had been given to Dian *specifically* for antipoacher work,
Crigler's proposals for "regularizing" Karisoke recommended that

the Center be completely removed from Fossey's control and placed under the umbrella of the mountain gorilla consortium being organized by his professional peer and close friend, Robinson McIlvaine. Crigler's support was much appreciated, as McIlvaine testified in a report to his trustees a few months later:

"In Kigali I stayed with our ambassador, Frank Crigler, who has been heavily involved in all this [the formation of the consortium under the aegis of the AWLF] since the beginning, and he was very, very helpful in many ways."

There is no evidence that Dian constituted any real political problem for the United States in its relations with the government of Rwanda. The State Department's interest in getting her out seems to have been due, as much as anything, to Cyrus Vance's desire to do a favor for his old friend Dr. Payne.

The early months of 1979 had produced revealing evidence of the scope of McIlvaine's grand design.

In January Dian learned that half of a ten-thousand-dollar grant promised to her personally by philanthropist Gordon Hanes to assist in maintaining Karisoke had somehow found its way out of her reach into the AWLF/Digit Fund or, as it was now being called, Project Survival/AWLF.

Then, in mid-February, she received a disquieting letter from Geza Teleki, another leading woman primatologist, with close ties to the International Primate Protection League:

"The International Student Association spent a week soliciting funds on the streets of Washington for the Digit Fund . . . however, contact with Mr. McIlvaine has resulted in my advising the head of the ISA to hold the funds, pending word from you. McIlvaine has clearly indicated that he is collecting funds not for the Digit Fund, but for the African Wildlife Leadership Foundation. . . . The students launched the campaign on the premise that all funds they collected would go directly to you. . . . I am reluctant to assure contributors they are supporting you when, in fact, they might be supporting whatever McIlvaine has in mind."

Dian's reply reveals her own growing doubts.

"This is the second time I've heard what you've written. The first was from Jim Doherty, executive editor of *International Wildlife Magazine,* but I have known McIlvaine for many years and do trust him implicitly . . . yet in no piece of his correspondence have I seen the name Digit Fund applied, and I can tell you, that hurts."

When McIlvaine wined and dined her in Kigali, he dispelled some of her apprehensions. New ones sprang to life, however, when a confidential memo from him to his head office came into her hands. She interpreted its contents as evidence that McIlvaine was supporting Sandy Harcourt and the Mountain Gorilla Project against her. She unleashed a blast at McIlvaine, which he tried to counter by claiming it was all a mistake resulting from his having composed the memo while on an airplane.

A few weeks later he took off the silken gloves. "We must now go forward," he wrote Dian, "on the nitty gritty of money matters." This meant, he explained, working out a transfer of Digit Fund Inc. money to the AWLF-Digit Fund.

McIlvaine then proceeded to instruct her to write a letter to her fellow trustees, Snider and Brylawski, stating that inasmuch as the AWLF had set up its own Digit Fund to "accomplish the original aims of Digit Fund Inc.," she now recommended that Digit Fund Inc. be dissolved and that the remaining moneys in its fund be transferred to the AWLF-Digit Fund. McIlvaine also told her he was sending a copy of this letter to Frank Crigler "because he is, in any case, intimately involved."

Despite an extreme reluctance to admit to herself that Crigler might be hand-in-hand with those who wanted her out of Rwanda, Dian could not indefinitely evade the reality. A sympathetic embassy employee sent her a copy of a letter that had been given to Crigler for forwarding in the diplomatic pouch. It was from Bill Weber, addressed to the Research Committee of the National Geographic Society. In it Weber accused Dian of mismanaging the Karisoke Research Center and suggested that she was *herself* responsible for the deaths of Digit, Uncle Bert, Macho, and Kweli because her persecution of the poachers had drawn their retaliation.

The scales were falling from her eyes whether she wished it so or not. She reacted by making up her mind that *nobody* was going to *force* her to depart. If she left at all, it would be in her own good time. Meanwhile she dug in her heels.

On February 27 she wrote to Bettie and Frank Crigler, stating her intentions, then justifying them, as if in full awareness that her letter would reach other eyes:

"I did a great deal of mulling and my conclusion is that I will insist on staying here through August. This will give me time to finish my book, finish a National Geographic article I'm committed to, and do the photography I desperately need to do on certain behavioral aspects.

"It will also give me time to break in new students and hopefully find someone to run camp during my absence. . . . I could not possibly leave while the V-W couple were still around.

"It would also be financially difficult for me to support myself in the States when universities are not operating and public lecture schedules are reduced. I will not sponge off other people, nor is there any way I can live at 'home' in California. . . .

"I found the cable from Payne awaiting me when I got back to camp. That simply wasn't the ideal type of reception I needed. . . . You have most likely spooked him with your cables/letters—I really don't know. . . . Also, I don't care too much for threats."

Dian was now missing Ian Redmond's presence more than ever. At Christmas he had sent her a present—"a plaque, old-fashioned, imitation bronze, stating 'TAKE NOTICE THAT AS FROM THIS DATE POACHERS SHALL BE SHOT ON FIRST SIGHT AND IF PRACTICABLE QUESTIONED AFTERWARDS, NOV. 1968.'"

"This gave me," she wrote to him, "one of the few good laughs I've had in months." But her hopes that Ian might soon return were dashed by a letter in which he explained that his hand was still in bad shape. Specialists had told him the ulnar and median nerves in the wrist had been completely severed, with the result that the musculature of the hand was wasting away. He was hoping for a remedial operation in April, but had not forgotten Karisoke. "My thoughts always stray back to you and the incredible forest and the gorillas—I frequently dream about camp—sometimes frightening dreams of cars and roads and shops where the meadows used to be—too horrible for words.

"Dian, if things are really bad with poachers, etc., and you think my presence would make a difference, *please write* and say so and I'll come after August 18. I feel that my first loyalties and my heart lie with Karisoke and the gorillas. Please be strong and try to be just a little optimistic—there must be an end to the killing soon."

Dian could be strong, but retaining even a little optimism was another matter.

On Saturday, March 3, David Watts came back into camp with Nemeye after having gone far out onto the saddle for a contact with Nunkie's Group. David was wearing that face which spells doom. He said either young Lee or young N'Gee (he couldn't tell which) was caught in a trap by one leg and surrounded by all the rest of the group, who were in a terrific state. He didn't know what to do so he ran most of the way back to camp.

I sent him out again right away with three of my men, armed with two pistols, in case the poachers returned and slaughtered the whole group in order to capture the youngster. I set out fifteen minutes later with camp gear in case we had to stand guard all night, but took two hours to reach the spot.

When I got there I saw it was the four-year-old female Lee, but we couldn't get to her to cut the wire because Nunkie and the others were just having fits and would have charged for sure. I decided to see if a few shots fired into the air would scare them off long enough to release the snare from Lee's left foot. Three shots made everyone flee—including Lee, who broke free with the wire still attached to her foot.

The group fled in the general direction of Visoke, away from the line of traps.

We decided to spend the night in the forest as the group was still in a danger area, and Sunday is the poachers' big hunting day when they come up to look at their traps.

Today (Monday) David found the group back on Visoke, fairly high up. Lee isn't using her left leg at all, but David can't determine if the wire is deeply embedded or not. I will send the electric stun gun I've never used down to Ruhengeri for a thirty-six-hour charge, but can't expect it back before Friday. Unfortunately Lee is staying close to her father, Nunkie, who will charge, so I greatly fear both will have to be stunned; then what the rest of the group will do I can't even imagine. . . . The worst thing about this gun is that you have to be within fifteen feet, the length of the wire; secondly, it only shoots twice before it has to be recharged. The great thing is that it is guaranteed not to be lethal, something that can't be said for a dart gun.

I don't see, in good conscience, how we can sit back and watch Lee's foot rot off, which is the near certain alternative, when we have the means to try to do something about it, but some of the students don't agree that we should interfere.

Watts was not one of those who thought nature should be allowed to take its course. However, he strongly recommended that the stun gun be tested before anyone faced a furious Nunkie with it. They tried it on one of the tame duikers near Dian's cabin. The little antelope jumped in mild surprise when the metal contact struck it and a "fifty-thousand-volt" shock was administered; then it ambled nonchalantly away, pulling the electric cord behind it. Clearly this device was no match for Lee, let alone Nunkie.

On March 18, Dian wrote to Dr. Snider: "As the wire becomes more deeply embedded the foot is becoming increasingly swollen and is oozing pus. Lee will either lose her foot or die of systemic infection. Since the failure of the stun gun I have been trying to contact the game warden at A'Kagera Park. He has had years of experience with a dart drug gun. . . . In my opinion only ten days remain before Lee enters her crucial state. The incident has created controversy in camp—the Peace Corps trio saying she should be allowed to die before interfering with the group; David Watts and myself saying that, if able, darting should be done to remove the wire. I *deplore* any artificial interference with the gorillas, but I remain convinced that the seriousness of this case warrants the extreme measure of darting . . . the accident might never have happened had there been a student at camp willing to continue with trap cutting, a student such as Ian Redmond. . . . Current students are either afraid or not interested in this type of work."

Dian concluded with an appeal to the arbiters of her destiny at National Geographic:

"We now have invested twelve years in the few remaining Mountain Gorillas. I would like to secure that investment, for the sake of the animals, for the sake of the research center. I think it is difficult for someone on the other side of the world to understand all of the problems involved; it is also unfair to draw absolute conclusions without fully understanding all the innuendos, political and otherwise, now involved in maintaining the center for the future of the gorillas. It is only their future, if they have one, that should be considered."

The young gorilla, Lee, had no future.

Unable to arrange for a professional to render the injured animal unconscious so she could remove the snare, Dian had no choice but to stand helplessly by while gangrene weakened Lee to the point where she contracted pneumonia. On the morning of May 9, Craig Sholley visited Nunkie's group and found Lee huddled in Nunkie's night nest, apparently unable to move.

Instead of leading the group off on the usual morning foraging expedition, Nunkie remained close to the sick youngster, answering her pathetic whines with low rumbling noises that were clearly intended to encourage her to come along. Lee tried, but collapsed and lay spread-eagled in the wet vegetation while a drenching shower swept over the clearing. Thereupon Nunkie—four hundred pounds of massive silverback—returned to Lee's side and lay down beside his suffering daughter as if to warm and comfort her.

Craig returned to camp to report that Lee seemed close to death.

**The thought of losing Lee was not to be borne. Sciatica and a broken ankle kept me out of it, but I ordered everyone out to try and distract the other gorillas and try to get the baby away from the group at least until I could give her some medical attention.**

This time there was no argument. While Bill Weber and a new student, Peter Veit, distracted Nunkie, Sholley slipped into the clearing, snatched up Lee, and ran. Early that afternoon Lee was carried in a litter down the mountain to the Ruhengeri hospital by Rwelekana, Mukera, and Basili. It was too late. That evening Lee became the seventh Karisoke gorilla to perish because of poachers. After her body was brought back to camp for burial, Dian sat for hours at her window staring out into the fog that had obscured the clearing. Mechanically she wrote one word over and over on her open journal.

**Digit . . . Digit . . . Digit . . . Digit . . .**

By mid-March, Dian's difficulties had multiplied to the point where they seemed almost insupportable. A miasma of mutual hostility and suspicion lay like poison gas over the camp, while beyond its borders the poachers were slowly regaining possession of the forests and meadows. The physical survival of Karisoke was itself in increasing jeopardy as the chief grant givers and the consortium of conservation agencies choked off the flow of funds that paid the staff and maintained the infrastructure.

Dian's health, always somewhat precarious, was failing fast. She ate less and less. She smoked far too much, and racking bouts of emphysema became ever more frequent. The agonizing pain in her left hip meant sleepless nights. Years of inadequate diet had drained the calcium from her, and she had snapped a bone in her ankle while searching for Kima's favorite toy a few yards from her cabin.

**I had almost forgotten how it hurts to break a bone. The awful sweat, vomiting, and a green face.**

She set the ankle herself, but although it healed it was never again fully trustworthy.

Nevertheless she remained indomitable, doing her best to find solutions to her problems. She made conciliatory gestures to the V-W

217

couple, including sending Amy a birthday present. It was returned with a scathing note of rejection.

Since the students would not help stem the mounting wave of poaching, Dian hired four more Africans, most of whom had worked for her in the past as trackers or camp staff. After giving them a few days' instruction and equipping them with boots, clothing, and camp gear supplied by the Digit Fund, she sent them into the forest under the leadership of Vatiri, one of their own.

Against all odds, and contrary to the dire predictions of the other whites in camp, the African-led patrol soon proved its worth. A week after its formation Vatiri and his companions tracked and surprised a group of nine poachers on the southeast slopes of Visoke, jumped them, and with the help of several pistol shots fired into the air, captured one, drove off the rest, and seized some fifty traps. By the end of the month the patrol had regained control of much of the surrounding region, and the gorillas, buffalo, duikers, bushbucks, and hyrax were again relatively secure. It was with pardonable pride that on April 12 Dian wrote to Digit Fund supporters in the United States:

"My patrol Africans work three days a week—days and areas altered each week to confuse the poachers—and thus far have cut over three hundred traps and released at least eight duikers alive. . . . I am using both Zairese and Rwandans, paying them very good wages, feeding them and clothing them. They like the work. In fact they come up on unscheduled days to hunt for traps. For their own safety it would be preferable if they were accompanied by Europeans, but nobody here will go with them and I am not physically able to.

"This is what the Digit Fund is all about—*active* conservation as opposed to talking about conservation—and I can't tell you what it means to be able to put the donations toward proper use, in memory of Digit and all the others. . . .

"You may wonder what I am doing. At this very moment I am trying to make a pair of size 14 boots for one of my patrol, a full-blooded Tutsi. The soles are heavy plywood with inner-tube bottoms, laced together with duiker skin sides lined with sponge rubber. It takes me back to my occupational therapy days, and the Africans think it the most interesting invention since the wheel."

Dian resolved the problem of how to finance the daily operations of Karisoke in equally direct fashion. She began paying the bills out of what remained of her own savings.

The difficulties of finding a "caretaker" to see to things in her absence were more formidable. She had discussed the matter with

McIlvaine during his visit, and he had gingerly suggested Sandy Harcourt, who was currently doing a gorilla survey in Uganda for the AWLF. Dian's first reaction was to reject this notion out of hand, but later she began to give it consideration. Despite what had happened between them, she retained a high regard for Harcourt's abilities and, it has to be assumed, a soft spot for him as well. Besides, if he took over Karisoke in her absence, he would be seconded by Kelly Stewart, whom Dian still considered to be a friend.

On March 6, McIlvaine wrote to her from Nairobi.

"By sheer chance Sandy Harcourt returned here from Uganda. . . . I told him that I had asked you if there was anyone in whom you would have confidence to keep Karisoke going if you spent part of the year elsewhere and that you had replied—after some reflection—'Yes, Sandy and Kelly, at least they are serious workers.' As you might guess he was stunned. But after reflection he replied, 'If that should work out, it would certainly take priority over my present Ugandan project.' "

Dian began testing the waters. She wrote to Kelly, who was then in England working on her Ph.D. Kelly's reply was chatty, friendly, and enthusiastic, and Dian took heart.

"I know of only two serious scientists who might be able to continue the research at a scientific level," she wrote to Dr. Snider, "Kelly Stewart and her husband, Sandy Harcourt. Both, now that they have matured somewhat, have the ability to coordinate conservation with research; at least I think this is the case. Whether or not they would give in to the ever-increasing popularization of the gorillas as a tourist attraction I can't say. . . . I think both should finish their current projects before deciding on whether they want to return here to carry on their research and, also, to carry on with the objectives I've striven for during the past twelve years."

On April 6, Dian wrote joyfully to Anita McClellan, the young woman who was her editor at the publishing house of Houghton Mifflin in Boston, announcing that she had finished the first draft of her book. "It hasn't been easy, as you certainly know. There's still a lot to do, but it is such a huge relief!"

She was right about there still being a great deal to do. Anita would have to labor with her for the best part of three more years before the book would see the light of day. But considering the circumstances under which Dian had been working, completion of a draft was in itself no mean accomplishment.

The weather began to improve as April progressed, and on occasion Dian was able to sunbathe outside her cabin. Even the irritation of having her privacy invaded by tourists did not detract too much from the luxury of lying in the sun. She overdid it and got badly burned—a happenstance that might well serve as a metaphor for much of her life.

On the twenty-first of April the Criglers climbed to Karisoke for a last visit before leaving Rwanda to take up a new posting in Colombia. If their departure had come a year earlier, Dian would have been devastated, but as things stood she was almost relieved.

**Bettie was very uptight. I don't know what she is thinking. And I am just so confused about Frank and where he stands. But it was sad to see them go.**

Change was in the air. On the twenty-fifth Sandy Harcourt climbed to Karisoke—by appointment—and he and Dian were face-to-face for the first time in years. Initially the meeting was somewhat tense, with Harcourt very much on the defensive about the part he had played in establishing the Mountain Gorilla Project. Eventually his hackles subsided, and the two of them got down to business. Although no firm decision was reached, Dian opined that she would be content to have Sandy and Kelly run Karisoke for several months, subject to certain conditions. Harcourt responded that he and his wife *might* be willing to do that, subject to even more stringent conditions.

They parted rather like two terriers who, after prolonged nose-and tail-sniffing, agree to tolerate each other—for the moment.

Dian's mood was immeasurably lightened on May 15 when Amy Vedder and Bill Weber departed.

**This leaves me with only one Peach Core student, together with David Watts and a new, young student, Peter Veit, who is keen and hardworking; the third Peach Core, Craig Sholley, is not a problem now.**

By the end of May she could write to McIlvaine, "All is going very, very, very well at camp. The students are an absolute delight now that the V-W couple are gone. I can't tell you how well we are getting along together. I go out to the gorillas when I can, but that means taking so much Darvon for whatever is wrong with my left hip. The pain isn't to be believed, day and night. I detest taking Darvon for fear of becoming reliant on it, yet it's the only way I can locomote without nonsubtle screams of agony. Craig told me his mother, my age, had a sciatica operation and was down for a year! I simply don't have that kind of time or money. Aubrey wrote about Sir Jonas

Moore in the nineteenth century, saying: 'Sciatica, he cured it by boyling his buttocks.' That's one hell of a remedy!"

Meanwhile things were not going smoothly with McIlvaine's grand design. Although ORTPN's director, Benda-Lema, had enthusiastically agreed to accept a technical aid package in support of the Parc des Volcans, to be funded, organized, and administered through the African Wildlife Leadership Fund, there was resistance from other branches of the Rwandan government. This, together with internecine strife amongst the members of the conservation consortium, each jockeying for the position that would yield it maximum public credit, had brought things to a standstill.

As Dian herself was not slow to point out, it was now a year and a half since Digit's death, yet nothing concrete had been achieved by the conservation establishment in defense of the remaining Mountain Gorillas.

**The park guards are worse than ever. Though there is a new conservateur, he can't control them. He cannot force them to go on poacher patrols, thus none are being conducted. Instead, the guards hide themselves in the pyrethrum fields outside the park and wait for poachers to exit from the park. They then grab them and collect "fines" of five hundred or a thousand francs for themselves and then release the "prisoners." ... Conservation "talk" does not save gorillas; only *active* conservation can do that. And the only active conservation in the Virungas is what comes out of this camp!**

Dian was also proving more of an obstacle than McIlvaine had anticipated. Instead of permitting Digit Fund Inc. to be merged with Project Survival/AWLF, she was clinging to it with increasing obstinacy and using its funds to hire and equip more men to carry out antipoaching patrols. Attempts to remonstrate with her got him nowhere. The death of Lee had made her intractable.

**The day the park guards are trained and motivated to do their work, that is the day I will happily stop patrolling. Until then I don't have a choice.**

Nonetheless she was still cooperating with McIlvaine. Although he would later take the credit for it, it was Dian who was responsible for the selection of a young Belgian, Jean-Pierre von der Becke, to become the first "project manager" for the combined AWLF gorilla project. Formerly employed as an adviser to the Zaire park system, von der Becke had found himself out of work late in 1978 and had pleaded with Dian for a job with the Digit Fund. She did not have enough money to pay him a salary, but his professed enthusiasm for the cause of the Mountain Gorillas so impressed her that she warmly recommended him to McIlvaine. It was a recommendation she would regret.

The attempts to pry her loose from Karisoke continued, although after the departure of Frank Crigler she found them somewhat easier to resist.

In early June, Dr. Snider wrote on behalf of the National Geographic, which was still withholding the vital maintenance grant:

"I understand from Frank Crigler that you may have some concern about having to accept a research post or fellowship in the United States without a stipend. . . . There should, though, be lecturing and other activities that might earn you something. In addition, and I make no promises whatsoever, the Research Committee might be willing to help to some extent with your work leading to scientific publications."

Although she returned a fulsome answer, brimming with gratitude, Dian did not rise to this bait. She could see which way the land lay and was learning how to protect herself. When, after talking to Snider, McIlvaine followed up with the suggestion that if she applied to the Society for a $35,000, *three-year* grant to work on her scientific notes in the United States, it would "probably be accepted," she saw the trap at once.

"Never, never, never speak to me again about asking for a grant that would keep me away from Karisoke for two or three years!" she scolded in reply.

**Although I believe they want me out of here for good, six to eight months will be as much as I can stand. I will dreadfully miss being away from here even that long and can't imagine what it will be like. If it were not for the book, which I must revise with my editor in the States, I might not go at all. . . . There is tremendous joy here now, not only from camp rapport with the students, but with the buffalo and duiker and bushbuck every night. They are all coming in herds and getting so tame that you can crawl up to them and scratch them on their flanks. I always knew this could be done with gorillas, but never with buffalo.**

Restricted by the pain in her hip, which she now half-suspected might be cancer, to only occasional visits to the gorillas, she took pleasure in the company of creatures who could come to her.

One midnight she heard and smelled buffalo. She slipped out

and stalked them unseen to within a dozen yards, then got down on hands and knees and crawled in amongst a herd of seven of the mighty animals. She sat down and by the light of a waning moon watched them drift around her. Twice she slowly reached out and stroked the flanks of the closest ones, which responded by lowering their enormous heads and gazing at her with bovine indifference.

These were *wild* buffalo, which big game hunters have long regarded as the most dangerous animals in Africa. One had gored a park guard to death only a few weeks before Dian's midnight tryst—though with good reason, for the guard had shot it, hoping to sell the meat in Ruhengeri.

Although she could not often visit them, the gorillas were in good hands. Veit, Watts, and even Sholley went almost daily to the study groups. Three or four times a week Vatiri led his patrol up the mountain slopes, and he and his men did their job so well that poachers or their traps were now seldom encountered anywhere on Mt. Visoke. Constantly encouraged by Dian, the patrols pushed farther afield, eventually forcing the poachers to abandon not only the saddle region but the eastern slopes of Mt. Mikeno as well. As of July 2 the Digit Fund's all-African patrols had accounted for 987 poachers' traps, and this in the space of a mere four months.

During the same period, the two dozen park guards had accounted for none at all. Nevertheless they had not been entirely inactive. Three of them tried to shoot the new conservateur, but only succeeded in putting a bullet through his hat.

Except in the part of the park patrolled by Dian's men, the poachers held free sway. Even Munyarukiko felt emboldened to rise from the dead and emerge from his hideout on the Zaire/Uganda border. Armed with military rifles, he and others waged such bloody war on the park's remaining elephants for their ivory that these great creatures almost disappeared from the eastern portion of the park.

As many as a dozen gorillas were also slaughtered in the Virungas during 1979, although none were killed in the Karisoke study area after the death of Lee.

One of the stalwarts of the antipoaching patrols was Mutarutkwa, the statuesque member of the Watusi tribe for whom Dian had tried to make a pair of boots.

**Mutarutkwa badly wants boots "like the other men's." The only hang-up is that he has a size 14 foot, nearly as broad as it is long. For a number of weeks he went out on patrol in several pairs of my heaviest socks, lacing them around his feet. Then I tried to**

make him a pair of shoes, but they weren't a great success. Finally I sent an outline of his unbelievable hooves down to the Ruhengeri market, begging for a solution. A talented old craftsman made a very stout pair of sandals out of rubber tires and inner tubes—using practically one tire per foot—and Mutarutkwa went bounding along on patrols thereafter, seemingly content.

Last week ten pairs of boots arrived from the American Humane Society. Yesterday the patrol came up for their work along with a new trainee who also has very large feet. I took the two largest pairs of boots (11 and 11½) down to the Africans' cabin for a fitting of the new man. Mutarutkwa almost swooned dead away with envy when he saw them. He swore that the 11½ pair would fit him, minus laces, as they are made of very soft leather.

With as much effort as a size 18 derriere seeking its way into a size 12 pair of jeans, he managed to get the boots on. From his height of 6'7" he looked down, way down, at these miraculous appendages and pronounced them perfect.

I couldn't help but notice that his face appeared slightly pained, and mischievously suggested we all have a little dancing session. Within seconds a cupboard was resounding like a drum, and we were all stomping the dust out of the floorboards.

All, that is, except Mutarutkwa. He stood zombielike, able to snake his arms about in nearly the proper manner, but barely able to lift his feet off the floor more than a few inches, only to resettle them tenderly with an almost inaudible groan.

After a few minutes of wild dancing and whooping on the part of the other men, his condition was noticed, particularly his facial grimace of pure agony, though he tried to disguise it. Everyone collapsed on the floor in gales of laughter that he didn't mind as he just plain collapsed in relief, as well as determination that these boots would somehow fit. He decided that, rather than give them up, he would sleep in them overnight so that his feet would become accustomed to them and vice versa. He absolutely refused to allow us to cut the boot tops open, which, to my way of thinking, was an act of sheer martyrdom.

End of story: This morning it took all of us a good five minutes to pry the boots off his swollen feet and another fifteen minutes for him to reduce their size by soaking them in Camp Creek (our drinking water supply). Then with that same great smile, he returned to his inner tubes to limp out on another patrol.

**N**egotiations between Dian and Harcourt did not go well. On June 9 he wrote to tell her that he and Kelly would not be able to come to Rwanda before December, and would only come then if they had the titles and powers of joint "directors of Karisoke Research Center." Furthermore, Harcourt demanded a legally binding undertaking from Dian "that you are prepared to allow us to run the Research Center for at least a year—and possibly after that.

"Finally, we would like to say that between us (you, Kelly and I, National Geographic Society, and ORTPN) we ought to be able to make the Research Center a place to be respected far outside Rwanda."

The gratuitous suggestion that Karisoke was not already widely respected made Dian almost as indignant as the implication that her word alone was not good enough and must be secured by a formal contract. Nevertheless, she swallowed her resentment and agreed to the conditions as she understood them.

**Sandy will run the research aspects and supervise the students. This will leave me free, when I get back from the States, to concentrate on the antipoaching work and my writing.**

A short time later Harcourt announced that "Kelly and I have decided I will be able to come to Rwanda toward the end of September, if you are ready to depart for America by then."

Dian was agreeable and began making preparations for an absence from Karisoke of seven or eight months. That would be time enough, she believed, to obtain the medical treatment she needed; whip her book into final shape with the help of Anita McClellan; and comply with the demands of the National Geographic and the Leakey Foundation that she "write up" her gorilla field notes in proper academic fashion.

Packing was well under way when she heard some disquieting news. After leaving Karisoke, Bill Weber had been hired by the Mountain Gorilla Project, while Amy Vedder returned to the United States to work on her doctorate. Now the V-W couple let it be known that they would soon be returning to Karisoke, at Sandy Harcourt's invitation. Dian was not pleased.

**What Harcourt has done is use the FPS Digit money to set up Weber at park headquarters to "habituate" groups of gorillas for tourists. Weber dislikes the forest and is nervous of gorillas. To my way of thinking, and admittedly this is biased thinking, Digit blood money—the FPS Mountain Gorilla Project—is paying for him to play a role he is no more capable of than my grandmother. My porters are keeping a close eye on him, far closer than he realizes, and say that he is in Ruhengeri at least every other day at the homes of various Europeans while his African tracker and assistant are in the forest. Weber does speak excellent French and writes it as well. His wife, and she is a beautiful young girl who is very appealing, leads him around with a ring through his nose, and she hates my guts. She will be back in January. But neither one of them will get to camp again if I can help it.**

Dian wrote Harcourt explaining politely but firmly that under no circumstances could she permit Weber or Vedder to come back to Karisoke. She also told him she herself expected to return to camp during his and Kelly's tenure, but made it clear that they would continue in command as scientific directors.

Harcourt's response was notably uncooperative. Having categorically stated that it would be impossible for him and Kelly to continue as directors if Dian were at the camp, he made it clear that he would now require an agreement between them limiting the amount of time Dian might spend at Karisoke.

On the Vedder/Weber question, he was unyielding, having first refused Dian's request that they be excluded from Karisoke—"We cannot be scientific directors of a place that we are trying to turn into a well-run research center and have to turn away people of whom we approved simply because you disliked them." He demanded the final say on *everyone* who might come to camp while he and Kelly were in charge.

In case Dian had any doubts as to who was in the driver's seat, he also informed her that he could no longer guarantee a September arrival. In fact, he suggested she might consider staying on until early January, since it would not be convenient for him to be at Karisoke in December.

This was really pushing it, especially for someone who claimed to know Dian inside out, but a lack of confidence in his ability to get his own way was not one of Sandy Harcourt's problems. Dian's patience was now perilously near its end. Her plans for a September departure and for establishing herself in the United States were in ruins. She had been as good as told that Karisoke, under her, was a mess; that she couldn't even visit the place without Harcourt's permission; and that the V-W couple would be returning there in triumph. It was more than she could swallow.

She unburdened herself to Dr. Snider, whom she continued to regard as a trusty friend and ally.

"I must assure you it is not sheer stubbornness or pettiness that will not allow me to permit the return of the V-W couple. The stories I heard in Kigali in June from people, both Africans and Europeans, were absolutely incredible. I certainly deserve the option of not letting them return to the camp and the gorillas that I have put so much of my own life, love, and labor into."

Presumably someone advised Harcourt that he had overstepped the mark. On September 10 he informed Dian that because the Webers were to be funded by the FPS to carry out conservation programs for the park, he could "modify our previous conditions, and agree to your requirement that the Webers do not pursue further work at Karisoke during the period of your absence."

As a gesture of conciliation this might have been better received if he had not appended to it a brand-new condition.

"We cannot come to Karisoke unless we have priority of access to the main study groups and unless there is no more than one social behavior study of gorillas besides ours being carried out while we are there."

Preserving a degree of equanimity that her detractors would hardly have believed possible, Dian replied:

October 6, 1979

Dear Sandy,
    I think it best for all concerned that I go ahead and take up an offer of additional students who can begin coming immediately rather than in January. This isn't as I'd thought things would eventuate, but I need to salvage what I can of my previous plans.

227

I cannot adhere to your condition concerning my not returning during the next year or to other restrictions you may wish to apply.

I couldn't possibly grant you "priority" to the main study groups at the cost of halting the work of Peter Veit. It would be unethical to take Group 5 away from him to coincide with your stipulation.

In the same mail she told Dr. Snider that she had decided against Harcourt and was making other arrangements.

**What I didn't know at the time was that National Geographic had already arranged with Sandy and Kelly to give them a grant of sixteen thousand dollars to enable them to take over Karisoke. I suppose when Dr. Snider got my letter saying Sandy was out, he must have gotten in touch with him right away.**

Thoroughly alarmed, Harcourt flew to Kigali. On November 3 he appeared at Karisoke.

**I was in bed with one of those pneumonialike attacks. He zoomed into Peter's cabin first and clipped out a few questions before leaving. Peter's own words afterwards were: "What did I do?" Then he banged on my door and came barging in. He refused to discuss any of his reasons for changing his plans without telling me—in fact for the most part he just sat with a supercilious face and didn't/wouldn't say anything. Believe me, I didn't even yell or scream at him. If he would just climb off his pedestal, one might be able to communicate with him, but I found it impossible. There is no denying his intelligence and the fact that he is not lazy, but he certainly needs a lesson in manners. Butter would not have melted in his mouth when we talked last April, but a touch of power seems to have gone to his head. He went off down the mountain in a perfect snit.**

Presumably Harcourt realized that he had not done his cause any good, so he climbed back up to Karisoke again next morning. This time he was almost reasonable. It was too late.

"I've already arranged for three new students," Dian told him. "I'll pick one of them to be Director here till I get back. I'm sorry, Sandy, but that's the way it's going to be."

Harcourt returned to England, and on November 15 he and Kelly wrote separate letters to Dian in an attempt to bring her around. Harcourt explained that he had just heard from the National Geographic that his and Kelly's grant application had been approved and he sincerely hoped that some agreement about their return to camp could be arrived at. "It would be a great pity, having been given funding, to write to N.G. saying that we could no longer use it."

The letter from Kelly was the first Dian had received from her since negotiations began in April. It was almost abject. Kelly wrote that she had so much hoped that the differences between Dian and Sandy would be ironed out when the two met, but she admitted she was not overly surprised by the negative results. "Perhaps," she wrote, "if Sandy was better at being friendly and polite, things would have gone more smoothly. . . . I ask you to reconsider us as stand-in directors of Karisoke during your absence."

Dian remained unmoved.

The latter half of 1979 was filled with incident. During early July, Dian supervised the exhumation of a number of gorillas that had died in the Virungas during the past several years. These were not *her* gorillas, but unfortunate strangers whom she had buried in a sort of paupers' cemetery. The Smithsonian Institution in Washington wanted their bones, and the National Geographic Society had urged Dian to oblige. She did so with reluctance. For nearly two weeks the ripe odor of decay hung over Karisoke.

**My cabin looks like a boneyard—bits and pieces all over the floor as we try to fit them together. For sure, I wonder why grown men would spend their lives looking at bones when they could look at animals in life. There have to be some kinds of science I'll never understand.**

There were plenty of live animals around Karisoke. A herd of buffalo, perhaps the same ones Dian had crawled amongst earlier in the year, had become permanent residents in the meadow below her cabin. They were so blasé about the human presence that on one occasion she had to step over a cow buffalo resting on her doorstep.

Bushbucks, hyrax, golden squirrels, and duikers abounded, but there were also visits from rarer creatures, including a hyena that tried to raid the men's food store, and a leopard that narrowly missed making a midnight meal out of the dog Cindy.

Crippled by the pain in her hip—**I would use a crutch if no one could see me—I really hurt too much to believe in living**—Dian could barely manage to visit the gorillas except when they came close to camp. Kima was, as always, both a comfort and an unending cause of exasperation. When she lost a toy koala bear given to her years earlier, she went into a furious sulk, refused to eat, bit everyone who approached her, and vandalized the cabin used by the antipoaching patrol. Dian mustered the whole camp staff to search for the toy, and when after three days it was not to be found, she ordered a new one, by cable, from San Francisco. As a friend said, "She treated that monkey like a spoiled child and loved it dearly, though it was hard for those who had to put up with its tantrums to see why."

Near the end of July, Vatiri brought her a baby bushbuck with a badly mangled leg that had been caught in a poacher's snare. In a classic case of maternal transferral, the young antelope adopted Dian as its mother, refusing to be separated from her. So she took it into her crowded cabin, where she nursed it for almost a month before it was fit to be released. It insisted on sleeping with Dian and became frantic if she went out of its sight. *It* had adopted Dian, but Cindy decided to adopt *it,* with the result that Cindy, too, insisted on sharing the bed.

**No sleep again last night—sciatica and damn dog and baby duiker not enough. Kima jealous, had to join in too.**

Apart from the duel with Harcourt, life at Karisoke went smoothly. Relations between Dian and the students had never been better. Peter Veit was showing signs of becoming a real gorilla defender in the style of Ian Redmond. Free of the influence of the V-W couple, Craig Sholley had returned to the fold. David Watts continued to be a dedicated and effective scientist.

It was with real regret that, in mid-July, Dian bade good-bye to Watts. Although they had never become close friends, they respected each other, and this despite Dian's inherent suspicions of anyone who professed an interest in socialism. She wrote to the director of the National Zoological Park in Washington, "I worked with David a total of fifteen full months at Karisoke. Throughout his stay, he was always good-natured and highly self-motivated. He also proved himself extremely levelheaded."

She felt somewhat less distress when, in early August, Sholley returned to the United States.

**I guess I could never tolerate what I call the Peach Core approach—turning the other cheek to the poachers.**

Far from turning the other cheek, Dian had by now made her patrol system so effective that poachers had all but abandoned the region central to the southern trio of volcanoes, Visoke, Karisimbi, and Mikeno. Vatiri was now leading his men deep into Zaire as well as northeastward toward Mt. Sabyinyo, cutting traps wherever they found them. The work was not without incident. On one occasion the patrol encountered a party of Zairean poachers armed with a rifle, and Vatiri's men had to beat a hasty retreat with bullets whistling over their heads. Next day they returned to the offensive.

**They wanted a second pistol from me, which I gave them for today, but am not sure that was too wise. Will be on pins and needles until they get home tonight.**

Elsewhere in the Parc des Volcans the poachers did much as they pleased. Neither the original Mountain Gorilla Project employees nor those of the AWLF had organized a patrol system, and the park guards remained as ineffective as ever.

Hard evidence of this came to light on September 3 when Dian was informed by Dr. Vimont, in Ruhengeri, that two gorilla babies were being offered for sale in Gisenyi. She investigated at once.

**They reputedly come from Zaire, though not from any region we are patrolling. Two babies means at least one more group destroyed. They are offered for sale for 400,000 RWF! It seems the French want to get them for captivity in Europe—the Rwandans also know about them, and I want to get them to try to release them back to the wild.**

Despite intensive efforts, Dian was unable to locate the orphans. She concluded that they had been smuggled to France, possibly via a notorious Spanish dealer in wild animals and with the connivance of Rwandan or Zairean officials.

The influx of tourists continued unabated. On one occasion camp was invaded by a party from Chicago who demanded that Dian herself escort them to see the gorillas. She responded by pretending to a fit of dementia and firing a pistol over their heads.

**I should hate myself for such a "no-no" but just couldn't resist. They were so pompous and so sure they could have anything they wanted because they were from the States. I guess I scared the hell out of them. They went clomping down the trail like a herd of buffalo that had gotten into a bee tree!**

They later filed a complaint of attempted murder against Dian, but nobody in Rwanda except for a few of her perennial detractors took this seriously.

Camp was host to many welcome visitors that summer, amongst them a number of Rwandan nationals including Dian's bank manager, whom she always addressed with full formality as Mr. Joseph. He climbed to camp with his family several times, and Dian was delighted and touched when he named a newborn daughter after her.

On August 12 a professor from Cornell University in Ithaca, New York, arrived at Karisoke.

Dr. Glenn Hausfater did not know Dian personally, but had written some months earlier for permission to visit as part of an African tour he was making to further his studies in primatology. Dian had agreed rather grudgingly since she did not like "scientific tourists" much better than the ordinary breed.

When the professor appeared, Dian was bowled over.

**He is about six inches taller than I! But also about six years younger—he is *really* nice! We had coffee, sandwiches, and beer and drank his cognac up here at my cabin and had a neat, long conversation.**

Hausfater had only intended to remain two days before continuing on to visit A'Kagera Park, but he and Dian got along so well that he decided to remain at Karisoke. Despite a week of rain and mist, or perhaps because of it, the friendship bloomed.

**I really like him. Glenn and I talk so well together and feel the same about so many things. He told me all about his life and I told about mine. He's been very unhappy recently but keeps his sense of humor.**

Clad in rain gear, the couple plodded through the forest to visit Group 5, and Dian was overjoyed at the way the gorillas seemed to accept Hausfater's presence. Although he was living in a guest cabin, Dian cooked his meals at her place and they talked far into the nights. She unburdened herself of the whole sorry story of the attempts to get her out of Karisoke, and he listened sympathetically.

One thing that bothered her was that she quite literally had nowhere to go in the United States. Although Snider and McIlvaine had suggested an affiliation with one of several universities and research centers, nothing came of this. Furthermore, few such institutions offered salaries or grants, and Dian was in no financial condition to support herself.

Glenn Hausfater thought he could resolve this problem. "I believe a niche could be found for you at Cornell as a visiting professor, Dian. I know Ithaca's a bit out of the way, but it's a wonderful place to live. Lots of wilderness and wild critters close at hand. I've got a little plane and I could fly you to some really remote places. The college crowd is small and friendly, and they'd fall in love with you."

Hausfater had to leave on August 18 to complete his African tour, but he kept in touch with Dian by cable, and she sent off a long letter that would await him on his return to Ithaca.

"Glenn," she concluded, "your visit was of deep significance to me. I remain very grateful to you, though I can envisage you cringing at that word, for all that you gave me of yourself. I'm not getting schmaltzy. You have no idea what a special gift it was to have met a person of your depth and integrity. Please don't be personally disappointed if they don't allot me a visiting professorship grant. You've done so much already. In all sincerity though, and I speak intuitively, this is the first time that I feel absolutely 'right' about leaving Karisoke. . . . You've made Cornell seem a viable and empathetic place rather than a competitive factory. I've been identifying with it since you left and only need to get camp settled before I can be free to come. Thank you so much for the first positive line of thought I've had in a long time.

"P.S. The big poacher I told you about, Munyarukiko, the one responsible for all the gorilla killings over the past eleven years, died of 'mysterious' causes last week. He *really* died this time. Imagine that!"

In his reply Glenn described an energetic assault he was making on Cornell's establishment in order to find a place for Dian.

"There are two or three possibilities. . . . The first is for very senior scientists, silverbacks with long publication records and big egos. Nevertheless, Cornell is really concerned about not having enough women professors. The provost has a cache of funds specifically earmarked for women scientists . . . you would be perfect for this. I am working on a March 1980 or September 1980 residency date for a visiting professorship. But be forewarned, I have been absolutely unsuccessful in finding any handsome 50-ish men who would be suitable partners for you at the local disco. These matters may take care of themselves once you are here.

"I *like* the schmaltzy parts of your letter. The visit to Karisoke was as helpful to me, personally and emotionally, as it seems to have been for you. You just have so much to offer, have made such a contribution toward gorilla conservation, and just deserve so much good, that I can't help but want to try to get you into a comfortable position and see that some good things come your way. . . . With a little patience we can lick the bastards."

Dian now began to have some doubts about her professorial abilities. At the end of October she wrote Glenn, "If I can, as you state, get my travel expenses to Ithaca, a small amount of research funding, office space, secretarial help (you're kidding!), and stationery, I believe I would be wiser to come to Cornell initially as an unsalaried visiting professor. In this manner I could test my abilities to cope once again with civilization. . . . If all goes well once the 'adjustment' period is over, then I could prove myself. I would also be free to finish the book and do a few lectures.

"I can't wait to get to the State Diner and have pictured it in my mind just so. I hope you can learn 'em how to fry breaded pork chops without tomato sauce gluck slopped over them, for that would run into the mashed potatoes and create a bus accident scene. I am drooling. And so onto another of my bad habits—MUSSELS! I crave them, and reckon there is something Freudian in it. The only kind I have thus far found in Kigali are tinned in Spain and have seaweed merde in their innards.

"I now have a poacher's dog in the front room with a bad, bad, bad foreleg from having been caught in a trap. I can't bring myself to kill it as it is terribly sweet. I will feed it up, it is emaciated, and try to fix its wound and find a home for it. In addition to the dog the last patrol brought in eighty-eight traps."

Not only did Dian nurse the dog back to health, she persuaded Earl Haldiman, director of an ABC television crew who visited Karisoke early in December, to adopt the poor creature and smuggle it back to the United States. Poacher, as Haldiman named it, adjusted so well to California that she eventually became a television star in her own right.

On the same day that Dian sent Poacher off to a new life, she received a letter from the chairman of the Neurobiology and Behavior section at Cornell:

"The terms of your appointment will be from mid-March 1980 to mid-December 1980. You will be paid a salary of $13,500. . . . Your professional duties will be to give several public lectures in the spring and to teach a seminar on the Great Apes in the autumn. We believe this schedule will . . . provide you an opportunity to do the writing Glenn has told us you were anxious to do."

Dian was ecstatic.

**Christmas sure has come early this year! The times and place and everything are exactly right for me. Glenn is a miracle man!**

As the year approached its end, Dian's health improved. On October 2 she had gone to the Ruhengeri hospital for an examination of her hip. X rays revealed that she had neither sciatica nor cancer. The pain was being caused by compression of her fourth and fifth lumbar vertebrae. Her friends, Drs. Vimont and Lolly Prescado, prescribed drugs and therapy that greatly reduced the pain, pending remedial treatment when she returned to the United States.

Since Sholley's departure in early August, the only other white person in camp had been Peter Veit. No vacancies had been filled pending Harcourt's arrival, but once Dian decided against him she had moved quickly to make alternative arrangements through Dr. Ramon Rhine of the University of California. Rhine produced three research students eager to work at Karisoke. Dian was confident that at least one would be able to take charge in her absence. However, none could arrive until early in the new year, so she and Peter continued to soldier on alone. This was no hardship.

**Peter works better and better. I encourage him to work for his doctorate thesis and he spends all his time with the groups. . . . Life is really peaceful in camp; I don't even yell at the Africans. I guess Fossil Fossey is getting marshmallowy.**

If there was a fly in the ointment, it was Jean-Pierre von der Becke, whom Dian had recommended to manage the AWLF gorilla project consortium. Following his arrival in Rwanda in early September, he had showered Dian with notes and letters fulsomely attesting to his enormous gratitude for her getting him his new job, and assuring her of his undying loyalty to her personally and to the cause of active gorilla conservation. But it was not long before his center of emotional gravity began to shift. By the end of October he had become an integral part of what Dian contemptuously referred to as the Parking Lot Gang, so called because its members spent much of their time around the tourist parking lot at the base of the mountain.

The "gang" now included Monfort and von der Becke, together with Bill Weber and various other employees of the combined AWLF/FPS/WWF Mountain Gorilla Project. According to the reports from Dian's intelligence network, their contributions to poacher control and gorilla protection amounted to virtually nothing, their time and energy being devoted almost exclusively to gorilla "tourism." To assist in this enterprise they tried to hire trained trackers away from Karisoke, but with the exception of one whom Dian had fired for theft, these efforts were unsuccessful.

Despite ORTPN's guarantee that Karisoke's gorillas would not be bothered by tourists, Group 5 continued to bear the brunt of such visitations. In mid-September the group's tolerance came to an end. It abandoned its old range on the southeastern slopes of Visoke and migrated so far west into Zaire that even Peter Veit had trouble following.

This defection left the Parking Lot Gang with almost no habituated gorillas to display to paying visitors. So, with considerable trepidation, they undertook to habituate, à la Fossey, a family on Mt. Sabyinyo which they called Group 13.

The name was ill-omened. On December 1 one of the two silver-backs in the group was found dead. An autopsy revealed that he had been shot through the shoulder, had suffered a shattered arm as a result, and had finally succumbed to infection. When Dian heard about it she was outraged, not just by this evidence that poachers were still lethally active in those parts of the park not patrolled by her own men, but by the obtuseness of the Parking Lot Gang, whose members had remained unaware for weeks that the silverback had even been wounded.

Her comment was pithy.

**They didn't notice he was wounded, sick, and dying! But most of them wouldn't notice an elephant if it dumped a ton of merde onto their heads.**

To Bill Weber she wrote: "Two months ago Sebahutu, one of the killers of Uncle Bert and Macho, etc., was released from prison after only ten months of a ten-year sentence. Also Seregera has been released after serving eighteen months. I am kept informed of the activities of both men. Both have rifles. They are in the park continually, and Musido-Sabyinyo is their main working area because of elephants. Subahutu shot an elephant near Ngezi about 1½ months ago, but the animal, a young one, fled and died near the summit of Visoke.

"You can take it for what it's worth, but in my mind one or both of these men are responsible for the death of your silverback. If you want, and I won't take it on without your approval and von der Becke's, I will organize a *legal* raid on their huts through the Substi-tut and the military, NOT through the park conservateur. . . . I certainly won't do it if you think I am interfering."

They did—so she didn't, which was no more than was to be expected. However, Bill Weber sent her a revealing personal note.

"I've now seen nine gorillas die since I got here, and each has taken its toll personally. Between the deaths and the other things going on in Rwanda, I think I might now understand you a little better; just a little."

Unfortunately he did not understand the gorillas any better. Barely a week after sending her this note he found himself in Ruhengeri hospital, a badly bitten man with several shattered ribs. He wrote Dian an apologetic explanation of what had happened. The previous Thursday eleven paying tourists had come to see gorillas, and Weber had ill-advisedly agreed to guide them all. When the straggling group finally found the gorillas, the animals were almost invisible in the thick vegetation. Bored or disappointed, three of the tourists began to wander away from the main body and were complaining loudly among themselves. This frightened the gorillas away. Weber doggedly led the tourists in pursuit. Coming upon a tunnel in the vegetation, he decided to crawl into it in order to see where the animals were. "Inside I saw a young-looking silverback about eight meters above me. We looked at each other for about eight seconds before he ran at me. All I remember is being hit with a lot of force, feeling his teeth sink into my neck and rolling downhill for about thirty feet before he let go and ran away. . . ."

Whatever his faults, Weber knew enough to be contrite. He begged Dian to tell him what he had done wrong.

She replied with sympathy, kindness—and good advice.

"You were definitely handicapped by having so many people with you, not to mention three unruly ones. The gorillas cannot be expected to tolerate such hordes of strangers, and for their own future—sense of security for breeding and carrying on with the natural behavior—it would seem that only small groups of people should be allowed to go to them.

"As you well know, I am very, very, very permissive, even overly considerate of the animals I work with. I detest standing upright with them, talking or smoking around them, pointing at them, splitting groups of people around them, etc. I've just always put their moods first before anything else, but that's my nature. . . . I also do not believe in following a group once they have moved off. Always one must think about the next day—are you going to leave them with a sense of trust in you, or are you going to push that sense to the breaking point? I believe in leaving the animals contented even though much of the time I was left very discontented about a day's contact, only having seen some rumps fleeing."

She sent some light fiction with this letter to help Weber while away the hours. Once again the Lone Woman of the Forest had failed to live up to her reputation.

Dian was not, however, naive enough to believe that all would now be well between them. She wrote to Rosamond Carr, "I guess you've heard the news about Weber's getting bitten and two ribs broken. I'm truly sorry for him as he has always been terrified of gorillas, and now it might be even more difficult for him. I've been exchanging letters with him, all very, very polite and honest. This will change when that $@/#& of a wife of his arrives."

Three days before Christmas, Dian received a long letter from her Boston editor, Anita McClellan. It was not a pleasant yuletide gift.

"Over the past four or five weeks," Anita wrote, "I have had a number of enlightening conversations with primate people, including Dr. Hal Coolidge. . . . All of them led me to believe there is a large movement to replace you with a 'more scientific' person, one who would work to develop the gorilla sanctuary as an economic resource. Alan Goodall is energetically lobbying to be the person to take over when you leave. . . . Barbara Holecek confirmed Coolidge's and the Geographic's attitude as generally held, that 'Fossey is considered to have gotten too close to the gorillas to be able to remain scientific about them.' "

By strange coincidence, the porter who brought Dian this letter also delivered a note from a *bazunga* down at the car park—Alan Goodall himself, asking permission to visit camp. Although she had just read his recently published book and had been irritated by some of its contents, she nevertheless sent word that he could come.

The following day Goodall and Peter Veit, led by Rwelekana, made a trip to Kabara in Zaire to visit the meadow where Dian had begun her gorilla work—and where Carl Akeley had died and been buried so many years before. They found his grave empty. His bones had been stolen from it only a few days earlier—perhaps to be used in the making of *sumu*.

Then it was Christmas and for once there was no Wog Party. Dian and Peter Veit celebrated alone.

**Peter came up at six-thirty and I wasn't ready as had cooked all day. Peach pie, fried chicken, baked stuffed chicken, mashed potatoes, gravy. I also made a chocolate cake, ice cream, canned artichoke hearts, breaded eggplant, and garlic bread. He ate too much. Then we gave gifts. He gave me an empty notebook, a labeling machine, a copy of *Brave New World*, and a very nice note. He told me that outside of his family, I'd done more to change his life than anyone else, and wished me happiness.**

When Dian awoke on New Year's morning, 1980, it was to the marvelous conviction that the worst of the turmoil and tensions that had been her lot for a year and more were well behind. She could now look forward almost eagerly to a "long vacation." Karisoke seemed secure. Her book was ready for polishing. And what made the prospect of several months in America most seductive, she was sure that a great new love awaited her there.

Dian turned Cindy and Kima loose for a romp, visited her hens and collected three fresh eggs, blew up the fire Mukera had already lit for her, cooked and ate her breakfast, then took a mug of coffee outside to sit and watch the burnished clouds streaming over the summit of Karisimbi.

Although a stack of the inevitable and interminable paperwork awaited her attention, she ignored it to slip off her jeans and sun her legs and hip while watching her world busy itself with the new day. A flock of multicolored parrots arrowed out of the forest into the big hagenia beside her cabin. A duiker doe minced down the meadow slope toward the stream. A blue plume of woodsmoke from the men's cooking fire rose slowly from the clearing below, and from far up the slopes of Visoke came the deep throb—felt as much as heard—of a silverback beating out the assurance that all was well with him and his.

The sun was sliding high by the time Dian put out her third cigarette of the morning and reluctantly entered the cabin. There were scores of letters to write, and she had been hard at it for hours when there came a timid knocking at her door.

She opened it to find one of her porters carrying a bulging potato basket on his head. She was annoyed by the interruption.

"What are you doing here, Mutari! I didn't ask for any more potatoes!"

"Not potatoes, mademoiselle! *Iko ngagi*—this is a gorilla!"

Dian's heart sank. Mutari lowered the heavy basket and, at her gesture, brought it into her living room. Slowly, and with apprehension, Dian removed the lid and turned the basket on its side. Out crawled a very weak infant gorilla.

Very early that morning in Ruhengeri, Dr. Vimont had been visited at his home by two furtive Africans who, after much hesitation, asked if he wanted to buy a gorilla.

Once he realized they were talking about an animal that had already been captured, he agreed to purchase it for about one thousand dollars. He and the two men then drove some fifty kilometers in his car to the place where the baby was being kept—a potato shed adjacent to Mt. Karisimbi.

Prior to leaving home, Dr. Vimont had told his wife to alert the authorities. When the three men got back with the baby, he proceeded to get the two sellers drunk while the military surrounded his home and then arrested them. He then arranged to have the baby sent up to camp where it arrived so unexpectedly.

As yet I know very little about the details of its capture, except that it had been kept by the poachers for at least two weeks and that it probably came from the far side of Mt. Mikeno. Apparently both its mother and the group silverback were killed during its capture.

It is in far better health than Coco or Pucker in that it has no

239

capture wounds and has made the transition from artificial back to natural foods (wild celery, thistles, galium leaves, bracket fungi, blackberries) within a short time. But it remains extremely lethargic, is possibly developing pneumonia, and has horrid diarrhea. For the first week it slept with me, but the diarrhea and lakes of pee made sleep impossible for both of us. I now have a sleeping box built into my bedroom, turned into an artificial "jungle," and have been able to catch up on sleep. But it will prove difficult to care for as it needs constant company.

It couldn't have come at a worse time, since I'd planned to leave for Cornell in mid-February. As grateful as I am to have it here where it will be taken care of properly, I remain very concerned as to its future. Have not yet received any word from Rwandan officials, whom I assume will want it to go to a zoo, nor do I feel I can permit the new students who are coming to take the serious responsibility of releasing it in the wild. For sure it won't be ready for any decision as to its future by the third week in February. I'm really in a bind because of my obligations to Cornell.

The peaceful interlude was at an end. Three days after the arrival of the orphan gorilla (a three-year-old female that was initially called Charlie), the first of the new research students arrived. He was Stuart Perlmeter, a soft-spoken twenty-six-year-old graduate in anthropology from the University of Oregon. Dian made one of her instant assessments.

I really quite like him as he seems to be mature and has integrity. I really think he will be the one to take charge here while I am gone.

Meantime she showed him how the camp was run and introduced him to the gorillas.

On January 12 the other students arrived: twenty-four-year-old John Fowler, a zoology major from the University of Georgia, and thirty-four-year-old Carolyn Phillips, an attractive woman whose qualifications for the job consisted of a B.A. in English and a general interest in animal behavior. Together with Peter Veit, now the old veteran, the quartet comprised, in the words of a visitor to camp, "something of a mixed bag."

Carolyn Phillips' stay was short. On February 1 she returned to the United States. With her departure the three young men sorted out their relationships anew, rather like Group 4 had done when deprived of female members.

Dian was now as busy as she had ever been with caring for Charlie, trying to pack her belongings and papers, breaking in the new students, and supervising her antipoaching patrols. Because she did not have much faith in Perlmeter's ability to maintain sufficient pressure on the poachers, she decided to wage a preemptive blitz before her own departure. To this end she hired extra men, and through January and February her patrols scoured the surrounding countryside to such effect that poaching virtually ceased within a radius of four or five kilometers from camp. In addition Dian "arranged" (there is no indication of how she did this) for the arrest and imprisonment of the notorious Sebahutu.

**I have jailed the man I feel is responsible for the shooting of the silverback, Brutus, in Group 13 in December—the same man who killed Uncle Bert and Macho.**

Although the conservation establishment continued to look askance at her antipoaching activities, she had her supporters. One such was the manager of the Nippenose Equipment Company in Williamsport, Pennsylvania. Having heard the sad tale of Mutarutkwa's boot trouble, he had a pair of size 14 Vesque boots especially made.

**Wow, I don't know who was the most amazed—the Africans, myself, or Mutarutkwa. . . . We all joined in, showing him which boot was worn on which foot and then lacing them up for him, still kind of unbelieving that such huge feet could actually be shod.**

**Mutarutkwa simply sat there at first with a dazed smile, then he slowly stood up from the bench outside my cabin, took a few steps, lengthened his stride, and broke into a run around the side of the cabin where he thought nobody could see him. Here he stopped, gazed lovingly at his feet, and began bounding through the big meadow just like an antelope, until he fell into a deep drainage ditch. He hauled himself out with a chagrined expression but, fortunately, with no broken bones.**

**He went out on patrol several minutes later with his eyes riveted to his feet, and if he'd run into an elephant, I don't believe he would have noticed it.**

**Some people believe that conservation requires the use of airplanes, jeeps, tarmac roads, and fancy buildings—they should learn about boots!**

As January ended Dian entertained the new U.S. ambassador, Bob Melone, together with the French ambassador to Rwanda. She was forced to endure another scolding for her "illegal" activities and to swallow a warning that the State Department would be unable to protect her in the event that the Rwandans moved against her. Dian got the strong impression that such an action might even receive State's support; but she was more amused than angered. She knew that her stock had never been higher with the president of Rwanda, who had just ordered that the baby gorilla, Charlie, should remain in her custody until it was well and that she could then release it back to the wild if she so wished.

Five days later she was unexpectedly visited by Robinson McIlvaine. On February 10 he wrote a memo from the AWLF office in Nairobi to the several partners in the new, expanded Mountain Gorilla Project describing his visit.

McIlvaine was met at Kigali Airport by project manager Jean-Pierre von der Becke and U.S. ambassador Melone. He stayed with Melone except when he was "up country." The day after his arrival von der Becke drove him to the bottom of the Karisoke trail but did not accompany him as he climbed upward in the pouring rain. According to McIlvaine, Dian no longer spoke to von der Becke or to the Webers, who were camped at the foot of the mountain.

McIlvaine reported that Dian was suffering from acute sciatica, a bad hip, and emphysema, but was also experiencing severe trauma over her imminent departure and forthcoming assignment at Cornell University. He thought it quite possible that at the last minute she might not muster the courage to leave Karisoke at all. "In her more rational moments," he wrote, "she thought of forming an oversight committee of distinguished American scientists to govern the research center." Meanwhile, "having refused Sandy Harcourt's bid to take over," she was prepared to leave the camp in charge of one of the two new students. McIlvaine suspected that once Dian was gone, Benda-Lema would invite Harcourt to take over.

The report also discussed the progress of the Mountain Gorilla Project, now almost two years old. Having noted that the Rwandan government had still not signed the agreement initiated by him, McIlvaine described the Parc des Volcans headquarters at Kigali as a "shambles." According to him, the conservateur was seldom there, was often drunk, and had run up 20,000 kilometers on a WWF-donated Land Cruiser before rolling it into a ditch. "Obviously the park guards have no morale, and five of them are in jail."

McIlvaine concluded his report with these brave words: "Although the situation could hardly be worse . . . we decided we must push ahead."

Dian's reaction to this memo, which she received from a sympathizer in Nairobi, went unrecorded. Perhaps it is just as well.

To further complicate her last weeks at Karisoke, a three-man Japanese movie team arrived on February 3 to spend a month filming her and the gorillas. She was already well-known in Japan, but this film would make her famous there.

The filmmakers were delighted with Charlie. Now restored to health, the young gorilla was in the process of taking over Karisoke.

**She has become a spoiled brat who does what *she* wants. But we now have to start getting her ready to go back to the forest. Fortunately John Fowler has turned out to be a great baby-sitter and is now changing her back into being a gorilla. She must be withdrawn from all of the fruit and bread she craves and become accustomed to out-of-door temperatures at night rather than sleeping above my fireplace in my bedroom in her lovely sleeping box that she has torn apart dozens of times. Fortunately Fowler is willing to sleep outside with her.**

As February drew on, Dian had a worrisome problem to resolve. Should she attempt to introduce Charlie into one of the study groups before her own departure, now scheduled for March first, or leave it up to Perlmeter? In the end, although she did not feel Charlie was sufficiently prepared for a return to the life of a free gorilla, she decided to make the attempt herself.

**We began the reentry plans in mid-February. My choice of the wild group was Group 4 since it had no infants or "hot" females or any approaching parturition who might have been jealous of the appearance of a new baby out of the blue. I turned down Group 5 partly because of this, and also it was now too far away and therefore vulnerable to poachers.**

**A week before I was to leave, I sent John Fowler and Nemeye to set up a bivouac camp in Group 4's territory. They had no fire and no food, only sleeping bags. The idea was to keep the baby away from camp to adjust to being in the forest again.**

**We chose the twenty-ninth to make our attempt. Wouldn't you know that would be the day when Group 4 was having an interaction with one of the fringe groups? The rain was pouring down, and the gorilla trails were horrid, horrid, horrid, filled with fear dung and fear odor, crisscrossed like a plate of noodles. In the confusion and rain we lost Group 4 and ended up with the fringe group, whose silverbacks charged John, who was in the lead with Rwelekana, while I followed with Charlie and the cine crew.**

**We went back to the bivouac camp and I pondered what to do. I had only two days left, and the students did not want to take**

the responsibility to reintroduce the infant without me. Very reluctantly I decided next morning to attempt reintroduction into Group 5. I was very apprehensive because one of the young females, Tuck, was "hot" and another older one, Effie, due to have her own baby anytime—like yesterday.

To make a long story short, we set out early next day with Charlie riding piggyback on John's shoulders. And we were all very nearly killed!

Reaching Group 5, John and I climbed a tree with baby so she would have the option of staying with us, going down to join the wild group, or coming back to us. I also thought it would give us a bit of advantage if there was aggression from the group.

Beethoven, Group 5's leader, saw us first, then the others. Tuck and Effie sniffed and stared, then both came to the base of the tree and Charlie wiggled out of John's arms and climbed straight down to them. For just a moment all went well with Tuck embracing the baby, then everything went wild! Tuck and Effie began to pull the baby like a rag doll. Icarus, the young silverback, then came over and began to bat the baby. It was mauled and hauled, bitten and nipped, thrown and dragged, and the noise of gorillas screaming and roaring was blood-chilling. Even Beethoven charged to the base of the tree.

I retrieved the baby once from Tuck and Effie, screaming and cursing like only Fossey can, but she climbed back down to them of her own accord and the mauling began again. After nearly an hour of this, heavy rains began and most of Group 5 took shelter under nearby bushes—Pablo carrying off my camera, which I'd dropped. Finally the baby limped over to our tree, and I again retrieved her and shoved her up to John, who put her under his rain jacket. I felt that was enough horror and we would have to take her home.

We had to wait another hour before we could go, as Icarus and Tuck maintained a threatening watch four feet from the base of our tree. Every time we moved a fraction, they pig-grunted and snarled and he beat his chest. His head hair stood straight up, and he gave out that bad aggression odor. They knew we had the baby, even though they couldn't see it, and they sure did want it.

This second hour was one of two (the previous hour was the first) times in my life I've ever been afraid of gorillas. Finally the rain let up, and Beethoven led the group slowly off, except Tuck and Icarus, who tried to climb the tree, and I had to kick them. Finally they all left and we sneaked home.

I had to leave for the States next day, with the baby back in my bedroom and nothing solved.

Three weeks later Stuart Perlmeter and the Karisoke native staff successfully introduced Charlie—now renamed Bonne Année—into Group 4, where she quickly became one of Peanuts's family.

The fears of McIlvaine and the Mountain Gorilla Project sponsors that Dian might not be able to "muster the courage" to depart were set at rest on the morning of March 3, when she descended the long muddy trail to the car park, accompanied by a train of porters.

The farewells at camp had been, to use one of her special words, schmaltzy. Parting from Cindy and Kima was hard, and parting from her staff not much easier. Nemeye, who had now been with her for eleven years, begged for and got her promise that she would soon return, then broke into tears. Vatiri and the six men of the antipoaching patrol volunteered their services to help carry her sixteen wooden boxes, cartons, and suitcases down the mountain. When she climbed into the front seat of the pickup waiting at the parking lot, chief porter Gwehandagoza gave her a small effigy of a gorilla carved in gleaming hardwood. "He didn't say," Dian noted, "but I think it was good *suma*."

She had need of a little benevolent magic as her time of exile began.

On the fourth I left Kigali and flew right on to Ithaca from New York—it was a long haul and a big jump. Glenn Hausfater and some other people from Cornell kindly met me, then I had to start in looking for a place to live. After a week I got flu and was flat on my back for ten days between changes of motels/hotels. The transition from camp to here was grim enough without having my temperature fluctuate from 105 to 100 and back in five minutes' time. My brain was totally broiled. I kept screaming for my Africans. A bad scene, and I felt as if all was finished.

Finally found an apartment—not what I had in mind but not bad. It is somewhat naked but does have a bed, a color TV, and an ironing board that I can use as a table to eat, sort slides, and type on. The thought of having to find and buy everything again from scratch is depressing. I am often inclined to feel I should quit playing the fool in trying to set up housekeeping again at my age. I keep wanting to yell for Kanyaragana to give me a hand—in fact I was told by a friend that I actually do this in my sleep!

At least I've learned to remember to flush the toilet and how to turn on the lights—a remarkable achievement after only three weeks in this country. Have also bought a '76 car, a bit on the rusty side. I will eventually get a driver's license—perhaps.

On March 23 I went to Washington for a meeting with Mr. Brylawski and others about the Digit Fund, but also to get my stuff that was shipped there with the Criglers' when they left Kigali. It was stored in Fidelity Storage, and their fidelity was so strong they wouldn't even let me in to look at it, let alone take it away. So I don't know when I'll be able to get my African furniture, pictures, and clothing. For sure, life isn't as simple in the States as in Rwanda!

Spring term at Cornell ends about May 10, before when I have to give two public lectures and am supposed to work on scientific papers. Cornell has given me an office with the use of a secretary at Langmuir Laboratories. Have been able to do really up-to-date reading thanks to Dr. Hausfater's library and the campus library. Have become quite stimulated by all the reading, notes taken, ideas formulated for lectures, and the opportunity to get on with my writing. All is made simple by the ease in which one is able to commute to Langmuir along near-rural roads, even though my car is not great. It blew up the first day and today had to be towed to a garage.

The ABC film made at camp last December was aired last weekend, and I wanted to crawl into a box after watching it. I looked like my own great-grandmother and was just about as articulate as she would have been without her teeth! Amazing to think of all the money they spent just to produce a half an hour filled with advertisements.

Have found a good doctor in Ithaca who has diagnosed a long-term internal condition, and his medication really seems to be working. Have been on it two days and feel like a wobbly colt. Perhaps I may eventually become "humanized" here at Cornell. For sure it is a great place to rehabituate long-term field-workers,

**but every time I think of camp I feel knives turning over in my heart.**

It is difficult to see how Dian would have been able to accomplish the "grim transition" from Karisoke to an utterly foreign way of life in Ithaca without the powerful and sympathetic support of Glenn Hausfater. Within ten days of her arrival in Ithaca they had become lovers.

Hausfater proved to be the kind of considerate and compassionate man who could tolerate Dian's emotional idiosyncrasies with no lessening of his affection for her. He was also, in her own words, "so full of fun and understanding." During those first, hard weeks of readjustment, he was her guide, mentor, companion, and "family." Not only did he pilot her through the intricacies of academe, he introduced her to people with whom she could feel at ease and to the homey comforts of an upstate college town. He took her to such sancta as Curry in a Hurry and the State Diner, and to roadhouses and discos. In addition he explored with her the woodlands and open fields within walking distance of her apartment, where she could find squirrels, raccoons, deer, and even an occasional fox.

But Karisoke remained very much with her. During her visit to Washington on March 23, Fulton Brylawski summoned a meeting of the Board of the Digit Fund Inc. in his offices. It was attended not only by the three directors—Dian, Brylawski, and Dr. Snider—but by Melvin M. Payne, Chairman of the Board of the National Geographic Society, and by Secretary-Treasurer Robinson McIlvaine.

Dian reported on the use she had made of the fund's money in training, equipping, and paying antipoacher patrols, and on their accomplishments—"four thousand traps destroyed in a single year." With regret she told her board that the patrols had been suspended since mid-March because in her absence nobody at camp was willing to supervise and organize them.

Then it was the secretary-treasurer's turn. According to the minutes of the meeting:

"Mr. McIlvaine proposed that the board consider a dissolution of the Digit Fund Inc. as a separate entity, to allow it to be merged into the activities of the African Wildlife Leadership Foundation."

He ran headlong into trouble. The tractable Dian Fossey he had known in other days was not at that meeting. In her place was a woman who refused to countenance such a merger and who proclaimed in no uncertain terms that the Digit Fund would continue in existence until the last poacher had been driven from the Virungas.

248

She finished with a ringing repetition of her battle cry—"I will *not* allow* Digit to have died in vain!"

It was the august Melvin Payne who oiled the troubled waters with the suggestion that a decision be postponed for a year, "upon the understanding that if at that time there was still a consensus for the continuation of the Fund as a separate entity, Mr. McIlvaine might feel compelled to withdraw from an active role in managing the affairs of the Fund." The meeting was adjourned.

Meanwhile trouble was brewing in Rwanda. The V-W couple had befriended Peter Veit and through him had sounded out Perlmeter about returning to camp and reoccupying their old cabin. Politely but firmly Perlmeter rejected this attempted infiltration. But then, a few days later, von der Becke, who had become friendly with Perlmeter, confided in him that Sandy Harcourt still planned to come to Karisoke and not only had the funding support of the National Geographic Society, but had been told by Benda-Lema that he could return whenever he wished.

The three young men at Karisoke were shaken by the news. None believed he would last very long under Harcourt. So Perlmeter wrote Harcourt a carefully worded letter pointing out that Karisoke was *not* currently being funded by the National Geographic but by Dian herself, and that the center could accommodate no additional researchers. He concluded bravely: "I feel it is my responsibility as on-site director to discourage any attempts by you and your wife to return to the center during the upcoming year."

Harcourt did not reply. However, he informed the V-W couple that he would soon be arriving in Kigali. When this news reached Stuart, he began to panic. On March 27 he wrote to Dian:

"*Harcourt is coming in April*—no doubt to visit camp to see what the situation is. What *is* the status of the camp, Dian? If National Geo gives him money and authority, what course of action do I have to take to prevent his coming and taking charge? You were counting on his pride preventing his coming, but that doesn't seem to be deterring him in the least!"

No longer isolated on an equatorial mountain, Dian could now fight back more effectively. She appealed directly to the mandarins at the National Geographic Society for support, pointing out that she had fulfilled the conditions demanded of her and asking that the long-deferred maintenance grant that she had been promised be released to the Karisoke Research Center immediately. Perhaps feeling some compunction, the Society agreed to do this. Furthermore, Dian

249

was told that Harcourt's grant would be withheld, pending clarification of the situation.

This seemed like victory, but if Dian thought she had checkmated Sandy Harcourt, she greatly underestimated his tenacity. She would also have had to overlook the fact that he was still the first choice of those who wanted her replaced or, depending on how one looked at it, supplanted, at Karisoke.

On April 11, Stuart Perlmeter wrote again:

"This afternoon I was called upon by Mr. Sandy Harcourt, who proceeded to inform me in his customary style that he was coming to Karisoke whether I like it or not." Harcourt informed Perlmeter that he had authorization from ORTPN and grant money from the Guggenheim Foundation to support both Kelly and himself. "I knew at that point I was dealing with a very ambitious man who was intent on taking this place over as soon as possible."

Perlmeter concluded that if Harcourt *did* return to Karisoke, he would have no alternative but to leave, even though, "if I leave I'll be giving in to what Harcourt is hoping for and ushering in a new dynasty."

This letter did not reach Dian until late in April, which, until then, had been a good month for her. She had given free rein to her deep-rooted domestic instincts, and the apartment was becoming a home. It became uniquely hers when her crates and cases arrived from Washington, and the walls could be hung with African mattings, spears, carvings, and gorilla portraits, giving this otherwise sterile cubicle in a concrete cliff at least an illusion of the ambience of Africa.

During this period she delivered two well-received public lectures and settled into her office at the Langmuir Laboratory. Anita McClellan, a pretty young woman with a strong romantic bent, arrived, bearing an edited copy of Dian's manuscript. Although the two had previously known each other only through correspondence, they discovered during the next four days that they could become boon companions.

Upon receiving Perlmeter's *cri de coeur*, Dian dispatched a cable reassuring him that Harcourt and the Mountain Gorilla Project interlopers could and would be kept at bay. To make sure that he stood firm, she proposed to return to Karisoke for a brief visit in July, at which time she would undertake to clear the air with ORTPN.

Ten days later another letter from Perlmeter reached her. Its contents were devastating. Paulin Nkubili—"Uncle Billy"—the one Rwandan official she trusted implicitly and who had been her shield through the years, had been accused of involvement in a coup against the president and would probably be executed. Perlmeter then told Dian that he could no longer endure the pressures of Karisoke: "I've loved the work up to this point, but I'm afraid if I don't leave soon I will no longer be able to perform the job I was assigned to do. . . . Since you are planning to return in July, would it be possible for you to find an interested student who would like to take over the position until you return permanently. . . . I am serious about a replacement, Dian. I don't know how much longer I can survive at Karisoke."

This letter effectively shattered Dian's fragile sense of well-being.

**A horrid, horrid day. Bad letter from Stuart. Harcourt will never give up. I don't know what to do.**

Perlmeter's threatened defection was not the only circumstance fueling a feeling of defeat and depression. She now heard that the National Geographic grant to Harcourt and Kelly was "only on hold" and that a growing number of prominent primatologists were convinced that Harcourt would do a better job of running the center than she had done because:

"He is a more objective and a better-trained scientist." Despite her long experience in the field and her Cambridge Ph.D., Dian realized that she was still an amateur in the eyes of the scientific establishment.

Throughout May and early June new blows continued to descend upon her. The discovery that she was not the only woman in Glenn's life temporarily turned what she had called her "rhapsody in Ithaca" into an emotional cacophony.

On May 13 she was told by a prominent neurologist that the damage to her spine was probably irreversible and that she should prepare herself for the likelihood of becoming a paraplegic. She was still suffering from emphysema and undiagnosed thoracic pains. The internal infection (having to do with her kidneys), which she had so optimistically believed defeated, returned to plague her. To further compound her bodily ailments, she had missed several menstrual periods and was afraid she might be pregnant.

The fates gave her no respite. On May 19, McIlvaine abruptly resigned from the Digit Fund Inc., leaving her with the problem of finding someone to sort out the financial tangle between that fund and the AWLF/Digit Fund. Mercifully, the doughty Dr. Shirley McGreal of the International Primate Protection League volunteered her services.

During these weeks Dian's depression deepened. Night after

night she lay awake thinking about Karisoke and yearning for it.

**It is my creation. Twelve years of my life! How can I lose it now? What RIGHT have they to take it away from me just because I wasn't born with a Ph.D. in my mouth? It will be the end of the gorillas if they win.**

Cindy and Kima began to haunt her too. Not only did she find herself missing them with almost unbearable intensity, but their photographic images by her bed seemed to be accusing her of abandoning them. The gorilla portraits on her walls stared down at her reproachfully.

**I'm having horrid, horrid dreams that they will all be killed and it is my fault, my fault, my fault. . . . I can't even look their pictures in the eye.**

Another of the now-dreaded letters from Perlmeter arrived in late June. Dian spent a few minutes nostalgically examining the colorful array of Rwandan stamps—delaying the moment when she would have to face news of more disasters at Karisoke. What actually awaited her inside the pale blue airmail envelope was worse than anything she might have anticipated.

"Kima's death took us all by surprise," Perlmeter wrote. "I've rewritten this letter three times and a hundred times in my head but can't seem to find the right words."

He did his best. He described the events of June 4 when he awoke to find Kima almost comatose in her box in Dian's cabin, where he now slept. After he, John Fowler, and Kanyaragana had tried everything they knew to rouse her, they wrapped her in a blanket and carried her down to Ruhengeri hospital. Unfortunately Dr. Vimont was on holiday and they could find nobody willing to spend time on a monkey. "The last person we asked happened to be Dr. Weiss, who just about threw us out of the place. . . . It was only after Jean-Pierre told us who he was that we realized our mistake."

By then Kima was beyond recall. The three men brought her body back to camp and buried it next day, "just past the large hagenia tree in front of your cabin. John is carving a small plaque with Kima's name on it. I don't think anything I can say will help at a time like this. Kima led a good life and chased more porters than there are stars in the heavens and gave you more comfort and love than probably any other creature you know. Please, Dian, hang in there and keep your head up."

Dian tells us little of how this tragedy affected her, other than, "Received news of Kima's death and went bonkers." Glenn abandoned his work and spent the next two days comforting her, and the solace he brought was sufficient to carry her through the worst of her mourning.

It was not so much that Kima had given Dian, as Perlmeter wrote, "more love than any other creature you know"—it was that Kima had been the recipient and repository for the outpourings of a woman's love that could find no other certain channel. Yet Kima was no mere child-surrogate, as some have said. She was a being whose needs kept Dian's capacity to love alive through years of disappointments with her own species. Her grief at Kima's loss was intense and long-lived—but not so long-lived as the guilt she felt at having left Kima behind at Karisoke.

Karisoke had now become a frail vessel at the center of a maelstrom generated by agencies of three national governments and such powerful organizations as the Fauna Preservation Society, the World Wildlife Fund, the National Geographic Society, and the African Wildlife Leadership Foundation.

It was painfully clear to Dian that the center could not continue to exist as the ad hoc structure she had originally created. If it was to endure, it would have to be provided with a power base of its own. Early in 1980 she had conceived of something she called an "oversight committee." This was to be a board of directors recruited from among prestigious primatologists and conservationists in the United States and abroad, who would form an impregnable defensive phalanx to protect the future of Karisoke.

Somewhat to her surprise, even some of those whom she knew to be among her antagonists applauded the idea. By the end of May 1980, sixteen influential men and women had agreed to serve as members of the Board of Scientific Directors of the Karisoke Research Institute. The first meeting was called in Ithaca for June 26 to discuss policy and organization—and to select a field director to run the center in Dian's absence.

Dian felt confident that her personal choice, Dr. Hal Bauer, would be accepted. But less than two weeks before the meeting, Dian received a confidential telephone call during which she was told that Harcourt had *already been selected* as the new director of Karisoke and would be attending the Ithaca meeting to discuss terms. No alternative would be considered. Unless she accepted Harcourt, there would be no further financial support for Karisoke, and the imprimatur of the scientific establishment would be withdrawn.

Without Harcourt, Karisoke Research Center would not be permitted to survive.

Coming hard on the heels of so many afflictions, this ultimatum was a vicious blow. Yet, in all fairness, many of those involved sincerely believed they were acting in Dian's best interests. As one participant, who does not care to be identified, explained:

"She was a very sick woman. The life she had led and the terrible physical disabilities had worn her down. They had also seriously affected her judgment. All that she had built at Karisoke was in danger of falling down because of her fixation about poachers. That would have been a terrible loss to science. The only hope was to get her out of it. Not just for a few months, but permanently. In order to save her, we had to outmaneuver her. I don't think anybody liked it, but it had to be done. She was such a great fighter, you know."

Dian was a fighter whose reservoirs of endurance and indomitability had yet to be plumbed. But she was also possessed of the intelligence to know when she had been outflanked and of the ability to fall back and regroup.

Only five directors actually attended that first board meeting. They were Drs. Stuart and Jeanne Altman, Glenn Hausfater, Emil Menzel, and Ed Snider. All were pleasantly surprised and some vastly relieved by Dian's tractability. Although she gave an impassioned résumé of the history of Karisoke, and took a trenchant and unrepentant stand on the subject of "active conservation" and the vital necessity of continuing it, she proved remarkably amenable to allowing Harcourt to assume the position of acting center director for one year. In recognition of this unlooked-for cooperation, the board proposed that she accept the post of program coordinator.

This was not much of a sop. In return for being allowed to serve as "liaison between the board and individuals wanting to carry out research at the center," she was required to "attempt to obtain funds for the maintenance and basic operating costs of the Karisoke Research Center as well as for the salary for the center director." This meant finding money to keep Karisoke going at least partially for Harcourt's benefit, together with money to pay him a salary—something Dian had never had. But she swallowed even this dose of wormwood and gall.

Several explanations have been proffered as to why she so passively accepted what was intended to be her permanent ouster from Karisoke. The most widely accepted one is that she really was almost at death's door, had deteriorated mentally, and secretly wanted nothing so much as to be allowed to grow old and die in peace in some academic backwater, but was too proud to admit it.

This hardly jibes with her own sardonic observations on the meeting.

Rather than knocking her out of the ring for good, the first meeting of the Karisoke board of directors revitalized Dian. Perhaps this was just the tonic and the challenge she needed. At any rate, she now buckled down to her book with a single-mindedness that startled Anita McClellan. Up until this time, she had viewed the book as her obeisance to science. Now she began to see it as a way to appeal to the general public to support the cause of the Mountain Gorillas.

**For people who come to my lectures, a gorilla isn't just a stack of scientific data. It is alive. They can feel for it in life and death. They *care* about Digit and Uncle Bert and all the rest. My book can help them do the same.**

Anita McClellan encouraged this point of view, and the revisions proceeded apace.

Dian's health also began to show improvement. A new specialist prescribed a treatment for her back that worked well enough at least to postpone the prospect of radical surgery. Her kidney infection responded to new drugs. She was not pregnant, and hormone treatments brought her gynecologic problems under control.

By mid-July 1980, she was feeling well enough to swoop down on Karisoke for a quick visit before Harcourt arrived. She told only a few friends of her intention because she had been warned that Harcourt's Rwandan ally, ORTPN director Benda-Lema, would do all he could to prevent her from returning. She did not fly the usual route via New York and Brussels—she went first to Tokyo to deliver a public lecture and conduct some seminars at the invitation of the Japanese film company with whose team she had worked at Karisoke. It was here she obtained her visa for Rwanda.

Despite these precautions, when she arrived in Kigali on July 26, it was to be met by a perturbed American embassy official.

"I have to tell you, Miss Fossey, there might be some trouble about your admissibility to Rwanda. There could be an incident at Immigration, and we certainly don't want that, do we? The ambassador sent me along to ease the way."

Nervously he guided Dian through the formalities of entry. There were no difficulties, although as she would later discover, Benda-Lema had indeed asked the Rwandan Foreign Office to exclude her. The request had been ignored by the foreign minister, who was an intimate of President Habyarimana. Dian still had friends in high places.

Benda-Lema did what he could to make her visit difficult. ORTPN had been refusing to renew the visitor's permits of the current set of Karisoke researchers, and Dian determined to put this right, but for four days was unable even to find the elusive Benda-Lema. It was not until she appealed to higher authority that he emerged from hiding.

They met at last at ORTPN headquarters.

**He and I had about an hour's meeting, and it was hard to tell who was the phonier—a fly on the wall would have enjoyed the sweet syrup that flowed. . . . But he knew, and I knew he knew, he had his orders. With absolutely no difficulty I got Peter Veit extended through January 1981. During our meeting, eventually joined by others of ORTPN, I swear I could hear harp music and the chattering of little angels overhead. B-L himself admitted that Harcourt had advised him that Peter's work was "unscientific" and, therefore, should be terminated.**

An extension of John Fowler's permit was also arranged, but there was no need to do this for Stuart Perlmeter, since he had no desire to remain. In fact, on the same day Dian finally climbed the long trail to camp, he departed from a place and situation that had become intolerable to him.

**From Ruhengeri I hired a taxi to drive to the base of the mountain and climbed, and it was really emotional to see the Africans crying, laughing, dancing, and beating their heads over my return. Arrived at camp at about 3:10 and went to the graveyard first. The sadness of seeing again all the names of the dead gorillas was overwhelming . . . the sadness of not seeing Kima alive left me with such a void and feelings of depression. Many people didn't like her too well, but I loved her so very much. . . .**

**Seeing Cindy was nearly as bad. She was all bald on her back and legs, just skin and bones, and could hardly walk. Like Kima, she hadn't been fed properly. I knew right away that I couldn't leave her again.**

**Everything looked shabby and run-down; unpainted cabins and overgrown trails. Most of my chickens had died, and I only saw two duikers in the four days I was there. The paperwork was in such a mess I had no time to visit the groups, except one. Saw Group 5, but it was a bad contact, with tourists on the trail before we got there and no chance for a get-together because the gorillas were so nervous.**

Mutarutkwa, the Zairean Tutsi who works on the patrols, came to say hello as soon as he heard I'd arrived. Two or three weeks ago he was attacked by three poachers, and I guess he just picked them up and shook them out. He heard from them that another infant gorilla was captured from the other side of Mt. Mikeno. Patrols from this camp have just about stopped, and as usual the park guards are hardly doing anything. I wonder how many more gorillas have to die before people realize what *really* needs doing in the Virungas. . . .

Ian Redmond, who is currently training guards at the park on a short-term contract, also came to camp to say hello. It was like old times to see him, but unfortunately we only had an hour together. He thinks even the parking lot gang are apprehensive about Harcourt's return now. Well, they made their bed, they can lie in it.

On August 3, Dian descended the mountain, leaving John Fowler and Peter Veit to run things as best they could until the new regime took over. This time she did not go alone. The old dog followed close at Dian's heels, and when her stiff legs would carry her no longer, Kanyaragana picked her up and draped her gently around his neck.

I'm ever so pleased I brought Cindy away with me, though as one might imagine, it was one chaotic trip! In Bujumbura they wouldn't let me see her in the belly of the plane, but I won out in Nairobi. The stewardess took me to the ramp where they were unloading cargo; the ramp ground to a halt while I climbed up to find Cindy's cage right near the front door. I put in water and the crappy food given to passengers for a "snack" and talked to her, and the local Africans were really pleased with the show until the military came running up wondering what the hell was going on! Then *they* got into the act since many of the older men remembered me passing through when the Nairobi airport was just a *toto*—a baby. I finally had to leave for the terminal since the dog act was holding up the cargo delivery; and I didn't see Cindy again until Brussels.

Now Cindy is very very housebroken, and I'd been very worried about this. At Brussels airport there was a "greeting girl," and I told her I had to get my dog out of cargo to be with me during the nine-hour layover.

There were also two little boys, sons of an American embassy guy in Kigali, on the flight, and the three of us were taken into a special lounge for kids. I felt like I too should be wearing an identification tag and sucking a lollipop. Finally the "greeting girl" came back to our kindergarten to tell me I could go down into the pits of the airport among dozens of revolving belts, noise, and utter chaos.

There was Cindy in her cage without water or anything. I took her out immediately, but she still wouldn't pee on the cement, so I had to take her through immigration and finally found a bit of grass right in front of the airport. I thought she was going to flood the whole of Brussels. One of the little boys had come with me, and he kept saying, "Wow! Look at *that!*"

Cindy's ordeal was not yet over. Somehow she weathered the long trip across the Atlantic, a mad taxi ride between John F. Kennedy Airport and La Guardia, and a final flight to Ithaca—again demonstrating her remarkable ability to retain her water.

Dian and her weary old dog were met by Stacey Coil, a young secretary at Langmuir who had been assigned to work for Dian, and who had developed an admiration for her bordering on hero worship.

"My mom and stepfather were up from Florida and had rented a cottage on Cayuga Lake that was big enough for fifteen people. Well . . . I somehow invited Dian to stay with them.

"When my husband and I arrived with Dian from the airport, my poor mom had heard so much about her and read everything I had been able to give her and was keyed up to the hilt with nervousness. When we finally got to the cottage it was late and dark. . . . You would have convulsed with laughter if you could have seen my mom's face when my husband unloaded an empty, very large cage from the back of the car. Of course, Dian was very much in charge and made herself at home and started bringing in everything while we got this surprise out of the other side of the car (my mom could only see this very large, dark, moving animal being taken out).

"We all went inside and had coffee to get acquainted. Then Dian went to the door and hollered in her big, booming voice for Cindy (my mom by this time is a little hysterical, but I thought it was just from having this famous person staying with her).

"In comes big, old, slobbering Cindy. Well, my mother almost cried she laughed so hard. She had thought Dian had brought a gorilla with her."

Temporarily leaving Cindy with the Coil family, Dian made her first visit to her own family since her return to the United States in early March. She was in California ten days and has left no record of what took place. By August 22 she was back in Ithaca, sharing her

North Lansing apartment with Cindy and concentrating her energies on her book and on preparing a lecture course on Comparative Behavior and Ecology of the Great Apes, which she would begin delivering in September.

With her return to Cornell she began making a strenuous effort to compartmentalize her life and to relegate that aspect of it concerned with the ongoing feuds and tensions surrounding the Karisoke Research Center to a kind of limbo from which she could remain emotionally detached. Although in her role as program coordinator she continued to receive and reply to letters from Harcourt, the board of scientific directors, and others of that ilk, she dealt with them distantly, almost ritualistically.

Like a wounded and exhausted animal, she withdrew herself until she could heal her hurts and renew both her physical and psychic strength. Cornell, and the easygoing and self-contained academic life of the town and the university, provided the refuge she so badly needed. But Dian never intended it to become a permanent shelter for the rest of her days. She saw it as a sanctuary from which, in due course, she would emerge to renew the fight for what she believed in—and for what was hers.

She did not develop a large circle of friends, but did enjoy a special warmth with the half dozen or so men and women whom she came to know with some degree of intimacy. These included one or two students, Stacey Coil, and some other Cornell staff members. Glenn Hausfater continued foremost among them. What had begun as a passionate and all-engrossing love affair had now burned down, but Glenn remained an enduring pillar of support throughout Dian's time of need. In late September she wrote to him while he was away in Colorado:

"I love it here tremendously and my lectures are going well, even though each takes an entire week to prepare. . . . Cindy and I have walked Monkey Run about six times. We also did Sapsucker Woods, though apparently no dogs are allowed there. It was beautiful and we saw a huge stag. Other than write and do lecture notes, I honestly don't do anything except walk Cindy. It sounds rather boring, but I feel myself falling into place again for the first time since Digit was killed in December 1977.

"I will stop now and take Cindy back to Sapsucker Woods to see the lovely beaver pond with all the turtles and birds. I love it there. I do miss you so much and wish I could be the only one to meet you once you return to Ithaca. I know that can't because of —— and probably others. Just know, please, that your return is special to me."

Not all her autumnal excursions into the countryside were so pleasant. One Saturday afternoon she drove Cindy north to a state forest Hausfater had shown her. She and the dog went for a ramble through the fields at the edge of the woods. Dian was reveling in the first flush of fall colors when she was startled by a barrage of shotgun fire. A few minutes later a party of camouflage-costumed hunters emerged from the woods nearby.

**They were dragging the body of a yearling deer and it was just a bloody mess, its intestines dragging behind. When they saw me and Cindy, they stopped and grinned as if their faces would split. One of them yelled, "Hey, lady, look at what we just got ourselves!"**

**There were *five* of the big bastards, and the yearling was hardly bigger than Cindy, but they were so damn proud of themselves. Fun hunters make me vomit!**

She wrote Rosamond Carr in Rwanda:

"Cindy now looks like a puppy; well, almost, has a beautiful coat and is sleekly healthy. I know she misses camp, but I spend about two hours a day walking her in the woods around the apartment and around the laboratory where I work in the country. She still isn't accustomed to being kept in the apartment except when I am with her, but they are always on the hunt for dogs around here as so much experimentation is done by the Cornell vet school that dogs are in constant demand. I am so glad I brought her back and only wish I could get rid of the guilt that I didn't bring Kima.

"I love my apartment, which is scarcely five minutes from work. But I don't like the proximity of neighbors—upstairs, downstairs, and next door—and would like to find a more rural place. All of the mattings, pictures, and carvings are now on the walls just as they were in my cabin.

"You won't believe it, but my lectures at Cornell are going just great! I can't believe it either, I was terrified of trying to teach since I only knew about gorillas and not about orangutans or chimpanzees. You'll never know how frightened I was that first day of class. Have now managed seven lectures, each of two hours, and can't get over the receptiveness of the twenty-five to forty students that show up each Tuesday. More and more people continue to show up, and we all learn from one another. The students range from freshmen to graduates to professors, so there is a great exchange of thoughts.

"WOW, I am working eighteen hours a day preparing the lectures and doing a second rewrite on my book, plus giving gratis lectures to schools in upstate New York. I don't recall ever working so hard in my life—mentally that is, but not physically. It's nice to get fat on junk food and I am finally FAT!

"No, Rosamond, I am not meeting very many people because I have so much to do, and everyone is so much younger than I am. I *am* inclined to get very, very lonely, but that is only because of missing the gorillas and Kima and the home that was, in Rwanda. But you know me well enough to realize that I am not giving up all that for good. I'm not just going to settle down here and 'reap my laurels.' But first I have to fulfill my obligations to Cornell and, above all, finish my book. I must also get all my health back, or as much of it as I can. At the end of December I hope to spend a week in Toronto for enzyme injections in my spine to take care of the sciatica that gets progressively worse in the cold weather.

"I think of you so much and would give anything to visit you for tea this afternoon! Honestly, for me, going from Ithaca to Gisenyi would be far less traumatic than going there from Karisoke, where I am, I guess, an alien now."

This was no overstatement. On September 25, Sandy Harcourt had arrived at Karisoke to take command. Although he only remained for a month before giving himself a leave of absence in England that lasted until January of 1981, he made it abundantly clear that Dian was, and would remain, persona non grata at camp during his tenure as acting director (he did not use that title, but always referred to himself either as center or scientific director).

Winter came to Ithaca, and Dian worked diligently at her lectures and her book. She saw enough of Glenn to assuage somewhat her loneliness, but for the most part was reclusive, spending her spare time reading or walking Cindy. She spent one entire weekend counting Canadian geese flying south. On another occasion she lost herself and the dog while trying to track a band of white-tailed deer. Then the snows came and restricted her excursions because the cold and the hard going made walking too painful an ordeal.

The human being she probably saw most was her secretary and busy young housewife, Stacey Coil. One November day she took Stacey with her in her rusty little car, into which she had to fold herself like an accordion, while she went for her driving test. It was a disaster. A white-knuckled driver at the best of times, Dian was so infuriated by a testy examiner that she ended the ordeal by slamming on the brakes, pulling hard into the curb, levering herself out of the driver's seat, and threatening to abandon car, Stacey, *and* examiner.

Her lectures continued to be well received. In fact, her students voted her the best professor of the year, a compliment she accepted gruffly in class and wept over in her apartment afterwards.

All through December she was preoccupied by thoughts of an appointment that had been made for her at a Canadian hospital where she was to undergo a new and radical procedure for her damaged back. On the second-last day of the year she flew off to Toronto on what she described as "maybe the last chance to beat being a cripple the rest of my days."

Her appointment was with Dr. John McCulloch, an orthopedic surgeon who had pioneered the use of a papaya enzyme to dissolve fused spinal disks. On a bleak winter afternoon she reported to St. Michael's Hospital.

Later she shared her experience with a friend afflicted by the same problem:

"Try and get a private room if you can (I couldn't) and prepare for horrid food. You go to the operating room in a wheelchair, totally awake with no prior shots. Once there you lie belly down on a cold, flat slab that wakes you up even more. Then the anesthesiologist starts an IV of liquid Valium.

"Still very, very, *very* much awake, you lie there as the doctor injects the enzyme into the particular disk involved. It takes about fifteen minutes for all of the joy juice to get into you. Part of the reason you are kept awake is so that McCulloch knows he is hitting the right spot! I got the impression that the more it hurt, the better a job he thought he was doing. That's all there is to it.

"Dr. McCulloch's success rate is now in the ninety percent area simply because of his cautious approach, and people have gone to him unable to walk because of pain and have walked out of there Lourdes-style. They told me I could leave at 10:00 A.M. next day, but seemed to ignore the fact that I couldn't stand up! Finally they found me an oversized corset that helped a lot, but getting back to my hotel with my luggage was a nightmare. One should never go alone for a job like this. . . .

"Within one month my pains were half gone; within two months practically all gone; and after four, no pain at all. It's like a new life to be without it. Since I'd had it for some three years, I found it difficult to break the habit of limping.

"A lot of American doctors disapprove of the procedure, thus it is illegal in this country. Thank God for Canada!"

t took Dian some time to recover from having her disks "digested by the papaya monster." A spring, 1981, teaching semester was offered by Cornell, but she was in no condition to cope with it. After a few weeks of rest, however, she was able to drive between the apartment and her office at Langmuir in her dubious little car.

January had another nasty surprise in store. Early on the sixteenth, one of Karisoke's trackers came running to Peter Veit to report that Dian's cabin had been broken into. Veit, who had been the only white in camp since the beginning of the new year, hurried to investigate. He found that someone had used tin snips to cut a crawl hole through the corrugated tin wall directly below a corner window of Dian's bedroom. Two intruders had thoroughly rummaged the room, stuffed their loot into six bedcovers converted into makeshift bags, and then fled down the main trail. They must have been singularly powerful individuals, since they took with them a movie camera together with fifty pounds of batteries and accessories, three typewriters, two microscopes, two pairs of binoculars, a desk chair, a pillow, ten towels, six sleeping bags, four camera tripods, and a variety of smaller objects.

They were never caught and no trace of the stolen property was ever found. This was the first time that Karisoke had been burglarized during the dozen years of its existence. The worst aspect of it, from Dian's point of view, was not the loss of equipment, valuable though this was, but the feeling that her home, the place she had helped build with her own hands and that was an essential part of her, had been violated.

**It would never have happened had I been there. It's like an omen. Karisoke is coming apart at the seams, and things will probably get worse.**

This gloomy prediction was undoubtedly inspired by the knowledge that, on the day after the robbery, Sandy Harcourt had finally taken up permanent residence as the new master of Karisoke.

Harcourt's regime was rigorously devoted to ensuring that Karisoke function as a *research* center. He had no intention of allowing anything to detract from what he conceived to be the camp's legitimate purpose—the collection of data. The nature of the data was not a matter of much moment so long as it had scientific merit. During his time, researchers would concern themselves with such disparate subjects as the weather, insect pests in the native shambas, regeneration of hagenia trees, and high-altitude vegetation. The compilation of esoteric facts and fragments of facts about Mountain Gorillas also continued, but this aspect was largely the private province of Harcourt and Kelly Stewart.

His priorities were not Dian's. In her view the most important role for Karisoke was to ensure that the creatures of the park continued to exist *in life*, rather than in the abstract as mere accumulations of information.

**Data gathering surely is important, but things haven't changed that much from the days when scientists shot everything in sight to gather data. They built their reputations then on mainly dead animals. Now they use live animals too, but the principle is the same. Alive or dead, you use the data to pile up a lot of research papers until you've got enough to get "silverback" status. Nothing terribly wrong with that, except that many modern scientists, just like their predecessors, don't seem to care if the study species perish, just so that they get all the facts they need about them first.**

It was, of course, inevitable that trouble would result between the acting director at Karisoke and the program director in Ithaca. What was not foreseen was the intensity of the battle royal that did ensue.

An exhaustive, and exhausting, account of the conflict is preserved in a vast accumulation of paper shot-and-shell exchanged between the two combatants, their allies, and supporters. What follows is only a synoptic record.

On September 27, 1980, just two days after he took command,

Harcourt complained that he had been given no money to run the camp and that the extensive back-files of gorilla data were missing. He wanted both matters rectified immediately "so this place can begin to function again." Soon thereafter, he informed the board that ORTPN wanted only "park-relevant" studies to be conducted at the center. These would emphasize such subjects as tourism and would downplay the behavioral studies of gorillas for which Karisoke had been established and had become famous. Harcourt announced that he intended to make ORTPN's requirements the center's top priority for 1981, although he and Kelly would, of course, continue with their own behavioral studies.

His next step was to write Dr. Jeanne Altman, chairperson of the board, to inform her that Benda-Lema had "formally, and in writing," accepted him as director—not *acting* director, be it noted. "ORTPN has recognized that the position is tenable for two years," he added, in what seemed a rather transparent attempt to gain similar recognition from the board.

Dr. Altman did not take kindly to these "communiqués from an appointee of the board," and Dian prematurely concluded that Harcourt had been put in his place. She wrote jubilantly to Rosamond: "He is Acting Director now . . . but although he may be allowed to burp on December 20 (or whenever) at 2:00 P.M., he will have to get permission first."

On January 26 he lobbed a volley over Dian's head with a demand to the new board chairman, Dr. John Eisenberg, that all of Karisoke's facilities surplus to his own and Kelly's needs be made available to workers in "applied research" relating to park administrative and procedural problems. Harcourt warned that unless up to *ten* such workers were admitted to the center, ORTPN might simply take over the whole place. Nobody took this threat very seriously, but Dian was quick to point out that any such arrangement would leave no room for new students who wanted to study gorillas.

There was a continuing exchange of small arms fire about money. Harcourt took the position that the large National Geographic grant he had received was his and Kelly's to spend entirely on their own projects. The responsibility for Karisoke's operating costs, he insisted, rested with Dian. It was up to her to find funds to pay the staff, keep the center's combi running, and keep the buildings and equipment in repair. He complained bitterly that, as things stood, he was being forced to pay camp costs out of his own pocket.

In July he suddenly reversed the field by announcing that he would be willing to find the operating funds himself *if* confirmation of an additional year or two as director was forthcoming. Robert Hinde of Cambridge, once Dian's doctoral tutor, now a board member and a strong Harcourt supporter, thought this seemed eminently reasonable. He recommended that Harcourt's directorship be extended to *three* years—a suggestion to which Eisenberg, also a Harcourt man, responded favorably.

Nevertheless, the board as a whole was growing restive. Although many of those who had initially supported Harcourt continued to do so, some few were becoming concerned that all was not as it should be. It was therefore decided that Glenn Hausfater, who was due to become the next chairman, should visit the center and bring back a firsthand report.

Harcourt was told to expect Hausfater at the end of September. "His Imperial Majesty," Dian noted, "was not pleased." In letters to all concerned Harcourt made it clear that the board's representative would not be welcome. He wrote Hausfater to tell him that nobody would be available to meet him at Ruhengeri Airport, that he was expected to bring his own food with him and pay "a per diem for use of my staff during your period here."

In response to a politic suggestion by Hausfater that the visit should help pave the way for Harcourt's reappointment as center director, Harcourt claimed that he had already been reappointed as director. He therefore wondered "if your visit is in fact necessary."

One of the board members who was having second thoughts was Dr. Snider of the National Geographic. Dian was delighted to find this old friend in her corner once again and quick to take his advice that she apply personally to the Society for the funding of Karisoke in 1982.

Presumably because he would not have controlled this money, Harcourt flatly rejected the proposal, adding that, in the event such funding was forthcoming, both he and Kelly would refuse to sign the standard literary release form required of all recipients of National Geographic grants.

Even some of Harcourt's loyal supporters were now becoming alarmed by his behavior. Dr. Hinde wrote to his protégé, pleading with him to be more gracious. "I can see that there are a lot of things that irritate you . . . but it really doesn't help to write such prickly letters. It doesn't make it easier for those who are trying to oil the wheels." An only slightly chastened Harcourt replied that, considering his perception of Dian Fossey's behavior, past and present, he found it extremely difficult to be polite to her—let alone gracious. He then unburdened himself of his feelings about Glenn Hausfater. "I don't think that Glenn will work as chairperson . . . my paranoia about Dian Fossey is too great." The letter concluded with an enigmatic phrase suggesting that all was not well in camp.

Hausfater arrived in Rwanda on September 30 and found the country in some turmoil as the result of another suspected coup. He described what ensued in a letter to the board:

"Prior to reaching Kigali, the taxi I was in was stopped and my bags, in particular, searched. All hotels, including the Catholic mission, were under government orders not to provide rooms for foreigners or strangers. After finding accommodations at a friend's house I was awakened, interrogated, and searched by the intelligence section of the police. Upon nearing the park headquarters next day I met an army blockade and was told they were . . . under strict instructions not to allow any visitors to the park.

"After returning to Kigali I was assisted by the American embassy in obtaining permission from the vice-president's office to pass through the Ruhengeri barricades. However, ORTPN now refused me permission to visit the Karisoke Center, and so with only two days remaining of my allotted time, I gave up and went on to Kenya."

However much the threat of a coup may have contributed to Hausfater's discomfiture, both he and Dian believed that ORTPN's action had little to do with a state of emergency and much to do with a willingness to cooperate with the current center director, who was himself so cooperative with ORTPN.

Harcourt now lobbed another bombshell at the board in which he registered displeasure at the prospect of Hausfater's becoming even interim chairman. Not a few board members reacted with indignation at what they viewed as this unwarranted interference.

Much alarmed, Robert Hinde immediately wrote to Sandy *and* Kelly: "I am sorry about Sandy's letter; it won't increase his reputation or help to get the committee on his side."

Harcourt apologized, but the effect was marred by his disclosure that he now intended to leave his post at Karisoke at the end of 1982—unless the Rwandan government (meaning ORTPN) asked him to stay on. Some board members took this as a threat: if they did not mend their ways, ORTPN might lose patience and "foreclose" on Karisoke. Whatever Harcourt's intentions may have been, this expression of them was unfortunate. Support for his cause had already been considerably eroded—now it began to dwindle rapidly away.

By the end of October the "Karisoke Gorilla Wars"—as one exasperated board member called the feud—seemed doomed to an inconclusive stalemate. The antagonists were exhausted by the wrangling, bickering, and recriminations. Harcourt was probably suffering more than anyone, and eventually it became too much to bear.

On November 19 he decided to abandon the struggle he had been waging off and on over the past four years. He wrote to Eisenberg tendering his official resignation, to take effect at the end of 1982.

Now it only remained for the two major combatants to conclude an armistice. The olive branch was extended by Kelly Stewart in late December during a flying trip to the United States. On the twenty-second she telephoned Dian from California, and the two women figuratively fell into one another's arms.

Next morning Dian cabled a peace missive to Karisoke:

DEAR SANDY HAD WONDERFUL AND LENGTHY CONVERSATION WITH KELLY LAST NIGHT. SHE EXPLAINED HOW HARD YOU ARE WORKING AND THE DEPTH OF YOUR CARE. . . . I SO MUCH WANT 1982 TO BEGIN WITH COOPERATION, NOT COMPETITION. MEANWHILE PLEASE KNOW I REMAIN VERY PROUD OF YOUR ACCOMPLISHMENTS. GIVE MY LOVE TO THE MEN. DON'T THINK OF YOURSELF BEING ALONE DURING THE SO-CALLED HOLIDAY SEASON. CINDY AND I SEND OUR BEST GREETINGS WRITING LOVE DIAN

Apart from the "Karisoke Gorilla Wars," 1981 had been relatively uneventful for Dian. While her back improved, she spent most of her days working on her book and collating research material.

The even tenor of her ways was pleasantly disrupted toward the end of April by a reunion of Louis Leakey's famous "trimates"—the three woman primatologists who had spent years of their lives in remote corners of the world learning to understand something of the nature and qualities of mankind's closest living relatives. The Leakey Foundation had arranged for Jane Goodall, Dian Fossey, and Biruté Galdikas to present a symposium at Sweet Briar College in Virginia on April 29, and the three women had agreed to rendezvous at Dian's apartment in Ithaca.

Jane was the first to arrive. Having flown almost nonstop from Africa to England, then on to New York and Ithaca, she was sorrowing for her husband, who had died only a few months earlier; and she dreaded the ordeal of a public lecture tour across the United States, which was to follow Sweet Briar. Dian did not know Jane well, but had always held her in esteem verging on awe, and so was somewhat nervous as she drove to the little airport to greet her illustrious peer.

She need not have been apprehensive. As she wrote to Jane's mother in England:

"I felt, upon seeing her, as if I was picking up a little wounded pigeon; I just hurt for her. Within a few minutes we were in my horrid apartment, and she just unwound. I felt myself the most fortunate person in the world just to be able to help her unwind. It was she who gave *me* a gift, not the other way around. . . . I've never felt as close to her—I guess because before there were always so many people around her, and I would never intrude upon her friends."

Even the subsequent arrival of Biruté Galdikas, with whom neither Jane nor Dian was especially sympathetic, did not interfere with the development of an enduring and affectionate relationship.

**This was the first time I'd ever been able to see so much of Jane, and I came to appreciate her even more than in the past. She is certainly an example that I have much to learn from— patience, dignity, graciousness, not to mention her wonderful sense of humor.**

After a "tryout of their act" at Cornell, the three flew to Sweet Briar for the symposium. There they were interviewed by Nan Robertson of *The New York Times:*

"This week Dian Fossey, Jane Goodall, and Biruté Galdikas came together in a rare meeting to talk about "What We Can Learn About Humankind From the Apes" at a symposium on the Sweet Briar College campus, which was drenched in the white dogwood and azalea of a Southern spring.

"They have become three of the world's foremost primatologists . . . with Dr. Fossey specializing in mountain gorillas, Dr. Goodall in chimpanzees, and Dr. Galdikas in orangutans.

"In conversations over two days, wedged between lectures and gala meals, the three talked about their lives and what made them tick. Dr. Fossey, forty-nine years old, is a San Franciscan, a brawny six-footer with a shock of black hair and coltish movements who somewhat resembles Julia Child. By contrast, Dr. Goodall, forty-seven and English, is wraith-thin and almost ethereal, with blond hair pulled back in a bun. The youngest of the three, Dr. Galdikas, thirty-four . . . a Canadian citizen . . . has masses of chestnut hair and bright blue eyes. . . .

"The physical discomforts in camp are often extreme. Dr. Fossey works at ten thousand feet on an extinct volcano, and there is altitude sickness and depression as well as rain, fog, and hail. Dr.

Goodall must often crawl on her stomach through bush pig tunnels to reach her subjects, and Dr. Galdikas is often neck-deep in leech-infested swamps looking for her orangutans. . . .

"This has been their life. Dr. Goodall, to whom the others defer as the pioneer, has been in the field for twenty years, Dr. Fossey for thirteen years, and Dr. Galdikas for almost a decade. . . .

"It is the solitude that finally breaks many. . . .

"Dr. Galdikas calls it 'bush fever.' Dr. Fossey calls it 'astronaut blues.' She said that 'if they can't endure the isolation, they get the sweats, they scream, shake, or cry.' The three women pooh-pooh any thought of danger, for they are comfortable with their animals, who have never hurt them seriously, not even Dr. Fossey, who works with what the early explorers called 'fearsome beasts' and what she calls 'the gentle giants.' . . . Both Dr. Goodall and Dr. Fossey imitated some of their calls, hoots, and pants, rising to hair-raising crescendos. Dr. Galdikas was asked to imitate an orangutan call and replied, somewhat sniffily, 'The adult female is virtually silent except when she's being raped.' . . .

"Dr. Fossey told of 'the silence of the forest,' putting her hands over her ears at the sound of a nearby cocktail party in the Sweet Briar president's house. 'I can't stand the noise back here,' she complained.

" 'I feel more comfortable with gorillas than people,' she said. 'I can anticipate what a gorilla's going to do, and they're purely motivated. It is true that there comes a time when I do literally dream of supermarkets and drug stores, potato chips and the Sunday morning paper. That's the beginning and the end of it.'

"And Dr. Goodall repeated what she once told Dr. Leakey: 'I don't care two hoots about civilization. I want to wander about in the wild.' "

The return to civilization certainly posed it problems. In a letter to Jane, Dian recalled how, during the seminar, "we were asked to comment on what aspect of civilized life we find most difficult to adjust to upon returning from the bush. I immediately thought of my inability to remember to flush toilets and responded with that answer without a qualm. I was going to expand on other difficulties like that, but you immediately reacted in typical English manner by punching me on the arm and saying in a semishocked voice loud enough for all to hear: 'Oh, Dian!' It was the spontaneity of your reaction that brought the house down."

On May 1 the "trimates" flew west for a joint lecture in Pasadena, but by now there was mounting friction between Dian and Biruté, and Jane had to mediate between them.

On her return to Ithaca in late May, Dian wrote to Jane:

"I don't know how to tell you just how much it meant to me to be with you on those parts of the tour we shared. Your presence truly made some of the bad scenes bearable. I have a great deal to learn from you in the way of being tactful, graceful, gracious, and businesslike. I missed you so when you got on the plane in L.A. In retrospect, that was kind of a funny departure. The 'two camps' so to speak, with Biruté in one corner and I in the other, and you so diplomatically kind in the middle."

Brief as it was, the time Jane and Dian spent together had been good for them both. Dian's genius for mothering the wounded had brought some solace to Goodall, and Jane's calm and sympathetic analysis of the Gorilla War proved a powerful antidote to the bitterness that had been festering in Dian. They parted as sustaining friends, and although they were to see each other only rarely in the years ahead, the friendship would endure.

As summer progressed and Ithaca grew increasingly hot and humid, Dian began to wilt. Work on the book dragged to a halt, so in early August, Anita McClellan rented a cottage close to the ocean at Bar Harbor. Here she and her aged dog, Boo, and Dian and Cindy spent six productive weeks. It was a marvelous and healing time for Dian and seems to have been no less memorable for Anita.

"I do want to tell you again, Dian, how wonderful it has been for me to be your editor and your friend and your peskiest fan. . . . Remember those days in Maine with our four-legged ladies and how we hammered out Chapter 5 for Coco and Pucker? Then our walks along the shore, looking at the birds and sea life, our talks in the cabin, our giggles, curses, and groans at the town library lectures? . . . How the locals ogled us on the lawn when we were yelling at each other? How Cindy insisted on supervising your every move when you picked shells on the beach?"

Dian returned to Cornell as a visiting professor when the fall semester began. As 1981 drew to its end, and the long battle with Harcourt seemed to be reaching its conclusion, she was in good mental fettle. Physically she was in better shape than she had been in years. With Anita's help she had made so much progress on the book that she could believe it would soon be completed. The publication of several scientific papers had somewhat muted the carping of her scientific peers. Good relations had been restored between herself and the National Geographic Society. She and Glenn had settled into the roles of comfortable and understanding friends. For once, the universe seemed to be unfolding as it should.

Dian spent January of 1982 holed up against the bitter winter weather in her now-familiar apartment. She worked away at the book, which by January 4 still lacked only two chapters of the twelve it would eventually contain. She went out occasionally for dinner or to a show with members of a small circle of casual friends. On January 16 some of them helped her celebrate her birthday. It was her fiftieth.

**I guess the Lone Woman of the Forests is turning into the Tame Matron of Langmuir . . . but I have to admit I feel younger today than five years back. Cindy seems to feel the same though she is fifteen now. There's life in us old dawgs yet!**

There was perhaps more truth in her jest about the transformation than she herself realized—or was willing to admit. The fact is that she was becoming increasingly reconciled to America. In dress and habit she was almost indistinguishable from the sometimes smartly turned-out female faculty members. Students and staff alike treated her with a degree of respect she had never known before—and had never wanted. Although her face was lined now and there were glints of gray in her black hair, she retained her physical attractiveness for men, even if she had much less interest in them. Although she still missed the gorillas and other animals as much as ever, and still yearned over memories of her years at Karisoke, the compulsive drive to return in the flesh had lost some of its impetus.

Furthermore, the truce with Harcourt had proved to be of the short-lived variety, and his continuing presence at camp undoubtedly did much to quench her thirst to be there.

"I begin to know I can never go back as long as he is there," she wrote to Jane Goodall, who was one of the few people to whom she still continued to address discursive letters. Long letters were becoming too much of a drain on her time, and besides, there was not the need for them in Ithaca that there had been in the isolation of the mist-shrouded volcanoes.

Harcourt began the New Year by writing to both Dian and Dr. Snider, complaining at length of having suffered financial loss and of not receiving proper financial support. He concluded his letter to Dian:

"I am not prepared to continue working as center director responsible to the KRC program coordinator and Board of Scientific Directors under such conditions. I will continue to work as center director responsible to the Rwandan government, but as far as I am concerned, all my commitments to the program coordinator and BSD . . . are ended until I receive the debt owed to me and receive funding for the running of the center in advance of expenditures."

In effect, he had quit the job—but would not leave.

The National Geographic Research Committee, which had recently granted $16,800 toward the cost of running Karisoke, was not pleased by this letter. However, Kelly Stewart acted swiftly to limit the damage. Her apologies on behalf of her husband calmed the storm somewhat, and a long and chatty letter that she sent to Dian ten days later soothed some ruffled plumages amongst the Karisoke board members. Dian herself was remarkably unperturbed by Harcourt's new eruption and was even slightly sympathetic.

**The boy is getting "bushy." Kelly should take him to England for a rest.**

Houghton Mifflin Company, Dian's American publisher, was now pressing for a title for the book, and Dian obliged with *Gorillas in the Mist*. It did not generate an outburst of enthusiasm.

**They don't like it. Nobody likes it. It seems only the gorillas aren't complaining!**

Like it or not, Dian stuck to her choice.

**Am now undergoing the grind of the appendices, tables, charts, references, etc. I deplore it. I am finding it very difficult to know how to divide time on a daily basis between book, updating course work, analysis of field data, correspondence. There are simply not enough hours in the day, particularly in this country where there is no incentive to wake up in the morning.**

By March 12, Dr. Eisenberg had had enough. He wrote to the members of the board:

"We seem to be entering a new phase in the continuation of studies at Karisoke. . . . I suggest the board phase out its involvement and that Dr. Fossey take a more direct hand in matters. In any event a new chairperson will have to be selected shortly since I would like to relinquish this position."

Many other board members also felt that Dian should now be encouraged to pick up the reins that had been so firmly taken out of her hands. More and more of those who had earlier been convinced that she and Karisoke ought to be divorced were now concluding that they might have erred.

Work on the book was disrupted at the end of February when Dian flew west to give some lectures in Oklahoma, including one at Tulsa, at which she was introduced to a young graduate, Wayne McGuire, who was keen on going to Karisoke as a research student. Although he did not make much of an impression on Dian at the time, McGuire was to loom large in her future.

Lecture tours were not an exercise in ego feeding—they were Dian's bread and butter. While she had been based at Karisoke, lecture fees had helped keep the center going; in exile in the United States, they made up a large part of her somewhat meager income.

On March 18 she and Cindy flew north to Plattsburgh, a small city not far from the Canadian border, where Dian had been hired to teach a month-long course. Although she had rather dreaded having to go even further "into the tundra," the interlude turned out to be a pleasant one.

**I'm teaching a mini-course in comparative behavior of the three Great Apes and am living in the country for the first time since leaving Africa. There is no way to explain what it means to me to have space and trees and animals and birds around once again. Cindy and I are both doing very well considering our ages, and the spring weather makes our old bones young again. I'm expected to remain here until the end of April. The students are super as are the faculty. Everyone is friendly, inquisitive, and enthusiastic over the course. I'll be sorry to leave.**

Back in Ithaca again she found herself required to make a difficult decision. The Karisoke board had delegated to her the task of choosing an interim replacement for Harcourt; someone to keep things going until she herself was able to resume command at Karisoke.

The temptation to return to Rwanda herself was strong, but several factors militated against it. Her current contract with Cornell would not be completed until September, and she considered it a matter of "integrity" that contracts be fully honored. *Gorillas in the Mist* was still not complete. Harcourt remained "in residence" at Karisoke, and there was no way she was going to return until he had vacated camp for good. Finally, there was Cindy—and the welfare of the old dog was by no means the least of Dian's considerations.

"I imagine Cindy would also like very much to return to camp," she wrote a friend, "but I don't believe she could endure the trip . . . her hind legs just don't work and she can't get up without assistance.

I've bought her an electric fireplace that looks almost like a real camp fireplace. In front of it I've put down a 'people' mattress and pillow, and that is where she spends most of her time, stretched out like a queen-in-waiting.

"Like Cindy, I too am now fat and menopausal (thus, very pleasant and congenial!). . . . I don't want to go through another winter here though. I do want to get back to camp and also get into writing full time rather than the half-teaching, half-writing schedules that now pay the rent."

In the end she decided to consider an application for the post of center director from David Watts, who had been with her at Karisoke from March 1978 to July 1979. She arranged to meet him in Chicago in mid-May to discuss arrangements. But first there was to be another "trimate symposium," this time at Hunter College in New York City.

By prior agreement, Goodall, Galdikas, and Fossey decided to use this opportunity to emphasize the urgent need for an all-out effort for the preservation of the remaining Great Apes. Dian was the last of the three to speak. *The New York Times* reported:

"Dr. Fossey described the fight to save the endangered African mountain gorillas, which are threatened both by the encroachment of farmers who want to cultivate the land and by poachers.

"Dr. Fossey's voice broke as she told of a group of mountain gorillas that were hunted down and killed.

"The audience was hushed as Dr. Fossey showed a slide of a graveyard near her campsite where the gorillas were buried. 'I keep the graveyard as a memorial,' she said, 'in the hopes that the day won't come when there are only graveyards and memories in the mist.' "

Dian and Jane had too little time together on this occasion. After a convivial gathering at the Explorers' Club, Dian caught a flight to Chicago. Her meeting with Watts went well, and it was agreed that he would take over at Karisoke as soon as Harcourt moved out. The assumption was that Harcourt would be cooperative about departing.

When Dian returned to Ithaca in May, she received a copy of a letter written by Harcourt to her British publisher, Hodder and Stoughton, threatening legal action if the book contained anything about him that he considered derogatory. Harcourt believed she might have made such comments, not only about himself, but about other people "concerned with conservation of the Virunga Volcanoes." If this was indeed the case, he warned the publisher, "you might have not just one, but several, lawsuits for libel on your hands, some of them international."

Dian and her publisher chose to ignore this challenge, but she sent a note to Anita McClellan about it.

"Oddly enough, on that same day, Kelly also wrote to me—a very fine, newsy letter signed 'Love, Kelly.' Kind of makes one wonder."

While Dian persevered with the book through the long, hot summer, Harcourt and Kelly flew off to England, then on to the United States, leaving a Japanese biologist, Juichi Yamagiwa, in charge of Karisoke. According to the accounts Dian received, the camp had not run as smoothly since her own departure.

For a time Dian and the board believed Harcourt and Kelly had left Karisoke for good. Watts was making preparations to go to Rwanda when, in mid-September, the couple arrived back at camp and settled in again as if they had no intention of ever leaving.

A new stalemate had apparently developed. Although most members of the board had acquiesced in Dian's choice of David Watts as the new acting center director, there was opposition from the Harcourt camp, which preferred that an Oxford graduate, thirty-two-year-old Dr. Richard Barnes, should succeed him. Apparently Harcourt did not wish to hand over to a Fossey appointee.

Finally Dian offered what seemed to her to be a workable compromise. She proposed that Barnes and Watts should share the management of Karisoke as codirectors. This appeared to be such an eminently reasonable solution that the board gratefully accepted it, and left Harcourt with little choice but to acquiesce.

Early in December, Dian received a letter from Juichi Yamagiwa that poured acid on her heart:

"I was so afraid to inform you of bad news. On the sixteenth of November guards and Vatiri found four poachers hunting the Musakama Group and chased them to get back a baby (one month female). Unfortunately Sandy and Kelly were absent from Karisoke. I sent the baby down the mountain quickly to get the care of doctor, because I was afraid it got damaged seriously.

"On the seventeenth ORTPN did not send up any guards in spite of my strong request. So I went with Vatiri to check the hunting place. My God! There were several bloody trails and we found a dead silverback killed by the poachers with spears. Bloody trails showed that another gorilla must have been killed or seriously wounded.

"In that evening Nemeye and Mukera, who had been tracking Group 5, reported they got attacked by several poachers with dogs on the eastern slopes of Karisimbi. Poachers seem to know that we are disarmed these days. I went down to Mountain Gorilla Project headquarters, and we arranged six armed park guards to stay at Karisoke and to escort us for at least a week, and sixteen porters to carry the poor silverback down to camp."

Dian had known for almost two years that her antipoaching program had been effectively abandoned, but this evidence of just how bad the situation had become was almost more than she could bear.

I had in mind to fly right away to Kennedy and take a chance on standby for Brussels and Kigali. Friends talked me out of it. They said it was too late to help the Musakama Group for now, and we had to put our efforts into getting things straightened out at camp. I wonder if we ever will . . . meantime the gorillas go on dying.

Dian had been able to entertain the spur-of-the-moment impulse to fly to Rwanda, and was perhaps impelled toward it, because she was now alone in her Lansing apartment. On October 19, Cindy had come to the end of her time.

Okay, Cindy, I promised you that I would do this, the only epitaph I can give you, but now in the first few hours after your death, I am wondering what life is all about. I so wished I had touched your body beneath that blue blanket at the vet hospital. I didn't because I did not accept the fact that you were dead, I guess. And I guess I was afraid that I would cry. Remember, you and I had a pact that we wouldn't cry in front of one another, but of course that was after you became a mature lady.

You were no ordinary dog. I know most of us like to think our dogs are extraspecial, but you were just that. Your mother was a registered boxer, born in Poland and brought to Rwanda by a real, honest-to-God count. Like most Europeans there, he kept your mother chained up as a watchdog. Well, somehow that fine lady of royal blood met an unknown male and the inevitable happened. I don't know how many of you there were in the litter, but that highfalutin count only kept three, and one was you.

In 1968 I'd been living in the Virungas more than a year. My company, in the way of talk-to folks, were my Africans and my chickens, Wilma and Walter. Walter liked to sleep in my tent at night and even rode on the carriage of my typewriter—which made for messy type. A good friend thought I needed more company than a couple of chickens and gave me this little, stump-tailed puppy. Of course you weren't born stump-tailed, but the Polish count wanted you to look real smart so he had your tail lopped off. It wasn't terribly clever of him, but still you kept that old stump wagging all these years.

Lord, were you ever an unwelcome visitor when you first came. While Walter was doing his thing all over the typewriter, Wilma was laying eggs in a corner of the tent, and you sure made their lives pretty rough. But as you grew up your playmates also grew in size. Nothing you liked better than playing at night, especially full moon nights, with the elephants that came to drink at the creek in front of my cabin. I'll never forget watching you with your little stump wagging madly, running in between the legs of those old mammoths, making them squeal and trumpet and flap their ears. Your play partners increased as you learned about buffalo, antelope, gorillas, mongeese—and the list was probably a lot longer, but that only you can tell.

Cindy, you were one lesson in courage, but remember, you loved people so much you failed as a watchdog. When Sebarari came into my cabin and swiped my valise with all the money I had in the world plus all my jewelry, you didn't bark. He just petted you on the head. No big deal, right? Everything being relative.

And so you grew and grew, not just in body, but in love. Seems you loved everybody—all the porters, the animal guests around the camp, the sick or wounded gorillas and duikers you helped look after, even the European visitors. Remember how each morning you would make your rounds from cabin to cabin just to give all a good-morning kiss with that big, wet tongue. Yes, Cindy, you were the "love" in Karisoke. Cindy, Cindy, there are too many memories, I'm sorry. . . .

The epitaph was never finished, but at the bottom of it one additional paragraph was scrawled.

Wed. 6:30 A.M. Cindy, remember the little newspaper boy who came over here after you died and really made more sense than most adults who try to express their sorrow but lack the words? This little boy said, "You must be really lonely now, and you must cry a lot. Whenever I'm lonely I cry too—but only when no one can hear me."

arly in January 1983, Dian wrote Rosamond Carr about the Karisoke situation:

"Another little gorilla was taken from poachers on November 16. I heard most of the details from the Japanese student who has been at Karisoke for some time but had to return to Japan. Just about everything I learned factually about camp came from him, and I shall miss his letters. Kelly sends on the monthly reports, which are very brief and positive, yet a number of students and visitors who have been at camp give me a whole new slant. Poaching is as bad as ever, but one simply doesn't hear about it now. The slaying of the silverback and others from the group from which the newest captive came would also have been hushed up had it been possible.

"I should very much like to return for about three months, but only after Harcourt leaves. He was due to leave at the end of December, but is staying on. He refuses to say when he intends to go.

"I'm sure my men must think I've dropped off the edge of the earth, and I so want to come back to convey my love and gratitude to them. I do want them to know that they, and the camp, are deeply etched in my heart and mind. . . . The students who have returned say that the cabins are falling apart. . . . It will be disheartening for me to see what I worked for for so many years getting in disarray, but if the men are cheered up and the camp gets a new sparkle, then I think the three months will fly by. I would obviously prefer to stay longer, but I don't know yet if I am capable because of the high-altitude breathing problems that are bound to be more acute now."

And in a more personal vein: "Have cut down on my smoking a lot—only one cigarette an hour, which must still sound excessive to you, however it sure beats three and four an hour! Rosamond, I am TRULY quite a mellow person compared to what I was. It must be the fat, or perhaps getting over the horrid menopause. So, the new Fossey is a jolly old lady who needs glasses to find her glasses, though she still has her own teeth. . . .

"The book is done at last. . . . I am so glad! I hadn't realized just how depressing it was to wake up each morning knowing how much more writing had to be done about the animals I so loved—those that had been killed. It was, at times, unbearable, and I was often close to giving up on it completely."

January had seemed to be going well this year, but on the twenty-fourth a missile with multiple warheads was dispatched from Karisoke targeted on the offices of M. Le Directeur, ORTPN; the African Wildlife Leadership Foundation; the Fauna Preservation Society; Cooperation Belge (the Belgian aid program in Rwanda); and the National Geographic Society.

It was a denunciation by Harcourt of the Digit Fund. Having vehemently denied that the fund and/or Dian deserved credit for driving the cattle out of the park or, for that matter, for saving what was left of the mountain gorilla population, Harcourt gave the credit to the park authorities and to "international organizations that have between them donated many thousands of dollars to active conservation of the mountain gorilla."

He went on to state that, though the KRC did indeed play an active role in gorilla conservation, it did so "in the absence of D. Fossey, in the absence of funds from the Digit Fund, and in the absence of any representative of the Digit Fund." As the director of the KRC, Harcourt formally disassociated himself and the center from all statements in the fall 1982 *Newsletter from the Karisoke Research Center.*

This outburst was sparked by the rejuvenation of the Digit Fund.

By mid-1980, Dian had decided that, in good conscience, she could no longer solicit donations for the fund since the antipoaching campaign it was intended to support was not being implemented by the new director. She therefore stopped publicizing it and, of course, sent no further monies from it to Karisoke. However, in the autumn of 1982, in anticipation of her return to camp and of renewing the patrols, she reactivated it. The newsletter announcing this decision and describing the Digit Fund's accomplishments was what had so stirred Sandy Harcourt's wrath.

At the end of January, Dian got something of a dressing down from Anita McClellan, who had been trying to persuade her to put more about the core conservation issues into *Gorillas in the Mist*.

"Your being polite and reluctant to describe Africans' attitudes toward government or park regulations; conflict of interest; misuse of cash from conservationists; bad land use; capture of animals for foreign zoos, etc., will not save gorillas' lives. Such reluctance to confront the tough issues is a bit like advocating theoretical conservation, which doesn't save the animals from traps and guns, but sounds okay."

Even though the implication that she was acting like a "theoretical conservationist" made Dian see red, she remained unpersuaded. She was not afraid of legal action if she exposed the sleaziness of the internecine wars engaged in by players in the "conservationist game"—she was just genuinely reluctant to pillory anyone in *Gorillas in the Mist*.

**This book is about *gorillas*, not people. It is not even about me, and there is too much "me-itis" in it already as a result of editorial decisions. I would prefer there be no people in at all, good or bad, but I guess that's too much to ask.**

February 1983 brought good news from Dr. Snider to the effect that the National Geographic's Committee for Research and Exploration had authorized a grant of $21,860 for 1983. This manna was accompanied by a warning: "Our committee is reluctant to make grants to support a facility [as opposed to an individual]. We are making a rare exception for Karisoke. However, I don't think the committee will do so indefinitely, and the committee urges you to seek funding from other sources for the center itself."

February also produced its share of problems. By the twenty-fifth Dian still did not know when Harcourt planned to leave Karisoke, nor had she heard whether ORTPN had issued work permits for her new students—Americans David Watts and Karen Jensen, and the Englishman Richard Barnes—without which these three could not proceed to Rwanda. She wrote urgently to Kelly:

"I know only that you intend now to leave in March, though when in March I don't know. Do you have any idea if the work permits will be ready for Watts, Jensen, and Barnes by the time you leave? They are, naturally, ever so eager to get on their way."

Kelly's reply, written on March 10, was disconcerting—and ominous. "We have not received Watts's application forms, so he has not been applied for," to which was added the information that Barnes and Jensen *had* been accepted by ORTPN, "and so we have sent Dr. Barnes a telegram, and I have written to Jensen." The letter closed on this pessimistic note: "Even if we received David's application next porter's day, I don't think there is much chance he will be able to come here before June."

Watts's application for a work permit had been mailed to Karisoke almost four months earlier, in November 1982, for forwarding to ORTPN.

On March 22, Richard Barnes arrived from England. Eight days later Sandy Harcourt and Kelly Stewart took their much-belated departure. The Harcourt era was at an end—but the shadow lingered.

One day before their departure, Watts's application turned up. Harcourt sent it on to ORTPN, but neither Watts nor Dian heard anything more about it until late May when Watts got a letter from Jean-Pierre von der Becke, who, it will be remembered, was the director of the Mountain Gorilla Project. The message was that ORTPN had refused Watts a permit because it would not "accept the fact to have two directors for KRC. Indeed they do not think the station is important enough, and I must say, I understand their point of view."

This was too much for Watts, who could plainly read the writing on the wall. He withdrew his application to work at Karisoke—whose new and now sole director would be Harcourt's choice, Dr. Richard Barnes.

The effect of all this on Dian was to precipitate a bout of depression, but it also convinced her that she dared no longer delay her return to Rwanda if she ever hoped to regain control of her creation.

She wrote to Ian Redmond with something of the old fire of earlier days:

"Remember that horrid, horrid night when I asked Rwelekana to bring you over to my house when I thought I was going 'bonkers'? In many ways I am going through those same unearthly feelings now, though certainly to a lesser extent, for I was leaving the animals then, and there is nothing here in the United States to leave except junk food or TV. . . .

"I am nearly packed up to go back to Karisoke, but for only three months—mid-June through mid-September. I have been told that someone is trying to arrange for me not to get a visa back into Rwanda—he did try same in September 1980, but to no avail.

"Most of my news comes from sources not connected with Karisoke, obviously. I *know* that poaching is heavier there, and within the Virungas as a whole, than ever when I was there. I *know* that young gorillas are being captured. . . . I also *know* the physical facilities at Karisoke are nearly rotted out because no one cared about the upkeep of the cabins; the car is finished for the same reasons. Everything I worked for nearly single-handedly over thirteen years is just about finished.

"What really bothers me, Ian, about you is that you say you will give proceeds from your lectures to the Mountain Gorilla Project, when *you*, of all people, know that cutting a trap is one hell of a lot more important than showing conservation education cine to Africans. . . .

"If you have suddenly joined the 'aren't we great, 'cause we teach the Africans how to conserve their country' scheme, I guess our paths have diverged. That plan is super, super fine, *but* it is putting the cart before the horse, and you *know* it. It takes one bullet, one trap, one poacher to kill a duiker, a buffalo, a gorilla, an elephant. No number of cute cine films are going to stop the slaughter now going on. It takes one small, preferably five small, patrols to cut traps, confiscate weapons, capture poachers, to preserve the animals remaining in the park. You know that also. The more popular the Mountain Gorilla Project grows, the less chances the gorillas have—that has been *proved* in the last two years."

As May progressed and the time for action grew closer, Dian rallied. Writing to Craig Sholley, who had been with her at Karisoke in 1979, she sounded almost buoyant:

"I am returning shortly. Perhaps not for a long stay, as I am quite too far over the hill—God, fifty-one years of indulgences—for a full-time stint up and down those hills; but I need to bring things to the wonderful men (no way to explain how I miss and love them) and to work on the cabins Fossey-style. . . . I bet I will be going up there, even if carried, with paint, new mats, stovepipes, lamps, and nails every year until I join my betters: Digit, Uncle Bert, Macho, and all the others."

Dian was now receiving mail from the new director at KRC, addressed very formally to "Dr. Fossey." The arrival of Karen Jensen, an attractive twenty-seven-year-old, on May 10 was good news. However, a report on the physical condition of the center made worse reading even than Dian had anticipated. Barnes wrote: "We have no cooking facilities and no lamps here other than the ones Karen and I are using at the moment; all the other stoves and lamps are broken, so it is essential that you bring something to cook on and to see by."

Dian was incredulous—"There were sixteen pressure lamps and eight working stoves in camp when I left"—but there was worse to come. Due to several years of neglect, the combi was a write-off, and a replacement would cost fifteen thousand dollars; guns for the patrols, much of the optical equipment, cutlery and dishes, even a large proportion of the bedding had also vanished. The list of replacement items Barnes begged Dian to bring with her from the United States or Nairobi kept growing until it was pages long. The disappearance of the bedding seems to have been the last straw. Dian replied to Barnes's appeals: "I will bring everything needed for writing, eating, seeing, but bloody @#$% if am bringing sleeping bags or linens. If these are all gone, the shit is going to hit the proverbial fan!"

With her arrangements nearing completion she booked a flight to arrive in Kigali late on June 20, 1983. Her stay at Karisoke would be shorter than originally planned. Publication of *Gorillas in the Mist* was scheduled for August 25, and Houghton Mifflin was arranging a promotional tour beginning only a week later.

**Everything I own is packed now as I get ready to wing back to camp. Much will be stored but I have five suitcases—UGH— filled with everything, literally, from soup to nuts. I have to take all this on to camp because just about nothing remains. In preparation for that I'm trying to pack my temper along with my belongings! Am only able to stay until August 27 when am due to return to the States for a bloody lecture tour arranged primarily for the book. My heart is certainly not in this. I reckon if people want to buy a book, they will buy it. They don't need the author shoving it down their throats. I don't know where I am going to go after the tour. If my old bod can take the altitude and the work, then I shall plan on returning to camp, but only if I can function there. I really can't tell. The first thing is to get Karisoke functioning again the way it used to, for the good of the students and of the gorillas. Then we'll see.**

She arrived in Kigali on schedule—and had to spend the next four days in the capital. ORTPN had decreed that she too must now have a work permit and was reluctant to give her one. When a permit *was* finally produced—it was good for only six months. Nevertheless, her waiting time in Kigali was well spent, literally, shopping in the dingy little *dukas* scattered along Kigali's dusty streets for yet more replacement items needed at Karisoke.

On the morning of the twenty-fourth she finally climbed to camp.

In the midst of a horrid hailstorm that had to be meant for me, since this is the beginning of the dry season.

Once she reached camp the sun began to shine.

The return was very emotional as I once again met my African staff (nine men), some of whom have worked for camp since 1967. We simultaneously hugged one another, shook hands, cried, laughed, and exchanged all kinds of gossip and tales. They kindly said that I seemed ten years younger (good old Miss Clairol), and they liked my new "fat" look. . . . About ten minutes after I had arrived, bathed and cleaned up, Kanyaragana, my houseboy since 1968 (now about thirty years old), came into the living room and said, *"Habari Mama yako?"*—How is your mother? Basili asked the same question next day. This isn't just politeness; they have a real concern for the families of close friends, and I believe they think of me as one.

I then had tea with Richard Barnes and the American girl, Karen Jensen. They are enjoying a sweet, new love affair and are both actually very nice, particularly Richard, who works hard; but the Africans are still the backbone of this place.

In the afternoon I took my first good look around. My heart really sank. I had never imagined such decay and neglect. The Africans watched me, and when I got so mad I was really crying, Kanyaragana said, "It hurts us too. But now you will bring it all back again."

My own cabin—some people call it the manor—was worst of all. Everything I loved was broken or removed. The big fireplace in my room was closed off; the stoves all removed; the pens for chickens and other animals destroyed; the gorillas' graveyard totally obscured by vegetation; outdoor tables all rotted; wall mats rotten and paint peeling off everything inside and out. The whole camp has been totally neglected as white people have come and gone, taken what they wanted, never bothering to replace or refurbish anything. Where the hell am I going to find stovepipes in Rwanda just now? BUT I will find them somewhere in Africa! I just do not understand how or why anyone could hate me this much.

The work of restoration began next day, and within a week—such was the fervor Dian brought to the task—the little world of Karisoke was looking considerably better, although it would take the best part of two months to finish the job. Meanwhile there were other old friends whom Dian urgently wished to see. The meeting, when it came, was unforgettable.

One of the outstanding moments of my life happened on July

5 when I set out with some degree of mixed anticipation and anxiety to renew acquaintance with Group 5, who were the only gorillas fairly close to camp. Would they remember me after three years' absence? I doubted it sincerely.

To reach them meant a bloody long climb lasting two hours and filled with such oaths from me that the long-dormant volcanoes should have erupted, because a new tracker, Kana, took the most energy-wasting and zigzag route. We finally found them in a bowl between First and Second hills south of camp. Kana headed back right away, leaving me huffing and puffing like a run-out old buffalo.

The females and youngsters of the clan (sixteen in all) were resting in thick vegetation in the warm sun on the steep slope of the bowl where they had made their day nests. When I got my breath, I worked my way down toward them, though I could see only the occasional one. When I got twenty feet from them I sat down and began making Fossey-style introduction noises—a soft series of rumbles like gorillas make when expressing content-ment.

The nearest female was old Effie, mother of six, whom I had known since 1967. She'd had a new baby in my absence, little Maggie, who sure didn't believe in making shy. Maggie came scrambling over right away—not to look at me, but to investigate my clothing and equipment. This dismayed me because I thought it was the result of too much habituation with the tourists the park gang has kept on sending to Group 5.

But my dismay only lasted a second or two. Effie glanced my way while chewing on a stalk of celery. She looked away, then did a double-take myopic scrutiny as if not believing her eyes. Then she tossed the celery aside and began walking rapidly toward me.

Meantime Tuck, another female I had known nearly as long, appeared out of the underbrush and started to pick up Maggie, I guess to take her off to safety, then Tuck too did a second take. She dropped Maggie and walked right up in front of me, resting her weight on her arms so that her face was level with mine and only a couple of inches away. She stared intently into my eyes, and it was eye-to-eye contact for thirty or forty seconds. Not knowing quite what to do, for I had never had this reaction from gorillas before, I squished myself flat on the bed of vegetation. Whereupon she smelled my head and neck, then lay down beside me . . . and embraced me! . . . embraced me! . . . embraced me! GOD, she *did* remember!

Tuck began crooning, and I crooned back. Effie had come up by then and she too stared straight into my eyes, sniffed me, then piled up on the two of us and I was really squished. Her and Tuck's plaintive murmurs reached other clan members in the dense foliage nearby, and one by one the other females came over to us. All the older four that I knew best repeated the eye-to-eye contact, then settled down with long arms entwining all of us into one big, black, furry ball. As they settled in, each one was making prolonged, inquisitive "hmmmmm" sounds as if to ask: "Where the hell have you been? Is this really you?"

Not to be left out, the youngsters joined us too: Jozi, Cantsbee, Pablo, and Maggie really took advantage of the trust their mothers were showing to work me over, gently hitting, nibbling, pinching me, and pulling my hair, and trying to carry off everything loose. They tried to take my camera, water jug, panga, and my glasses, which, unfortunately, I have to wear in the field now. They did kidnap my new leather gloves (two hours later I found the right one, but the left one is forever on the mountain).

I could have happily died right then and there and wished for nothing more on earth, simply because they had remembered.

While the kids cavorted a few feet from us, Effie, Puck, Poppy, Tuck, and I settled down to enjoy a forty-five-minute palaver, all nestled up together amidst the thistle and celery clumps. I'm ashamed to say I did most of the vocalizing, but with an audience like this how could I resist? The problem was that when I used their language I didn't really know what I was saying, so I talked English. I told them of Cindy's death, then strayed to life in America (that got me a few sympathetic grunts), and apologized for inflicting Harcourt on them, then ended up just trying to tell them how happy I was to be back. Believe it or not, I'm sure they understood that part at least.

While we ladies had our confab, old Beethoven, the leader of the group, with the two blackbacks Ziz and Shinda, fed their way down into the bottom of the bowl, paying us no heed. The other silverback, Icarus, stayed on our slope about fifteen feet from the ladies' gossip circle but didn't interrupt. Eventually Beethoven looked up at us and barked that the party was over. Time to go. The ladies and their offspring moved off slowly, leaving me with absolute disbelief at what had happened. They *knew* me—they *welcomed* me back! Perhaps they were even happy to see the Lone Woman of the Forest again.

I tried to visit them next day, but they had returned to the high part of the saddle, above eleven thousand feet and five hours' walk away. I couldn't make it.

I had gone out with Rwelekana; and when we were coming back (I was totally exhausted), he very seriously said, "Yesterday the gorillas had to come a long way to say hello and greet you near camp. Today they have to go on with their own business." I absolutely choked up at this idea, but he was serious.

The effect of the reunion with Effie's clan was transcendental—and enduring. Whatever doubts Dian may have had about her future place in the scheme of things had been resolved.

I know now that I've truly come home. No one will ever force me out of here again.

Restoration went on apace during a long stretch of warm and sunny weather. Dian was reveling in Karisoke, as this letter to Anita McClellan testifies:

"Heard the weirdest sound today. Took about fifteen seconds to identify it. The drone of a distant airplane! Now I know I've really escaped. Well, not quite. Every now and then I think I hear the phone ringing and just freeze. That particular Ithaca symptom might take another week to disappear. DAMN, phone just rang again. . . .

"Magical afternoon. Off and on sunshine, warm, quiet. I'd been four hours working on the six-month summary report for National Geographic and couldn't stand one more minute of same. So in my lavender Nikes and matching windbreaker, I sneaked away from camp chores to go out to Mzee's grave." Mzee had been the patriarch of the Karisoke duikers.

"On the small protected glade where he last lay down, the turf is now filled with neat piles of bushbuck and duiker dung, and buffalo circle the glade. It was spine-tingling, as if the remaining antelope (the population is more than halved since I left here) held nightly séances with the spirit of the wise old sage, seeking the secret of longevity in their doomed habitat. . . .

"Mikeno, Karisimbi, Visoke, all loomed out of the mist on cue, and there was such tranquillity as I have not known in years and years. Within a couple of dozen feet of Mzee's grave grows a special orchid known to no one but myself. The striped flowers, a slightly pink shade, were in full bloom. I bade it greetings and once again resisted the urge to take a small sample. Never, never! Nothing is quite as magical as having forest secrets like this—perhaps seashore secrets run a close second. I might share them with you if you are willing to run the risk of having your tongue cut out.

"Muse time took up a large portion of the afternoon's two-hour allotment of freedom, leaving just time to Nike-christen my favorite meadows and visit more secret places, of the serval family, touraco family (not home today), and oh, so many squeaky friends."

To human friends in Ithaca, she wrote:

"Wish you could have a little slice of this gorgeous forest with its majestic hagenia and hyperium trees. . . . I can't believe I'm saving $475 monthly rent by being surrounded by beauty instead of cement. . . . There are eight cabins here. My own we built in 1974 from saplings as supports; tin sheeting painted green for outside walls and roof; lovely, durable matting to form inside walls, ceiling, and floor covering. Every one of the rooms has large, large windows through which you can look out at the age-old hagenia trees (somewhat similar to giant oaks, but covered with moss, strands of lichens, and orchids). They look like they are floating, in all the shades of the green rain forest, particularly at dusk when the animals of the little meadows surrounding the camp come out to graze. Sure does beat Lansing North!"

And a somber touch:

"It is lonely without my old dog Cindy and my old monkey Kima, both of whom played such a large part in my life over the past fifteen years. I have Cindy's ashes with me, but I must await a private moment to spread them in her favorite spots around camp and along some of her favorite trails."

To Stacey Coil:

"The Africans and I have now virtually rebuilt half of the whole damn camp—matting, painting, rewiring stovepipes, fixing broken ceiling supports, replacing outside tables and benches, totally rebuilding the johns and the men's kitchen. I have spent two thousand dollars on the job so far, but inch-by-inch the men are restoring this place as it was. No rain for the first thirteen days, but now it is hailing like hell every day, so we stay in and repair lamps, stoves, sew the ripped-up sleeping bags, tents, even boots.

"As far as Barnes and Jensen are concerned, I again have the luck of having two kids all of a sudden madly, passionately, forever in love. I am really and truly happy for them—I do not joke, for it will be another Karisoke marriage.

"The gorillas remain very far away, thus I have not had another contact with them since July 5. Not seeing them hurts, but I do have six weeks left and am feeling stronger and more fit than ever. However all four study groups remain at over eleven thousand feet, which means more than three hours' climbing. And the oxygen support system I brought back with me doesn't seem to work at this altitude. The nose tubes simply *shoot* out oxygen—nearly blew my head off!"

Not all the gorillas were inaccessible. On July 30, while hiking toward the Zaire border with Kana, she had "another extraordinary contact."

This time it was with Tiger, now a lone silverback, whom I had observed on the day of his birth in November 1967. He was born into Group 4, the group that was decimated by poachers in 1978. Since then he has had rather a tough time. For a time he batched it with some of the other surviving Group 4 males, but for three years he has been traveling alone, trying to find some females with whom to mate and start a clan of his own. This means "interactions" with the silverbacks of other groups, in which he has been rather badly beaten up despite his tremendous size and strength.

Even though I have known him since his birth, when I found him this time near the old cattle path I was following, I did not expect the kind of reception I had received from Group 5, because he is a lone animal, and they tend to be temperamental and unpredictable.

When I spotted him he was about fifty feet away, feeding in dense foliage, most of which was celery. I motioned Kana to go and hide, which he was glad to do because Tiger is one big gorilla! I then sat down to give all the proper gorilla introduction vocalizations and quickly get my camera out of my knapsack, though I was sure I wouldn't get any pictures because he would flee as soon as he realized someone was near.

I had just barely taken the camera from the bag when— zoooom—he came right at me at a loping run. Reaching my side he lopped down a big lobelia with one hand, then raised his arm again as if he was going to whack the @#$%& out of me! Then, to my relief, he slowly lowered his arm and gently stroked my arm before sitting on the base of a tree not two feet from my side.

There he sat gazing down at me, seeking eye contact, and for about fifteen minutes we exchanged "remarks" in groans, grunts, and croons while I also took picture after picture. The reason for all the pictures was that I couldn't see him clearly without my glasses, but he might not have known me with glasses on, so a compromise had to be reached. I could see him through the viewfinder, in fact I could have counted the hairs on his great big head!

My tracker was nervous, since he was only fifty feet away, and he cracked a branch. Tiger swung over there to investigate, and Kana went back to camp somewhat hastily! After that Tiger and I spent the rest of the afternoon together, munching celery stalks and just keeping each other company.

When heavy fog and rain moved in at four-thirty I had to go, but felt great compunction about leaving him alone in the forest. I half expected him to follow me home and half wished he would. Poor "little" fellow. It was really quite sad as every now and then he would gaze over in the direction of Karisimbi and give one or two plaintive hoots as if bewailing his sad, lonely single status. My anger at the poachers who destroyed his family kept me cussing all the way back to camp.

The depredations committed by poachers during her three-year absence haunted Dian. Even before she began putting the camp to rights again, she had reactivated the antipoaching campaign. This entailed reestablishing long-range, overnight patrols usually led by Vatiri, and short-range daylight patrols by the camp trackers, sometimes accompanied by Richard Barnes, who turned out to be a conservationist after Dian's own stamp.

Writing on July 24 to Rane Randoph, the accountant for the reinvigorated Digit Fund, Dian reported: "The Africans and I are really accomplishing miracles, what with rebuilding, repainting, sewing, cleaning, scouring, resupporting floors and roofs—the list is absolutely endless—but the cabins are beginning to shine, both inside and out.

"Of far more importance are the patrols. I remain deeply grateful that not one franc/penny of Digit Fund money was sent to camp during Harcourt's two and a half years here. He never went on patrols . . . nor did the other staff members. . . . He has now been replaced by Richard Barnes, in his early thirties, who has had previous experience in Africa working with elephants. He speaks Swahili fairly fluently and is strong on *active* conservation. His opinion of the park guards is the same as mine.

"No week has passed that patrols are not supervised by either Richard or one of my old, trusted Africans. They bivouac as before in the forest overnight to trap poachers unaware of their presence, or leave Karisoke at five in the morning to intercept poachers working their routes.

"Richard did not know anything about the Digit Fund until my arrival because Harcourt had informed him only about the Mountain Gorilla Project—the theoretical conservation group that sanctions tourism rather than trap cutting or poacher capture.

"Would you believe that in the past month only, some four hundred traps have been cut and two poachers caught. A third poacher tried to cut up one of my men ten days ago, but ended up getting the worst of it."

This incident took place on July 13 when Rwelekana, out on a day patrol, encountered the most notorious and dangerous Virunga poacher still on the loose. This was Sebahutu, one of the killers of Uncle Bert and Macho, and a great destroyer of elephants as well as gorillas, duikers, and smaller animals. Although Sebahutu usually carried a high-powered rifle, he had only his panga and spear with him on this occasion.

Armed with a .22 starter's pistol that could only fire blanks, Rwelekana sneaked up behind Sebahutu, who was setting a duiker trap, and demanded his surrender. The poacher did not hesitate. Swinging on his heel he thrust his spear at Rwelekana's belly. The tall tracker threw himself sideways and the spearhead cut a long but superficial gash in his thigh. Grabbing the spear, he wrenched it out of Sebahutu's hands, turned it on him, and stabbed the poacher in the arm. Sebahutu fled, leaving his spear, traps, and a bloodstained jacket that he peeled off and abandoned in order to speed his flight.

Rwelekana hastened back to camp with his trophies.

He sauntered up to my outside table where I was typing up long-overdue reports. His pants were very bloody, and his face looked rather odd, but that was because he was trying to appear very casual and serious while in fact he was bursting with pride and the desire to grin from ear to ear.

Rwelekana had recognized Sebahutu, so Dian hastened to report the incident to the authorities in Ruhengeri and to demand that the poacher be arrested. Easier said than done. Although everyone knew who Sebahutu was, nobody seemed to know where he could be found. Dian thereupon had Gwehandagoza pass word around that knowledge of the poacher's whereabouts was worth a *prime* (reward) of one thousand francs. The details of what followed are obscure. What is certain is that the prime was paid by the Digit Fund and that Sebahutu was put away with a five-year sentence. Active conservation, indeed.

One of the two other poachers captured during this period was found to be in possession of the freshly severed head of an adult male gorilla. Although the man remained mute under interrogation, Dian's information network eventually uncovered a horrendous tale.

It seems a rich *bazunga* came to Gisenyi while on a hunting safari. His guide passed the word that the boss (a German, I believe) would pay fifty thousand Rwandan francs for a guide to help him shoot a silverback. The sportsman was led to a group on the west side of Karisimbi where he shot two gorillas, one probably a female. To avoid risks he had the guide carry the silverback head out for him, but never got it because the man was caught.

That's all the gorillas need now! It is like the thirties when sportsmen calling themselves "scientists" would come to the Virungas and kill a dozen gorillas for the biggest head to hang in their trophy rooms. Hunting safaris are still the bloody plague of Africa, though they are quieter about it now.

Well, poachers and hunters have been doing just about what they liked around here for the past three years. There'll be no more of that!

The pace of the antipoaching campaign picked up steadily. Just a few days before her return to the United States, Dian was able to exultantly inform Fulton Brylawski that "the Digit Fund, thus far this year, has been responsible for the cutting down of 1,701 traps!"

Immersed in the tasks of re-creating Karisoke and supervising the war against the poachers, Dian had almost forgotten about her book, until on July 29, Gwehandagoza brought her an airmail package. It contained "the first copy of *Gorillas in the Mist,* hot off the press today."

Either the book was something of a disappointment to her, or as is more likely, she felt obliged to suppress the exquisite, once-in-a-lifetime thrill every author experiences when he or she has the first copy in hand. Whatever the cause, Dian sounded quite grumpy in a letter to the Prices:

"The picture quality is poor." However, she could not suppress a triumphant note: "Twenty-five thousand copies have been printed and advance sales have reached thirteen thousand! All the reviews I have seen so far are extremely favorable, but then, maybe I have been sent only favorable reviews."

On August 10 Stacey Coil sent her one of the other kind, written by her onetime student, Peter Veit, for the magazine *Natural History.* It was sharply critical.

"The Veit review: Wow. What can I say?" Dian wrote to Stacey. "You asked me not to get hyper about it—well, I really have not with regard to speaking to anyone, but oh, oh, what my insides did by themselves! Tonight I read it over real cool like (took four Scotches)."

Like many neophyte authors she could not resist the impulse to strike back: "I will write a letter to the editor, simply for communication's sake; it does not need to be published. In addition to actual literary mistakes, my review of Veit's review asks about the role of the reviewer. Is it, as it should be, to discuss a book's merits or downfalls, or is it to give space to a reviewer's rantings?" It is doubtful if Dian ever received an answer to this excellent question.

Publication brought other problems. Seemingly everyone who had ever taken a photograph at Karisoke now asserted ownership of one or more of the pictures reproduced in the book, fiercely disputing the credits as ascribed and demanding punitive payments. While some of the claims were legitimate due to crediting errors, most were not, and some were deliberately mischievous. The battle of the photographs was to be an ongoing irritant in Dian's life for a year and more.

With the book in front of her, Dian now had to face the terrifying prospects of a promotional tour. She reached back into her childhood for a word that sufficiently conveyed the apprehension she felt.

**The thought of having to go through all that bloody interviewing gives me the collywobbles. I do so wish I had said no, no, no and stuck to it!**

She was distracted somewhat from the coming ordeal by a flood of visitors, including Jenny and Warren Garst, who arrived in Kigali on July 30 en route to Karisoke to make another gorilla film for the *Wild Kingdom* series. Dian sent them a quick and somewhat apologetic welcome note that concluded: "Either at the Economat or in Ruhengeri, try to buy some glasses, cups for coffee and tea, soup and flat dishes, and pots. You will also need some towels, thermoses, and sheets. I'll pay for these things, of course, but they just don't exist at camp."

The Garsts climbed on August 4 and settled in for a month-long stay in a cabin Dian had refurbished for them. She was delighted to have them, but the high moment of the month was undoubtedly a brief visit from Ian Redmond, en route to an investigation into the mysterious use of a cave complex by elephants in east Africa. He was followed by a spate of other visitors who turned Dian's remaining days at Karisoke into a pandemonium.

She wrote somewhat desperately to Anita McClellan: "The Garsts from *Wild Kingdom* have come; there are two African students from Butare University here now; the boy, Richard Barnes, and the girl, Karen Jensen, and on top of that, Debre Hamburger's little sister; then in a few days, the American ambassador, his wife and daughter! I feel like I'm running a damn hotel!"

Nevertheless, when she and her porters descended the muddy trail to the car park on the morning of August 26, she was in better shape than she had been for several years and ready, if not willing, to face the ordeal ahead.

Much of that readiness came from the certain knowledge that, even as she had restored Karisoke, so had it restored her—and had been restored *to* her. She was no longer a wanderer in limbo.

Arriving in New York on August 26, Dian flew on to Ithaca, there to be greeted by Stacey Coil, who was now acting as the more-or-less-unpaid secretary of the Digit Fund. Glenn Hausfater was away, and most of the other people Dian knew at Cornell had not yet returned for the autumn semester. Nevertheless, Ithaca at least provided her with a breather before she embarked on a Herculean program of travel and public engagements.

Deborah Spies, deputy director of the L.S.B. Leakey Foundation, had arranged a month-long lecture tour for Dian, into which the publicity people at Houghton Mifflin had injected as many television, radio, and press interviews on behalf of *Gorillas in the Mist* as could be managed. The result was an itinerary whose demands might have given pause to an Olympic athlete.

On September 6, Dian flew to New York to attend a launching party for her book at the Explorers' Club, followed by a full day of publicity. Then it was on to lecture in Philadelphia, Washington, Detroit, Chicago, San Francisco, Los Angeles, back to San Francisco to visit the Prices, then more lectures in San Diego, Albuquerque, Birmingham, and finally on October 7, to Columbus, Ohio, for her last appearance in the series.

During this month she gave ten illustrated talks before audiences of up to a thousand people, appeared on more than sixty television programs, was interviewed by scores of newspaper and magazine reporters, and endured an unspecified number of autographing sessions. By the time she returned to Ithaca on October 10, she was "as exhausted as if I'd climbed the summit of Visoke twice in one day."

Unwilling to stay at yet another hotel, she went in search of a furnished apartment. None was available, but by an astonishing coincidence, the second-floor apartment in the North Lansing block she had occupied after her arrival in Ithaca in 1980 was vacant. It had been nakedly empty then—it was as empty now; nevertheless it offered a roof over her head, independence, and privacy. She moved in, equipped with a sleeping bag, a portable typewriter, three wooden crates, and her luggage and called it home . . .

. . . for just five days. Then the Houghton Mifflin publicity staff flung her into action again. The "national promotional tour" that followed took her through many of the southern, central, and eastern states, and lasted until October 29.

By the time she staggered back to Ithaca and her Spartan refuge in North Lansing, she had lost thirty pounds—and most of her vaunted new joviality.

It hadn't been all bad. The lectures had earned nearly eleven thousand dollars to help support Karisoke. Publicity from the talks and the book had triggered a generous flow of donations to the Digit Fund; and Dian had been truly moved by the interest ordinary people had shown in the fate of the mountain gorillas. She wrote to her New York agent, Gina Maccoby:

"I hope the tour really was the 'smashing success' you say it was. It certainly got off to a rocky start in New York and braked to a pit stop in one other location. For the most part I was awed by the public's interest and empathy with the gorillas. It was a great privilege to have been able to represent the species to large audiences who seemed to care about the animals. The experience would have been almost ethereal were it not for the fact that so many of the gorilla individuals were dead, and that Anita McClellan was also absent from receiving her very just rewards for making *Gorillas in the Mist* possible."

This last was a reference to the fact that Anita and a number of other Houghton Mifflin employees had been fired a few months earlier as part of an economy measure. Dian's sense of loyalty had been outraged, and she had been waging war with her publishers ever since.

Although she had been physically drained by the past two months—her physician of many years, Dr. Ralph Spiegl, was now adjuring her to "preserve yourself; throw away the cigarettes; gain some weight; do some exercises; stop phoning your parents"—the experience seems to have stimulated Dian's imagination.

**I'm going to introduce an entirely new idea for the protection of the remaining mountain gorillas; one that, hopefully, will**

eliminate once and for all the barriers that continue to divide native blacks from white expatriates, pit one country against another (Zaire/Uganda/Rwanda), and one organization against the other. My idea is based upon the very simple fact that gorillas live in groups.

I call it the Guardians for Gorilla Groups plan.

I would like to see each of the forty-five or fifty gorilla groups scattered throughout the Virungas made the sole responsibility of a small staff of "guardians" consisting of one or two park guards, perhaps some of their family members, and a few black or white assistants.

Ideally each gorilla group would be contacted by a guardian at least every second day so that the location and status of every gorilla within the Virungas would constantly be known to a central registry. In addition to regular salaries, the guardians would be rewarded on a merit basis.

The American and European public, instead of being asked to give toward the general cause of gorilla conservation, would be invited to adopt a gorilla group and contribute to the expenses of that group's guardians. These sponsors would receive accountings of the work of the guardians and reports on the status of the groups, and of named individual gorillas within the groups.

The idea is so simple it can hardly help but work, and I do not understand why I have not thought of it before. The surviving gorillas are now very unevenly distributed because of the very unequal degree of protection they receive. For example: Mt. Muhabura, shared by Uganda and Rwanda. In 1955 there were over fifty-five gorillas living on that mountain. The Karisoke Research Center census of 1981 found only six survivors in two tiny groups, and a solitary silverback. This is because this area gets no protection from the Parc National des Volcans guards, and none from Uganda. Yet Mt. Muhabura is ideal terrain for mountain gorillas. My Guardian plan could save what individuals remain and help the buildup of a new population there.

I don't believe I am being unduly optimistic, not after all my years of experience with the local people. I will present the proposal to the new director of ORTPN upon my return to Kigali. At worst, he can only turn it down, but I intend to be convincing.

While Dian was still in Ithaca, devoting her depleted energies to refining her gorilla guardian plan, a letter arrived from Richard Barnes. It was a shocker. "The center is now bankrupt," he announced curtly. "There is no money left to pay the staff. . . . On

Tuesday I will pay the men's wages out of my own pocket, and then it seems that I will have no other option but to close down the center. . . . If that happens the consequences could be serious: the news will get around outside the park and (a) potential poachers will realise that our gorillas are unguarded, and (b) robbers will know that it is easy to raid the camp."

Dian received this doomsday announcement with incredulity and bewilderment. She had left Barnes what she believed to have been more than sufficient funds and as recently as October 18 had sent him an *additional* five thousand dollars by bank transfer. She was still trying to make sense of the situation when Dr. Snider telephoned in great perturbation. He too had received a copy of Barnes's dire warning and wanted an immediate explanation of what had happened to the National Geographic grant monies.

Very much on the horns of a dilemma, Dian had no ready answer. She had convinced herself, and wished to believe, that Barnes was the right man in the right place—an able lieutenant who not only could assist her in restoring the center to its former state of effectiveness, but one who could exercise effective command during her absences. "He is calm, reasonable, and above all, reliable," she had insisted.

Her written reply to Snider was defensive of Barnes. She maintained that Karisoke could not possibly be short of money. As for Barnes, "he is an exceedingly conscientious person who has, I fear, become overly fatigued by patrol work and trying to keep up with various fringe groups of gorillas. Therefore he is not putting the camp's objectives into their proper perspective; fatigue is the biggest cause of 'bushiness' that I know of, and who could be a better spokesperson on that topic! . . . It is my fervent hope that the camp will live up to its past standards despite the current slump, which I feel certain will be remedied."

These hopes were dashed when a worried Warren Garst, recently returned from Rwanda, called to tell her that conditions at Karisoke had become chaotic and that Barnes had also told *him* that the center was closing down. Bewilderment was followed by disillusionment, then anger as Dian heard from another source that Barnes and Jensen would be joining the staff of the Mountain Gorilla Project under the ubiquitous Jean-Pierre von der Becke.

By then it was time to fly back to Rwanda, accompanied by Warren Garst, who needed some additional footage for his film. The pair arrived in Kigali on November 22 and remained in the capital for the next several days while Dian tried to rally the Rwandan authorities and other interested parties in support of her gorilla guardians scheme. On December 15 she sent the National Geographic a formal account of what had transpired in Kigali, and of what had awaited her when she climbed to Karisoke.

As if fearful that the Society might not credit what she had to tell, she invoked the services of a witness:

"I have been fortunate in having Dr. Warren Garst present . . . during most of the events that occurred following my arrival in Rwanda. . . .

"I had a meeting with Laurent Habiyaremye, the new director of the Office Rwandais du Tourisme et des Parcs Nationaux (ORTPN). Mr. Habiyaremye has been a friend of mine for some ten years at least, from the time when he used to direct an import company. . . . We had an excellent meeting. He appeared very pleased with the new plan, Guardians for Gorilla Groups. . . .

"Dr. Garst and I invited J.P. von der Becke to dinner, along with Drs. Alain and Nichole Monfort, who serve as advisers now for the A'Kagera Park. J.P. had just returned from a six-week stay in America and Belgium as you know.

"J.P.'s attitude could only be described as a mixture of hostility and smugness. He stated that he had been asked to lecture at the National Geographic Society . . . and that he had had 'discussions' with members of the N.G. Research Committee. If this is so, could I be informed about any decisions made, please? He was not talking.

"J.P. alone, of those I spoke to in Kigali, did not care for the Guardians for Gorilla Groups proposal, stating that it required too many extra guards, which is not so at all. Personally I feel that he was miffed that he had not thought of it first. . . . In quite an outburst he stated that my 'book was all lies,' as were my lectures.

"Dr. Garst and I climbed up to camp on Sunday to find that Karen Jensen and two family members of Richard's had packed up their belongings and left the previous Thursday for J.P.'s home near Ruhengeri. Dr. Garst went to Richard's cabin to invite him for dinner, which was refused; but a 10:00 A.M. meeting was scheduled for the following morning. Dr. Garst was present throughout.

"Without any formalities Richard announced, 'It will not come as any surprise to you, but we are quitting.' He then proceeded to hand over a check for 270,000 Rwandan francs (which were the unspent funds on hand). . . . No accounting was given of any money spent since the end of June. . . . I asked about my .32 Walther pistol. . . . He responded, 'I threw the gun away in the forest. It was not registered and was therefore illegal in this country.' . . . No answers except 'Bullshit' were given to my inquiries about three missing Olivetti typewriters. . . . There were no reports or summaries of research activities after the end of September. As well, the Karisoke seal is missing.

"Richard left at 10:45 along with the rest of his belongings. . . . During the course of cleaning up the mess in his cabin, I found several letter copies from J.P. von der Becke to the director of ORTPN stating that Karisoke should be part of the Mountain Gorilla Project, therefore under his jurisdiction. . . . This explains, to a great extent, why work·permits have been held up. Without researchers, a research camp is simply a collection of buildings awaiting occupancy by tourists. I don't intend to let that happen.

"I had a lecture series arranged in South African universities beginning January 25, to be followed by a book tour in England through February. Unless something in the way of a miracle happens, I don't see how I can now keep these schedules."

Not only had Richard Barnes failed to live up to Dian's expectations, his departure with Karen Jensen stripped the Karisoke Research Center of researchers, leaving it—in the opinion of her detractors—without legitimate purpose. It also left Dian effectively rooted to her volcanic aerie in the role of caretaker and general factotum.

In this emergency she began beating the academic underbrush in the United States for new students. She also bethought herself of David Watts, to whom she wrote and cabled, asking him to reconsider taking on the job of center director.

She needed researchers not just to keep von der Becke and his ambitions at bay, but also to justify continuing financial support for the center.

**Without research data's being generated at camp, it is not possible for me to ask N.G. for funds to support Karisoke. For the time being, until new students can be found, I am monitoring the gorillas as best I can with the aid of the trackers. When N.G. funds run out—probably at the end of January of '84—I will have to keep the camp going entirely on my own funds for at least three months until research gets properly under way again. For the time being, because of the money earned lecturing in the United States, we can survive.**

Although Dian was beset with difficulties, Karisoke comforted her. On the first morning after her arrival home, even before the somewhat bizarre meeting with Barnes, she had spent an hour on the meadows watching the biggest, most inquisitive bushbuck she had ever seen; and had been greeted there by the resident pair of white-necked ravens accompanied by two young-of-the-year. The adult birds flew directly to her and lit on the ground only a few feet away. Dian could not be sure that they had recognized her, but felt they had.

On her second day home, "feeling very fit," she accompanied Garst on a filming foray to Nunkie's group where that sage old silver-back obliged the camera by staging such a convincing mock charge that Garst fell over backward with his tripod on top of him. "If gorillas could laugh," Dian noted gleefully, "Nunkie would have been having hysterics."

Garst departed on December 18.

**I am now alone with my white elephant, Karisoke, my wonderful Africans, my gorillas, and all the other animals. It would be ideal, if not for future problems having to do with money and the efforts of outsiders to make as many difficulties as possible.**

A few days later Anita McClellan arrived for a two-week visit. This was a happy time. Dian introduced her friend to the forest world and to the gorillas, and they spent long evenings in front of the restored living room fireplace talking of their dear departed dogs and other subjects close to their hearts. They also made excited preparations for the revival of one of Dian's cherished Karisoke traditions— "the Wogs' Christmas party."

**Anita and I had to work nearly to dawn wrapping extra presents and making more food because Gwehandagoza came up with the news there would be one hell of a big crowd coming. The party is supposed to be just for the Africans who work here and their close relatives, but now they have the idea it's for the _whole_ extended family!**

**Well, we had it on the twenty-fourth as per schedule. Eighty-one men, women, and children climbed up here—and eighty-_two_ went down. Yes, I delivered my very first baby yesterday, in between passing out lunch and passing out the Christmas presents!**

**No, I did not pass out too, but it sure was an odoriferous and intriguing experience to say the least. The mother was the wife of my tracker Kana, and he and she are both Batwas. Most of the other women present were Bahutu, and so none of them particularly wanted to help her out, so that left you know who to order the boiling water (I never saw so much boiling water in my life) and take up where the poor lady had to leave off.**

**The problem started after the whole crowd had spent two**

hours dancing and singing and drinking pombe and just generally having a good time. I got into this myself, and I guess Kana's wife and I both overdid it, but the results were worse for her. I had started taking Polaroid pictures of each family group for presents, when it became obvious that Kana's wife wasn't able to smile. He poked her and ordered her to smile, which she did momentarily, but that poke was the "straw that broke," only in this case it was the bag of waters.

I had her carried to the guest bed in my spare room and rolled up my sleeves the way they do on those TV movies of a prairie homestead.

When the baby was out, I cut the cord properly with my bread knife (fortunately just sharpened) on the breadboard, then tied the cord with whatever was handy—a pipe cleaner—then slapped the hell out of the baby, who didn't seem to be breathing at all. The mother seemed in too much pain to be much interested (the baby was a month early) as I held him upside down and slapped away. But she smiled when he finally screamed and began breathing.

Then she sucked the gluck out of his nose and ears (there are limits to my abilities), after which I cleaned off the debris adhering to his tadpolelike form. (Why is it that newly born television babies come out pink and clean and unscummy?) I then swathed him in a towel swiped from the Mille des Collines hotel, handed him back to his mum, and ordered her to nurse him, just as I had seen it done on TV.

Well, was I ever laughed at by the assembled ladies who had crowded into the room to see the fun. According to what I was then told, babies are usually born in the field, and other work usually has to be completed before baby gets a chance to have its first meal. They truly didn't know that the neonate could suckle in its first hour of life! I didn't either, but *it* knew, and it did!

The crowd was now getting restless for their gifts, so I left the mother and child to begin distributing the loot, but before I could get started, Kana gave a speech announcing a successful birth and then he named the new son KARISOKE! How about that! Then the women, some nineteen of them, began a birth chant that was simply spine-tingling. There are no words to describe it, but I shall never forget it.

About 5:00 P.M. the guests left along with Kana and most of his children. An eighteen-month-old had to stay behind too because it was still suckling, and a young girl stayed to spend the night with the mother, change pots, and switch the two babies to and from the lunch table.

Next morning Kana returned along with his mother-in-law, the most gnarled, sweet-smiling, dignified old lady all dressed up in her very very best finery. She had climbed the mountain for the first time in her life to say thank you and to chant prayers of thanksgiving over her new grandson. I was truly touched by her graciousness. It was an extraordinary experience, and a humbling one.

The wife and babe descended at 10:00 A.M. in the rain after Kana and the grandmother had cleaned up the room to the best of their ability. I never thought about it at the time, but the birth of a Batwa baby at Karisoke might have a good influence on controlling poaching activities. Kana and his family are related to all the Batwas in Mukingo, the biggest poaching village in the Virungas. So word will spread that Nyiramachabelli chose to deliver a Twa baby, rather than chase the mother and child into the woods. So this fortuitous event may turn out to have been an effective measure of *active* conservation!

Kana's son was not the only unexpected gift to arrive at Karisoke that Christmas. On December 26, Dian received a letter from Rane Randolph enclosing a photocopy of a check for ten thousand dollars—a donation to the Digit Fund from two Californians, Harold and Sandra Price—no relation to Richard Price.

Apart from atrocious weather—"Daily rain, fog, and hail"—January of 1984 was unusually kind to Dian. There was still no word of new students on their way or of whether Watts would accept her offer, but Anita remained in camp until the tenth, and on January 5, Dian welcomed another visitor.

Carole Le Jeune is a Belgian "girl" of forty-one years who was born in Zaire and has lived there most of her life. She is an artist specializing in paintings of flowers, very shy and sort of peculiar. She is willing to stay here during the three weeks I might be gone, but I don't feel totally secure about this since she is subject to attacks of malaria and isn't feeling so well just now.

Gorillas are doing fine—though I can't keep up with them as before because my foot is infected again and of course my lungs are bad—and they are ranging so very far away. My biggest problem at the moment is that I am due to leave for South Africa on January 25 and then on to England, but I don't feel I can leave responsibility for camp just with Carole and the Africans (though they are as loyal as always) because of what might eventuate from down below. So I am on the verge of having to decline these long-planned tours. Won't cable the sponsors just yet as I am hoping for a minor miracle in the form of "replacements."

The miracle occurred. On January 18, while driving back to the Karisoke car park after a visit to Gisenyi, Carole Le Jeune encountered that rare phenomenon in Rwanda—a European hitchhiker. Being a kindly soul, she offered him a lift. The sunburned young man explained that he was a farmer's son from the French Alps working his way around the world before settling down. He had heard about the gorillas of the Virungas and had decided to stop by en route to Uganda. Carole decided to risk Dian's ire—all too easily roused by tourists—and take him back to camp with her. It was an inspired decision. Dian liked him, and when he volunteered to spend the next three or four weeks at Karisoke, she was happy to accept.

Claude Glise is a boy of real integrity who will give my Africans a feeling they have not been abandoned. I believe he and Carole can hold things together in my absence.

Reassured that Karisoke would survive, she departed at the end of January.

The South African part of the tour, nine days, was unbelievably hectic with an average of ten interviews a day (radio, television, newspapers), not to mention giving lectures every second night. Sleep and meals were sparsely distributed.

Part of the reason for the trip was to promote the book; but Hodder and Stoughton had only shipped one thousand copies, and all were sold before the tour ended. My expenses were split between them and Air Zaire, who want to promote tourism among South Africans. What a prick the Air Zaire guy turned out to be! On the pleasant side, the H&S promotions person—Nicole—was just a dear. She is a very petite, little, pretty young blonde who is just the spitting image of Lady Di and stopped traffic wherever we went. You can imagine the contrast between us two.

I was able to see very little of S.A., which I resented, since the scheduling was far more demanding than any American tour I've ever been on. What I did see, mainly from airplanes, was cultivated and built up—a far cry from the Africa I know and love.

If South Africa failed to delight Dian, some of its citizens were less than delighted with *her*. In several interviews and in at least one lecture, she was sufficiently critical of apartheid to attract the attention of the authorities. Subsequently she received word from the

American Embassy in Kigali that she would not be welcome if she returned to South Africa.

Was shunted off to England on February 6 on an absolutely horrid two-day journey on ancient planes that stopped everywhere, frequently leaving me in transit and as a standby passenger for nearly a day in Lisbon, and all on account of that skinflint Greek Air Zaire representative. If he comes to Karisoke as he says he will, I will introduce him to the most bloody-minded buffalo in the Virungas.

Was met at London airport by a Mercedes and uniformed driver and the Hodder and Stoughton rep—a 36-year-old girl/lady named Monica whose conversation consisted almost entirely of "ta ta" and "how lovely."

The schedule was just as hectic as in S.A., but I saw lots of Ian Redmond and was ever so proud of the way he has matured, what with marriage and a full-time job as writer-reporter with the BBC *Wildlife* magazine.

One Sunday I invited him and myself to Cambridge to visit Robert Hinde, my professor when I was there working for my degree, who used to be a very very good friend. To my sorrow Robert had little to say to me now because of what he claimed was my unfairness to Harcourt and Barnes, both of whom are here at Cambridge.

Although I knew Harcourt and Kelly were here, I sure didn't expect to run into them; but I did so in the library. Kelly looked up at me and her face registered shock, surprise, sorrow, maybe a little guilt and fear, and an instant of happiness before she totally closed down all emotions and simply said, "I'm so surprised to see you." I said a few insane words of greeting, felt compelled to hug her, then followed her gaze some fifteen feet to where Harcourt sat immersed in a book that he held around his lower face. Kelly just sat staring at him; he did nothing, so I left. I remain very saddened by that meeting.

A second weekend was spent more pleasurably.

I took Ian as a guest along with me to visit John Aspinall's HUGE country estates, which contain hundreds of species of wild animals, including twenty-four lowland gorillas in an enormous outdoor enclosure who are living very much as they would in the wild. WOW, what an experience! Like myself, Aspinall often gets bad press, but I found him to be basically a humble man who has a passionate love and appreciation of animals. Every weekend he goes into the enclosures with his gorillas, lions, tiger, rhinos, ele-

306

phants, wolves, etc., because he feels the animals need a personal relationship with humans if they are going to trust their surroundings, breed, and remain content.

We spent two days with him and his family at Howletts and Port Lymphe, his two castles (literally) and game preserves. All of Aspinall's wealth is based on gambling, and he is reputed to be the wealthiest man in the U.K. outside of the royalty.

Well, on the sorry side, he asked how his contributions to my work had helped. Naturally, in turn, I asked, "What contributions?" Same old story—he has sent thousands of dollars, so I learned, to the Mountain Gorilla Project for Dian Fossey's work with the mountain gorillas!

Aspinall's "zoo" was exceptional. One week previously I had visited a zoo enclosure in London of the same dimensions but where most of the space had been wasted on a huge moat. There sat five gorilla adults, one male and four females, involuntarily tapping their bodies much like patients in a geriatric ward. I was told by the zoo official accompanying me that "they were saved from the pot in West Africa by being bought for the zoo." As I watched the animals sitting there, alternately patting themselves aimlessly or pulling out their own hair, I could not help but think that "the pot," if that *had* been the only alternative, might have been a better solution.

Other things that happened: Had to give a lecture at the Royal Society, which was spooky for me. Ian had forewarned me that members of the Mt. Gorilla Project from the Fauna Preservation Society would be there taping every word I said. It was indeed the case, but as Ian later described it, they all went out with their tapes between their legs. I stated that tourism and trap-removing sponsored by the Mountain Gorilla Project *have* aided the gorillas' plight—and then spent three times as much time describing how the Digit Fund runs patrols six days a week, etc., etc., and in fact does most of the antipoaching work.

Tired, but in good spirits, Dian flew back to Kigali on February 20. Before proceeding on to camp she had another meeting with Laurent Habiyaremye, director of ORTPN, concerning her gorilla guardian proposals.

"I can't tell you how much I like the new park director," she wrote Stacey Coil. "He is the first director I ever met who has real integrity. In turn, he also likes me and has spoken out strongly for the continuation of Karisoke as a research center and as the main hope that remains for the gorillas."

Her mood was further buoyed when, on reaching camp, she found a letter from David Watts accepting her offer of the director's job. He was prepared to come within the month if she could obtain the requisite permissions. These she succeeded in arranging with Habiyaremye in the unprecedentedly brief span of ten days. She cabled Watts, who arrived at Karisoke on March 22, after an absence of almost five years.

Dian, who had been alone since the first of the month when Carole Le Jeune and the young French cattleman both went their separate ways, was delighted to show him around a restored camp. Watts was pleased to be back and anxious to get to work on a new gorilla study funded by a grant from the Leakey Foundation. It was as well that he had his own funding, since Karisoke's financial state could now only be described as perilous.

On February 27 Dian had written Stacey Coil: "I know my bank account must be nearly defunct by now. . . . It is a little spooky running Karisoke on only the traveler's checks I brought with me from Ithaca and the Digit Fund, but I can manage for a while before I put out a plea to the powers that be." She had been counting on royalty income from the book to bridge the gap, but sales had not been as large as expected, and she had incurred heavy charges against royalties for additional artwork and extensive changes to the book's page proofs.

In a letter to Shirley McGreal she noted wryly, "Let's face it, the book wasn't that great a seller; but I still have my gold fillings to fall back on. I don't know whom to ask for money since the Mountain Gorilla Project appears to be soaking up all available contributions from the major funding agencies and the public at large. Most people with whom I have spoken while in America, South Africa, and the U.K. seem to think they are donating to Karisoke when they give to the MGP."

She had not approached the National Geographic.

I don't think it right to ask N.G. for money when there is actually no behavioral research going on here because no students yet.

This was not the whole story. She was apprehensive about asking the Society for help because she was fearful that the senior officials there had once again turned against her.

What disturbs me tremendously is that von der Becke inferred following his return from America that I am finished with N.G. If this is the case, and I have only the absence of answers to my letters to feel that it might be, I am extremely dejected. Dr. Snider hasn't written a word to me in ages. That hurts!

This was not paranoia. While her articles in the Society's magazine and films about her life with the gorillas had served the Society's
purposes very well, she was no longer the stellar attraction she had
once been.

Although Dian must have been at least dimly aware of this, she
stubbornly refused to realize that Karisoke's fairy godmother of more
than a dozen years was now departing from the scene.

During March and April she kept herself preoccupied with
antipoaching work, a training program for park guards, and in trying
to establish her Guardians for Gorilla Groups. She made little progress with the latter. Although ORTPN's new director had praised the
idea, he would take no steps to implement it. He would not even
commission a study to determine its potential. This intransigence was
due, in part at least, to the hostility evidenced toward the plan by
those whose vested interests would have been put at risk had Dian's
scheme been approved.

In close cooperation with the Belgian Aid program, conservation organizations were now funneling hundreds of thousands of dollars into various divisions of ORTPN, which had come to depend
upon this source of funds. Laurent Habiyaremye may have been
Dian's good friend and warm supporter when he first took over his
new post, but he had quickly found himself influenced by more prac-
tical considerations.

Unable to persuade the Rwandan government or any established
conservation agency to espouse her plan, Dian was nevertheless encouraged by a few individual supporters. One of these was Joan
Travis, a longtime friend of the Digit Fund who wrote: "I would love
to know if you have actually started the new regime of assigning a
local family to each gorilla group. As I recall, you said that this would
require about one hundred dollars a month. If you have embarked on
this program, Arnold [her husband] and I would like to become responsible for the support of one such unit."

Dian was now sending guardian patrols three times a week to
each of the several gorilla groups in the study area, and to an additional three fringe groups on the northern slopes of Mt. Visoke.

This was all very well, but the guardians had to be paid and
there were too few Joan Travises around. The financial drain on
Dian's resources was assuming the proportions of a hemorrhage.

**I am now personally paying the upkeep of Karisoke, its track-
ers and camp staff, as well as most of the Guardians for Gorilla
Groups we have set up, all from the proceeds of the book. But
these are now down to very little. I really do not know whom to**

ask for funding since the camp is essentially conservation-oriented rather than scientifically oriented for the moment.

She wrote Stacey Coil, "I desperately need money and am now having to borrow from everyone." By early April it looked as if the bankruptcy Richard Barnes had prematurely predicted for Karisoke might become a reality.

**I feel like an abandoned mother of fifty-seven, the number of gorillas now in the study area. To care for them I have to get work or sell something. I could try selling my body, but there wouldn't be many takers for Fossil Fossey, so I must try something else.**

Although she loathed the idea, her only real hope rested in intensifying her activities as promoter and saleswoman for the mountain gorillas. "It is truly like being some kind of a hooker," she had once remarked. Perhaps so, but there was no help for it. She decided to return to the United States in May to scout for funds.

The timing of Watts's arrival had been fortuitous. A week after he climbed to Karisoke, Dian came down with yet another bout of pneumonia. As usual she aimed to cure herself but, by April 10, had become so sick she was lapsing into unconsciousness. At this point David sent for a litter and had her carried down the mountain to Ruhengeri Hospital. There she remained until April 20, by which time she was sufficiently recovered to return to camp to greet the first of the new students, a young Englishman from the University of Bristol named Michael Catsis.

Still too weak to attempt anything strenuous, Dian mooched about in and near her cabin for the next several days. She was hatching a new project—a book about the human and animal history of the Virungas to be based on interviews with the elders of the native population. Acceptance of her declining health, combined with the need to earn a living for her dependents, had reactivated the writer's itch that had been with her on and off since childhood.

She was wasting no time feeling sorry for herself, as she makes clear in a letter to Shirley McGreal written in early May:

"I am *not*, as you suggest, 'killing myself by neglect.' In 1963 a lung specialist in Louisville warned me that it would be suicidal to climb to Kabara on that first memorable safari to Africa. He subsequently died of lung cancer! At any rate, I take extremely good care of myself in full realization that I live at ten thousand feet in a rain forest, and in a cabin whose fireplaces smoke more than I. I take vitamin pills, have bought a small oxygen machine, eat a couple of bananas a day to avoid potassium deficiency, and thrive on potatoes and eggs (my main diet because of budget problems). In other words, I

310

spoil myself. My only regrets are that I cannot go to the gorillas on a daily basis anymore, but Karisoke trackers and research students can and do. As long as I can function to train guards and new Africans in duties related to the *active* conservation of gorillas and other inhabitants of the Virungas, then I happily exist."

She was not entirely separated from the gorillas. They occasionally came close enough so that she could reach them. On April 2 she and Group 5 had their first visit together since January.

**They were quite near camp, but it is ever so cold and rainy. Virtually all we did was exchange grunts of empathetic misery, though young Tuck managed to swipe my three-hundred-dollar altimeter, so tonight it sits in the rain, and hopefully tomorrow a tracker will find it. But Tuck was so funny. I thought I had everything portable hidden in my pockets and my knapsack, but she managed to spy a bit of the string connected to the altimeter just protruding from my knapsack. Zoooom! In a flash she grabbed it and ran to old Beethoven, a couple of yards away, all the time twirling it around and around on the end of the string like a deadly missile. It frightened the @#$%&\* blue cheese out of the old man! He screamed as this alien object was whirled around his head and hurriedly moved off. Tuck then directed a "just try and get it" look at me. I hope I gave her my cold—it is a green/red one, and not much fun.**

It was this cold, exacerbated by the day in the rain, that turned into pneumonia; but for Dian this was a small price to pay for a few hours of communion with the mountain kings.

ess than three months after
her return from England, Dian was on the road—or in the air—again.
Leaving Kigali on May 14, she retraced the now tediously familiar
route via Brussels to New York, then went on to Louisville for a brief
visit with members of the Henry family, but chiefly to check on the
state of her personal finances. It was with no great surprise that she
found her current account overdrawn.

**My savings, which aren't exactly Rockefeller-type, are
mostly from Uncle Bert's legacy and are my old-age pension. I
guess I'm old enough to start drawing on them now. Not that
there is any choice.**

During the next ten days she shuttled back and forth between
New York and Washington, attempting to regain the support of the
National Geographic Society. Although she was treated kindly by old
friends such as Dr. Snider, it was painfully apparent that the Society
had no intention of taking her back into the fold.

She spent hours on the telephone trying to interest other potential sponsors in funding Karisoke. Receiving an absolute rebuff from
the Leakey Foundation, she tried a number of private donors to good
causes, but found that those inclined to support gorilla conservation
were mostly committed to the Mountain Gorilla Project or its parent
organizations.

At the end of May she retreated to Ithaca to spend a few days
pondering her lack of success as a fund-raiser. Her gloom was not
much lightened when she learned that Biruté Galdikas had recently
received a grant of $60,000 from the Earth Watch Society and that

one of the members of the oil-fed Getty family was supporting Jane Goodall's work to the tune of $250,000.

Although rejected by the conservation establishment, Dian was becoming a heroine to rank-and-file activists in the conservation movement. These were mostly people who had very little surplus income, but they gave what they could. By the time she left Ithaca she had the satisfaction of knowing that there was at least enough money in the Digit Fund to cover the costs of antipoaching patrols and her gorilla guardian program for the immediate future.

Her next stop was Chicago, where she worked for ten days on the *Wild Kingdom* gorilla film, thereby earning enough "to pay camp costs and the men's salaries for two months at least."

While in Chicago she consulted a doctor about a new and disquieting ailment. The doctor diagnosed a heart disorder, probably due to stress. He gave her a prescription and recommended that she rest and take life easy for at least six weeks. He particularly enjoined her not to travel and to avoid high altitudes!

**He might as well have told me just to stop breathing and be done with it. I thanked him nicely and settled his bill, which would have paid for a solid month of antipoacher patrols. Well, if my heart is as tough as my old lungs, I guess I'll make it.**

Next day she was en route back to Karisoke.

Not long after her return she wrote to Warren Garst:

"I have never known this camp to function better, without friction, etc. Twice a week I send detailed reports on the patrol and guardian work to the director of ORTPN and to the park conservateur. Their appreciation of same is *real*. Have two good assistants in the form of David Watts, who is far happier this time since the V-W couple aren't here, and the young English boy, Mike Catsis, who works very well and speaks perfect French. In the next month or so three more people are expected—general researcher, botanist-artist, and veterinarian. Karisoke is going to POP with output!"

To Joan and Arnold Travis, who continued to fund one of the Guardian Groups, she reported: "Things continue well at camp, though I am still paying for its upkeep out of my pocket and everything connected with patrol work out of the Digit Fund. So far this year (end of June) we have cut 1,101 traps and caught two poachers. The patrols are running seven days a week. We are covering fringe groups, but not as often as I like since most are so far away from Karisoke. We are now guarding eighty-four gorillas, nearly half of all there are in the whole of the Virungas. . . . I was going to send you

313

some cute little dung dollops from infants in the fringe groups as 'baptism/adoption' gifts but thought better of it.

"The director of ORTPN really liked the adoption idea at first. He was so excited and happy that something new was going to be done, but the Belgian head of the Mt. Gorilla Project did not like it. That killed the scheme for the entirety of the mountains, but not for us up here. We have taken the heartland of the volcanoes to protect. I'll say this, all is most effective, as traps are getting harder and harder to find and poachers are running scared."

Although Karisoke's human society was in equilibrium, the same was not true of the gorillas. This summer witnessed some extraordinary disruptions of their social structure.

**Tiger had been wandering like a lost soul since leaving Peanuts's bachelor group. Recently he started to shadow Nunkie's Group. On June 21 there was one hell of an interaction. Nobody saw it, but Nemeye heard it from a kilometer or two away. Said it sounded like a war. I think he was too scared to go over and see what was happening.**

**Tiger succeeded somehow in splitting Nunkie's group apart. Nunkie's six females and their offspring were scattered all over Visoke. On the twenty-seventh one of my trackers found Jenny, a three-year-old female, wandering and whimpering all alone in the forest. When she saw him she came right to him and climbed into his arms before he knew what was happening. She wouldn't let go so he headed back to camp. I couldn't believe my eyes when I saw this guy outside my cabin uncomfortably being hugged by the youngster.**

**I didn't want to keep her away from her group, so gave her no encouragement and she climbed a hagenia tree outside my cabin where she rested all day. In the evening we could all hear chest beating up the mountain, and the youngster climbed down and went off to rejoin her father, Nunkie, some one and a half kilometers away. Next day her mom, Simba, found her way back to Nunkie too, so there was this happy reunion.**

**For a while two others of Nunkie's females, Pandora and Petula, stayed with Tiger, but then he evidently decided he wasn't a family man after all and gave them the slip to pursue his lone way again. Petula had left her four-year-old with Nunkie but has lost an eighteen-month-old infant that can't now be found. These two females are now trying to join up with Group 5!**

**All of the above sure sounds like a gorilla soap opera. Will Tiger ever find his perfect mate! Are Pandora and Petula really lesbians? Is the King of the Mountain, Nunkie, over the hill?**

A month went by.

Gorilla Soap is continuing. Petula split with Pandora and disappeared on the other side of Visoke in search of Nunkie, who by then was back on *this* side again! Pandora just rejoined him and Simba and his two remaining females yesterday after traveling all over the countryside.

THEN. Last week Tiger struck the group again, just behind camp, and everything is in chaos once more! This time Tiger took off with Simba who is his half sister, but her daughter, Jenny, is *again* missing. Simultaneously another of Nunkie's females, Fuddle, and *her* two offspring split off and now are doing the same thing that happened to Pandora—wandering around looking for Nunkie. Nothing like this has ever happened before in all my years in the Virungas and none of it makes sense.

On August 20, Dian added a footnote to this confusing roundelay.

The crazy, unheard-of interaction between Tiger and Nunkie's Group thankfully seems to be over. Petula is still missing. Our hero, Tiger, ends up with his half sister, Simba, whose daughter, Jenny, finally rejoined Nunkie, whose group is now back together except for two females and the lost baby. But I'm not counting on the story's being over. Tune in tomorrow, and we'll see what happens next!

Strange events were taking place even in the staid purlieu of Group 5.

That Group is having problems too because old Beethoven is allowing his sons Ziz and Pablo to copulate with his oldest female, Effie. And none of the three males seems to be interested in the sexually mature, hot and eager young females Puck, Tuck, Poppy, and Pansy, so they are now doing their thing together and fighting and squabbling like mad. All this is behavior such as I never thought could occur. It is just too humanlike!

Visitors abounded this summer. During the first week in August a dozen scientists attending a world primate conference in Nairobi climbed to Karisoke. They were surprised to discover that the derogatory reports they had been hearing about Dian had been grossly exaggerated. An English primatologist was subsequently heard to say: "Dian Fossey has been the victim of an unconscionable hatchet job."

On August 17 the arrival of Lady Amanda Aspinall created something of a sensation.

She is twenty-six years old, an extraordinarily beautiful, well-bred girl about my height with the same color hair. She is extremely thin, as I was at her age, and the gorillas just went crazy over her, the older ones particularly, as if they confused her with me many years ago.

On her first night in Rwanda, Amanda ran into a prof from N.Y. traveling with a young male student. The man assured her he was a good friend of mine (I've never laid eyes on the creep) and talked her into letting them come up to camp with her. A young Spanish couple glommed on too, and all were adamant about staying the night here. WOW, what a scene ensued! Happily one of my trackers showed up with lots of fresh, hot gorilla dung from Nunkie's Group. So I spread out and examined the nice juicy lobes with great gusto on the dining table in front of my cabin until the freeloaders left in disgust.

Guess who they met coming up, on their way down, Ian Redmond! He was guiding a group of English nature tourists through Rwanda and Zaire but took the day off. What a surprise and delight to see him again in camp! We talked till the wee, wee hours. I do so wish he could be back here to stay. He is the one person with whom I have worked at Karisoke (outside of the Africans) that I fully trust. I can't stay here all the time, much as I wish. The constant gray skies, altitude, and work are kind of getting to me/my lungs/heart. But Ian had to go down again next day.

Before leaving, Ian mentioned that the faggy prof and friend, and the Spaniards, were calling me every name in the book on their way down the trail and even he wasn't able to calm them down.

Dian and Ian were amused by the incident, but it would turn out to be no laughing matter.

The first week of September was memorable for two events.

Dian acquired a pair of gray parrots—a gift from one of her pilot friends. Although they could never fill the gap left in her life by the deaths of Cindy and Kima, they provided some focus for her affection and brought some animal vitality into her lonely cabin.

On September 3 the park's assistant conservateur, Jean Burgeri, climbed to camp to tell her that the infamous poacher Sebahutu, the killer of Uncle Bert, with whom she had been waging war for a decade and more, was dead.

He was killed by a buffalo last week!!! Burgeri only learned about this when all of Sebahutu's many wives and children, dressed in mourning, went past park headquarters yesterday, and the yelling was so loud he came out to ask what had happened. The story is that the death occurred in Uganda. Now only Gashabizi remains of the six principal poachers, and then Digit, Uncle Bert, Macho, and Kweli will have been avenged.

Sebahutu had been freed from prison far short of completing a five-year sentence, after paying a fine that was, in effect, a bribe. This was common practice, and it enraged Dian on two counts. In the first place, it allowed poachers to return to their nefarious trade. In the second place, "in order to pay the fines and bribes, poachers and their partners in crime work twice as hard in the forest killing more and more animals to make up the money." There was nothing she could do about this, but she could and did celebrate Sebahutu's demise with a party that included everyone in camp.

Alas, as had once been the case with Munyarukiko, the report of Sebahutu's death was false, undoubtedly contrived to delude the authorities, and perhaps Dian as well.

On September 9 she descended the mountain for the first time since her return from the United States in mid-June. She did not go because she wanted to, but because her visa, which was now being issued for only three months at a time, was running out. Climbing up or down the porters' trail had become such an ordeal that she would not undertake it even to please such a close friend as Rosamond Carr. If the weather was good—not pouring rain or hissing hail—she could manage to slither down the steep track in a couple of hours, but in bad weather it might now take her as long as four hours to scrabble back up to Karisoke, and that only with the help of the strong arms of her porters.

She found a disturbing change in the atmosphere at ORTPN's headquarters. Her "good friend" Laurent Habiyaremye had become invisible. When she persisted, she was told by an underling that she was wasting her time; the director was angry at her, because of her treatment of the tourists who had climbed to Karisoke with Lady Aspinall, and did not wish to see her.

Worse was to follow. When she applied for her new visa, she was brusquely informed that would take several days.

A visit to the American embassy did nothing to resolve the difficulty or to ease her mind. There she was told that ORTPN was displeased with her and was intent on making difficulties. Dian arrived at a familiar conclusion.

**Same old story. Mt. Gorilla has got around this director too. They are in, Fossey out.**

She still had a string to her bow—a Rwandan friend was able to take her request for a visa direct "to the number 2 man in Foreign Affairs. My visa was ready next day."

Dian had planned a second journey to the United States in 1984 to raise money from a lecture tour, but for unexplained reasons no engagements were ever booked. Meanwhile she had committed herself to travel to San Diego to receive the Joseph Wood Krutch Medal from the Humane Society of the United States, in recognition of her work with the gorillas. She had also intended to visit her mother, whom she believed to be dying. When the lecture schedule failed to materialize, she decided to go anyway.

For once she did not worry about the security of Karisoke during her absence. Her fortress on the mountain was now well manned. In addition to David Watts, Mike Catsis, and Carole Le Jeune (who had returned to continue her plant portraits), the troops had been augmented by Jan Rafert, a young gorilla keeper from the Brooklyn Zoo, and by an Australian veterinarian.

**They are all ACTIVE conservationists, and I don't believe any of them would go over to the MGP as has happened in the past.**

She departed at the beginning of October, flying first to Ithaca where she spent two weeks with Stacey Coil and accountant Rane Randolph clearing up a backlog of Digit Fund paperwork, then on to California to find that reports of her mother's state of health were greatly exaggerated. Nevertheless it was a gloomy visit, during which Kitty Price dwelt mournfully on her desire to be buried in Piedmont, California. Perhaps not wanting her daughter to feel left out, as it were, she announced that she was giving Dian a plot she owned in a cemetery in Fresno.

Dian's sight had been failing for some time, so she consulted an eye specialist in San Francisco. He found a growth over the left cornea and recommended surgery. With some hesitation Dian concurred, and an operation was scheduled for October 20; but when she found that the procedure would entail several days in the hospital with her eyes bandaged, she canceled it.

On October 27 she was presented with the Joseph Wood Krutch Medal at the Humane Society's annual convention in San Diego. She was deeply moved by the experience, the more so since this was the first such honor she had ever received. Mavericks and medals do not often go together.

Then it was back across North America for a few days with old friends in Louisville, and on to Brussels and Kigali—but *not* on to Karisoke. Dian had to make a slight detour first.

In early September she had received a cable from her agent.

**The Dutch publishers of the book will pay for me to go to Holland for three days, November 5–8. After long self-debate I decided to take the offer though the travel arrangements are mind-boggling. I'll be bringing back mountains of stuff from the States, mostly for my Africans, but there is no way this over-**

weight can be worked without costing me a fortune I haven't got if I come home via Amsterdam. So I will have to first fly to Kigali, stash all the baggage, get a night's sleep, then turn around and go right back across the African continent, the bloody ocean, and end up in Amsterdam. My God, I really dread it! One jet lag will never catch up with the one before it!

It wasn't *quite* that bad; Dian did manage two nights and a day in Kigali.

Arrived in Amsterdam at 6:00 A.M. on the morning of November 7 and was told that I had to meet Prince Bernhardt at his palace at 11:00 A.M. Panic! It was about one and a half hours from Amsterdam to the palace at Geitz, so I primped and ironed like mad and set off finally with two charming male escorts, feeling like Cinderella but looking more like her stepsister. The prince is actually quite nice and casual. I had been told it was to be a morning tea affair, but I was the only one who stuck to the tea (how about that!), with the prince on sherry and his male secretary on Scotch. We spent forty-five minutes talking about gorillas, and he claimed to have read the book since he wrote a brief foreword to the Dutch edition. In it he claims that the WNF (the Dutch branch of the World Wildlife Fund) has helped my work considerably—well, there we go again.

Dian was also taken to Burgers Zoological Gardens in Arnhem to see a group of seven young adult lowland gorillas that had been collected in West Africa for the zoo trade by an animal dealer with headquarters in the Republic of Cameroon. Unfortunately for him, Shirley McGreal's International Primate Protection League got wind of the captures and raised such an international stink that the Cameroon government intervened. McGreal, backed by Fossey and others, wanted the animals kept in Africa and reintroduced to the wilds. They were overruled by the prestigious International Union for the Conservation of Nature, which arranged to have them shipped to Holland. The sight of the Cameroon Seven, as they had become known, confined in a sunless indoor enclosure, infuriated Dian. On her return to Karisoke she wrote to the director general of the I.U.C.N.

"Please keep in mind . . . that a gorilla is its own owner. Albeit the 'Cameroon Seven' may be the nominal property of the I.U.C.N., it has sold its soul by their exportation. . . . I would detest being in the position of the person who signed the release papers for the 'Cameroon Seven' to go to Holland, thereby robbing them of their natural heritage, probably forever.

"It is certainly not for me to judge the decisions of the I.U.C.N. However, I will ask you to weigh your consciences as to what you are currently doing or avoiding doing toward the *active* conservation of an endangered species."

This was not the sort of action calculated to endear Dian to the conservation establishment, but by now she had come to consider that a lost cause in any case.

Her Dutch publishers took her to another zoo, at Apeldoorn, which had six lowland gorillas. This was a press event, and while photographers and TV cameramen clustered close, the inevitable publicity person handed a copy of Dian's book to one of the caged gorillas. Writing to the Prices about this incident a few weeks later, Dian quoted a newspaper headline: " 'Local Gorillas Eat Up Fossey's Book.' Which is exactly what they did. Maybe that is why the book has sold so well in Holland—seven thousand copies so far, which is a lot of gorilla fodder."

During her last day in Holland the stress of her recent peregrinations caught up with her and she almost passed out during a book-signing session.

Very lung-sick and really worried if I could make it back to Rwanda. Left next morning with temperature of 105° and flew directly to Kigali, where I crawled into the Mille des Collines Hotel and slept for twenty-four hours. Then I called the embassy and Ambassador Bland and his wife took pity on me and sent a car to take me to the residence, where they looked after me for the next three days. Probably saved my life, which is what I told them anyway.

On the fifteenth, armed with all kinds of pills, I unwisely tried to climb the mountain but collapsed and had to be carried up by stretcher. On my arrival found David had raised all the men's salaries and told them to stick with the new salaries and also make larger food demands. If he goes on like this, the sooner Watts is out of camp the better for all of us, particularly the Africans, who have become confused by his doctrines. Jan Rafert, a nice, quiet person with a sense of integrity, has taken over running the Digit Fund patrols. They have cut down 2,262 traps this year, released eighteen animals alive from traps, and have captured and imprisoned eight poachers. Not one gorilla from study of fringe groups injured/killed/harmed by poachers, though several have been caught in traps in other parts of the Virungas and some killed.

Effie had a new baby on October 20, likely sired by old

320

Beethoven, who is perking up. Tiger remains with Simba, who is pregnant now and should give birth in April. All of the groups are two hours or more from camp, even for the trackers, and it rains on a daily basis, so I don't see them. But I have my parrots (not very sociable), and the ravens come every day for food. Toby, the hyrax by my cabin, is the father of twins and sits on his log with momma and babies below, in absolute confidence of me even when I am within five meters.

I am still maintaining Karisoke by the payments from my book and the antipoacher patrols by the Digit Fund. The Mountain Gorilla Project continues to use my name as well as that of Digit for their own collection of funds. I have met, during the past eight months, a number of organizations and wealthy individuals who claimed they had given thousands of dollars to the M.G.P. to help my cause. This kind of news is really defeating.

Dian's concern about money was eased a little in mid-December when the trust committee of the Humane Society of the United States made her a grant of five thousand dollars for "the work you have been doing in the cause of animal protection.'" This was the kind of recognition she could appreciate.

Another useful bit of recognition had come her way at the end of November when she had attended a fete to honor the establishment of Rwanda's other national park, A'Kagera.

The fete was well done and most enjoyable. Laurent Habiyaremye was there; and though at first he snubbed me, he became more friendly toward the end of the festivities. That was likely because the president was also there. He came up and shook my hand, laughing with delight that I was still in the country, for he had thought I had left permanently. Because I *really* like this man I was thrilled to pieces. Habiyaremye noted this real honor and seemed duly impressed, but von der Becke was furious. Too bad! I guess I still have some friends higher up.

One final bit of good cheer reached Karisoke before Christmas—a letter from Houghton Mifflin announcing the release of a trade paperback edition of *Gorillas in the Mist*. "As of December 5 we've advanced 11,760 copies—which is wonderful news to carry into the new year!"

As if to balance the good news, another bleak episode in the story of Tiger took place on December 22.

My beloved Tiger has been severely if not mortally wounded in a fight with Ziz, Group 5's young silverback, and he has lost Simba to Ziz. Apparently, from the tracks they left, the interaction took place about an hour from camp on Mt. Visoke. When the two groups almost met, Simba evidently moved to the Group 5 females, perhaps just for a visit. Tiger must have gone after her and met Ziz head-on. Albeit gorillas have extraordinary recuperative powers, Tiger now has a huge hole into his pleural cavity, not to mention other severe bite wounds. I have a very unscientific "schmaltzy" feeling about "little" Tiger, now a huge silverback, whom I saw on his first day of life in 1967. Now he is alone near camp, eating little, traveling less, and passing blood in his feces. I cannot put him out of my mind but don't know what to do for him.

The little village of green-painted cabins on the edge of Karisoke's mist-shrouded meadows was very quiet as Christmas approached. Carole Le Jeune had left camp to be with her dying mother. Mike Catsis was spending Christmas in Kigali. And, as Dian reported in a letter, "Watts, the pompous, socialist ass from Chicago, has gone to France for three weeks of holidays."

He and Dian had been at odds ever since he had taken it on himself in her absence to increase the men's salaries. Matters had come to a stormy head on December 10.

Today Basili told me Watts was going away to France, but Watts says nothing. I go to his cabin tonight to find out. Lots of yelling and screaming in front of Jan and all Africans—pretty bad scene, and Jan wanted to disappear into the woodwork.

Next day she added:

Watts up today to apologize for yelling at me, says, "I only wanted to do something good for the men because of rough economic times below."

Fortunately the two antagonists respected each other enough to come to terms. Although Dian was adamant about not raising salaries, she volunteered to give each man a special *prime*, which would have the same effect. Unredeemed capitalist that she was, she was also a reasonably soft touch.

Only Dian and Jan Rafert remained at camp to host the annual Christmas party, which for financial reasons was much scaled down.

No way I can afford to have a party for all the eighty-plus Africans and families. Only the men will be here, but ought to be content with very bulky packages of gifts for them and families from America and Europe as well as their substantial *prime*. I "did" eighteen boxes, all wrapped in red and white and also "did" a small tree with Jan. On Christmas Day I had a stocking for Jan and made Christmas dinner.

On the twenty-sixth it was the men's turn, and did we have a party! I don't think Karisoke has ever done better or had more fun. It was in my living room, with lots of food and beer, followed by lots of singing and drumming, and then such dancing that we will have to take up all the floorboards to get the beams back into place.

Then I started pulling out the Halloween nonsense I brought back from the States last trip, silly false noses, plastic glasses, and eyebrows and mustaches, and the men went bonkers over them, looking into my mirror and killing themselves laughing at the results. Little Kana, the one whose wife gave birth here last Christmas, put on black glasses and a scraggy mustache and instantly looked like Monsieur X., a horrid, mean local burgomaster who is really disliked by everyone. Just for ducks I asked him the kind of question I might ask the burgomaster, concerning his illegal acquisition of parkland. Kana picked up the game and "became" Monsieur X.—pompous, grandiose, bumptious. His manner and voice just absolutely epitomized that particular type of "official" bigwig African. "You not be asking me silly rot questions, mademoiselle!" It was a riot. None of us, including Kana, knew he was such an actor. All the others were literally crying with laughter and rolling in their chairs. Me, I was on the floor laughing as I've never done in years.

It eventually turned into a full-scale play with each man taking on a role as a typical policeman, soldier, park conservateur, storekeeper, and even playing Jan and me, the two bazungas. Went on for hours. The finale was Kana's depiction of a Kigali-type "big man" that he did half in Swahili and half in Kinyarwandan until we were just worn out. Even Jan, a serious sort of person usually, was in hysterics. Gosh, it was fun!

Dian wrote to Anita McClellan giving an account of the culinary delights she had found among her own Christmas gifts:

"I did not receive pearls, diamonds, and emeralds, but I *did* receive two boxes of Triscuits. So who needs jewels? Salivating like mad, I put half a box of Triscuits covered with phony butter and Magi sauce under the broiler and went on a Triscuit orgy. I'm not going to share them with *anyone!* Next—the smoked almonds! Oh, God, this is living! They last longer if you suck them. Then something I've never seen before—canned bacon slices. Num num! I'm dying to get into them, but if I do my stomach will think it's died and gone to haunt a supermarket. I'll save them for company, and then begrudge them every slice. Ditto with the fancy, smoked oysters . . . three sacks of Colombos, the eating of which involves careful stripping with front incisors to get the full flavor and make them last longer. And let's hear it for peanut butter/cheese crackers. Too much! Also granola bars and raisins. Even though these are good for you, I like them anyway."

This letter crossed with one from Anita that may have been the nicest present Dian received:

"A wave of nostalgia swept over me this Christmas as I thought of the time spent with you and the elusive gorillas, the ever-naughty ravens, the shy, sweet duikers, the chatty hyrax and the night-visiting bushbucks. . . . Don't forget me, the Boston branch of the International Fossil Fan Club . . . and don't forget to be 'cranky' in between patrol reports; and baked potatoes; and forest walks; and camp chores. Hey, you're family to me!"

s had so often been the case, the new year began badly for Dian. On the morning of January 5 she took advantage of some watery sunshine to seek out Tiger and take him a few handfuls of precious blackberries collected by Nemeye and Vatiri. The injured gorilla seemed sicker than ever, and the stench of the badly infected chest wound was nauseating when he came slowly to her side.

**He wouldn't take the berries and wouldn't eat them when I put them down. Just sat there, whimpering a little. Not being able to help him made me cranky. I got worse when went back to cabin and saw two strange *bazungas* at the lower cabins. Basili came up to say they were tourists from Spain *demanding* to see me. They had a letter from the ORTPN director (*no* copy to me) saying they were welcome to stay at Karisoke for several months. This letter had been written in *November!* I told Basili, "No way!" and to send them down the mountain. They went but Basili said they were screaming and yelling to their porter and were absolutely furious.**

These were no ordinary tourists. As Dian had observed from the director's letter, they were from the Barcelona zoo, whose reputation in the world of primate protection was by no means of the best.

Almost alone among European nations, Spain was not a signatory to CITES—the United Nations–sponsored Convention on International Trade in Endangered Species—whose task it was to *prevent* such trade. In consequence Spain was being used by animal dealers as a way station for transshipping endangered species to buyers in other countries. Spanish zoos were notorious for the cooperation they extended to these dealers, especially with regard to the great apes.

What Dian did *not* know was that the director of the Barcelona zoo had met Laurent Habiyaremye while that worthy was attending a conservation conference in Madrid in October 1984, and had made it known to the ORTPN director that his zoo was keenly interested in adding a mountain gorilla or two to its primate collection. Habiyaremye seems to have been most sympathetic, and it was agreed that two members of the zoo staff would visit the Parc National des Volcans to observe the habits of mountain gorillas.

Dian heard no more from the Spaniards until, as she wrote to Rosamond Carr, "the 18th, when they showed up again, this time with a letter from the director asking/telling me to collaborate. 'I inform you that I allowed Mister Serrat and Miss de Dalman to stay in National Park for doing research on gorillas. I hear that you don't agree with me, their presence there disturbs you. I want you to be collaborator one time and let them do their research.'

"This simply blew my mind. I fired back, I guess in haste."

Hasty or not, her reply was certainly not calculated to improve relations with ORTPN:

"Monsieur le Directeur, may I remind you that you apparently authorized the stay of these people from the Barcelona zoo last November, BUT you *never* sent me a copy.

"On January 5 these two strangers showed up at Karisoke *without notice* demanding a cabin and full cooperation for their so-called research. Your note has *vastly* insulted the integrity of Karisoke Research Center, which you obviously consider a hotel."

There was more in the same vein, ending: "I have given them a cabin room, which they don't like. I don't believe this is happening!"

Dian's enforced cooperation was minimal. She gave the couple space—in the leaky half of the two-room cabin normally occupied by David Watts, who was still away on holiday. It contained no furniture, no bedding, no cooking or eating equipment, and no lamps. Consequently, the unhappy Spaniards were forced to climb down to Ruhengeri in a hailstorm and spend the next several days buying what they needed, wherever they could find it, *if* they could find it. Even Dian felt a little sorry for them.

I don't like being cranky, but sometimes I can't help myself. Anyway, on the twenty-second a park guard came up with a note from ORTPN *demanding* that I show up in Kigali to see the director before noon on the twenty-third. I contacted Kigali by radio to explain that I couldn't walk down the mountain because of spider bites. I was told "it" was a matter too serious to be discussed on the radio and to "be there or else." I assume "it" had to do with the Spanish couple, but at any rate I didn't go. I await the next missile with a bit of trepidation. Thank heaven for spider bites!

Nearly three weeks ago, I had found four little bites, almost in the shape of a small dog's bite, on the upper inside of my left leg. I didn't think anything of them until they began to itch like crazy, then began to ooze pus horribly, then hundreds of small bumps appeared all over the thigh and also began to ooze. Lord, what a mess, and what a place to try to treat! I changed from jeans to skirt to be able to pour medicine on more easily. Finally the blisters began to dry up, leaving big, fungus-looking scabs, but now similar "things" are beginning on both hips. Well, believe it or not, I can't thank the spider, or whatever it was, enough, because the bites saved me a trip to Kigali.

Dian remained deeply suspicious of the Spanish invasion and apprehensive of what it might portend. In a letter to the International Primate Protection League she wrote:

"These two aren't doing what I call research. From what the trackers tell me, they are just interested in what gorillas eat and other things that would be useful for a zoo. . . . As you know, in the past, several park officials were involved in the capture of young mountain gorillas for sale in Europe. . . . I don't encounter these Spaniards at all; they keep out of my way for sure; but I still know everything they do. Meanwhile I have told Vatiri and the other men to keep a sharp watch on all gorilla groups for any sign of poacher interest."

The ominous presence of the zoo technicians did nothing to soothe Dian's growing irascibility, nor did the return of Watts and the departure of Jan Rafert. As January ended, she vented some of her peevishness in a letter to Ian Redmond:

"I hear from my Africans that Bill Weber is back from the States to work below. To my knowledge he hasn't been up here, but I now have virtually nothing to do with the lower part of this camp where the researchers live since the only nice guy, Jan Rafert, had to leave. . . . I see Watts at most five minutes every morning when the trekkers go out with him, and that's about five minutes too long. When Jan left on January 18, I asked the Africans whom he reminded them of. To a man they first named you, and then Ric Elliot and then Tim White. So, you see, it can't just be me who evaluates people the wrong/right way.

"The holiday season passed relatively smoothly, but one day my ravens prompted me to ask Mukera and Nemeye to follow their squawks, and sure enough, they found a Twa poacher just across the creek and were able to get his bow and arrows. Cheeky bloke!

"Let me give you the 1984 summary for the Digit Fund: 2,264 traps cut down . . . 18 animals (bushbuck, duiker, hyrax, porcupine) released from traps alive; 7 poachers caught and imprisoned; none of the gorillas monitored from Karisoke were harmed by poachers. But I don't like the handwriting on the wall—refer to Spain, below. . . . It is now possible to walk by Digit's grave without the same, horrid, black aching void; for he alone has made all of the above possible, but how I wish that he, Uncle Bert, Macho, and Kweli were still on this earth propagating their kind, stripping thistles, pulling gallium vines off the old hagenia trees, sunning and purring on the rare days, and even shivering and steaming on the long rainy days. They so much belong here, instead of us humans.

"I learn from Shirley McGreal that someone in camp is getting grants to supply information on the feeding and management of mountain gorillas in captivity. . . . It was also brought up at the Madrid International Union for the Conservation of Nature conference that this year mountain gorillas will definitely be exported for 'survival's sake.' From another source I learn that Spain is going to get them from Rwanda.

"I feel very paranoid, yet this same kind of preparation happened in the case of the attempted capture of Kweli. . . . I am spending an awful lot of Digit Fund money just on keeping tabs on things down below.

"Now, I know you don't like people talk, but *please* tell me if you have any idea what is going on between Watts, Barnes, Jensen, and Harcourt, etc. There is a tremendous amount of correspondence between them, but on the soul of Digit, I haven't opened a single letter. I cannot really lose my temper anymore cause it makes my heart pound too much but . . . I think it is really shitty how J.P., Harcourt, V-Ws, and now Watts are turning me into a real monster."

On January 28, Dian received a letter from an American zoologist who had just visited the park's tourist-habituated gorillas and had been disturbed by the experience. "I was surprised at how blasé they were at having us so close by—is it good for them to be that habituated, I wonder . . . do you approve of the gorilla visits from the public? Is it 'sacrificing' those groups for the publicity and revenue? Does it jeopardize their safety?"

Dian's reply provides a fair and reasoned assessment of how she viewed gorilla tourism:

"I've met quite a few tourists who were absolutely *thrilled* with their contacts with the habituated groups and were returning home with a 'glow' in their hearts for the magnificence and dignity of the gorillas.

"To answer your specific questions, I approve of gorilla visits by the public as long as they are properly controlled. You have absolutely no idea what gorilla 'visits' were like before the past two to three years . . . literally hordes of people—twenty at a time—pushing and paying their way into the park using any African available as a guide. Because of the noise and quantities of people, my own study groups were shattered and retreated into poacher-endangered areas in Zaire or on the highest slopes of Karisimbi. Food wrappings, tins, and even Tampax littered the trails, but I'll leave out the even more gruesome details of the early tourist days. It is not good to dwell on the past.

". . . The Rwandan government is absolutely thrilled over this badly needed source of revenue for their truly poor country. Gorilla tourism is growing beyond their highest dreams, BUT, no one is thinking about the goose that laid the golden egg. . . .

"By concentrating on tourism, salaries for the expatriates, cars, staff housing, etc., the Mountain Gorilla Project has almost, not quite, neglected its responsibilities toward safeguarding the remaining gorillas in the Virungas. Yet if it were not for the M.G.P., you, and several hundred others, would never have had the privilege of meeting these extraordinary animals. So it would hardly be fair of me to say that they are all wrong and I am all right.

"Nevertheless, far away from the fanlight [sic] my Digit Patrols keep on working. . . . *None* of the gorillas being monitored by the Digit Fund were harmed or injured in any way by poachers during 1984, because of constant surveillance by Karisoke patrols; but four were trapped in the area patrolled by Mountain Gorilla Project. They actually lost eight gorillas to poachers last year, but of course the public won't hear about it.

"As an example of the problems here, three nights ago poachers' dogs killed a magnificent old bushbuck who had been King of the Forest long before any of us came around. He probably sired half the few remaining bushbucks around Visoke until these dogs brought him down by his testicles. Subsequently we have been spending many patrol hours trying to find these dogs, for this is the fifth bushbuck they have killed in the last two months. This kind of thing doesn't attract tourist or grant money, but it is what my work is all about—*active* conservation."

By mid-February, when she wrote to her old friend Glenn Hausfater, now living in Minnesota, she was in a better mood:

"People continue to come and go at Karisoke, some helpful,

some not. The majority of them are able to do good footwork, which I find next to impossible now. Their reports leave a lot to be desired, but this I can remedy with the help of the Africans—I have designed a neat check-sheet and map system that the trackers follow to every group religiously every day. It makes European observers almost superfluous. It goes without saying that my main purpose in life is keeping the Digit Fund antipoacher patrols going and training park guards for the gorilla guardian program. . . .

"One last project is now well under way—one that I've wanted to do for years, unraveling the meanings of all the names of hills, streams, rivers, etc., within the Virungas. This is truly proving to be exacting work and the men relish it as much as I. I have roughly six hundred such names with great history behind them, most dating back to the early days of the Tutsi, but many still used by the Hutu, almost with reverence. It's a constructive way for the old lady to spend her spare time. Needless to say, these work goals are slipped in between beating the Africans, starving them to death, or shooting at tourists! Would you believe, these stories are still flying hot and heavy down below."

The campaign of calumny against her no longer bothered Dian excessively. In fact, now that the fund-granting organizations had cut her off and she could suffer no further financial damage, she could find a flicker of amusement in the fearsome reputation her enemies had given her.

However, when that reputation threatened her continuing residence in Rwanda, she was *not* amused. On March 5, with her current visa about to expire, she reluctantly and with considerable apprehension climbed down the mountain and headed for Kigali. Word had reached her a few days earlier from the American embassy that there was a possibility her visa would not be renewed at all. "Representations have been made that you ought to be excluded from Rwanda on the grounds that you have abused the country's laws and hospitality."

Dian went straight to the ambassador's residence, where she was warmly received. After her return to camp she wrote to Deedee Blane, the ambassador's wife, "I can't thank both of you enough for all of your kindness and generosity. The five days in your company seemed like a five-star vacation. I only wish I hadn't been so worried about the visa, as this gray cloud sure didn't make me a very responsive houseguest."

The gray cloud seems to have been dispelled largely because of lobbying by Ambassador Blane. His arguments must have been impressive, because not only did the government renew the visa, it did so for a period of six months. Dian became euphoric when she heard the news—so much so that she managed to crash a borrowed car (her own combi had long been *hors de combat* for lack of money with which to repair it) with such gusto that she broke two ribs. When she returned, more-or-less triumphantly, to camp on March 10, it was in a litter carried by ten porters. Fortunately, the ribs had broken cleanly this time. They healed fairly quickly and without the agonizing complications she had endured in 1977.

Her relief at obtaining a six-month visa was immense. As she wrote to Stacey Coil, "I don't believe I could have borne it if they had told me to leave. The longer I work here, despite the fact that I cannot go into the field as often as I used to, I realize more and more just how important it is that I am here. Stacey, this is the only place where I belong."

By late March, Mike Catsis had returned to England and had been replaced by a thirty-four-year-old American, Peter Clay. Dian's feud with Watts was still being maintained, but had settled into a ritualized conflict without much animosity on either side.

**On March 17, Watts resigned but brought a paper saying what a good fellow he is on the eighteenth. So I guess he stays.**

Dian would probably have missed him if he'd gone. Clearly she did *not* miss the Spaniards, who departed on March 27.

**SPICS GONE. Thank God.**

She did not relinquish her vigilance after their departure, being now convinced that an attempt would be made to kidnap one or more young gorillas from the Virungas.

Tiger's illness remained a major preoccupation.

**He is doing better, though I am inclined to worry about the effect on him of the rainy season, which will surely last another month. He is just behind my cabin now and I visited with him yesterday, which wasn't easy with my two broken left ribs. He seems to be moving better and is perhaps perkier, but his chest wound hasn't healed and he has a deep cough, but since I am lung-prone myself it is quite possible that I overreact to such symptoms. He continues hanging around back of camp, either because of my scintillating company or the big bamboo clump in my front yard. On the sly (because I won't let anyone cut any living growth near camp) I have been taking him fresh bamboo shoots every day. Not enough to make him dependent on it, just enough to perk his spirits up a bit. I really believe he hangs around because he is lonely and knows this is a safe place where he can see/hear people every day.**

Ziz, who was a runt and a whiner as a kid, has now turned into the King of the Mountain. He has acquired five new females, which is a record for even an experienced silverback. I believe two came from Group 6, one from a fringe group, and Simba of course from Tiger. The influx of these new females into Group 5 led to a lot of fighting between them, so Ziz finally left Group 5, taking his harem with him. This leaves old Beethoven, the only silverback left in the group, with old Effie, his six daughters, two sons, and three grandchildren. If he meets up with another, stronger silverback, it could mean the end of Group 5. Ziz is wearing out his little thing covering his five females. If there isn't a gorilla baby boom it won't be his fault. Ziz the whiz!

The other groups remain far, far away, and I just can't get to anyone except Tiger. It is ever so frustrating after so many years of going out daily no matter how far the animals were roaming. I guess I shot my wad by overworking during the first twelve years here and in Zaire.

April was crammed with incident. The final contract with Universal Studios for a movie to be based on *Gorillas in the Mist* arrived, was signed, and sent on its way.

Dian received an invitation from a New Zealand advertising company.

They want me to do a TV commercial for American Express of, you've got it, Fossey sitting with a lapful of gorillas, saying, "and don't leave home without one." I think I'll pass on this assignment.

Another invitation arrived; this one from the Morris Animal Foundation of Los Angeles, asking Dian to speak at the foundation's annual meeting at Universal City, California, in mid-June, then attend a primate medical seminar in San Diego. Since the foundation would pay all expenses, Dian decided to take advantage of the opportunity. Tongue in cheek, she wrote to her agent in New York, "What a chance! Could go to Disneyland! Visit the Universal lot!! Got to be the dream of a lifetime."

Next she heard that paperback rights to *Gorillas in the Mist* had been bought by Penguin, which intended to publish in June, and that the book had already been translated into French, Spanish, Swedish, Finnish, Japanese, and Dutch.

To top it all came the news that the Humane Society of New York was awarding her its special medal in recognition of her work with the gorillas.

April in Rwanda had produced some of the worst weather in recent years. That month it rained or hailed at Karisoke on twenty-nine out of thirty days, with a total precipitation of almost fifteen inches! When it was not raining—and often when it was—the mountains and the forests were shrouded in black fog.

On May 1 the sun came out. Next day the poachers, who had been rained out of the forests, returned to the attack.

Vatiri's patrol, consisting of himself, Munyanchosa, and Sekaryongo, found the fresh footprints of four Batwa poachers along the Suza River. It was then late in the day, but they followed the tracks across the boundary between Zaire and Rwanda until it began to get dark and they had to return to camp.

Vatiri concluded the poachers hadn't made any kills yet, so would remain on the mountain. He also thought they might be interested in gorillas, so I felt a special effort was needed. I split the available men into two patrols, Vatiri and Munyanchosa in one and Sekaryongo and Nemeye in the other, both patrols armed with pistols.

They left camp at 7:30 A.M. While circling Five Hills, they found the fresh trail of one man climbing up the Suza ravine. Vatiri, the senior tracker, sent Nemeye and Sekaryongo to follow this one while he and his partner went off to search for other tracks.

Nemeye and Sekaryongo carefully followed the lone trail above the 4th Hill and across the Rugasa River. Continuing cautiously into Zaire, they smelled smoke and guessed there was a poacher's *ikiboogi* close by. They split up and closed in on it, pistols in hand, but the poacher saw or heard them coming and, clutching his panga and his bow, fled into a creekbed covered over with vegetation. Sekaryongo opened fire but missed. They were then all madly running down the gully, and Nemeye shouted not to shoot again for fear someone would be killed.

At this point the poacher must have thought *he* would be killed, and stopped. When the trackers reached him, they were amazed to find it was Sebahutu—the most notorious poacher left

333

in the Virungas, who had never before been captured in the forests because he could run like an antelope, hide like a mole, and was as aggressive as a tiger if cornered. Sebahutu had also been reported dead a few months ago, but that had been just a ruse.

The patrol brought him back to the *ikiboogi* and tied up his hands and ankles so he couldn't run while they packed up his stuff: a salt sack filled with red potatoes, corn, and beans, which showed he expected to be in the forest several days. At this time he offered my men five thousand Rwandan francs apiece if they would let him go and as many elephant tusks as they could carry. He said it was useless to take him back to the Ruhengeri prison because of his "connections" there and in the park headquarters. According to Nemeye, he wasn't worried because he said he was in the park to do a job for some of the "big men." I doubt that "job" was getting ivory. Probably it was to set up an attempt to get a young gorilla.

The patrol brought him back to camp, and I kept him in my living room, tied up of course, for twenty-four hours. Much like a man confronting a deathbed confession, he willingly (I didn't touch him) gave us over sixty poachers' names, and locations where they enter the forest; the names of those with guns; makes of same; where they obtain them; and where they hide them. Then he gave names and locations of dealers and middlemen that make a living off selling trophies such as elephant tusks and feet, gorilla skulls, hands, and feet and infants, and antelope and buffalo meat. Then Sebahutu came up with the names and descriptions of whites and Pakistanis who deal with the middlemen exporting the above trophies out of Rwanda.

The wealth of information was mind-boggling. If the government will truly cooperate, this capture will put the biggest dent in poaching within the Virungas ever known. Already it has set the park department and its guards on their ears—raids have been started everywhere by the judiciary in previously "secret" places. Nothing like this has ever happened before.

Unlikely as it might appear to Dian's critics, Sebahutu's confession seems to have been voluntary. Dian insisted that no force was used, and this was confirmed by Sebahutu himself in the course of an interview with Mark Condiotti, the one employee of the Mountain Gorilla Project Dian trusted. She sent Sebahutu down the mountain to the custody of the military, accompanied by a note from her to Condiotti: "I sure hope they don't mistreat Sebahutu after all this information he has so decently given." Mark responded the following day, "I felt you had been gentle with Sebahutu and he told me you were nice to him. So you need have no worries about any false rumors about you coming from M.G.P. or the park conservateur." To which Dian replied, "Am glad to hear that I haven't yet been accused of beating or castrating him, etc., etc. I actually became quite fond of the little fellow—he didn't have to open his mouth, but he sure did!"

The simplest explanation for Sebahutu's loquaciousness is that he feared the Lone Woman of the Forest would otherwise kill him for his many crimes against the gorillas. Perhaps the "law" would not have harmed him; but Dian was outside the law—and incorruptible. In any case she found herself in possession of a mother lode of information, some of it dynamite.

**There are names on the list that could mean big trouble if released. If there *was* a plan to capture mountain gorilla infants for Spain, it surely won't happen now.**

The sunny weather that had welcomed May proved short-lived. Ebony clouds again obscured the volcanoes, and Dian wrote to a friend in California, "Aren't you bored with sun nearly every day? Tell me, what *is* sun? What does it *look* like? What does it *feel* like? I keep telling myself this place can't be worse than Ithaca in winter, but after nearly three months of almost daily rain and fog, I just don't know."

Peter Clay knew. He left camp for good on May 20, although not without regret. In a moving farewell letter to Dian he wrote:

"There is a very real sense here of the world being created anew each day. That creation seems a miracle, so close and so stirring in its beauty. Perhaps it is the clouds moving silently through this ancient forest, the cool mist seeming to caress us. It has felt like a return to Eden, and to a kind of innocence, to spend these few months here. Though I know my species is despoiling this fragile earth and is tragically estranged from nature, here it feels not so. The gentle duikers and bushbuck, the strange little hyrax, and most of all, the gorillas seem to have forgiven man's shortsighted abuse of the earth."

The weather was not the only depressing factor in Dian's life at this time. Her lungs were again "hurting like hell," and she was out of money. In late May she wrote to Ambassador Blane:

"I am nearly broke and would like to borrow 100,000 RWF from the American embassy or anyone else who is willing to trust me for same and would be more than happy to pay a reasonable rate of interest. I'm expected in America on June 6, at which time I can collect more funds. In the meantime I must leave money for camp expenses during my absence. I hope this request doesn't seem outlandish. I make it in desperation!"

Blane responded by lending her the required sum from his own pocket.

On May 21, Karisoke was visited by Barry Schlachter, a reporter from the Associated Press, fresh from interviewing employees of the Mountain Gorilla Project and sources in Kigali about Dian Fossey. His feature story was representative of her treatment in the press at this period in her life:

"The visitors slogged on foot for about an hour and a half through sometimes thigh-deep mud and clumps of stinging nettles to reach Fossey's settlement in the ghostly beautiful rain forest. . . . Fossey has emphysema. She chain smokes the local Impala-brand cigarettes. She takes small steps, pausing for raspy breaths of air, while leading visitors to the gorilla cemetery. . . . She teaches the apes to fear blacks, but not whites, because most of the poachers are Africans. She admits the practice could be branded as racist.

"She has been known to spray-paint a four-letter word on an errant cow that wandered into the preserve. She once was accused of kidnapping a poacher's child to swap for a captured baby gorilla. . . .

"The habituation of gorillas has led to a money-making tourist industry in Rwanda, says Laurent Habiyaremye, forty-eight, director of parks and tourism. About sixteen percent of the national revenue comes from tourism, three fourths of that directly traced to gorilla-viewing activities, he says.

"The Rwandan park director credits Dian Fossey for making that possible and has a lot of praise for her.

" 'If my office could grant her sainthood, it would,' he says.

"Despite his high regard for Fossey, Habiyaremye flatly denies an allegation in her book that a ranking park official here conspired in the killing of a gorilla named Kweli. He also attacked her policy of teaching gorillas to fear blacks, but not whites. . . . 'It is scandalous. She makes a mistake because gorillas live in a country of blacks.'

" 'I have no friends,' the tall Californian says with no hint of regret. 'The more that you learn about the dignity of the gorilla, the more you want to avoid people.' "

The dichotomy evident in Habiyaremye's comments is significant. As to the paragraph about Dian's being friendless, this particular oversimplification proved damaging. It was, and still is, widely used by her detractors as confirmation that Dian Fossey despised her own species and had little concern for human beings. As a self-confessed misanthrope, she therefore deserved little sympathy or support from her own kind.

A week after Schlachter's visit, and just four days before she was scheduled to leave for the United States, came bad news.

On the twenty-eighth my trackers Celestin and Rwelekana got a message through to me on the park radio that they had found Nunkie dead on the slopes of Karisimbi where he had been living with his group of fourteen females and young. The trackers had sent the message to me via a park guard, but my radio went out and I couldn't get details. For most of that horrid day I thought that fine old gentleman had been killed by poachers.

When the trackers finally got back to camp, they said he had died of natural causes. It was something to be grateful for, that at least he had not been murdered. I had his body brought back to camp and Dr. Bertrand climbed and we did an autopsy. Although the findings are not yet conclusive, it would seem that intestinal parasites, coupled with lung disease, were highly contributive to his death.

One of the deep-rooted causes for Dian's distaste for tourism in the park was the disturbing possibility that the gorillas might contract human diseases from the visitors. In the latter part of 1978 she had been infuriated to discover that one of the Karisoke researchers was in the habit of defecating while with gorillas and permitting the animals to smell and even eat the feces. Ian Redmond's studies had shown how prone these great apes were to parasitic infestations, and she feared that exposure to parasites contracted from Westerners, against which the animals would have evolved no defenses, might prove disastrous to them.

With this in mind she decided to take samples of the contents of Nunkie's intestines with her to the United States for expert analysis.

We buried Nunkie, that good old man, in the cemetery near my cabin, but the problems are only now beginning.

A gorilla group cannot remain an integral unit without a silverback leader. Nunkie's females and offspring spent several days bewilderingly circling around the site where his body had lain, not feeding, not knowing what to do. The death occurred seven kilometers from their normal range on Mt. Visoke. So we are now in the process of trying to "herd" them back here, where the lone silverback, Tiger, seems the perfect candidate to take over the group's leadership.

The herding process is proving far more difficult than expected as the females want to return to the death site in search of

Nunkie, seeming not to grasp the concept of Nunkie's death. So far we've been able to keep them together and move them roughly four kilometers in this direction, but each day we become more apprehensive for fear they will just disintegrate all over the Virungas.

Well, it took a week, but eventually Nunkie's ten offspring and four females reached Visoke, where they totally relaxed for the first time since his death. Tiger moved in as I had hoped and was able to get Fuddle, who willingly went with him as she was the only female in the group with regular cyclicity. The other females and young fled from Tiger's further advances and went so far that they ran into Group 5, when Ziz acquired yet another mate, a second Nunkie female, Pandora.

The remaining two adult females and kids and adolescents fled west to get away from Group 5, and ran into Peanuts's Group, consisting of all adult males, mostly survivors of Uncle Bert's Group 4. You can well imagine the ruckus among the sex-starved males who hadn't laid an eye on a female in years! I wonder when they'll be able to settle down, if ever. I tell you, Peanuts and his gang are the busiest bunch of gorillas I've ever seen, but Nunkie's widows and orphans now seem to be taken care of.

Burdened by Nunkie's death, and of two minds as to whether it would be safe to leave Karisoke in Watts's hands, Dian was increasingly distrait as the day approached for her to leave. She hid all the valuables, including the binoculars given her by Jean Gespar and her few bits of jewelry. She could not decide what to do with an orange folder that contained the "evidence" linking certain Rwandan officials with the illegal trade in ivory and gorillas. At the last minute she decided to take this with her, concealed in the bottom of one of her travel-worn suitcases.

On June 5 she arrived in Ithaca, where she spent the next ten days dealing with Digit Fund affairs and watching too much TV.

There isn't that much else to do. Most of the people I knew are gone elsewhere now. I really like Stacey's family, but I can take just so much of that "cosy comfort." It hurts to watch but not be a part of it.

She was glad to fly off to Los Angeles and Universal City. On the nineteenth she did her duty by the Morris Animal Foundation and that night appeared on the *Tonight* show with Johnny Carson.

Since I was on Eastern time, the show was about six hours

too late for me. To try to look perkier, some four hours before the show I set my hair and put some eyedrops in my eyes. The eyedrops (I didn't have my glasses on) turned out to be insect repellent that was contained in exactly the same kind of tube as normal eyedrops. The right eye swelled to enormous proportions and turned totally red, so I decided to take a nap in my hotel room, but set two alarm clocks to awaken me prior to the arrival of the stretch-limo to the studio.

It goes without saying that I heard neither alarm. I did hear the phone ring to say that the driver was waiting at the hotel door. I finished dressing in the elevator, put on glooky makeup in the limo, met a lot of people at the studio, and was shown to my "dressing room," where makeup and hairstylists descended with very negative headshakes.

I guess I was on the show, but my psyche and soma were still in Africa. Johnny was very easy to talk to. He almost, not quite, made me forget I was wearing my only pair of black heels, purchased in 1978, and which had holey soles. My one thought prior to going onstage was to keep my feet flat on the floor, but a few minutes before the curtain opened one of the buckles flew off my shoe. A security guard ran to search for a stapler and stapled the buckle on rapidly just before I emerged into the glare of the lights. With my first step into the limelight I felt the staples digging into my feet and my new hose running amok up my leg. I knew the attention of the whole world was riveted on the runner and the trickle of blood from the staple holes. But people kindly told me later that it went very well. I only wish I had been there too!

On the twenty-second she was in San Diego to take part in a seminar at the San Diego zoo on primate medical problems. While there she arranged for an examination of the specimens taken from Nunkie's corpse. The parasitologists reported that Nunkie had been very heavily infested with hookworm, *Necator americanus,* a human parasite. It was their opinion that the infestation, even if not lethal in itself, would have fatally lowered Nunkie's resistance to other diseases.

"Those gorillas that came into close contact with tourists may get the parasite by eating human feces, being touched by humans, or simply being in close contact with them."

Dian was appalled by the implications.

The horrid thing is, it might not have been just tourists. He could have been infected by one of my own students!

Dian would also have had to come to terms with the fact that she bore the ultimate responsibility for having initiated and perfected the habituation procedure.

On June 26, Dian returned to San Francisco for the longest stay with the Prices she had been able to endure in many years. It was not intended as a filial visit.

**It was my chance to do a lot of patching on this old lady. I surprised myself to find out how much of the machinery needed fixing. Guess I have to spend considerable time in the body shop.**

Among the physical problems that engaged Dr. Spiegl and various other medical people were several teeth requiring root canal therapy; chronic obstructive lung disease; hypertension; paroxysmal auricular tachycardia; and a renewed sciatic condition of the left hip. None of these could be treated effectively in the brief time before Dian returned to Africa. In addition it was discovered that she was suffering from stress fractures in both feet at least partially due to a chronic calcium deficiency that had made all her bones increasingly fragile. On July 10, Dian underwent surgery that she had deferred for almost a year to remove the growth from her left eye.

This formidable list of ailments may sound worse than it actually was. At any rate, when Dian boarded the plane on July 18 for her flight back to Kigali, she was in good spirits.

**Nice engineer from New Orleans going to Nairobi sits with me on Sabena flight. Dinner in Brussels. I ask him to visit camp. Who can tell . . . ?**

ian's buoyant mood did not long survive her return to Rwanda. While still at the Kigali airport she heard that the American ambassador and his wife, who had become good friends and loyal supporters, had been abruptly recalled to Washington. As she wrote to Deedee Blane, "Only then did I fully appreciate the expression 'my heart churned.' I grabbed a taxi to the residence, only to find that the worst had indeed happened—total emptiness."

Back at camp, she wrote to Rosamond Carr, "The reason I was delayed coming back was because I finally got my eye surgery done and it required follow-up care. Also had been diagnosed as having a stress fracture. Wow, was it ever painful, and remains so. At any rate, six porters with a litter carried me up the relatively easy parts of the trail, while I slowly walked the hard parts.

"It was necessary to return to camp at once as Carole Le Jeune, the Belgian artist, had been there three days staying in a tent, since I had all the empty-cabin keys (simply could not allow Watts to get hold of them). Also there has been a Rwandan student, Joseph Munyaneza, here for about a week, and I didn't want him to feel as though he were being neglected.

"Much to my sorrow my visa expires on August 9, which means I have to go back down to Kigali to get it renewed. . . . I am anxious to see you about something that really has me worried sick. When I returned to camp—the only place I'm really happy and functioning on all eight cylinders—I talked with each of the men separately to find out what had happened when I was away. Each told me that David Watts has been meeting with von der Becke and other members of the MGP and ORTPN to formulate a means by which they could take the camp away from me.

"They said I was to be given time to take down my personal belongings and that it would then be turned into a tourist camp to be run by my ex-students, including Amy Vedder (now back in Ruhengeri with husband Bill), Watts, the Harcourts, Roger Wilson, and others who were here in the past. They would work for Mountain Gorilla Project and occupy one cabin on alternating time periods, and the tourists the remaining cabins.

"Rosamond, there are so many of them and only one of me. It really is frightening. The men said that David told them I am *costing* the Rwandan government hundreds of dollars every day I stay here because I keep tourists away from the study groups by my presence. He told them that it wasn't right that I had the cabins, furniture, equipment, trained men, and habituated gorillas that should be used by the MGP for tourists. Three of the men (out of four currently here) said they would quit if I was expelled from camp.

"They also said the President's son came up during my absence, and Watts took him to Group 5 and told him the same story. The men really seem to think this is all going to eventuate next month—they are, or seem, very apprehensive. I just don't know what to expect but take one day at a time and will breathe easier after I get my visa. I love this place and the work that I can do here more than life."

Next day Dian wrote to Deedee Blane, with wishful overtones:

"It could be that the meetings between Watts and the MGP and ORTPN officials were only about the upcoming 60th anniversary of the founding of the park and that Watts was deliberately provoking my Africans, knowing they would tell me. Nonetheless they seem awfully worried, and I am a basket case awaiting the eviction notice at any moment. I sure wish you were both still here."

On July 28 Watts resigned, for the last time, as field director of KRC. He wrote her a rather caustic note in which he referred to the center as "YOUR" camp and said that she could now reassume "YOUR" responsibilities for it.

He departed two days later, intending, as he told some of the staff, to enjoy a leisurely holiday. He began his vacation in Ruhengeri as the houseguest of Amy Vedder and Bill Weber.

Dian was not sorry to see him go. She wrote to Anita McClellan, "David Watts has finally left. Thank God! He always was a good field worker, BUT a real snot to have around camp."

In a state of acute apprehension Dian descended the mountain on August 7 to see about getting her visa renewed. Although this was becoming a familiar ordeal, each time she had to go through it seemed worse than the time before.

**To obtain a visa I have to have the authorization of the director of ORTPN. He at first was "unavailable," but when I persisted, said he wouldn't see me. Finally I was so pushy (after the third day) he saw me in the anteroom and told me in front of half his staff that the Mountain Gorilla Project would be taking over my entire camp for the sake of tourists and it would be staffed with scientists of their choosing. He would not talk further and slammed into his office.**

**I couldn't believe what I heard but went to the American embassy, temporarily being run by two nice ladies. They called people at the Rwandan Foreign Affairs and elsewhere and said that if Habiyaremye refused me, the entire Western world would screech loudly. Something worked, and I finally did get my visa— but *only* for two months and only after a week of trying. I'm traumatized by Habiyaremye's intended action if it is truly meant.**

Any hopes Dian might have nurtured that he did not mean it were dissipated when she climbed back to camp on August 15—"with Guam pulling me most of the way—it took two and a half hours though the path was dry." Lying on her kitchen table was an official letter from Habiyaremye:

"During a meeting I held end of June the status of our research center was redefined.

"I want KRC to become an International Research Station fully integrated with ORTPN and working in close collaboration with ORTPN and international scientific organizations [read: MGP and its parents].

"I fully realize it is important to study a few gorilla groups, but it is also urgent to start other uses in the interests of the country. A committee will soon be designated to list the priorities, and I intend to ask well-known scientific organizations [see above] to send experienced scientists to KRC. . . . From now on I will decide who will work at KRC and the MGP will be in charge of administrative aspects.

"No doubt you will understand and agree to my new policy."

Dian's response was amazingly calm. If, as she suspected, Habiyaremye's letter was intended to "get me to hang myself," it failed.

Pointing out that she and KRC had already hosted researchers "from America, Australia, Belgium, England, France, Japan, Kenya, Netherlands, Rwanda, Scotland, Spain, and Zaire," she welcomed further "internationalization." She politely pointed out that KRC's activities were already closely coordinated with ORTPN. With regard to the committee to list priorities, "I would very much welcome the opportunity to be a part of this committee since I believe we all have a tremendous obligation to work for preservation of the Virungas' wildlife resources. I have spent eighteen years of my life dedicated to this goal."

Only once did she bare her teeth. "Monsieur le Directeur, does your decision to decide who will work at Karisoke mean that you, personally, are excluding me, the founder and the source of Karisoke's continuing financial, scientific, conservation, moral, and *international public support* from taking part in such decisions? I hope not.

"In closing I would like to suggest that you not be further biased by expatriates who come and go in and out of Rwanda in accordance with their short-term personal goals that will never realistically contribute to Rwanda's future."

Although she appeared confident, this was hardly a true reflection of her state of mind. In truth, she was convinced that the ultimate battle in the long struggle to drive her off the mountain was now at hand and that the odds were heavily against her. She prepared to make a final stand. In mid-August she wrote several letters to friends, all more or less in the same vein.

"What is at stake are the habituated gorilla groups, trained African staff, and seven furnished cabins. I can't keep the gorillas out of their hands for tourism, but my Africans say they will quit if I am sent away. And there is such a thing as a scorched earth policy. Currently I have several large tins of kerosene and lots of matches. My men are scared, which isn't fair since they are so good, but they say they concur if I have to burn all seven cabins and their contents. That threat may be the only way I have to save a lifetime of work."

Whether she meant it or was bluffing, Dian made sure that the plan for "Fossey's Last Stand" was noised about, especially in Kigali where it would be bound to reach the ears of officialdom. Over the years she had learned much about internal politics in Rwanda, and she hoped that higher powers would rein in the director of ORTPN rather than let him push her to a flaming wall.

September 11 was the 60th anniversary of the establishment of the original Albert National Park by the Belgians. Although the existing Parc National des Volcans represented only a fragment of the original, ORTPN was determined to celebrate in style.

**The park director did not send me an invitation; but the current park conservateur, who is a truly nice guy and with whom I**

344

work well, sent me one together with an apology for what he felt must have been an oversight on the director's part. I know better.

My Africans and I had worked all month to make a beautiful big display board illustrating Karisoke's work in the park. The conservateur was thrilled with it and hung it right next to his office so everyone inspecting the new park headquarters couldn't help noticing it, including Rwanda's president.

It was kind of a gray, dismal, sprinkly day. The fete started late with the president's late arrival, followed by dancing and singing, which I love, and then boring long speeches. There was a big printed program put out by the director, but nowhere was my name or Karisoke mentioned, though there was a great tribute to the Mt. Gorilla Project.

Then the bloody director, Habiyaremye, got up and delivered an hour-and-a-half speech in Kinyarwandan—which was about 94½ minutes too long. I thought even the president was going to go to sleep. My men told me it was mainly concerned with the great profits of gorilla tourism and how much money that had brought into the country. Toward the end the director made presentations of two cardboard plaques for the greatest contributions to the Parc des Volcans since Independence. They both went to the Belgian heads of two travel bureaus.

After all was over I got a lift on the muddy, glucky road to Ruhengeri to snatch a very late lunch at the Muhavura Hotel. While I waited for it, out of the blue comes Benda-Lema, who now manages a bank in Kigali. He came running over to my table and seemed absolutely incensed because there had been no mention of me. He said he had been sitting right behind the president and claimed the president gave the director hell for ignoring Karisoke and my work there. Benda-Lema really seem so aggravated about it that he made me cry, just because I guess I was feeling kind of sorry for myself. Also because I hadn't gotten along too well with him while he was director, yet here he was taking my side. I was just so grateful for his going out of his way to express his feelings to me.

Benda-Lema then went back to a group of swanky officials in fancy uniforms, and I started in on my cold french fries and tough pork chop, to be interrupted a few minutes later by one of the swanky ones. This one asked in English, "Dr. Fossey, what did you think of today's affair?" Well, I didn't know who he was but decided to get some things off my chest. My basic complaint was that there had been absolutely no mention of the work done by the patrols to control poachers. Then I yakked about theoretical versus active conservation. He asked me to come outside so he could take my picture! Turned out he was the head reporter for Rwanda's weekly newspaper, *Kinyamateku*. Wow! Now I either get thrown out of the country for sure, or else something good will come of it.

I went back to my now-frigid, greasy french fries—I was famished—when another "bigwig" African in military uniform came into the dining room, looked about, then came straight over and sat down at my table. He introduced himself in French as the secrétaire-général in charge of immigration in the president's office. He asked what problems I had been having in obtaining visas. I nearly passed out with surprise! But I told him in my horrid French, as best I could, about the two-month visas doled out by the ORTPN director and how hard even they were to get. He gave me his card and told me to call him when I next came in for a visa. He ended by saying about the director, "What does he think you are, a tourist?"

By then I had to cut the frites out of the grease with a knife, but they tasted like elixir. We'll see. This may have been the most useful lunch I've ever had. On the other hand, sometimes these people get carried away by the mood of a festive day but forget everything the moment they've passed their beer.

One added note. As I climbed back to camp that night, I heard the hyrax calling and the barks of the bushbuck and duiker. They are voices I hear every night, but I realized that they were still here because I was here to help protect them. Nothing in the way of awards from the ORTPN director could have meant as much to me as that knowledge.

Next day I talked to my men. All fifteen of them (nine staff and six members of the Digit patrols) had been at the fete—specially dressed in uniforms I had made for them, with K.R.C. on the jacket pockets; and when there was no mention of them or me or Karisoke or the work they had done, they were badly disappointed. Now I told them the rewards for us had to come from seeing and hearing the wealth of wildlife existing around us in the park. If it had not been for all our efforts over the past eighteen years, I don't think there would have been much left. I think it made them feel a little better.

A few days later, Dian heard a rumor that Habiyaremye was on his way out. Although she knew better than to give much credence to

Kigali gossip, the simple fact that such things were being said about him made her feel somewhat less threatened.

**I had Mukera put the kerosene cans back in storage. But I still keep my matches handy.**

August saw much coming and going at Karisoke. At the beginning of the month David Watts's replacement arrived. He was a six-foot, shambling, blond, bushy-bearded doctorate student whose first application to work at Karisoke had been rejected by Dian three years earlier. Now, with only one other researcher in camp, Joseph Munyaneza, a young Rwandan entomologist, she was glad to get him, although during his first few weeks she had her doubts.

**Wayne McGuire from Oklahoma University arrived at noon today with four park guards as porters and settled into Watts's cabin without saying a word to me. By 6:30 P.M. he hadn't yet come up to my cabin even to say hello, although I had sent an invitation to come for dinner. This is really weird, but maybe not so weird. I know he has been in correspondence with the V-W couple, von der Becke, and Watts, who saw him last winter in the States. Gwehandagoza tells me he was met at Kigali airport by Bill Weber, who drove him to Bill and Amy's house, where he stayed overnight and met Watts and the other MGP people. I don't believe I'm truly paranoid, but it sure makes you think.**

**Vatiri came by with his patrol while I waited for the new boy. They had found fresh poacher tracks (two Twa, two Hutu—Vatiri can tell so much from a track I'm surprised he didn't know their names) following one of the fringe groups. We rapped together about tomorrow's work, then went outside to find an entire herd of bushbucks behind my cabin: two yearlings, two two-year-olds, two adult females, and the magnificent old buck I call Prime II, who is so old he can just barely walk/wobble. I was deeply touched to see him again as I thought he had long since been taken by poachers. The sight of him will forever remain etched in my memory, long after the wretched memories of "me-itis" students are gone.**

There were other arrivals. On August 3 a wealthy young American couple, Evelyn Gallardos and David Root, came to Karisoke to spend two weeks photographing gorillas and other animals, not for profit or for science, but for pleasure. They were the first manifestation of a new project of Dian's—one about which she was somewhat embarrassed. In order to pay the bills to keep Karisoke running, she had reluctantly decided to accept paying guests, *well*-paying guests, from amongst the rich dilettantes in the United States who had been everywhere and done everything—except visit gorillas in Rwanda. That this would be a form of tourism, and therefore an exploitation of the gorillas, was something of which she was uncomfortably aware. She rationalized it as best she could.

**There will never be more than four people here at one time, and visiting the gorillas will be bottom priority to ongoing research studies by students. Control of everything done will be superstrict. I don't like this, but if Karisoke is going to continue to save mountain gorillas, it has to be, because I cannot continue to support it on what is left of my savings.**

The arrival of the first of the new "visitors" coincided with the final departure of Carole Le Jeune. The shy, quiet little Belgian flower painter had become Dian's closest confidante in Rwanda. Her loss was a heavy one.

In mid-August, Dian made a crucial decision concerning her own future.

She had asked an agent in the United States to arrange a lecture tour, and the agent had reported that one could be booked for November and December. The timings were such that, for the first time in decades, Dian would have been able to spend a Christmas season in Louisville. The prospect delighted her.

**It would be so great to have a few days in that good old sun, which I miss more than anything else as I get older and crankier and my bones get sorer. But it can't be. I can't leave camp with the ORTPN director and the Mountain Gorilla Gang still hanging over it like vultures. Carole is gone, and Wayne McGuire, who has turned out to be a nice enough young man, is so woolly he gets lost going to the can. I may get one or two students at the end of the year but can't count on it. Well, I'll just have to postpone the tour until spring—if they still want me then.**

Several parties of French doctors and nurses, local friends of Dian's, climbed to visit her in August, their porters laden with hampers of good food and drink. Then, on the twenty-seventh, she was visited by two representatives of the World Conservation Center in Switzerland, who brought deeply disturbing news. Charles Darwin, the silverback leader of a group that had been habituated by the

Mountain Gorilla Project for tourism, had just died—apparently of hookworm infestation.

The suspicions with which Dian had been wrestling since Nunkie's death, and had been reluctant to accept, were intensified when the WCC's veterinary specialist concluded that "with the large numbers of visitors who are now taken into close proximity with the gorilla groups, the potential for the transmission of human diseases is very great."

Despite the implications for herself and her own work, Dian was almost ready to grasp the nettle. She felt increasingly impelled to do so when, at the end of August, Beethoven—the staunch old patriarch of Group 5—disappeared. First Nunkie, then Charles Darwin, and now Beethoven . . .

**I don't know what is going on. Maybe poachers aren't the worst thing to happen to the gorillas. Perhaps WE are. . . . ORTPN and the Mountain Gorilla Gang will go out of their minds if this infection of gorillas through human contacts is true. The whole of the Virungas would have to be quarantined. Tourism would be dead and so would Karisoke . . . but someone will have to get at the truth of what is happening.**

Fully aware of the violent repercussions that would follow any action seriously threatening the gorilla tourist business, Dian agonized over what to do through long days and sleepless nights.

**Last night I went to the graves again. It was black as coal and I could only dimly see the markers. I stood beside Digit a long time still not knowing what to do, but Digit knew, and Uncle Bert and all the others.**

She had made up her mind.

In mid-September she wrote to Evelyn Gallardos:

"Phillipe Bertrand, the Ruhengeri Hospital surgeon who did the autopsy on Nunkie in June, as well as on the newest silverback victim, told me this weekend that Jean-Pierre von der Becke and Mark Condiotti, both of the Mountain Gorilla Project, asked him NOT to give me any photos or information about the autopsy on Charles Darwin. As a proper scientist Phillipe was appalled; as a personal friend he was quite angry."

Phillipe Bertrand was one of the few local people with whom Dian felt she could safely discuss her growing certainty that gorillas were dying of diseases contracted from human beings. When she found him sympathetic and indeed already half-convinced, she took

349

the plunge. She proposed they form a team to investigate the matter. Very circumspectly they recruited a second medical doctor and two veterinarians. All were either French or Belgian, and none had close links with, or any great affection for, the Mountain Gorilla Project or ORTPN.

Whether from reasons of prudence or due to subsequent loss, nothing of record can be found to reveal what this group attempted or accomplished. One thing is certain. If the nature of the inquiry reached those concerned with gorilla tourism, it would have been recognized by those who profited from it as a serious threat to that activity.

All summer long, Dian had been bothered by a general sense of unease about the gorillas. Something strange and unsettling appeared to be disturbing the lives of the lords of the volcanoes, putting them into an extraordinary state of flux. They were becoming, as she said, *hiva-hiva*—Swahili for all mixed up. Her notes and comments from August through October reveal the perplexity she felt.

August 1: **Nunkie's females are scattered everywhere in different groups—Tiger only took Fuddle; Pandora is with Group 5, and Papoose and Augustus plus seven youngsters are with Peanuts's all-male Group, but they keep shifting like a crazy game of musical chairs.**

August 18: **Just last week Peanuts's Group split in half because the two silverbacks, Peanuts and Beetsme, simply could not share Nunkie's two females—Augustus and Papoose—so now Augustus is with Peanuts and Papoose with Beetsme. The younger animals are fairly evenly distributed between the two subgroups, which are now some four kilometers apart. At the moment I hardly know what to expect next. Don't know how we are going to follow all this, since only one gorilla student is now at camp, but it is really important that we do so.**

August 30: **Since Charles Darwin's death, his group of six females and their youngsters are scattered all about Visoke's slopes. The Mt. G. P. people cannot keep up with them, so it is up to us to try. My Africans can track a rabbit's breath in a hailstorm, but I would give my soul to be ten people and twenty years younger.**

September 5: **Peanuts and Beetsme have joined forces, then split again, and now three of Nunkie's survivors that were with them are missing somewhere on the northwestern slopes of Visoke and in the distant saddle areas. My trackers are working their guts out trying to keep up with these two groups.**

September 12: **Peanuts's Group has been made into Peanut**

Butter because Beetsme took everyone away from Peanuts except for the crippled blackback Ahab, who loyally hung on with the poor, deprived silverback. I just can't keep up with all these constant changes.

September 15: This is where it hits. Beethoven, the grand old silverback leader of Group 5, has disappeared and must be presumed dead. I'm heartsick about it. We have done little but search for his body but to no avail. At least his group remains under protection of his powerful silverback son, Ziz, who is the hugest silverback I've ever seen. He is having a bit of a struggle keeping the eleven sexually mature females he's got now from tearing one another's hair out.

October 8: Still have not found Beethoven's body; but as I shall never lose the memories of the old man, I can endure the loss of his body. Group 5 recently lost Poppy during an interaction with the Suza Group, yet gained old Flossie, originally from Group 4. It makes one dizzy with never-ending changes. Peanuts and Beetsme continue swapping partners and Nunkie's offspring, on the occasions when they come together in the far western saddle area. Charles Darwin's survivors are still all over, and about half seem to have disappeared to the eastward. Tiger and Peanuts, who might have taken them over, are miles away. *All* the gorillas now seem to be in the wrong places at the wrong times.

Bewildered by all this erratic behavior, Dian was harboring uncomfortable speculations.

Something has gone really wrong. Not only are the members of the groups switching back and forth, some of them leaderless, there is no kind of pattern to their ranging. Groups are wandering where they never went before, and bad interactions are more and more frequent. This just stirs up the pot and leads to more interactions as groups flee all over the mountains bumping into each other. I can't think what is the matter, unless it is the result of too many human contacts combined with too many poachers.

Poachers were certainly a major factor that autumn. Although they generally steered clear of the Karisoke study area, they were numerous and aggressive everywhere else in the park. Digit Fund patrols fought back vigorously.

On September 15 my people caught another poacher setting traps in the park—number three for this year. They took him down for the usual interview with the park authorities before he was supposed to have been taken to Ruhengeri prison. However, instead of prison, the park authorities, under orders from the director of ORTPN, fined him two hundred dollars and released him. Just like old times. There is not much doubt who gets the money.

On October 12 a Digit Fund—sponsored patrol captured three more poachers, their dog, and twenty-six traps. They took the poachers to park headquarters on the thirteenth, but I fear that they too will simply be allowed to pay a fine to ORTPN and then be released. I pray for the day ORTPN comprehends that pocketing profits will not stop poaching or gorilla killing.

Some such comprehension should have dawned on ORTPN's director at the end of October when a bloody little battle erupted between the poachers, who now felt they were operating under "pay-as-you-play permits," and a detachment of police outside the control of the park authorities.

The first I heard about it was October 30 when MGP radioed to ask if I was missing any gorillas from the study groups. When I said no, I was reluctantly told they had a two-year-old male infant that had just died from a "blood clot in the heart." They said it probably came from Uganda.

I immediately sent the only two trackers then at camp to check on the fringe groups northwest of Visoke outside our area. But they ran into five armed poachers and had to flee for their lives and hide out in the forest for hours, not getting back to camp until 10:00 P.M. Wow, was I frightened for them!

My men only got the true story of the capture for me later. A gang of six poachers, all Rwandans, attacked a gorilla group between Mt. Sabyinyo and Mt. Muhabura, in part of the park supposedly patrolled by park guards under Mt. Gorilla Project. At least three, and perhaps more, adult gorillas were apparently shot to get the baby. The poachers then got out of the park safely, but ran into a *sécurité* force who challenged them. There was a gunfight. One poacher was killed, one badly wounded, and the others captured. The baby was apparently injured. It was taken to park headquarters where it just died. I do so wish captured infants would be brought straightaway up here for the sake of altitude, food, around-the-clock care, and *quietness*.

Although all four men who were put into prison were *known* poachers, they were allowed freedom after only two weeks, *because they were caught outside the park*, it was said. Nothing said about how much they paid for their release. Isn't that sickening?

On October 7, Dian again visited Kigali to renew her visa. With some hesitancy, for she did not know if he would even remember meeting her on the day of the fete, she telephoned the *secrétaire-général* of Immigration.

**Well, par for the course. Much to my sorrow, Mr. Nduwayezu, the secretary-general, was out of town. So also was Mr. Habiyaremye, or at least that is what his office told me. It took three days before Mr. Etienne Nyangezi, the second-in-command for ORTPN, overcame what I reckon was fear to write out my authorization for another *two* months only to stay in this country.**

Returning to camp, she was delighted and somewhat awed to receive a letter from one of the grand old men of the science of ethology, Dr. Niko Tinbergen, professor emeritus at Oxford University. He had read her book and been so impressed that he sent her a four-page, handwritten letter of congratulations together with some cogent ruminations on behavioral studies.

"Tremendously honored and impressed," Dian responded in an even lengthier reply, in which she talked of times long past—a subject she normally shunned.

"I learned to avert my face and abase myself to the gorillas from working with autistic children and adults, whom I found I could best reach by hiding my face, assuming an obsequious posture, and feigning interest in stuffed toys or live pets. Such 'neglect' never failed to elicit responses from patients suffering from severe withdrawal, but all wanting inside themselves to make contact without knowing how. It meant, I think, that I posed no sort of threat and therefore was safe to approach.

"You don't have to read on, but this is now so vivid in my mind. John, twenty-six years old, was a brilliant student in his final months of veterinary training when he was bitten by a diseased dog. The disease turned John into a limping, drooling, howling, peeing vegetable. After he had been stricken for months, his parents asked me to visit him at their home. I made the mistake of the usual face-to-face, yak-yak approach, which only made him howl louder and urinate more frequently. I then tried just going to his room, ignoring him, and sitting in a corner playing with a kitten. Within two days he was nudging me for attention, but I wouldn't give him any until he used the urinal. This he did on the third day and thereafter whenever I was with him and even when alone. I made the kitten the common point of contact between us, directing my attention to him through it, and he did the same. After two months he no longer howled. After three months he began to speak to me, simply, and one day even opened the door for me and got my coat from the cupboard. This was his first 'shared' action in over a year. I wish I could end the story on a happy note, but John's father had a heart attack and the family had to put John into a home too distant for me to visit, where he quickly reverted and died of a seizure several weeks later. I cannot forget him.

"I don't quite know why I've told you this story, except that the incident has recently come strongly back to memory, and also because I am of the conviction that one can't work well with disturbed children or even adults without having worked with animals and, perhaps, vice versa.

"Thank you for asking about my current work. It continues with the blessings of the highest powers in this land (president and staff), but I have problems with the bureaucrats of the tourist and park department who eye my camp and the gorilla study groups as justifiably theirs. They are backed by a small group of whites salaried by the Mountain Gorilla Project all wanting my camp. Well, they'll have it over my dead body, if then."

Dian was still having trouble coming to terms with Wayne McGuire, the only white person now sharing Karisoke with her. Her feelings about him were ambivalent.

To Anita McClellan she wrote, "Wayne is really nice, but he can get lost between my cabin and his. He gets lost in the forest nearly once a week. He doesn't know how to turn on his pressure lamp, make a fire, sort out his clean from his dirty clothing, boil potatoes. Like I say, he is basically very very nice and polite, which is a relief, but no way I'm going to be his big mama. Hopefully, eventually, he'll understand that my diaper-changing days are over. . . . My Africans do not like him because they have had to search for him three nights, overnight, in the rain!"

And to Stacey Coil: "I just don't know if the McGuire boy is going to be able to stick it. Like I say, he truly is a nice, good person but so disorganized it is frightening. You can't walk into his cabin because of the clutter. . . . I'm really worried about him. Otherwise we get along fine."

October's visitors included some surprises—reporters and photographers from all three of Rwanda's newspapers. This was the first time any of the local press had visited Karisoke or shown an interest in Dian's work. For whatever reason, this long neglect was now made good. To her somewhat smug delight, Dian and Karisoke now became positive news in Rwanda.

All three papers have run big spreads about camp, our work, and the men and myself. It is all in Kinyarwandan of course, but my men have translated everything and they are FANTASTIC articles. We've been nominated, so it says, for special awards, like medals, from the president. The biggest article, two full pages in a twelve-page newspaper, makes me sound like the second coming and did everything but tell the director of ORTPN to resign. Maybe I am bragging, but I am so happy for my men, who are just floating and expecting the president to drop in by helicopter any day. Everywhere they go in Ruhengeri they wear their uniforms and are treated like heroes. Isn't that great?

In a letter to one of the reporters, she wrote, "How in the world can I ever thank you for your kindness, your heart, and your sense of integrity, of *umurava?* I have boxes and boxes of press clippings from all over the world, BUT never, never, has one meant as much to me as yours. Well, I got all teary with joy and gratitude and the men all laughed at me. We did an impromptu dance and have been going around with big smiles plastered on our faces ever since. . . .You have made us all so happy. It is the kind of happiness that lasts forever, for your words seemed to come from your heart and have therefore settled in our hearts."

In mid-October, only a few days after Dian assembled her group of doctors and veterinarians for the first time to begin inquiring into the recent silverback deaths, something very disturbing happened. Her two gray parrots abruptly sickened without evidencing the symptoms of any disease recognizable to her veterinarian friends. When one of them ventured the opinion that the birds might have been poisoned, Dian vehemently rejected the possibility. But next day she threw out the supply of food she had been giving them. And after feeding for a few days on a new stock brought up from Ruhengeri, both birds made a seemingly miraculous recovery.

Dian did not record her reaction to this incident except in a single, tight-lipped comment.

**It was extremely frightening.**

What followed on the night of October 27 was infinitely more so. Dian wrote her journal entry for this date while in a state of extreme agitation. The words sprawl all over the page.

As was so often the case, she had been unable to get to sleep and so, just before midnight, decided to step outside and enjoy the rare delight of moonlight gleaming on the peaks of Karisimbi and Mikeno. She was thunderstruck to find the wooden image of a puff adder on her doorstep.

This thing carved by someone TODAY. First indication of SUMU was parrots nearly dead, flipped on cage floor. . . . I have hidden it and will say nothing about it.

She was as good as her word. There is not the slightest mention of this fearsome discovery in any of her correspondence or other writings, and she evidently said nothing to Wayne, to her men, or to anyone else, not even Rosamond Carr.

During her years in Africa she had informed herself as to the nature and usages of native sorcery and magic. She understood full well what she had found—and what its message was.

Someone had laid the curse of death upon her.

lthough Dian did not record her feelings about the sinister discovery on her doorstep, assuredly she did not take it lightly. On the other hand, she knew that native sorcery had power only against those who believed in it and that the Rwandans considered whites immune to *sumu*. Working things out in the reassuring light of day, she would have reasoned that a Rwandan intent upon her death would, in all likelihood, resort to the use of poison, this being the preferred method of committing murder in Rwanda.

It may also have occurred to her that the death adder and the apparent poisoning of her parrots, were ploys designed to increase the pressure on her to abandon her mountain home. Unless—unless someone was laying the groundwork for eventual violence that could be blamed upon unlettered Africans such as the Batwa poachers. Perhaps it was with this dark thought in mind that she so rigorously suppressed any mention of what had taken place.

Whatever her conclusions may have been, the days following the discovery of the snake brought distractions that must have been very welcome. On October 30 a charming French journalist with the melodic name of Anne Marie Voisin-Romagnani arrived to research an article about Dian and Karisoke. She was closely followed by a French cinematographer whom Dian found less attractive.

**Yann is so pretty, suave, and delighted with himself. Some thirty years ago I would have fallen madly in love with this beautiful man (Clark Gable with blue eyes and long, sandy hair), but he was too arrogant for words. Thus we simply tolerated each other,**

and guess who had to do all the cooking? How do French women stand the brutes?

Of much greater import was the arrival of a young Dutchman Dian had met during her brief visit to Holland in 1984. Sjaak Van de Nieuwendijik had been given leave from his job as keeper of gorillas at a zoological park to learn the ways of the animals in the wild. Dian was delighted with him. **This "little" boy is about seven feet tall, blond hair, and just as nice as they come. I don't know when I've ever enjoyed such a refreshing, enthusiastic, intelligent, vital young person in camp. He is already speaking Swahili and never complains about anything, though the weather is HORRID. He just gallops through the forests every day and all day to be with the gorillas. I am hoping and praying he will stay until the New Year and beyond. I would have no hesitation leaving camp in his care when I go on my lecture tour to the States in March or April, but his boss may want him back too soon.**

Dian's journal notes for November 10 consist of a single brief entry:

**I get very, very, very sick & heart is bad. Why?**

There is no elaboration, but the question may relate to suspicions of what had happened to her parrots. It is certain that *sumu* was still much on her mind. Two days later Vatiri and his men caught another poacher, and a description of the event begins with the bald statement:

**Black magic is quite prevalent in these parts.**

**My patrols have captured four poachers in four weeks, all actively poaching in the park. This one turned out to be *really* nasty. They caught him skinning a lovely bushbuck taken from his trapline right next to a gorilla group. His name is Yavani Hategeka, and the strange thing is I captured him once before in 1974. It bothers me that he doesn't look any older than he did then, but I look a millennium older, which isn't fair. He wasn't the least bit cooperative with me. Although we grilled him all night, he wouldn't answer questions. As a result, I took away his black magic charms that had been sewn into his stinky, frayed jacket (I know where to look for such things now). They consisted of two little pouches containing dried vegetation and an inch-square piece of some kind of animal fur. It was like taking a nipple away from a baby—maybe not a nice thing to do, but I did it since he wouldn't give me any information about other poachers. I watched him shrivel up defensively upon losing his charms, but he had had over two hours to tell us things prior to his "rape."**

Now, according to my men, he will never poach again, once he gets out of prison, because I have his "sumu." Along with the "sumu" pouches we also found a letter in his pocket from a dealer in Zaire who is in the smuggling business with the poacher. Some kind of rare metal, probably gold, was involved.

Dian took no chances with Hategeka. Instead of sending him down to park headquarters in the manner prescribed by ORTPN, she sent him directly to the judiciary in Ruhengeri. There he was tried, convicted, and given a three-year sentence. Two weeks later his brother appeared at the prison offering to pay fifty thousand Rwandan francs for Hategeka's freedom, but to Dian's delight—and surprise—he was refused. Shortly thereafter she heard that the incorrigible Sebahutu had been the loser in a prison fight and was in the hospital suffering from mortal injuries.

At the end of November Dian wrote a long letter to a friend in the United States in the relaxed, story-telling vein that had once characterized her correspondence but which she now seldom seemed to have the energy or the inclination to indulge:

"I'm really sorry I didn't get the chance to go to America this fall, but Wayne, the new 'student' who came in August, just could not have held camp together by himself. He's a nice boy but with hardly the smarts to come in out of the rain. That is really hard on him because today was the FIRST day of sun in a good two months of daily rain. I sneaked off into a little meadow not far from my cabin, actually the same one where I wrote the very first pages of my book, and spent two lovely hours basking like a happy hound dog. Then the whistles sounded, meaning 'come home wherever you are,' and I had to go back to deal with one of my antipoaching patrols who had brought in a badly hurt duiker caught in a trap for me to fix.

"Your letter speaking of Christmas reminds me of one that happened about ten years ago. My mother had this wonderful, wonderful, and wealthy friend who was one of the most generous people I've ever known, but a little scatterbrained, which endeared her all the more to me. I had a Trappist friend in a monastery, Father Raymond by name, in Hardstown, Kentucky. This nice lady was a devout Catholic, so I introduced her to him via mail. He happened to mention in a letter how cold their cells were in winter, so she immediately sent him a huge, magnificent electric blanket! I don't think he's stopped laughing yet, though his abbot didn't seem to see the joke.

"Well, one November when I was home in California briefly from camp, she planned a Christmas shopping day for me that involved a lovely lunch and was to be followed by a spree in a big shopping center full of lovely stores. At lunch she tried to get me to open up as to what I *really* wanted for Christmas. There was only one thing I *really* needed and that was a meat grinder for camp.

"The minute I spoke my wish her face just fell, 'Well, ah, well, that wasn't exactly what I had in mind,' she stammered. Never mind. Off we went, she dressed up fit to kill, to find a grungy hardware store where a good hour was spent buying the most elaborate meat grinder they had. I still have it and it still works. You know, I don't think she had ever been in a mere hardware store before.

"On a separate piece of paper you have the list of things I *really* need *this* year, as you asked. Notice it begins with Triscuits—I dream of them, literally dream of them. I crave salted food like that, and nuts and pretzels, etc. Every time I go to America I plan at least one full day of supermarket shopping beginning, as always, on the right side of the store (I can't shop from left to right) with the biggest cart they have. I drift up and down the aisles in absolute heaven, neither seeing nor hearing anyone around me.

"Things for the men. Well, they just appreciate anything, which is part of the goodness of them. They go through socks like Kleenex. I buy these when in the States at army-surplus stores. They are hardly Saks Fifth Avenue items. Inexpensive watches are also badly needed. I hate asking you, but my not getting to the States this fall has put a dent into the men's (and their families') Christmas presents this year. There is so little one can buy in Rwanda—so much in America. I mention warm jogging pants and hooded tops not because my men go jogging for their health (they can hardly walk when they get home from a day in the forest), but because when I give them something nicer they won't wear it on the mountain. They save it for the big city of Ruhengeri—all four blocks of dusty *dukas* (little stores). We will keep the jogging suits up here for them to change into following a cold, rainy day's outing in the forest.

"I started this letter yesterday, then at 3:40 P.M. someone banged at my front door. I opened it to find a thin, bearded fellow whose greenish face matched his drenched rain gear. He was burdened with a heavy rifle and a panga. Because of the rifle I realized he must be a new man, a Belgian, working for the Mt. Gorilla Project, who occasionally do patrols with the park guards. All the Mt. Gorilla Project people are ordered to carry these big rifles when they go into the park, though I don't know why.

"At any rate, he squished into my cabin, collapsed before the fireplace, and told a harrowing tale. The park guard with him had turned on him several hours previously, attacked him with a panga, shattered his eyeglasses, and walloped him on the forehead with the flat of the panga before collapsing in some kind of seizure. Not knowing what else to do, the Belgian had dragged himself to my camp.

"I sent him back into the pouring rain and fog, with all of my men carrying a litter to find this man. They didn't get back here until 8:30 P.M. to report that the guard had disappeared. The Belgian was then in a horrible state, cold, wet, tired, shaking for good reason, and the lump on his head getting bigger and bigger. I fed him a stiff drink, and sent him down the mountain with one of my men. I *didn't* tell him I thought the guard might have rabies, which is quite common here. Even without that, it was a day I'm sure he'll remember.

"The gorillas are doing well, except they are cold and perpetually wet during this prolonged rainy season. The new fellow, Wayne, the one who kept getting lost, went to Ruhengeri to cash a traveler's check two weeks ago and hasn't been heard from since. I do hope you have a joyful turkey day. Eat lots of stuffing and exhale on your next letter. What better odor is there in the world?"

To which was appended "Fossey's Christmas List":

1 box of plain nummie TRISCUITS
Some Rice-A-Roni mixes
Some Lipton noodle mixes
Liquid hickory smoke!!!!
Potato chips
Salted walnuts or pecans or just any nuts at all
Pretzels
Vitamin supplement for parrots
A little tinned ham
A second box of nummie TRISCUITS
Sesame seeds and/or sunflower seeds (for parrots)
A hot-water bottle
A carton of Merit Longs cigarettes (shame, shame!)
Jell-O—any flavor
Unpopped popcorn
A package of freeze-dried mushrooms

A few days later an apologetic Wayne McGuire finally slogged back to camp to explain that he had contracted an ear infection while in Ruhengeri. Dian welcomed him home, although not without a note of some asperity.

The American boy is back, though I don't know for how long. If I could afford a nurse for him, I would.

With the beginning of December the weather broke. The seemingly eternal rains and mists no longer saturated the mountain slopes, turning them into a dim subaqueous world. The brilliant skies and piercing sunshine of high altitudes returned, and everywhere life quickened. The saturated lichen beards hanging from the ancient hagenia trees grew dry and fluffy and were filled with flamboyant little sunbirds. The camp hyraxes emerged to sit sleepy-eyed in the sun by day and to engage in their ultramundane songs by night. Although unable to visit them because of her breathing difficulties, Dian knew that the gorillas were lolling in sunlit glades, and she was happy for them in this time of warmth and relaxation after the months of somber fog and rain.

There was little relaxation for her. The dread day was fast approaching when she would again have to renew her visa. On December 3 she hid her pistols, her money, and the few pieces of jewelry she possessed (including the ruby ring given to her by Louis Leakey) behind the bottom drawer of her dresser and resolutely descended the mountain bound for Kigali.

She was accompanied by young Sjaak, and although she was heartened by the moral support his presence gave her, she was also saddened for he was leaving the Virungas to return to Holland. "Sjaak," she had written to his employer, "is not only an extremely gifted observer and field worker, he is probably one of the finest who has ever worked at Karisoke. I so wish there were more like him and that he could have remained at Karisoke into the new year."

It was with a brave front but inner trepidation that Dian presented herself at ORTPN's headquarters. The officials there proved even stickier than she had anticipated. Habiyaremye would not see her; and although some of his subordinates evidenced sympathy for Dian's plight, they could do nothing to help her obtain the all-important permit without which her visa could not be extended.

In mounting desperation Dian went to the American embassy, but the current incumbents, while polite, offered no assistance.

She then retreated to the Mille des Collines hotel for a badly needed drink, and there encountered the editor of one of the local papers who had recently written glowingly about Dian and her work. When she confided her difficulties to him, he smiled broadly and patted her hand. "Mademoiselle Fossey, I think you do not understand. In Kigali you have many friends. But not at ORTPN. And not, perhaps, among your fellow Americans and some other foreigners. Why do you not ask your *friends* for help?"

362

Dian needed no further prompting. She hastened to the presidential secretariat and asked to see Augustin Nduwayezu, secretary-general in charge of Immigration, whom she had met while trying to eat her cold and greasy *frites* in Ruhengeri on the occasion of the f ete some three months earlier. Nduwayezu was in his office and invited her to join him.

**When he asked what he could do for me, I'm afraid I really gave him an earful. I more or less told him the whole story about ORTPN and the Mt. Gorilla Project problems. He very kindly listened to all and even wanted to hear more. When I was just talked out, he merely said, "Why didn't you come and tell me all this before?" Then he said, "You are one of our cherished guests and can stay in Rwanda as long as you wish."**

**He called a secretary, who took my passport. Ten minutes later the man came back with it stamped with a special visa *authorizing me to stay in Rwanda for two whole years*. The Big Man handed it to me with a laugh and said the next one would be good for ten years if I wanted. Wow, if he had handed me a ticket to Cloud Nine I couldn't have been happier!**

Dian was ecstatic as she raced around Kigali, vigorously doing errands for the camp and telling everyone she knew of her good fortune. As one friend remembered it, "She was as exuberant as a dog let off her leash. Coughing and puffing at her Impala cigarettes, she was the perfect whirlwind—just as she had been in the early days. We were all so happy for her I felt like crying."

If her friends were delighted with the news, her antagonists must have been hugely dismayed. Nduwayezu, who stood close to the center of Rwandan power, had in effect confirmed Dian's suzerainty over Karisoke, not just for two years, but presumably for as long as she desired to remain. So the Lone Woman of the Forest would continue to occupy her domain and defend its animal inhabitants from human comers as far into the future as one could foresee. There were those who must have found this an intolerable prospect.

Dian returned to camp on December 7, still in a state of exhilaration. However, her body was unable to keep pace, and it took her three and a half hours to make the climb. At the long and frequent halts to rest, she coughed so much and so hard that blood trickled from the corners of her mouth.

**I couldn't have made it without Guam's help. He was so good to me. Tonight there was so much pain that I got X. First time in a long, long time.**

Through the succeeding days Karisoke was alive with people and vibrant with activity. While a jolly young Rwandan technician, Frederick Byandagara, constructed a weather-recording station, cheerful little groups of French and Belgian medical men and women climbed to camp to volunteer a hand with this project, which had long been dear to Dian's heart, and to revel with her in the burst of magnificent weather.

Whether because of the return of the sun or the assurance that mademoiselle would be remaining at the helm of Karisoke, the camp staff and the Digit Fund rangers were in high good humor as December slipped by. Even the news that the apparently indestructible Sebahutu had recovered sufficiently from his "mortal" wounds to escape from hospital, only to be recaptured by the police after an all-night pursuit, was greeted with hilarity by the Africans. Dian was moved to note, "The old scoundrel almost got away. . . . I almost wish he had." She made this comment in a letter written in Swahili to her longtime houseman, Kanyaragana, who was in Ruhengeri Hospital convalescing from surgery. She enclosed a bundle of Rwandan francs. "For your wife and children from all of us at camp." The letter was signed "Love to you, Nyiramachabelli."

As Christmas neared, she made this entry in her journal:
**Today, December 22, from Rosamond, a nice tray/picture from Nyundo, two bottles of face lotion—much needed—and a neat bamboo picture frame.**

In response to these presents from her closest friend in Rwanda, Dian began a letter on her old Smith-Corona portable:

"Your great gifts just arrived with Guam and I opened them right away. I know I shouldn't but I hate waiting for things. I didn't like it when I was a kid and now I don't have to wait, which helps make it worthwhile being grown-up.

"The frame is just right for my big color print of Digit. It is a welcome Christmas present for him too. The lotion will make me so beautiful even Habiyaremye will become my slave. Since I don't have tea and crumpets served too often here, I intend to hang the tray/picture in my bedroom where I can enjoy it all to myself.

"Rosamond, I do so wish you could have been here this Christmas. I can't manage a party for my men but will try and fix dinner for my wonderful Rwandan student, Joseph Munyaneza, who is leaving on December 26, and for Wayne McGuire, if he can find his way here from his cabin.

"A nice Swiss zoologist about my age is coming on the twenty-eighth to be the new research director of Karisoke, then there will be lots of American visitors. Camp will be bulging by the time I leave for America in March, but right now it is awfully quiet. . . ."

This letter, the last Dian Fossey ever wrote, remained unfinished.

Nor are there any further entries in her journal except for this, carefully printed in block letters on the final page:

WHEN YOU REALIZE THE VALUE OF ALL LIFE, YOU DWELL LESS ON WHAT IS PAST AND CONCENTRATE MORE ON THE PRESERVATION OF THE FUTURE.

The rest is silence.

As the sky began to lighten on the morning of December 27, Kanyaragana donned his shabby old suit coat and made his way across the chill and misted meadow toward Dian's cabin to light her stove and make her morning cup of coffee.

He moved silently through the wet grass, startling a duiker doe. She leaped high, ran a few paces, and then recognizing him, lowered her head and resumed browsing. As he continued on his way, a pair of ravens plunged from an overhanging hagenia tree to circle his head, raucously demanding a handout. He tossed them some scraps, then glanced toward the distant crest of Mt. Karisimbi. To his delight he saw that the roseate clouds of dawn were shredding away from the truncated cone. It would be a fine morning in the Virungas.

Adorned for Christmas with a red felt Santa Claus bearing the legend "Howdy," the front door of Dian's cabin stood partly ajar. Concluding that his mistress had wakened early and must be impatiently awaiting her coffee, Kanyaragana swung the door wide and hurried into the living room.

At ten minutes past six that morning, Wayne McGuire's disheveled bedroom was invaded by a mob consisting of the entire Karisoke staff, together with several park guards who had spend the night at camp. Waking in confusion, McGuire, whose knowledge of Swahili was rudimentary, could only distinguish one horrifying phrase in the babble of the men's voices:

*"Dian kufa! Dian kufa!"* Dian is dead!

Dressing so hurriedly that he thrust one foot into a brown boot and the other into a black one, McGuire found himself being half shoved, half led toward the building Dian's detractors called the Manor, but which she herself mockingly referred to as the Mausoleum. The duiker vanished into the nearby forest and the ravens retreated high into a pallid sky as the men surged to the door of Dian's house.

Peering myopically through his spectacles, McGuire stepped into the living room. It was in frightening disarray. Lamp chimneys had been smashed and the floor was gritty with shards of glass. Some of the furniture had been upset, but the Christmas tree stood unscathed by the front door, brooding over a mound of presents awaiting distribution to the staff.

Propelled by the press of men behind him, McGuire stumbled through the door of Dian's spacious bedroom. It too had been roughly treated. Drawers and cupboard doors stood open, and books and clothing littered the mat-covered floor. A table in the middle of the room had been overturned. The mattress of the double bed had slipped off its frame.

There was silence, except for the sibilance of mass breathing, as McGuire took a few slow steps forward. On the floor by the bedside, partially concealed from view by a small sofa, Dian Fossey lay sprawled upon her back, an automatic pistol and a clip of ammunition by her side.

Her skull had been split diagonally from her forehead across her nose and down one cheek to the corner of her mouth. Catching a glimpse of this ghastly wound, a sixteen-year-old apprentice tracker screamed wordlessly and plunged toward the door.

Awkwardly Wayne McGuire knelt down to check her pulse for a sign of life. But there was none.

"Oh, Dian," he whispered. "Oh, Dian."


On the gray and gloomy afternoon of the last day of 1985, Dian Fossey's body, encased in an unpainted plywood coffin, lay beside an open grave sunk into the saturated soil of Karisoke. While a missionary from Gisenyi, the Reverend Mr. Elton Wallace, delivered his simple eulogy, thirty Africans and nine whites clustered in a semicircle to one side of the grave.

"Last week the world did honor to a long-ago event that changed its history—the coming of the Lord to earth. We see at our feet here a parable of that magnificent condescension—Dian Fossey, born to a home of comfort and privilege that she left by her own choice to live among a race faced with extinction. . . . She will lie now among those with whom she lived, and among whom she died. And if you think that the distance Christ had to come to take the likeness of Man is not so great as that from man to gorilla, then you don't know men. Or gorillas. Or God."

Just beyond the grave, and facing the cluster of human beings, stood a small thicket of rough wooden posts bearing the names of some of those amongst whom Dian had come to the Virungas to live, and to die—Digit . . . Macho . . . Uncle Bert . . . Kweli . . . Nunkie—more than a dozen of them.

Rosamond Carr, tiny beside some of Dian's robust trackers, white-haired and looking very frail after the long climb up the mountain, raised her gaze from the coffin and looked across it to the gorilla cemetery.

"Some people wanted to send her poor body back to the States. What a terrible thing that would have been.

"But Dian wouldn't have it—her *spirit* wouldn't have it. They hadn't been able to force her out of the Virungas while she was alive. They couldn't do it now that she was dead."

# EPILOGUE

The circumstances surrounding the murder of Dian Fossey are obscure. The assassin may have gained entry to her cabin (which was always securely locked at night) by tearing away a section of the metal sheathing from the southeast corner of her bedroom. Significantly, the hole was made at the only point where entry through it would not have been blocked by the bed or by any of the numerous pieces of built-in furniture, which argues that it was cut by someone who knew the layout of Dian's bedroom.

On the other hand, it is equally likely that the killer was someone known to Dian whom she had admitted to the cabin. The piece of sheathing could as easily have been removed after her death to make it appear that the murder had been the work of an outsider, perhaps one intent on theft. But there was no theft. Although the interior of the house gave the impression of having been ransacked, nothing was missing. Dian's money and traveler's checks to the amount of more than three thousand dollars, plus her jewelry and thousands of dollars' worth of cameras and optical and other valuable equipment remained untouched.

Dian's good friend, Dr. Bertrand, who examined the cabin the day after the murder, believes the disruption could have resulted from Dian's frantic attempts to escape her murderer while trying to find a gun with which to defend herself. She often hid her guns, and not infrequently forgot where. In the event, she did lay hands upon a pistol and a clip of ammunition—but the bullets were of the wrong caliber and did not fit the weapon.

The panga used to kill her (and with which she had been struck several additional blows to the top and back of her head) was her own. She had confiscated it from a poacher years earlier, and it normally hung as a decoration on her living room wall. Any fingerprints that may have been on it were destroyed when it was handled by a number of people after the killing. Because the murder weapon was a panga, some of Dian's peers are convinced she was killed by a poacher seeking vengeance.

"It was a shock, of course," said one of them, "but we weren't particularly surprised. She really had it coming to her for the way she treated them."

The judgment that Dian Fossey got what she deserved has some supporters.

Bill Weber: "No one wanted to fight her. No one wanted to take over the place. She invented so many plots and enemies. She kept talking about how nobody could take it up there, how they all got 'bushy,' but in the end she was the only one who went bonkers. She didn't get killed because she was saving gorillas. She got killed because she was behaving like Dian Fossey. . . . She mistreated everyone around her and finally was done in."

Kelly Stewart: "Dian was no good as a scientific worker, but still she couldn't hand over control. She couldn't take the backseat. . . . She viewed herself as this warrior fighting an enemy who was out to get her. It was a perfect ending. She got what she wanted. . . . It must have been painful but it didn't last long. The first whack killed her. It was such a clean whack I understand there was hardly any blood."

Rwandan authorities gave little credence to the revenge theory. Knowing their own people, they were fully aware that the violent murder of a white by a Rwandan was extremely unlikely. There had only been one such incident during the previous thirty years. Nor were the Rwandan police blundering incompetents, as they have since been portrayed by various white expatriates and by some of the American media. The investigators concluded that the murder was an inside job or, at least, had been committed by someone fully cognizant of how Karisoke operated. Soon after the investigations began, most of the current Karisoke staff was arrested. So, also, was the tracker, Emmanuel Rwelekana, who had not worked at Karisoke since being fired by Dian several months earlier, but who had been employed during the interim by the Mountain Gorilla Project.

One by one, as their innocence was established, the Karisoke staffers were released. Rwelekana alone remained in prison—in solitary confinement. On August 21, 1986, nine months after Dian's death, he and Wayne McGuire were jointly charged with the murder of Dian Fossey. A few weeks later Emmanuel Rwelekana was dead, having reputedly hanged himself.

Wayne McGuire was never arrested. At the urging of American embassy officials in Kigali, he fled to the United States just two weeks before the charges against him and Rwelekana were made public. No extradition treaty exists between Rwanda and the United States. There is no doubt that McGuire was "permitted to escape" by arrangement between the U.S. State Department and the Rwandan Department of Foreign Affairs.

On December 11, 1986, Wayne McGuire was tried in absentia by a Rwandan tribunal. Ten days before the anniversary of Dian's death, McGuire was convicted of her murder and sentenced to die before a firing squad—if he ever had the temerity, or the stupidity, to return to Rwanda.

Although it was never any part of my purpose to try to solve the mystery of her death—my interest has been in Dian Fossey's *life*—I have some opinions on the matter.

Unless Wayne McGuire went berserk, I do not believe he murdered Dian Fossey. There is no credible motive and the evidence produced against him at the trial has all the earmarks of having been contrived. I think he was a sacrificial goat.

Nor do I believe Dian was killed by poachers. If one of them had really sought her death, he would have attempted to have her poisoned or, if absolutely desperate, would have killed her when she was in *his* domain—in the forest—where an arrow, a gunshot, or a spear-thrust could have ended her life with small risk to him.

Then who did kill Dian Fossey, and why?

I suspect she was murdered by an African with whom she was familiar and who was himself familiar with the camp and its day-to-day activities. I suspect he was hired, or suborned, by influential people who increasingly viewed Dian as a dangerous impediment to the exploitation of the Parc National des Volcans, and especially to the exploitation of the gorillas. I believe the extension of Dian's visa for two full years was her death warrant.

I have been told that soon after Dian's death a plan was prepared to turn her "Mausoleum" into a museum for the edification of gorilla-watching tourists who would be accommodated in the other cabins at Karisoke. I was told that the plan is temporarily in abeyance because it would not be politic to implement it now. Perhaps when the moviemakers, reporters, and writers of books have all finished their work, and the world at large has forgotten what Dian really stood for—and against—ORTPN and its associates will have their way.

Meantime Karisoke Research Center functions much as Dian Fossey would have wished. Research students continue to go there to study the gorillas, and Digit Fund patrols still sweep the forests to keep them free of poachers and their traps.

As for the mountain kings of the Virungas, who can say what fate awaits them at our hands? But if they *do* survive, it will be due in no small measure to the dedication of a woman who was in love with life—with *all* of life—a woman who did what great lovers must always do: who gave herself completely to those she loved.

# INDEX